CW00538387

Environmental Anthrop

Today, we face some of the greatest environmental challenges in global history. Understanding the damage being done and the varied ethics and efforts contributing to its repair is of vital importance. This volume poses the question: what can increasing the emphasis on the environment in environmental anthropology, along with the science of its problems and the theoretical and methodological tools of anthropological practice, do to aid conservation efforts, policy initiatives, and our overall understanding of how to survive as citizens of the planet?

Environmental Anthropology Today combines a range of new ethnographic work with chapters exploring key theoretical and methodological issues, and draws on disciplines such as sociology and environmental science as well as anthropology to illuminate those issues. The case studies include work on North America, Europe, India, Africa, Asia, and South America, offering the reader a stimulating and thoughtful survey of the work currently being conducted in the field.

Helen Kopnina is based at the Institute for Advanced Labour Studies at the University of Amsterdam, The Netherlands. Her books include *East to West Migration* (Ashgate) and *Crossing European Boundaries* (Berghahn).

Eleanor Shoreman-Ouimet teaches in the Anthropology Department at the University of Connecticut, USA. Her research focuses on conservation, agriculture and environmentalism amongst rural communities.

Environmental Anthropology Today

Edited by
Helen Kopnina and Eleanor Shoreman-Ouimet

Routledge
Taylor & Francis Group

LONDON AND NEW YORK

First published 2011
by Routledge
2 Park Square, Milton Park, Abingdon, Oxon OX14 4RN

Simultaneously published in the USA and Canada
by Routledge
711 Third Avenue, New York, NY 10017

Routledge is an imprint of the Taylor & Francis Group, an informa business

British Library Cataloguing in Publication Data
A catalogue record for this book is available from the British Library

Library of Congress Cataloging in Publication Data
Environmental anthropology today / edited by Helen Kopnina and Eleanor
Shoreman-Ouimet.
     p. cm.
  Includes bibliographical references.
  1. Human ecology. I. Kopnina, Helen. II. Shoreman-Ouimet, Eleanor.
  GF41.E417 2011
  304.2—dc22
              2011004694

ISBN: 978-0-415-78155-8 (hbk)
ISBN: 978-0-415-78156-5 (pbk)
ISBN: 978-0-203-80690-6 (ebk)

Typeset in Bembo
by Taylor & Francis Books

Printed and bound in Great Britain by
CPI Antony Rowe, Chippenham, Wiltshire

I would like to dedicate this book to my sister, Anna Kopnina, great
lover of humans and animals
(HK)

For Will
(ES)

Contents

List of Figures

List of Tables

Notes on Contributors

Anderson, E. N. (Gene) is Professor Emeritus of Anthropology at the University of California, Riverside. He has done fieldwork in Hong Kong, Malaysia, Mexico, British Columbia, California and (for shorter periods) several other areas. He is primarily interested in cultural and political ecology, ethnobiology, and the development of ideas and representations of the environment (especially plants and animals). He has also done research in medical and nutritional anthropology, branching out from a human-ecology focus. He has written several books, including *The Food of China* (Yale University Press, 1988), *Ecologies of the Heart* (Oxford University Press, 1996), *Everyone Eats* (New York University Press, 2005) and *Floating World Lost*, an ethnography of a Hong Kong fishing community (University Press of the South, 2007). He is currently working on the relationship between ideology, resource management, and cultural representations of the environment.

De Vries, Daniel H. holds a PhD from the Department of Anthropology at the University of North Carolina at Chapel Hill where he worked with historical ecologists, urban geographers, and social-demographers to develop his research agenda on the temporal dimensions of social vulnerability. Since 1994 he has focused on the integrative power of the landscape as a unit of analysis. In 1996 he graduated from the Department of Psychology at the Rijksuniversiteit Groningen (RUG) writing a thesis on how differences in classification of Nature influences landscape preferences, which was later published and instrumental in the development of a more cultural approach to landscape preference research in the Netherlands. After emigration to the United States he focused his research and work on the historical and temporal properties of complex systems, inspired by the work of historical ecologists tracing the evolutionary properties of cultural landscapes. Daniel worked as an applied researcher on projects financed by the U.S. Federal Emergency Management Agency (FEMA), the U.S. National Institute of Health, and the U.S. Agency for International

Development. He is currently employed at Amsterdam Institute of Advanced Labour Studies, Faculty of the University of Amsterdam.

Dunford, Christine Mary is an applied urban anthropologist at The Field Museum and a project manager on this project. She received her MA in Cultural Anthropology from the University of Illinois at Chicago in 2000, and her PhD in Performance Studies from Northwestern University in 2009.

Efird, Rob is an assistant professor of anthropology and Asian studies at Seattle University, USA. He has conducted extended fieldwork in both China and Japan, and has in the past written and published on Sino-Japanese relations, recent Chinese migration to Japan, and popular culture in both countries. Over the past three years he has been researching and writing on environmental issues in China, primarily in the southwestern province of Yunnan. His China research has focused upon Japanese and Chinese environmental NGOs that are working there on a range of environmental issues, including renewable energy, desertification, and environmental education. In addition to publishing a survey of Japanese environmental NGOs in China in *China Development Brief*, he is currently guest editing a special edition of the journal *Chinese Education in Society* devoted to Chinese scholars and practitioners of environmental education. A manuscript based on 2009 fieldwork entitled 'Learning the Land Beneath Our Feet: NGOs and Place-based Learning in China' is under review at the journal *Comparative Education Review*. In the summer of 2010 he collaborated with the U.S.-based China microfinance NGO Wokai and conducted fieldwork in Yunnan to identify potential microfinance recipients who are engaged in environmentally sustainable initiatives that also raise local standards of living.

Haenn, Nora is an Associate Professor of Anthropology and International Studies at North Carolina State University, USA. Her work on the politics of conservation includes the ethnography 'Fields of Power, Forests of Discontent: Culture Conservation and the State in Mexico.' With Richard R. Wilk, she is co-editor of 'The Environment in Anthropology: A Reader in Ecology, Culture, and Sustainable Living.'

Hirsch, Jennifer is an applied urban anthropologist at The Field Museum and co-principal investigator on this project. She received her PhD in Cultural Anthropology from Duke University in 2000. At the Museum, she leads ECCo's efforts to engage diverse communities in regional sustainability initiatives, through projects that link cultural diversity to environmental conservation.

Kopnina, Helen is an anthropologist (PhD Cambridge University, 2002) currently employed at Amsterdam Institute of Advanced Labour Studies, faculty of the University of Amsterdam. Kopnina is the author of four other books, *East to West Migration* (2005); *Crossing European Boundaries: Beyond Conventional Geographical Categories* (2006), *Migration and Tourism: Formation of New Social Classes* (2007) and *Health and Environment: Social Science Perspectives* (2010).

Labenski, Ed is a PhD Graduate Student at the University of Chicago, USA. He studies social developments and policy processes in indigenous/State relationships in Canada with particular attention to treaties and Cree/Saulteaux cultural identity.

Larsen, Peter B. is a Danish anthropologist, who has worked in Asia, Latin America and at the international level on environmental issues, particularly related to conservation and social equity issues. He has worked closely with international organizations such as WWF, IUCN and UNEP on protected area conservation, community-based management and wildlife trade management. He is currently finalizing a PhD thesis in anthropology on environmental governance in the Peruvian Amazon.

Maida, Carl A. is a professor of public health at UCLA, where he teaches medical anthropology and scientific research ethics in the Graduate Program in Oral Biology. He has a joint appointment in the Institute of the Environment in the UCLA College of Letters and Science, where he teaches courses on action research methods and conducts community-based research on natural hazards, community toxics, environmental disease, and urban sustainability. His research studies on how community-scale crises impact urban populations are presented in a recent book, *Pathways Through Crisis: Urban Risk and Public Culture* (Rowman & Littlefield, Lanham, MD & New York, 2008). At UCLA Geffen School of Medicine, he conducts studies of the impact of natural disaster on children, adolescents and their families as a member of the National Center for Child Traumatic Stress, and as a member of the UCLA AIDS Institute, among persons living with HIV. He has conducted community-based research and evaluation research funded by the National Science Foundation, National Institute of Mental Health, Robert Wood Johnson Foundation, Ford Foundation, Howard Hughes Medical Institute and The California Endowment, and currently serves as an evaluator for the Terrorism and Disaster Center at the University of Oklahoma Health Sciences Center, an organizational member of the National Child Traumatic Stress Network. He is a partner in a community-based participatory research project, Community Action for a Renewed Environment (CARE) Program – Reducing Toxic Risks, funded by the US Environmental Protection Agency. His recent book, *Sustainability and Communities of Place* (Berghahn Books, Oxford & New York, 2007) explores sustainable development as a local practice, worldwide. He is a member of the UCLA Campus Sustainability Committee, and chairs its Academic Subcommittee. He is a Fellow of the American Association for the Advancement of Science, the American Anthropological Association, and the Society for Applied Anthropology.

Moran, Emilio, F. is Distinguished Professor and the James H. Rudy Professor of Anthropology at Indiana University, USA, Professor of Environmental Sciences, Adjunct Professor of Geography, and Director of the Anthropological Center for Training and Research on Global Environmental Change (ACT). Dr. Moran is the author of nine books, fourteen edited volumes and more than 140 journal articles and book chapters. He is formally trained in anthropology, tropical ecology, tropical soil science, and remote sensing. He was Leader of Focus 1 of LUCC from 1998 to 2005 and has been engaged in land use and land cover change research for many years. His research has been supported by NSF, NIH, NOAA and NASA for the past decade. His three latest books, *People and Nature* (Blackwell 2006), *Human Adaptability*, 3rd edition (Westview 2007) and *Environmental Social Science* (Blackwell 2010) address broader issues of human interaction with the environment under conditions of change.

Peters, Troy is the Community Outreach Coordinator for Chicago Climate Action Plan, working with the Chicago Department of Environment. There he works to develop and implement innovative programs that engage local organizations and residents in sustainable community-based climate actions. Troy comes most directly from the Field Museum, having been a primary ethnographer for their CCAP research on neighbourhood level climate change awareness. He has a Masters in Social Science from the University of Chicago.

Pokrant, Bob Professor of Anthropology, School of Social Sciences and Asian Languages, Curtin University, Perth, WA, Australia (PhD University of Cambridge, 1982). Recent books: M. Gillan and B. Pokrant (eds) (2009): *Trade, Labour and the Transformation of Community in Asia*. London: Palgrave Macmillan. A. Atiq Rahman, B. Pokrant, N. Quddus and L. Ali (eds) (2006): *Shrimp Farming and Industry: Sustainability, Trade and Livelihoods*. Dhaka: University Press Ltd.

Shoreman-Ouimet, Eleanor is an anthropologist (PhD Boston University, 2009). She is currently an adjunct faculty member of the Anthropology Department at the University of Connecticut, USA. Her research focuses on conservation, agriculture and environmentalism amongst rural communities. Her current work is based in the Mississippi Delta where she is investigating 'anti-environmentalism,' the role of 'rural elite' in community-based conservation, and the environmental ethics of large commodity farmers. Her recent publications include: 'Regulation, Collaboration and Conservation: Ecological Anthropology in the Mississippi Delta' (*Human Ecology* 2009); 'Muddy Waters: Water Conservation and Environmental Ethics in the Mississippi Delta' (*Anthropology News 2010*).

Sponsel, Leslie E. earned his BA in geology from Indiana University (1965), and an MA (1973) and PhD (1981) in anthropology from Cornell University, USA. Over the last four decades he has taught at seven universities in four countries, two as a Fulbright Fellow. Since 1981 he has been on the anthropology faculty at the University of Hawai'i where he is currently a Professor and the Director of the Ecological Anthropology Program. There he teaches ecological anthropology, environmental anthropology, the anthropology of religion, spiritual ecology, and sacred places, and the anthropology of Buddhism, among other courses.

From 1974–81 Sponsel made several field research trips to the Venezuelan Amazon to study human ecology. Almost yearly since 1986 Sponsel has made field research trips to Thailand to explore various aspects of Buddhist ecology and environmentalism together with his wife, Dr. Poranee Natadecha-Sponsel of Chaminade University of Honolulu. In recent years they have been developing a new project exploring the possible ecological interrelationships among Buddhist monks, sacred caves, bats, forests, and biodiversity conservation. Among Sponsel's extensive publications are more than two dozen journal articles, three dozen book chapters, and 29 articles in seven different scientific encyclopedias. He edited two books and co-edited two others. Currently he is working on contract with a publisher to complete a book titled *Spiritual Ecology: A Quiet Revolution* (forthcoming).

For more information see his personal homepage: http://www.soc.hawaii.edu/ Sponsel.

Stocker, Laura, an Associate Professor, is a marine ecologist by training. Currently, she researches and teaches in the area of coastal sustainability, climate change policy, sustainability education, sustainability mapping, cultural models of the coast and conceptual aspects of sustainability. She completed her BSc and MSc at the University of Auckland's Marine Laboratory at Leigh, on the ecology of subtidal marine invertebrates. She then completed a PhD on subtidal marine invertebrates at the University of Sydney. She was employed at Murdoch University in 1989 where she shortly established Australia's first course in sustainability, focussing on the interaction among social, economic, economic and ecological fields. In 2008 she was employed by Curtin University, along with several other colleagues to form the new Curtin University Sustainability Policy (CUSP) Institute. Here she coordinates the Masters Course in Sustainability Studies. She is deputy leader of a nationwide project, the Coastal Collaboration Cluster, researching the uptake of climate change knowledge into coastal governance.

Trusty, Teressa, an anthropologist and business consultant, has studied environmental management, conservation, and development in the Bolivian Amazon and Pacific Northwestern U.S. Her research focuses on the role of values and beliefs in environmental behaviors and decision-making and the factors that affect the development of conservationist attitudes. When not conducting research or teaching field courses in Latin America, she provides consulting services to organizations in the areas of operations and product development. She holds undergraduate degrees in computer science and earth systems, and she received her PhD in Environmental Anthropology from the University of Washington in 2010.

Van Deusen Phillips, Sarah is the project coordinator for human rights at the Center for Research Libraries-Global Resources Network and periodically serves as a consulting ethnographer in the Field Museum's division of Environment, Culture, and Conservation. She received her PhD in Comparative Human Development from the University of Chicago in 2008.

INTRODUCTION

Environmental Anthropology of Yesterday and Today

Eleanor Shoreman-Ouimet and Helen Kopnina

Theoretical trends and schools of thought in the field of anthropology evolve rapidly. Anthropological literature must keep abreast, not only of these intellectual shifts, but also of pressing global, political, and social issues. Thus, this volume, like others before it, seeks to provide updates on the state of the science and the theoretical and methodological trends of the day. Yet, there is another, more important reason why such a volume is necessary now, 'today', of all days, and another reason why this will serve as more than just another update on the discipline. Today, we face some of the greatest environmental challenges in global history. Understanding the damage being done by communities, large and small, and the varied ethics and efforts contributing to its repair is of vital importance. For these reasons, environmental anthropology today is different and arguably more critical than ever before. This volume thus poses the question and raises the challenge: What can increasing the emphasis on the environment in environmental anthropology, along with the science of its problems and the theoretical and methodological tools of anthropological practice do to aid conservation efforts, policy initiatives, and our overall understanding of how to survive, culturally and physically, as citizens of the planet?

Anthropology of the Environment or Environmental Anthropology is a specialization within the field of anthropology that studies current and historic human-environment interactions. Environmental anthropology is largely considered to be the applied dimension of Ecological Anthropology which encompasses the broad topics of primate ecology, paleoecology, cultural ecology, ethnoecology, historical ecology, political ecology, spiritual ecology, human behavioral and evolutionary ecology, and the like (Biersack 1999; Sponsel 2007). The recent shift towards the applied side of the study of the human-environment relationship is driven largely by environmental concern. This volume is also a product of such concern and is thus based on the belief that environmental anthropologists can offer a unique contribution to the study of our modern society and the environment on which this society is dependent. The following chapters demonstrate how innovative and intensive new methodologies, questions, and broader subject pools are bridging the gap between environmental anthropology as an academic discipline and environmental anthropology as a policy-tool and applied science.

This volume builds upon the existing work in the field by distilling the most important theoretical as well as methodological and ethnographic contributions from ecological and environmental anthropology. This is accomplished by including chapters written by several of the field's prominent scholars whose earlier work has defined the field of environmental anthropology. We also include the work of young scholars in order to create a cross-generational conversation that encompasses the past achievements, the current state of the art as well as the future of environmental anthropology. Both established academics and newcomers to the field address the types of interdisciplinary, environmentally focused projects that complement or sometimes challenge traditional anthropological approaches. While much of the literature within the field of environmental anthropology draws upon the existing anthropological practice and methodology applied within the environmental or ecological context, our volume promotes both innovation in theory and methodology, as well as engaging in the interdisciplinary dialogue with other social scientists addressing environment or ecology. Unlike most volumes in environmental anthropology, which stress either theoretical or applied approaches, contributions to our volume represent a meeting ground of both applied and more theoretical approaches.

As the following chapters demonstrate, this volume is premised on the idea that it is truly in this nexus of theory and methods that anthropologists offer their greatest gifts to environmental preservation. This is the arena in which environmental anthropologists can demonstrate how the wealth of ethnographic and ecological information that they accumulate and process, as well as their familiarity with individual cultures and cultural affinities to local landscapes, can enhance environmental policy, education, activist efforts, and the design and implementation of culturally and environmentally sensitive conservation programs. This is perhaps nowhere more effective than in recent interdisciplinary efforts that combine ethnographic data collection with biological ecology and ecosystem science, cultural and ecological history, survey methods, mapping technology, and public policy initiatives, just to name a few. Many recent works, for example, address pressing environmental concerns such as climate change, natural disasters, biological diversity, etc. These efforts are exemplified by anthropologists such as Anthony Oliver-Smith, Susanna Hoffman, Susan Crate, Barbara Rose Johnston, Carole Crumley, Michael Dove, James Brosius, Luisa Maffi, Andrew Vayda, Kay Milton, Patricia Townsend, and many of this volume's contributors. Such research demonstrates first-hand how environmental anthropologists are contributing to our understanding of global environmental problems and conservation efforts while also participating in the construction of local level solutions by providing a window into the impacts of environmental change and globalization processes, as well as environmental perception and behavior.

The marriage of anthropology with the hard sciences is penetrating all areas of environmental anthropological investigation – from the most positivistic analyses of changing soil chemistries to the study of spirituality and conservation. The following chapters demonstrate exactly this range. Research presented in chapters by Gene Anderson and Leslie Sponsel, for example, demonstrate how in-depth analyses of spirituality and traditional belief systems correlate to resource use and long term sustainability. These works combine the study of traditional beliefs with the local history of environmental change, resource use, sustainability and/or degradation in traditional societies, and demonstrate how a thorough understanding of communities that have successfully maintained equilibrium with their environment may provide a model for sustainability in other areas. Daniel de Vries applies a similar analysis of belief systems and the link between environment and cultural behavior to a western problem in his analysis of Hurricane Katrina and the long overlooked link between accurate risk assessment in natural disasters and cultural beliefs about the local environment. On a similarly environmentally pressing note, Bob Pokrant and Laura Stocker examine the contribution of anthropology to climate change research and policy through a focus on the relationship between development planning and climate change policy and practice. Meanwhile, Emilio Moran demonstrates how to document and map such examples of cultural and environmental change with the use of GIS mapping systems. Such technology, Moran demonstrates, enables researchers to directly analyze landscape change and note the connection to changes in land-use, population size, and sociopolitical relationships between regions. These examples reinforce the current move in environmental anthropology towards supporting local, regional and global conservation efforts by providing well-rounded analyses of human-environment interactions by emphasizing the links between biological ecology data, cultural dynamics, and human behavior.

This volume also highlights other interdisciplinary ventures, as well as innovative methodologies and rejuvenations of traditional anthropological theories. For instance, several of the volume's contributors combine 'traditional' anthropological theory with interdisciplinary theoretical approaches drawn from political science (Larsen), pedagogical studies (Efird, Kopnina), site-based planning, environmental change analysis, special analysis and impact assessments (Moran), and eco-system services (Trusty). Others engage in socially involved, rather than strictly scientific and/or detached debates, arguing that their research may serve to motivate community conservation projects (Shoreman-Ouimet), local awareness of environmental problems (Hirsch et al.), environmental justice (Maida), environmental policy and politics (Larsen), conservation economies and regional scale analyses (Haenn), greater engagement of schools in environmental education (Efird, Kopnina), and increased attention to emic temporal perception in climate-related risk assessment (de Vries).

Methodologically, this volume evaluates the already-existing practice of ethnography of human-environment interaction as well as calls for greater interdisciplinarity. Rather than relying solely on the systems approach formerly applied to the study of the interrelationship between culture and the environment, this volume also introduces new methodological tools, including consumption diaries and concept mapping, designed to track the use of resources from food to electricity (Kopnina); and Participatory Action Research (PAR), which has proven particularly helpful in community efforts to improve local environments (Maida and Hirsch et al.) Ethnographically, this volume adds new case studies from around the world to illustrate how the theoretical domains of environmental anthropology can be explored through innovative and environmentally engaged fieldwork.

In addition to working with biological and ecological data, mapping systems, and a range of new methodologies, many of today's environmental anthropologists are also finding value and inspiration from the humanities and other social scientists. Following this trend, many of the chapters of this volume reference the work of environmental sociologists and the ways in which they have integrated the environment into their discipline through the New Ecological Paradigm (NEP). Developed by environmental sociologists William R. Catton and Riley Dunlap (1978a and 1978b), the New Ecological Paradigm is a way of conceptualizing human beings and human behavior in the context of the larger environment in which all species live, as well as a method of assessing environmental values and beliefs. The paradigm was pioneered around the same time as many anthropologists (Vayda and Rappaport 1968; Hardesty 1977) were cultivating the study of the relationship between culture and the environment. The point of revisiting its applications to environmental anthropology comes both from the insight to be gained from interdisciplinary efforts, but more so from the ways in which the NEP situates human beings in the environment as opposed to viewing the environment strictly from a human or cultural perspective. Although anthropologists will rightly remain foremost dedicated to understanding human culture – this volume argues that anthropologists also have a role to play in and tools to stave off environmental destruction. Thus we see combining anthropological method and theory with the emphasis that the NEP puts on the environment and human vulnerability to, and dependence upon it, as a productive way to elicit more environmentally-engaged research among environmental anthropologists.

The following sections will address the rise of environmental anthropology and reflect upon the current developments within it. They also address the anthropocentric nature of much environmental anthropological research and present an argument for shifting from a relativistic approach to the study of human-environment interaction to one that more objectively addresses the role of human communities in environmental degradation and repair. Finally, the following sections discuss environmental anthropology in the context of the New Ecological Paradigm, addressing its usefulness to the field of anthropology and demonstrating the ways in which environmental anthropologists are becoming increasingly environmentally conscious in their research topics and ethnographic emphases.

What is Meant by Environmental Anthropology?

The contributors to this volume argue that the discipline of environmental anthropology is well suited to address the causes of recent environmental degradation. As Kay Milton (1996: 24) so articulately noted, any discipline that can claim to be the study of human ecology should also be able to claim a central place in the way environmental problems are examined and addressed. Cultural studies of particular (local, cultural) incidences of human interaction with nature can contribute greatly to the understanding of such interaction at the grass-roots level. At the theoretical level, environmental anthropologists can contribute both their unique cultural explanations, which are particular to the contexts in which environmental problems are studied, and general or universal explanations, based on the theory of human nature.

However, it is not just the ideology that is of importance but the subject matter itself that dictates the impact of environmental anthropological research. As Marxist anthropology is often concerned with the study of interaction between social classes, and feminist anthropology is often concerned with the study of women, environmental anthropology has at its core (while not the only subject), the human relationship with ecology, the environment, and environmentalism. The field of environmental anthropology draws upon various domains within anthropology from ecological to cultural anthropology and across disciplines from the humanities to the social and natural sciences.

According to Barnard and Spencer's (1996: 169) definition, ecological [or environmental] anthropology focuses on the complex relations between people and their environments and directs our attention to the ways in which a particular population purposefully or unintentionally shapes its environment, and the ways in which its relations with the environment shape its culture and its social, economic and political life. Moreover, according to the Society of Applied Anthropology, ecological anthropology assists policy-making and program planning by combining expertise in ecology with methods and tools for understanding the social and cultural dynamics of communities potentially affected by policy decisions. Simply stated, ecological or environmental anthropology is 'anthropology which puts more than usual emphasis on the interface between cultural and ecological factors' (Barnard and Spencer 1996: 186). The extensive body of relevant scientific knowledge in environmental anthropology includes: understanding and building on the social organization of communities in larger social systems for use in identifying and solving environmental problems; understanding local environmental knowledge for use in the preservation of local and global environments; recognizing and addressing differences in cultural perceptions, categories, linguistic terms, values and behaviors related to the environment in order to confront differences and improve communication among specific cultural/ethnic groups with respect to addressing environmental concerns; as well as identifying and utilizing culturally specific styles of communication and rhetoric typical of designated groups to enhance communication and mutual understanding among groups.

In this volume we hope to demonstrate how these uses for and tools of the discipline can be expanded to include a more direct concern for the environment itself, as well as with the local communities that engage with it. The contributors to this volume demonstrate that studies need not choose between dividing culture from nature nor unifying them as an interactionist whole. Instead, the following chapters demonstrate examples of, ways of thinking about, and the execution of projects that examine environmental problems, and the ways in which human communities, regardless of size or status, affect the environment; as well as how they may be adapting to environmental change.

In general, ecological anthropologists investigate the ways that a population shapes its environment and the subsequent manners in which these relations form the population's social, economic, and political life (Salzman and Attwood 1996: 169). Ecological anthropology, as described by one of the discipline's prominent scholars, Tim Ingold, is 'an understanding that proceeds from a notion of the mutualism of person and environment' (Ingold 1992: 40). This type of mutual understanding is only possible because environmental anthropologists study such a range of topics, often emphasizing the non-Western viewpoint, sometimes working together with non-governmental organizations (NGOs), participating in policy debates and acting as advocates and allies of local populations of farmers, indigenous peoples, or urban minority groups. They also draw attention to the socio-cultural aspects of environmental problems, contributing a much-needed counter-balance to the emphasis on the ecological, physical, and economic dimensions that often dominate debates and decision-making. The authors of this volume argue that anthropology of the environment affords valuable insight into our relationship with the environment, which may assist policy-makers, project designers, and peoples impacted by today's environmental problems.

According to Orlove and Brush (1996) environmental anthropologists have also been credited for pointing out the importance of the participation of local people in conservation programs, such as in the participation of local populations in protected area management or of farmers and traditional communities in plant genetic resources. The work of environmental anthropologists has also helped to more effectively link local populations, national agencies, and international organizations to the natural environment in which such groups operate. Examples of such anthropological work include the documentation of local knowledge and practices that influence the selection and maintenance of crop varieties and the conservation of rare and endangered species in protected areas, as well as addressing different concerns and definitions of biodiversity held by local populations and international conservationists (Orlove and Brush 1996: 329).

A Brief History of Environmental Anthropology

Dove and Carpenter (2008: 61), note that a number of key developments in the history of environmental anthropology can be identified. First, there is a move from the studies of communities as self-enclosed entities towards recognizing them as part of wider political-ecological systems and questioning their 'boundedness'. Secondly, there has been a move away from synchronic and toward diachronic approaches, as well as a general shift in the field away from assumptions of equilibrium toward assumptions of disequilibrium (Crumley 1994; Balee 1998). As in all general trends, major exceptions exist. While the shift in emphasis from equilibrium to disequilibrium largely reflects biological ecology and observable patterns in nature, many scholars emphasize the important examples of cultures in which equilibrium has been maintained for generations, arguing that they have maintained a sustainable system of existing in their local environment (see Sponsel and Anderson in this volume). These examples, it is argued, provide excellent models for the possibility of sustainability as well as for the role of belief systems in environmental preservation.

Third, environmental anthropology is not just becoming more involved with politics, but starting to become more political itself. Fourth, environmental anthropology has become increasingly influenced by post-structural theory. This is manifested through greater reflexivity, an interest in studying environmental discourse, and a view of the environment as both material reality and a product of discourse. Finally, environmental anthropology is becoming increasingly interdisciplinary, freely crossing the boundaries between the natural and social sciences, as well as the humanities. The following section provides a brief history of the major periods in the evolution of environmental anthropology.

While ecologists and environmental scientists had begun to acknowledge nature's characteristic dynamism as early as the 1950s (Cronon 1996a), ecological anthropologists at this time were reacting against Franz Boas' and Alfred Kroeber's subordination of environmental forces to cultural influence, and seeking constants in the relationship between humans and the environment. Characterizing this early period in the history of the specialization is the work of Julian H. Steward, which analyzed the adaptations of human labor to available natural resources and examined the role of ecology in ethnic relations and the symbolism of culture in relation to the environment (Steward 1949; 1955). Julian Steward (1955) was one of the first to emphasize ecological forces in the evolution of culture. Steward's notion of cultural ecology theorized that adaptive responses in similar environments gave rise to cross-cultural similarities. The theory centers on the concept of the 'culture core', or the constellation of features that are most closely related to subsistence activities and economic arrangements (Steward 1955: 37).

Cultural ecology distinguishes between different kinds of socio-cultural systems and institutions, it recognizes both cooperation and competition as processes of interaction, and it postulates that environmental adaptations depend on the technology, needs, and structure of the society and on the nature of the environment (ibid 44). Steward was adamantly opposed to reductionist, particularly cultural reductionist theories of culture change. He argued that while the culture of any society constitutes a holistic system in which technology, economics, social and political structure, religion, language, values, and other features are closely interrelated, the different components of a culture are not similarly affected by ecological adaptations (Steward 1955). He believed, much to Boas' dismay, that it is social structure that responds to environmental requirements. This basic structuring, Steward argued (1968: 50), is related most immediately to cooperative productive activity, and it is manifest in community and band organization and in essential kinship systems. According to Bennett's (1999: 213) analysis, Steward's ultimate goal was for human ecology to be recognized as an instrument for the solution of problems: in the biological realm, human adaptation to the environment; in the cultural, 'how culture is affected by its adaptation to the environment.'

This period in ecological anthropology was also largely marked by the work of Fredrik Barth in his study of the relations between ethnic groups, demonstrating the importance of environmental factors (1966; 1969); and Clifford Geertz's analysis of the role of ecology in the symbolic 'passion' of a culture (Geertz 1959; 1963). Both Barth and Geertz built on Steward's work by describing complex and interdependent cultural and ecological systems.

The extent to which ecology could potentially frame and shape the cultural condition had a powerful impact on anthropology and led to a number of theories on the interaction between culture and the environment. After all, as Kroeber himself once argued, 'no culture is wholly intelligible without reference to … environmental factors with which it is in relation' (Kroeber 1963: 6). Though quite different in their own right, E. E. Evans-Pritchard (1940), Alfred Kroeber (1963), and Marvin Harris (1968) working with the concepts of cultural ecology and cultural materialism, exemplified efforts to understand the influence of environmental factors (Kottak 1999: 23). Derived from Herskovits' (1926) study of a boundary between the livestock and agricultural spheres, Evans-Pritchard and Harris further developed the concept of the 'cattle complex', or in Evans-Pritchard's words, 'cattle idiom' and in Harris' term 'sacred cow.' Harris is best known for his history of anthropological theory and development of the cultural materialist approach. Clearly influenced by Steward, cultural materialism is based on the idea that similar technologies applied to similar environments produce similar arrangements of labor in production and distribution, and that these in turn call forth similar kinds of social groupings, which justify and coordinate their activities by means of similar systems of values and beliefs (Bennett 1999: 231). Translated into research strategy, Harris' principle of techno-environmental, techno-economic determinism assigned priority to the study of the material conditions of socio-cultural life (ibid). The effect of this deterministic theory, however, was the materialist characterization of all ecological theories of culture, thereby instigating a shift away from the study of human-environmental interactions in anthropology.

In an attempt to rectify this materialist reputation, the majority of ecological anthropologists pulled away from causational theories of culture and began to apply the methods of cultural ecology on the micro-level. Thus ecological ethnography was born, pioneered largely by the work of Roy Rappaport and Andrew Vayda through the development of the concept of 'ecological populations.' Although largely influenced by his scholarship, Rappaport and Vayda saw Steward's approach as somewhat inadequate. They believed that the original concept of cultural ecology implied correlation to mean causation, and to treat the 'culture core' as if it included only technology (Netting 1977: 10). Furthermore, they found Steward's selection of ecological features to be lacking important factors such as other organisms, other human groups, and the study of the interaction between culture and biology and genetic and physiological effects (ibid). As a way of incorporating these various factors into a cohesive cultural ecological analysis of the Tsembaga rituals, Rappaport (1968) adopted a functionalist framework, which not only allowed him to present the interrelatedness of cultural features, ecology, and behavior, but also accommodated these theories about how cultural and ecological institutions relied on one another to maintain a homeostatic balance. The problem with this however was that Rappaport's ritual analysis implies a constant, unwavering pattern of fluctuation, and makes no mention of the possibility that the system will give way to growth or development of any kind. Furthermore, the boundedness, or micro-level nature of Rappaport's study, as Moran (1990) notes, forces the questions: how do ecosystem boundaries change through time and how do shifts in boundary definition relate to internal and external structural or functional relations?

Together with the 'cultural materialism' of Harris, the 'ethnoscience' of Berlin, Conklin (1957), and Frake (1980) Rappaport's 'ecological ethnography' highlighted the fact that indigenous groups have traditional ways of categorizing resources and regulating their use (Kottak 1999). The basic units of ecological anthropology in the 1960s were thus, not surprisingly, the 'ecological population and the ecosystem' (often discussed as discrete units characterized by distinct cultural features), and ethno-semantic domains (such as ethnobotany). Methodologically, this period of the sub-discipline's evolution was characterized by the development of systems theory and negative feedback (Ellen 1982; Hardesty 1977). Systems theory, as proposed by Clifford Geertz (1963), offered insights on the future of such a society, but was ulti-mately disregarded by anthropologists who recognized its neglect of history. Focused on the complex networks of mutual causality, systems theory requires the delineation of a system's boundaries and a model from which the system's behavior can be stu-died and predicted. Geertz believed the concept of 'eco-system' to be the logical conclusion to the interplay of culture, biology, and the environment. Geertz descri-bed an eco-system, theoretically, as 'a dynamic set of relationships between living and nonliving things through which energy flows and materials cycle and because of which other problems of survival are worked out' (Hardesty 1977: 14). Geertz believed that if one can determine the constellation of features which are most unequivocally related to the processes of energy interchange between man and his surroundings in any given instance, then they can also determine which environ-mental features have primary relevance for those same processes (Geertz 1963: 8). These early ecological anthropologists, however, were criticized for their presumed preoccupation with stability rather than change, and the simplicity of their systems (including self-enclosed cultures unaffected by global forces of technological and social change) (Friedman 1974; Wolf 1982). Many critiques pointed out that few groups could exist on local resources and live in clearly demarcated areas or ecosys-tems free from intrusions of globalization. Volumes, such as Hardesty's (1977) *Ecological Anthropology*, started adding global perspective to human-environment interaction.

Breaking from the deterministic, equilibrium-based approaches of the above cul-tural ecologists, researchers in the field of historical ecology attempted to present a more holistic perspective on the relationship between humans and nature, empha-sizing the idea that the subject of study is indeed a changing, fluctuating relationship rather than any objective 'thing', in particular (Balee 1994). While many historical ecologists of this time acknowledged the role that equilibrium plays in environmental development and human–nature relationships, their historical research illustrated the inconsistency of equilibrium and proved that it may not be as sensitive or so easily destroyed as environmentalist arguments indicate. Netting (1981) exemplified how an ecological anthropologist can use the concept of equilibrium without depicting it to be the life-blood of the environment. In *Balancing on an Alp*, Netting (1981) extended the ecosystem analysis from its typical appraisal of how people survive in their surroundings and respond to life-threatening situations to include how those factors can change from one generation to the next and the ways that people meet novel challenges and unprecedented problems outside their local subsistence system. While the goal is still to trace strategies of sustainability, which inherently connote the presence of mechanisms of equilibrium, Netting describes equilibrium more as a descriptive tool than an ecological law. Equilibrium, Netting concludes, is not the result of natural forces and a burden for humans to maintain, rather, it is created by humans in the first place, for the physical benefits it has shown to confer (Netting 1981: 225). Life is just simpler, it seems, when we are at one (literally) with the world.

In the 1970s, theory (such as functionalism and cultural materialism) became more blended with political awareness and policy concerns, and is largely related to the rise of the environmental movement and emergence of non-governmental organizations (NGOs). According to Conrad Kottak's (1999: 23) review of new ecological anthropology, the emerging discipline attempt[ed] to understand and devise culturally informed solutions to such problems/issues as environmental degradation, environmental racism, and the role of the media, NGOs and environmental hazards in stimulating ecological awareness and action. Concerns about the loss of biodiversity led to the creation of protected areas and the realization of the importance of the local populations' participation in conservationist efforts and the value of traditional ecological knowledge and history in the preservation of local environments.

One such study exemplifying this interdisciplinarity of theory and methods was historical ecologist, William Balee's (1994) analysis of the Ka'apor of the Amazon. By focusing on the interpenetration of culture and the environment, instead of human adaptation to the environment, he was able to comprehend the historical bases for the current relationships and dominance hierarchies between local indigenous groups. In *Footprints of the Forest* (1994), Balee's main concern is with how the Ka'apor interact with the plants in the diverse vegetational zones of their homeland. According to Balee (1994: 1), ethnobotany focuses on the similarities and differences among societies in the use, management, classification and nomenclature of plants. Brought together, the methods of ethnobotany and historical ecology help Balee to synthesize historical, cultural, ecological, and sociological data into a comprehensive theory about the history of the Ka'apor.

These techniques provide evidence supporting Balee's claim that knowledge of the natural world not only helped the Ka'apor to control their territory, but also that indigenous environmental knowledge, itself, can act as a dating technique by illustrating how long a certain group has occupied a territory and the linguistic roots of their ecological vocabulary. Balee was able to argue that differences in historical ecology lead to differences of mental economy among Lowland South American cultures (Balee 1994: 114), no doubt a broader conclusion than many previous ecological anthropologists were able to derive from their data sets. As Moran (2006) aptly points out, this type of inclusion of a historical dimension in ecosystem studies provides an appreciation of the processes of stability and change in human ecosystems.

During this period in the history of the sub-discipline, research in cultural and environmental history and cultural ecology converged on the environmental politics of protected areas (Stearman 1984; Stearman and Redford 1995). Several distinctive features of anthropology that make it particularly well suited for studying protected areas are outlined in multiple articles published in the *Annual Review of Anthropology* (Oliver-Smith 1996; Smith and Wishnie 2000; Moran, King, and Carlson 2001; Maffi 2005; West, Igoe, and Brockington 2006; Dove 2006; Acheson 2006; Muhlausler and Peace 2006; Charnley and Poe 2007). Orlove and Brush's (1996: 333) article 'Anthropology and the Conservation of Biodiversity' stresses the commitment to long-term field studies in the relatively isolated regions in which protected areas are established; the exposure to biology in four-field departments; and the willingness to study not only local populations but also reserve managers, international conservationists, biologists, government officials, and staff of NGOs.

The period between the 1980s and 1990s is distinguished largely by the way in which environmentalism itself became an object of study for anthropologists interested in discourse, ideology, and postmodernism. In addition to conducting scholarly research, anthropologists also engaged in the debates over protected areas in other ways: as advocates for indigenous rights organizations such as Cultural Survival (Clay 1988), as observers of local communities' interactions with NGOs (Conklin and Graham 1995; Kottak 1999; Tsing 1999), as political analysts in interactions between Western activists and non-Western governments (Brosius 1999), as policy-makers in international institutions such as the World Bank (Davis 1988) and the World Wildlife Fund (Wells, Brandon and Hannah 1992). Anthropologists also acted as cultural intermediaries who arrange for the publication of interviews with local inhabitants of protected areas, and as expert witnesses in court cases in which indigenous land claims are adjudicated (Kemf 1993; Merlan 1991). In both academic and advocacy roles, anthropologists have argued strongly for the participation of local populations in the planning and management of protected areas. These arguments are sometimes based on social justice claims (Clay 1998)—that the often poor and marginal inhabitants of protected areas should not bear the costs of conservation—or on human rights claims, in which local populations have entitlements as citizens of the states that administer the protected areas, as native or indigenous peoples with specific claims to sovereignty over their territory, and as human beings who participate in the planet-wide interactions among different species (Johnston 1994, 1995).

Insights from the work of contemporary environmental anthropologists have been particularly valuable in providing both culturally specific; context grounded case studies of human interaction with the environment (McElroy and Townsend 1989; Milton 1996; Haenn 1996; Townsend 2000; Vivanco 2006; Argyrou 2005; West 2005; Haenn and Wilk 2006; Moran 2008; Dove and Carpenter 2008). Some anthropologists argue for a greater understanding of native perceptions of nature and environment, rather than adopting Western top-down approaches and epistemologies (Blaser 2009; Kalland 2009). Some have pointed out those factors missing from the study of human-environmental relationships and our methods of assessing long-term sustainability (Moran 1990; Netting 1993). Others address global politics and developmental or industrialization issues and their effect on the local communities (Browder & Godfrey 1997; Chetham 2005; Maida 2007). Yet other groups of anthropologists focus on the human-nature relationship from both historical and cultural perspectives (Strang 1997; Moran 2006). A number of researchers have also recently taken it upon themselves to write volumes solely devoted to the theories and methods of environmental anthropology (notably, Kay Milton, Nora Haenn and Richard R. Wilk, Patricia Townsend, Tim Ingold, Emilio Moran, Andrew Vayda, Carl Maida and Veronica Strang).

The latest period in environmental anthropology is marked, according to Dove and Carpenter (2008: XIV), by the continued influence of postmodern theory which adds yet another self-reflective, subjective, and interpretive dimension to anthropological interest in the interaction between humans and their environment. Work on 'ethno-ecological landscapes', 'environmental discourses', 'environmental narratives', 'environmental perceptions', 'cultural ecologies' and all sorts of 'social constructions' (of nature, of environment, etc.) may seem like a far cry from the more political, applied and even activist trends in environmental anthropology (for example, Escobar, 1996). Yet, 'constructions' can be used not only in postmodern rhetoric of conceptual deconstruction, but also as a potent political tool used by policy-makers and indigenous communities. In Peter Brosius' words (1999: 37),

> … A broader, transdisciplinary florescence in environmental scholarship in the last decade has had a decisive influence in alerting us to the importance of recognizing the cultural and historical contingency of 'nature' and the significance of this contingency for understanding the ways in which various kinds of political agents construct and contest nature.

These reflective, constructive, interpretative works are currently complemented in the field by the efforts of more solutions-oriented researchers aiming to develop more effective methodologies for understanding human behaviors towards, and relationships with the environment. For instance, researchers Vayda and Walters (1999) question the rationale for establishing spiritual and political ecology as subfields. Critical of the conceptualization of culture in human ecology, these authors also argue for events rather than culture, structure, or system as the main object of inquiry. Together, these approaches are making strides towards reconciling the antagonistic relationship between culture and the environment and may give theoretical guidance for the further development of environmental anthropology.

Recently, research centers and institutes focusing on Environmental Anthropology have emerged. The Anthropological Center for Training and Research on Global Environmental Change (ACT), for instance, is an interdisciplinary training and research center focusing on the human dimensions of global environmental change headed by Emilio Moran, one of this volume's contributors. The center specializes in the study of variable local causes of human activities and provides solutions to the use, conservation, and restoration of human ecosystems. ACT's research and training objectives focus on how particular local populations manage resources and how those activities may be monitored using remote sensing technologies and field studies. Furthermore, Anthropology of the Environment, a section of the American Anthropological Association, the professional society of American anthropologists, hosts a forum for over a thousand anthropologists interested in ecology, the environment, and environmentalism (http://www.eanth.org/index.php). A number of American universities have also started offering degrees in environmental anthropology in the last decade and many international universities host anthropologists specializing in environmental or ecological anthropology.

The Environment In Environmental Anthropology

In an article published by *American Anthropologist*, reviewing the history and present state of the art of the ecological anthropology, Kottak (1999: 33) issues a remarkable statement:

> People must come first. Cultural anthropologists need to remember the primacy of society and culture in their analysis and not be dazzled by ecological data. Funding sources that give priority to the hard sciences, fund expensive equipment, and support sophisticated technology should not lead us away from a focus on cultural specificity and social and cultural variables. Ecological anthropology must put anthropology ahead of ecology. Anthropology's contribution is to place people ahead of plants, animals and soil.

In contrast to Kottak's polemical ideal, this volume highlights current research that investigates the environment and environmental issues in order to balance the attention paid to environmental and human wellbeing in environmental anthropology, policy initiatives, and conservation efforts. Considering the richness and diversity of literature in the field of environmental or ecological anthropology to date, it may seem like an oversimplification to assert that human exceptionalism is still part and parcel of mainstream anthropology. Yet, we do dare to assert that mainstream anthropology often focuses on people or cultures and the(ir) 'environment' as a dependent variable and tends to overshadow human agency in the destruction of the natural habitat, by focusing on topics such as access to resources and/or by not paying close enough attention to physical, chemical, biological, and socioeconomic factors in ethnographic analyses (Netting 1993). In the recent article in *American Anthropologist*, signaling the danger of marginalization of anthropologists in (environmental) policy debate, Charnley and Durham are concerned that the danger is not in anthropologists 'being dazzled by ecological data,' but rather that 'environmental anthropology is becoming anthropology without environment' (Charnley and Durham 2010: 411).

The danger of marginalization of environmental anthropologists from the policy debate stems from anthropologists' reluctance to engage with quantitative and environmental data, and the discipline's phobia of the tables and figures, 'which are effective for communicating research findings to policy makers' (Ibid). In this volume, our contributors address both Environment and the People or People as part of the Environment, rather than relying on traditional reification of human(ity) and culture; and discuss broader-based, more holistic methodologies for assessing the long-term impacts of human communities on the local and global environment. Some of the contributors to this volume, notably Moran and Kopnina, show that anthropology's methodological reach is not limited to 'traditional' ethnographic studies, and that methodologically mixed approaches may aid both anthropologists in their daily practice and indeed instruct policy makers, urban planners or environmental educationalists.

Ironically enough, one of the fundamental obstacles to putting the environment back into environmental anthropology, is culture. This stems from the dilemma in anthropology as to whether culture is itself an object of analysis, or whether it is simply part of a broader framework for the analysis of something else, usually something that is seen as part of culture and therefore as 'cultural' in nature (Milton 1996:10). Because studies in environmental anthropology inevitably, and rightly so, involve culture, culture often becomes the focal point to the extent that it obviates the environment and the stresses upon it. When taken to the extreme, in the form of constructionism, this perspective makes the environment little more than a product of culture and therefore further minimizes the objective existence of nature and therefore the gravity of human-induced environmental damage. This situation is further compounded by the frequent reliance on the assumption that cultures are structured systems, which has led anthropologists to exaggerate the problematic nature of cultural change and to focus on minutiae without seeing the bigger picture when it comes to the impact that communities can have on local environments. Anthropologists, as Milton (1996: 17) phrased it, have been more inclined to use the microscope than the wide-angle lens. This, combined with an ambivalence over the role of globalizing processes in cultural analysis and a preoccupation with relativism, can lead to the neglect of or simply an inability to see, not only large scale culture change (Milton 1996) but also large-scale implications of local-level environmental damage. Without conversely minimizing the significance of cultural adaptation to and modification of the environment, this volume seeks to re-emphasize the environment in the discipline of environmental anthropology and demonstrate the ways in which, when conducted with the environment, as well as culture, in mind, environmental anthropology can aid environmental efforts at the local and global scales.

Although anthropologists, in general, are moving away from the human-nature dichotomy some recent work seems to be reconstructing such a perspective in its efforts to reverse the notion that people degrade nature (Posey 1998; Fairhead and Leach 1996). Posey (1998) and Fairhead and Leach (1996) argue, for instance, that what we have assumed to be remnants of natural forest surrounded by degraded savanna, were in fact created by people. Posey's ethnographic accounts of natural habitats created by the Kayapó' Indians are classic examples of environmental anthropology's ethnography. Much more rare are examples of those groups instrumental in felling hectares of pristine forest just next to such human-planted enclaves. However, this work has received much criticism from other researchers. Turner (1993) noted that the Kayapó's relationship to 'their' forest (as well as their experience and participation in wage labor) was ambiguous. Posey's conclusion was also criticized by geographer Eugene Parker, who argued that far from being created by the natives, the forests' islands were natural, the result of forest advance at the edge of savannah (Parker, 1993: 721). The fact remains that what may appear to be objective facts about human-environmental history and their current relationships are often subjective observations that deserve further analysis and consideration.

Typical of many anthropologists, the aforementioned authors are defending the weaker position of the local community and their local land use practices against the dominant policymakers (Fairhead and Leach 1996: 260). Despite popular sentimentality popularized by the recent Hollywood blockbuster *Avatar* (2009) depicting alien 'people' living in close harmony with nature and struggling against the utilitarian ambitions of the Earthlings, critics continue to discredit this 'noble savage'-like depiction of tribal peoples who are at 'one with nature' and represent the true 'natural men' (see Sponsel in this volume). Aside from the outdated straw-man arguments critiquing those who might claim that all traditional societies are 'at one' with nature, more grounded arguments simply attest that indigenous peoples have 'human vices just as we do' (Wagley 1976: 302), do not necessarily view animals and plants as something worth protecting (Allendorf et al. 2006; Infield 1988), are capable of overuse and poor decision-making (Netting 1993), and that the majority of traits that perhaps once enabled traditional societies to live in greater harmony with the environment than more industrialized groups, are slowly diminishing (Brosius 2006).

In turning their gaze to the processes of 'development' and its effect on local communities, anthropologists have noted that factors such as population growth, the inequitable distribution of wealth, and the growth of industrialized nations have served to widen the relative gap between the rich and poor (Bodley 2008a,b). In fact, in examining the relationship between economic and technological progress and the health and welfare of local communities, Bodley (2008) argues that increased consumption, lowered mortality, and the eradication of all traditional controls have combined to replace what for most tribal peoples was a relatively stable balance between population and natural resources, with a new system which is imbalanced.

An example of the negative effect of population growth on the health and welfare of local populations is described in Warren M. Hern's (1992) article 'Family Planning, Amazon Style' which links high fertility to health and economic problems of the Shipibo Indians. While in the field, Hern received multiple requests to supply the villagers with Western contraceptives as families, and particularly women, admitted to having many more births than wanted. In explaining this unprecedented growth, the author lists a number of Western interventions that disrupted traditional means of controlling population growth, such as abstinence, abortion, infanticide, use of herbal contraceptives and polygyny. Starting from the influence of Christian missionaries and in recent years, 'Westerners' who prohibited 'parochial practices' and introduced Western medicine, the Shipibo experienced a population growth of 4.9 percent per year, with an average of ten births per woman. The Shipibo watched the timber cutters, cattle ranchers, commercial fishermen, and the farmers of commercial crops cause deforestation and flooding that eliminated traditional crops and game on which the Shapibo relied. Spurred by economic necessity, the Shapibo 'themselves are drawn into the money economy and sometimes sell products from scarce animals (such as water turtle eggs) in order to get cash' (Hern 1992: 172). Imported goods became the norm as traditional resources became rapidly exhausted. As a result, depletion of natural resources, poverty and disease have followed. While (Western) medical technologies, and 'progressive social practices' that prohibit traditional methods of population control, and wage labor are praised as goods for 'progress', the native population seems to succumb more and more to poverty and disease. Due to such 'development', Hern (1992: 174) concludes,

> many human societies that controlled their fertility in the past have lost the tradition of doing so in the frenzy of modern cultural change. The old methods that reduced births have not yet been replaced by the new technologies of fertility control. The result is chaos, suffering, more cultural change, and in some cases, even more rapid population growth.

Reflecting on the dangers of 'progress,' to local cultures and the relativity of the very concepts of 'progress' and 'quality of life' many anthropologists question the 'goodness' of industrialization and the whole enterprise of 'development', including the 'democratic sharing' of the green revolution, medical technologies and other 'seductive blessings' (Diamond 1987). In stark contrast to development anthropologists employed by organizations such as IMF and the World Bank who may be sympathetic to the ideas of 'development', many environmental anthropologists are wary of such ideas when they are imposed on local populations (Tsing 1999). Indeed, in this endlessly complicated time of growing economic need and environmental deterioration, the internalization of the ideas of 'progress' as well as the seemingly global acceptance of wage labor and consumerism (in which 'native' populations contribute to the further degradation of their own culture and environment) pose new ethical challenges for the increasingly 'engaged' anthropologists.

While the contributors to this volume recognize that environmental problems most frequently originate from top-down policies, they remain objective to the fact that environmental damage can be caused by communities of all sizes. Small size or adherence to traditional lifestyles should not, necessarily, exempt a population from its environmental responsibility, just as it doesn't exclude them from suffering the repercussions of ecological deterioration. The point is not to determine which is to blame for the global environmental crisis, the industrial or non-industrial world, but rather simply to assess on a case by case basis and as a part of larger ethnographic studies, what it is that communities are doing for or against their habitat that could have long term ramifications. In general, we believe that this type of emphasis could bolster anthropology's understanding of areas where education, aid, or intervention may be needed; as well as garner local ecological knowledge, and a more complex understanding of the human-environment relationship that may be helpful in other areas around the world.

Notions of Nature

Environment, interpreted in the most common contemporary (Western) sense, may mean anything from 'nature' to 'surroundings'. When we speak of 'nature' we may refer to what in the words of the philosopher and poet Ralph Waldo Emerson, consists of 'essences unchanged by man; space, the air, the river, the leaf.' When we refer to environment as surroundings, we often speak of influences, contexts and conditions surrounding human existence and activity. Of interest to many post-modern writers, especially those following a constructionist view (Mason 1990; Chaloupka and Cawley 1993; Burr 1995; Escobar 1996), however, is the notion that the concept of nature is a socially constructed entity, created by the 'actors' themselves, and largely a product of language. From this perspective, nature is not only represented by language but created by it and ultimately becomes little more than an offshoot of social reality (Kidner 2000: 264). This makes it impossible to judge one attitude toward nature as better or worse; more beneficial or more harmful than any other for, according to this logic, there is no nature outside the human perception of it (ibid). Thus from the constructionist viewpoint, to paraphrase David Hume's famous dictum, 'if the tree falls in the forest but nobody hears the sound', the tree has not really fallen. While Emerson depicts nature as independent of the human place in it, the latter, constructionist view, refers to a dependent construct wholly connected to the human perception of it (Kopnina and Keune, 2010).

According to Catton and Dunlap (1978a and 1978b), the environment can be defined in terms of the following categories: Biophysical (the world outside humans); Natural (greater emphasis on 'ecosystem' including all living organisms); Built/modified (human-constructed surroundings); and Social (culture and society that people develop). The biophysical environment is conceived of as the world outside humans. The natural environment is similar to the biophysical one, with the greater emphasis on 'ecosystem' including all living and non-living organisms that occur naturally on Earth. Catton and Dunlap (1978a) distinguished between built, modified and natural (physical) environments and social environments. The biophysical and natural environments in common discourse are mostly associated with nature or wilderness. The other two types of environment, built and social, refer to, respectively, human-constructed surroundings, including public and private homes and urban landscapes; and to the culture and society that people develop and in which they interact. In Durkheimean terms, humans depend upon only three kinds of environment: the organism, the external world and society (Durkheim [1893] 1984: 285–86).

As discussed in a previous section, ecological anthropologists working in the 1960s and 1970s (Vayda and Rappaport 1968) emphasized the importance of the environment outside of but influential upon human cultures – often 'biologizing' cultural ecology by adding concepts like population, energy flow and ecosystem from the field of biology. With the surge of post-modernism, however, that perspective was largely overshadowed by the notion of the environment existing as a human construction. Today, the shift towards the environment as important in its own right, for its own sake as well as for that of all human beings, is again dominating environmental anthropological literature with the emphasis shifting towards the human impact on the environment. This is not surprising for the applied social science given the fact that current public discourse often associates environment with 'issues' or 'problems' that are often lumped together under one umbrella. These include climate change, aridification and desertification (drying up of regions, often associated with erosion), risks involved in nanotechnology, air and water pollution, and many others. Placing environment in the context of globalization, we may note that environment is also presently seen as a commodity, or as a public good. Biological diversity is defined in the Convention on Biological Diversity as 'the variability among living organisms from all sources including, inter alia, terrestrial, marine and other aquatic ecosystems and the ecological complexities of which they are part; this includes diversity within species, between species and of ecosystems' (Reid et al. 1993). Environment in the narrow sense of 'nature' (pristine wilderness) which exists independently of humans (or to use the judicial or moral jargon, having a 'right to exist') is often relegated to the domain of environmentalist groups. Policy-makers, developers, and (social) scientists often have divergent perspectives which are sometimes at odds with environmental activists. But it is the interplay between both human and environmental interests that earns a focal point in this volume.

Environmental 'issues' or 'problems', viewed both as historical developments and scientific, as well as socially constructed controversies are often grouped under 'degradation discourse', where the 'underlying narrative in fact tells us that people degrade nature, and thus that nature should be saved from culture' (Dove and Carpenter 2008: 3). However, some anthropologists question the assumption that culture threatens nature (Posey 1998) and assert that nature, in fact is socially constructed (Escobar 1996). The controversy concerns the very definition of 'environmental problems' or 'degradation', the extent and origin of these problems, and the ways these problems can be addressed. Lomborg (2001), for example, argues that claims of overpopulation, declining energy resources, deforestation, the loss of biodiversity, and climate change are not supported by scientific data. Conservative think tanks, often supported by industrial lobbyists, promote skepticism as a key tactic of the anti-environmental counter-movement (Jacques et al. 2008). Most observers, however, agree that the increase in human activity adversely effecting the environment is particularly linked to the processes of industrialization, urbanization and population growth (see recent publications of UN Environmental Programme; Intergovernmental Panel on Climate Change (IPCC); The Global Environment Facility (GEF), US Global Change Research Program; Millennium Ecosystem Assessments (MEA), etc.). Recently, Lomborg himself revised his position regarding mitigation of anthropogenic global warming and announced his agreement with 'tens of billions of dollars a year to be invested in tackling climate change' and declared global warming to be 'undoubtedly one of the chief concerns facing the world today' (Lomborg 2010).

This volume is based on the assumption that the unprecedented loss of biodiversity as well as climate change, in the twenty-first century, are largely due to human activity. It is from this objective stance that the following chapters make their claims regarding the role of environmental anthropology in the larger effort to understand human-environment interactions and to preserve the environment for itself and its inhabitants.

Introducing the New Ecological Paradigm to Anthropology

'Anthropologists often share the concerns of sociologists or political scientists but come to them through a different route'

Kay Milton (1996: 9)

William Catton and Riley Dunlap wrote a series of articles defining environmental sociology (Catton and Dunlap 1978a; 1978b; 1980; Dunlap and Catton 1979; 1983; 1994). Referring to paradigmatic definition of environmental sociology, Catton and Dunlap (1978a; 1978b; 1980) assert that Western society shares a variety of background assumptions that they termed the Dominant Western Worldview (DWW) (Dunlap et al., 2002). Frustrated with anthropocentric bias within sociology, they argued that contemporary sociologists needed to address the relationship between society and the biophysical environment, just like many anthropologists have done in various ways since the turn of the nineteenth century. Catton and Dunlap accounted for the oversight by examining the taken-for-granted assumptions of mainstream sociology and explaining how those assumptions led the discipline to ignore the biophysical environment (Bowman 2010). The authors described a sociological paradigm termed Human Exemptionalist Paradigm (HEP) based upon a shared anthropocentrism that – irrespective of particular theoretical orientation (Marxist, functionalist, symbolic interactionist, etc) – led sociologists to treat modern societies as 'exempt' from ecological constraints. To rectify the situation, they advocated the New Ecological Paradigm based on an alternative set of background assumptions. Instead of assuming, for example, that humans have a cultural heritage in addition to (and distinct from) their genetic inheritance, and thus are quite unlike all other animal species, as expressed in HEP, the authors argued that environmental sociology (should) recognize that despite exceptional characteristics, humans remain one among many species that are interdependently involved in the global ecosystem (see also Hornborg and Crumley 2007). A similar approach, many of the contributors to this volume argue, can be developed for environmental anthropology.

There is a traditional preoccupation in anthropology with the position of the 'underdog,' and 'traditional way of life' that has to be defended against Western encroachments of, for example, conservationists that want to ban people from using natural resources. However, mainstream anthropologists often do not address factors such as population growth, increasing use of natural resources, and the spread of capitalist materialistic values when defending the traditional way of life. Little has been said, for example about the role of the 'poor', the 'native', the 'indigenous' in participating in the global process of environmental degradation. Although very often orchestrated from the top (the West, the wealthy, the state, or corrupt local governments), the destruction of natural habitats both by over-consuming upper-classes and the struggling poor is rarely the subject of participant observation. This poses methodological challenges, to be sure. Access to communities openly committing such crimes and/or opening up the lines of communication with such individuals is much harder than doing so with underprivileged victims of environmental tyrants, (see Shoreman-Ouimet in this volume). As it stands, however, narratives of the brave struggle of indigenous peoples or the urban poor against those in power often neglect the possibility that the real 'power' destroying biodiversity may, in some instances, lie within the people—be they poor and indigenous, or the rich and cosmopolitan. It is the notion of the 'power to destroy' that we emphasize here—the idea that in today's world few communities are spared the pressure to adapt to their environment in such a way that doesn't require manipulating the ecosystem. While not all of these communities could possibly be considered 'anti-environmental', they represent the hastening deterioration of local environments. As a result, we believe they offer prime opportunities for contemporary environmental anthropologists interested in documenting human-environmental relationships as well as slowing or repairing environmental damage to examine the connection between local environmental knowledge, decision-making frameworks, and behavioral outcomes (Nazarea 1999).

The time has come for ethnographies to be more complicated—they need not stick to one side or one cause. They can depict cultural reality and reveal conflicting truths. In fact it is hard to imagine a community in which individuals' actions or agendas don't somehow contradict the group's larger environmental, social, political, or religious ideologies. Although we could never deny the paramount importance of 'native' or 'local' involvement in shaping environmentally sound practices and protection of their own natural heritage and environment, the tendency of ecological anthropologists not to also note the opposite side of the coin and the ways in which that same society might also cause environmental injury is consistent with HEP ideology and the prioritization of culture over nature. Such ethnographic over-simplification, in short, ignores human agency in both the negative and positive aspects of environmental preservation.

The goal here is not to eradicate cultural relativism from environmental anthropological research or condemn marginal groups to takeover by big conservation. The fact remains that no one formula can be realistically or conscientiously applied to environmental problems in different cultures, in different geographical regions; and local perspective, participation, and perhaps even initiation, should be considered as basic to environmental repair as it is to its destruction. However, we are questioning the dependence upon relativism that can keep the social scientist from objectively recognizing and commenting on the environmental damage caused by even the most marginal communities, and which therefore also impedes their ability to thoroughly understand the link between local knowledge and environmental behavior. If the goal is to depict or protect a community's way of life, are we not working against them and ourselves by neglecting the degradation of the environment on which they and other communities depend? This volume is thus intended both to highlight the productive work currently underway by anthropologists concerned with environmental degradation as well as serve as a plea for more environmentally-engaged, conservationist anthropology that crosses disciplinary lines and combines information such as the history and biological ecology of local environments with ethnographic data. As the following chapters demonstrate, such work has much to contribute to environmental education, community-based conservation, policy initiatives, and outreach programs.

However, equally important to recognizing and analyzing the environmental damage done by a given community is, conversely, analyzing and describing the ways in which a community may be making an effort to repair and/or protect the environment. Sometimes this type of behavior is rooted in cultural and religious beliefs (see Anderson in this volume); while at other times such actions can seem to contradict past behavior (see Shoreman-Ouimet in this volume). By analyzing these beneficial behaviors and their origin, we garner local environmental knowledge, and learn something about native perceptions of the local environment and methods of classifying and prioritizing various elements in the ecosystem (Conklin 1961; Nazarea 1999). Furthermore, we can make associations between their cognized world, and the cultural beliefs and values that are powerful enough to inspire communal action in the name of the environment (see Maida and Hirsch et al., in this volume). This type of research and these sorts of details demonstrate the positive aspects of human-environmental relationships, which one could argue is equally as, if not more important then, emphasizing the negatives in terms of perpetuating environmentally beneficial behavior and motivating environmental conservation elsewhere. The following chapters thus take into account a range of environmental and social issues in populations around the world. They present various examples of environmental degradation, ethics, and knowledge, as well as instances of environmental conservation efforts and learning. Furthermore, they provide valuable methods of accessing such knowledge and provide insightful theoretical frameworks for assessing and synthesizing such information. All this, we believe, can aid anthropological and conservationist efforts to understand various cultural perspectives and mediate environmental problems.

Organization of the Volume

The remainder of the book is divided into three sections: Theoretical Perspectives, Methodological Challenges, and Anthropologists and the Real World.

The Theoretical Perspectives section includes conceptually motivated chapters building upon the theoretical framework in anthropology as well as other social sciences. Chapters by Leslie Sponsel, Gene Anderson, and Peter Larsen open up interdisciplinary dialogue, as well as elaborate on the 'classical' themes in anthropology, outlined in this Introduction.

Lesley Sponsel bridges the gap between politics and spirituality in his chapter entitled 'The Religion and Environment Interface: Spiritual Ecology in Ecological Anthropology'. Sponsel begins by defining spiritual ecology as a diverse and complex arena of intellectual and practical activities at the interface of religions and spiritualities on the one hand, and on the other, of ecologies, environments, and environmentalisms. His chapter reviews in historical perspective anthropological contributions to the development of spiritual ecology since the late nineteenth century from the work of pioneers such as Edward B. Tyler and James G. Frazer, in the mid-twentieth century from O.K. Moore, Ake Hultkrantz, Roy A. Rappaport, and Gerardo Reichel-Dolmatoff and then the more recent contributions of Stephen J. Lansing, Philippe Descola, Eugene N. Anderson, Kelly D. Alley, Kay Milton, and others. The chapter identifies the main trends, questions, and issues in research, and then identifies key needs and problems for future research. Finally, it places the actual and potential contributions of anthropology in the larger context of the multidisciplinary and multi-faith activities in basic and applied work on spiritual ecology.

In his chapter 'Drawing from Traditional and "Indigenous" Socioecological Theories', Gene Anderson exemplifies Sponsel's broader discussion of spiritual ecology by presenting research and findings from his own research on traditional and 'indigenous' socioecological theories. Here, Anderson discusses a possible future for environmental anthropology by arguing that although traditional ecological knowledge and belief systems continue to be disregarded as sources of serious social theory, traditional and local people have managed, in most cases, to conserve environments and manage resources sustainably. According to Anderson, these wider systems of consciousness and ideology are ignored partly because many are founded on beliefs in 'spirits' or 'supernaturals' that 'rational' social scientists do not accept. Yet, quite apart from the highly debatable meanings of the words in scare quotes, most of the actual moral and ethical teachings involved do not necessarily depend on the 'supernatural' material. For instance, Native American societies of the Northwest Coast of North America construct personhood to include all beings, and their societies include local trees, bears, and mountains. They therefore treat all these beings with care and respect. These moral messages are in turn propagated through oral traditions and through spectacular and aesthetically compelling visual arts. Anderson believes that this presents opportunities for using traditional cultural materials to motivate conservation and sustainable management, while also providing some knotty problems for philosophers. According to Anderson, 'our universities have quite literal walls between 'ontology,' 'epistemology,' 'religion,' 'social science,' and 'art.' Indeed, they are often in different buildings.' The Northwest case shows these distinctions are not only shaky, but are possibly dangerous. Anderson ends with a plea for an environmental anthropology that takes traditional cultures seriously, including their philosophies of knowledge and emotion.

Peter B. Larsen closes this section with an interdisciplinary piece entitled 'Environmental Politics and Policy Ambiguities in Environmental Anthropology'. Here, Larsen discusses the evolving relationship between environmental anthropologists, policy, and politics. According to Larsen, anthropological approaches to

environmental policy and politics are today at the forefront of social theory inter-
linking with political science, human ecology and the wider social sciences. Whereas
the wider epistemological field arguably is more dominated by environmental law-
yers, economists and natural scientists, there is growing recognition of the kinds of
socio-cultural and context-based analysis anthropologists bring to the table. Larsen's
chapter portrays a number of different ways in which environmental anthropologists
have engaged with policy processes and politics in their work. It seeks to describe
both the theoretical and empirical diversity at stake ranging from hands-on involvement in policy design towards conceptual debates in political ecology. Larsen presents
various cases to demonstrate that anthropologists have approached the environmental
policy field in both creative and far-reaching ways, ranging from analyses of global
level environmental processes and transnational environmentalism to local level studies of natural resource management politics. In so doing, Larsen addresses some
common themes characteristic of environmental anthropology and identifies new
directions for research, with particular emphasis on emerging conceptual challenges
associated with the fields of environmental policy-making and politics, not only specific to environmental anthropology, but also linked to the wider ethnographic and
anthropological enterprise as a whole.

In the Methodological Challenges section, Emilio Moran, Helen Kopnina, Daniel
de Vries, and Carl Maida present detailed discussions of the methodological challenges
and innovations in environmental anthropology today.

The section begins with Moran's chapter on the application of GIS to environmental anthropology research. Moran reviews the evolution of spatial thinking within
anthropology, particularly in environmental anthropology, pointing out that while
spatial thinking has been central to theorizing in geography, it has had a less important place in anthropology. Moran explains how the growth of anthropological
engagement with the importance of place has roots in archeological approaches, the
use of aerial photography by some cultural ecologists, and has exploded since the
1990s as more anthropologists have begun to use GIS and satellite remote sensing
data in their environmental research. This increased use of spatial analysis has also led
the field to be more interdisciplinary, more team-based in its field research, and more
integrative than in the past. The chapter reviews this progress and points to future
directions that this integration is likely to take or require from environmental
anthropologists in both training and in practice.

Moving from a technical to a more engaged approach, Helen Kopnina addresses
an innovative methodology in the case of environmental education in her chapter
'What About That Wrapper? Using Consumption Diaries in Green Education'.
Here, Kopnina discusses her preliminary findings on the use of consumption diaries in
green education. Consumption diaries are chronological documents recording the
purchase, use and waste of material, including edibles and utilities. Consumption
diaries are both analytical tools and a means of stimulating environmental awareness.
This chapter discusses both the technique and the results produced by analyzing
the diaries collected from upper-elementary school-aged children and their parents
in Amsterdam, The Netherlands. Kopnina combines qualitative and quantitative

methods to unravel childrens' and parents' perceptions and awareness of consumption and draws from recent research on the role of green education as an important driving force behind the 'greening' of society to help answer the underlying questions: How successful is green education in the Netherlands? How can green education be stimulated further? Focusing on the critical role of education in building a sustainable future and preparing students for green jobs, this chapter examines the possibility of including the study of (responsible) consumption in the school curriculum.

Continuing with the theme of innovative methodologies, in his chapter 'Time and Population Vulnerability to Natural Hazards; The Pre-Katrina Primacy of Experience', Daniel de Vries discusses how anthropologists can better understand and utilize the connection between social time and population vulnerability to natural hazards. de Vries argues that while environmental anthropologists have made progress in showing how perceptions of reality are dependent upon culturally specific assumptions, the modernist tendency to see time as a chronological, quantitative, measurable ordering of events has remained a particularly stubborn scientific premise rarely challenged in the analysis of human-environment interactions. Furthermore, while the changing relationship of humans to time can be seen from the way in which globalization has 'compressed' time and space, hegemonic discourses of linear time are reflected both in objects, such as time-measurement through nuclear clocks, or scientific practices, such as the favoritism of historical analysis over the 'subjective' investigation of culturally shared memory. Linear, Newtonian time, de Vries argues, can be seen as one of the final frontiers of the paradigm of environmental control which underlies the Dominant Social Paradigm. Here de Vries reviews the potential implications that this cultural bias disfavoring the 'social' aspects of time can have from the perspective of risk perception in urbanized floodplains. Based on qualitative fieldwork among residents, engineers, and planners historically dealing with flood hazards, de Vries demonstrates how social time can be studied anthropologically by focusing on the relationship between community wide experiences of surprise and the quality of temporal reference making practices, such as landscape monitoring, memory-networks, and the attribution of meaning. In doing this, he argues that the lack of recognition of non-linear temporal practices in shaping cultural models of risk can seriously increase a population's vulnerability to natural and/or man-made hazards, and as such increase the potential for disaster. The chapter ends by proposing a better integration of social time in emergency preparedness and early warning management programs, and concludes that building system resilience is for a large part dependent on effective management of the temporal aspects of stakeholder cultural models of the environment.

Turning the discussion back to a more traditionally ethnographic methodology in 'Participatory Action Research and Urban Environmental Justice: The Pacoima CARE Project,' Carl Maida discusses the usefulness of participatory action research (PAR) in environmental anthropology, specifically in the area of environmental justice. Based upon long-term ethnographic fieldwork in Pacoima, an urban community confronting toxics, such as household lead, toxic dumping, and diesel pollution, his work investigates how, through resident coalition-building on behalf of the community, PAR has helped to mitigate these toxic threats to area homes and neighborhoods. Pacoima, a community of 101,000 persons in the northeast San Fernando Valley in the City of Los Angeles has endured multiple crises, including deindustrialization, transnational migration, and environmental degradation, compounded by natural hazards, including the 1994 Northridge Earthquake. A largely African-American community until the mid-1990s, Pacoima is predominantly Latino. The trauma of the earthquake forced residents to acknowledge that their community's built and natural environments had become progressively degraded well before the earthquake. The shared experience of the disaster helped to establish a place-centered community identity among neighbors, many recently migrated into the area, as they began to reconstruct after the temblor. As neighbors set out to repair their homes and to clean up their blocks, they also extended their helping resources to people in adjacent neighborhoods. A grassroots organization, called Pacoima Beautiful, which was initially formed to help residents clean up but then grew to promote environmental education, leadership development, and advocacy skills to residents, has an agenda of civic engagement on behalf of environmental awareness and community building. An action research approach designed to enhance the quality of life in the community, together with the cultivation of an aesthetic sensibility, informed the various projects undertaken by Pacoima Beautiful. Maida's chapter focuses on the tension between lay and professional knowledge among stakeholders as they set priorities and develop strategies to carry out a broad-based action research agenda on behalf of identifying toxic substances, understanding the health implications of potential toxic risks, and ameliorating those risks. The chapter introduces the process of community-based PAR, and through ethnography, demonstrates how the Pacoima-based CARE (Community Action for a Renewed Environment) project followed a PAR approach that resulted in long-term community capacity to improve the local environment.

In the last section, Anthropologists and the Real World, Bob Pokrant and Laura Stocker, Teressa Trusty, Nora Haenn, Eleanor Shoreman-Ouimet, Robert Efird and the joint chapter by Jennifer Hirsch, Sarah Van Deusen Phillips, Edward Labenski, Christine Dunford, and Troy Peters present a wide array of ethnographic case studies depicting the ways in which environmental anthropologists are making conservation and environmental well-being part of the larger discussion of culture and the human-environmental relationship. Building upon theoretical and methodological insights from the previous sections, these chapters present rich, context-specific ethnography that is characteristic of environmental anthropology today. However, the contributions in this section also provide valuable interdisciplinary data that could complement scholarship in other social science areas, as well as aid informed policy makers in the fields ranging from urban ghettos to rural communities.

In 'Anthropology, Climate Change and Coastal Planning,' Bob Pokrant and Laura Stocker discuss humanity's response to climate change as one of the main global challenges of the twenty-first century. This chapter examines the contribution of anthropology to climate change research and policy through a focus on the relationship between development planning and climate change policy and practice. The first part of the chapter examines the contribution of Environmental Anthropology to the study of human–nature interactions. It shows that present-day Environmental Anthropology and cognate areas are actively engaged in both academic and policy-oriented research relevant to climate change and climate variability. Such research includes historical understandings and adaptations to weather and climate variability; debates over the social construction of climate change science; the relevance of local knowledge to natural resource management; environmental discourses; unequal ecological exchange and world systems theory; local responses to environmental globalization; and the relationship between development planning and climate change. The second part of the chapter focuses on current debates over the relationship between development planning and climate change, drawing from on-going research on adapting to climate change in coastal Bangladesh and Western Australia for illustrative purposes. The authors critically examine various approaches to coastal planning that seek to integrate development and climate change objectives; the contribution of anthropology to improve culturally informed governance practices among researchers, policy-makers and local communities; and their implications for the promotion of more socially and environmentally sustainable futures for coastal populations.

On a more culturally specific note, in her chapter 'From Ecosystem Services to Unfulfilled Expectations: Factors Influencing Attitudes Toward the Madidi Protected Area,' Teressa Trusty examines communities, attitudes and conservation in the Madidi National Park and Integrated Natural Management Area, Bolivia. According to Trusty, in Bolivia, very few protected areas are created at the behest of indigenous inhabitants and other rural residents. Instead, these parks and reserves reflect national and international interests in conserving biological diversity. It was concern for the quiet voices of those impacted by the creation of these areas that led Trusty to this research, which explores the patterns and variations in environmental values and beliefs amongst residents of rural communities located within and along the north-eastern border of Madidi protected area in northwestern Bolivia. Since its creation in 1995, the park has become a focal point for a range of ideas and attitudes about conservation, rights to resources, and development. Residents of the region, both natives with a long history in the area and more recent migrants from the Andean highlands, share a similar understanding about the park and its purpose. However, they diverge in their attitudes toward the park, reflecting their expectations for benefits from the park and how these have been fulfilled or not. Here, Trusty integrates ideas from political ecology and cognitive anthropology to explore these divergent views and the factors that influence them ranging from the actions of conservation actors in the region to the distinct characteristics of the study communities.

Further investigating the impact of conservation and national park bureacracy on local communities, in her chapter, 'Who's Got the Money Now?: Conservation-Development Meets the *Nueva Ruralidad* in Southern Mexico,' Nora Haenn draws on anthropology's holistic tradition to address a prickly question: Does environmental conservation exacerbate social inequality? Researchers currently debate whether or not conservation practices widen the gulf between rich and poor and whether conservation organizations have focused on cultivating wealthy donors at the expense of strengthening local programs that serve lower income households. Haenn's chapter follows the holistic tradition to show that, at least in some cases, conservation programming may have little effect, one way or the other, on the economic well-being of local peoples. Haenn demonstrates how holism emphasizes the idea that the context surrounding any given phenomenon is as important as the phenomenon itself; and illustrates how in applying holistic approaches to human-environment relations, anthropologists have made surprising findings. For example, Fairhead and Leach, examining the historical context of forest cover in West Africa, found that claims to deforestation there may be exaggerated (Fairhead and Leach 1995 and 1996). Anthropologists working in the area of political ecology regularly seek answers in geographical contexts, examining the ways distant and powerful actors might affect local ecologies. Since its earliest days, political ecology has shown how some local environmental actors may knowingly act unsustainably but are powerless to do otherwise, as they work under the direction of state and international authorities (Stonich 1993). Applying a holistic perspective to the Calakmul Biosphere Reserve in southern Mexico, Haenn outlines a 'regional economy' and compares this depiction with a 'conservation economy' to examine conservation's financial impact. Haenn compares this 'conservation economy' to a broader set of financial flows, including states subsidies and remittances from international migration. The article concludes that, in light of this comparison, the impact of conservation programs on local livelihoods is relatively small.

Like the inhabitants of the Calakmul Biosphere Reserve, many rural US communities have been dubbed 'anti-environmentalist' for their utilitarian view of the land and opposition to outside conservationists. In her chapter, 'Middle Out Conservation: The Role of Elites in Rural American Conservation,' Eleanor Shoreman-Ouimet demonstrates how wealthy landowners and social elites have successfully established water management districts and conservation organizations that are improving environmental quality and redefining the role of agriculture in environmental preservation. Focusing on what Shoreman-Ouimet refers to as 'Middle-out' conservation whereby local elite negotiate between local landowners and federal authorities, this chapter examines the role of social influence and local history and the relatively small role of Western environmentalism in the development of conservation programs. It furthermore demonstrates the need for anthropologists to expand their communtity base by paying increased attention to supposed 'anti-environmentalists' and other communities who have been excluded from the environmentalist discourse for their use-based environmental philosophy. Minorities, rural landowners and commodity farmers have much to contribute to the global discussion on environmental preservation and in the United States own and operate large amounts of valuable land. Emphasizing their efforts to improve land and water quality is thus not only important for what it may teach anthropologists and ecologists about the connection between land use and its preservation, but also for the positive message it sends to other communities who may be encouraged to make similar strides towards environmental preservation.

In his chapter 'Learning By Heart: An Anthropological Perspective on Environmental Learning in Lijiang,' Robert Efird reiterates Kopnina's earlier point that anthropological studies of the ways in which we learn about our environments are both remarkably scarce and increasingly significant. Environmental learning is not just a means of acquiring empirical knowledge; it can also play an important role in shaping our attitudes and behaviors towards our environments. Efird thus argues that knowing more about the intergenerational process whereby people acquire this environmental knowledge and belief may help local communities preserve this knowledge and its effective transmission. As governments in nations ranging from the U.S. to the People's Republic of China officially endorse the teaching of environmental education in schools, studies of environmental learning in sustainably managed ecosystems may also serve as a useful reference in worldwide efforts to teach children to live more sustainably.

Like Carl Maida's work in the previous section, Jennifer Hirsch, Sarah Van Deusen Phillips, Edward Labenski, Christine Dunford, and Troy Peters demonstrate the applicability of and ethnographic vigor involved with the PAR approach in their chapter 'Linking Climate Action to Local Knowledge and Practice: A Case Study of Diverse Chicago Neighborhoods.'

This work was done by The Field Museum in concert with the US Forest Service, social network researchers from Northwestern University, community leaders, and the City of Chicago Department of Environment (DOE) staff. The chapter presents ethnographic research commissioned by the City of Chicago DOE to understand socio-cultural viewpoints on climate change as it works to develop locally relevant programs for engaging the city's diverse communities in its recently released Chicago Climate Action Plan. The overall focus of the chapter is on the importance of taking an anthropological approach to climate change mitigation and adaptation in order to facilitate the development of effective climate action programs, addressing this issue in terms of three specific points: 1) To address climate change, it is important to consider socio-cultural perspectives on climate change and the environment. Hirsch's et al. research illustrates that top-down policy models make cultural assumptions that potentially clash with local cultural models based on communities' understandings of the environment and the impact of individual behaviors on climate. 2) The socio-cultural perspectives that anthropologists uncover in diverse communities can be incorporated into climate action programs, which the authors illustrate through programs that the City of Chicago has adopted based on their ethnographic findings. 3) Finally, the authors address the role of anthropologists in developing climate action programs and how traditional anthropological methods might be tailored to have the greatest impact on policy implementation. The authors consider questions of how to translate anthropological research into actionable items to help mediate between policy agencies and communities. The focus here is on how their participatory action research methodology allows us to engage both with the diverse communities of Chicago and the DOE as a social entity, and as a cultural broker.

As these brief summaries indicate, the contributors to this volume confront the theoretical, methodological and ethnographic challenges that face environmental anthropologists today. It is our hope that this volume might serve as a resource, reference and perhaps even as an inspiration for students and practicing anthropologists, as well as for people everywhere interested in the environmental and social sciences and concerned with the future of our planet and its population. Enjoy.

References

Acheson, J. M. (2006) 'Institutional Failure in Resource Management,' *Annual Review of Anthropology*, 35:117–34.

Allendorf, T., Swe, K. K., Oo, T., Htut, Y., Aung, M., Allendorf, K., Hayek, L.-A., Leimgruber, P. & Wemmer, C. (2006) 'Community Attitudes toward Three Protected Areas in Upper Myanmar (Burma),' *Environmental Conservation*, 33: 344–52.

Argyrou, V. (2005) *The Logic Of Environmentalism: Anthropology, Ecology and Postcoloniality (Studies in Environmental Anthropology and Ethnobiology)*, Oxford: Berghahn Books.

Balee, W. L. (1994) *Footprints in the Forest: Ka'apor Ethnobotany – the Historical Ecology of Plant Utilization by an Amazonian People*, New York: Columbia University Press.

——(1998) *Advances in Historical Ecology*. New York: Columbia University Press.

Barlett, P. F. and Brown, P.J. (1985) 'Agricultural development and the quality of life: An anthropological view,' *Agriculture and Human Values*, 2(2): 28–35.

Barnard, A. and Spencer, J. (1996) *The Encyclopedia of Social and Cultural Anthropology*, London: Routledge.

Barth, F. (1966) 'Models of Social Organization,' *Royal Anthropological Institute of Great Britain and Ireland*, Occasional Paper, no. 23.

——(1969) *Ethnic Groups and Boundaries: The Social Organization of Culture Difference*, Boston: Little, Brown and Company.

Bennett, J.W.(1999) *The Ecological Transition: Cultural Anthropology and Human Adaptation*, Chicago: University of Chicago Press.

Biersack, A. (1999) 'Introduction: From the 'New Ecology' to the New Ecologies,' *American Anthropologist*, 101(1): 5–18.

Blaser, M. (2009) 'The Threat of the Yrmo: The Political Ontology of a Sustainable Hunting Program,' *American Anthropologist*, 111(1): 10–20.

Bodley, J. H. (2008a) *Victims of Progress*, 5th edition, Lanham, MD: AltaMira Press.

Bodley, J.H (2008b). *Anthropology and Contemporary Human Problems*, 5th edition, Lanham, MD: AltaMira Press.

Brosius, J.P. (1999) 'Green Dots, Pink Hearts: Displacing Politics from the Malaysian Rainforest,' *American Anthropologist*, 101(1): 36–57.

——(2006) 'Common ground between anthropology and conservation biology'. *Conservation Biology*, 20:683–85.

Browder, J.O. and Godfrey, B.J. (1997) *Rainforest Cities: Urbanization, Development, and the Globalization of the Brazilian Amazon*, New York: Columbia University Press.

Burr, V. (1995) *An Introduction to Social Contructionism*, London: Routledge.

Catton, W. and Dunlap, R. (1978a) 'Environmental sociology: A new paradigm,' *The American Sociologist*, 13: 41–49.

——(1978b) 'Paradigms, theories, and the primacy of the HEP/NEP distinction,' *The American Sociologist*, 13: 256–59.

——(1980) 'A new ecological paradigm for post-exuberant Sociology,' *American Behavioral Scientist*, 24, 15–47.

Chaloupka, W. and Cawley, R. M. (1993) 'The Great Wild Hope: Nature, Environmentalism and the Open Secret,' in J. Bennett and W. Chaloupka (eds) *In the Nature of Things: Language, Politics, and the Environment*, Minneapolis: University of Minnesota Press.

Chapin, M., Lamb, Z., Threlkeld, B. (2005) 'Mapping Indigenous Lands,' *Annual Review of Anthropology*, 34: 619–38.

Charnle, S. and Poe, M.R. (2007) 'Community Forestry in Theory and Practice: Where Are We Now?' *Annual Review of Anthropology*, 36: 301–36.

Charnley, S. and Durham, W. H. (2010) 'Anthropology and Environmental Policy: What Counts?' *American Anthropologist,* (112) 3: 397–415.

Clay, J. (1988) *Indigenous Peoples and Tropical Forests. Models of Land Use and Management from Latin America,* Cambridge, MA: Cultural Survival, Inc.

Conklin, B.A. and Graham, C.R. (1995) 'The Shifting Middle Ground: Amazonian Indians and Eco-Politics,' *American Anthropologist,* (97) 4: 695–710.

Conklin, H. (1961) 'The Study of Shifting Cultivation,' *Current Anthropology,* 2: 27–61.

Crate, S. A. and Nuttall, M. (eds) (2009) *Anthropology and Climate Change: From Encounters to Actions,* Walnut Creek, CA: Left Coast Press.

Cronon, W. (1996a) 'Introduction,' in W. Cronon (ed.) *Uncommon Ground: Toward Reinventing Nature,* New York: W.W Norton and Co.

——(1996b) 'The Trouble with Wilderness, or Getting Back to the Wrong Nature,' in W. Cronon (ed.) *Uncommon Ground: Rethinking Human Place in Nature,* pp. 69–90, New York: W. W. Norton and Co.

Crumley, C. L. (ed.) (1994) *Historical Ecology: Cultural Knowledge and Changing Landscapes,* Santa Fe, NM: School for American Research Press.

Davis, S. (1988) 'Indigenous peoples, environmental protection and sustainable development,' *World Bank Off. Environ. Sci. Affairs Occas. Pap.* Washington, DC: World Bank.

Diamond, J. M. (1987) 'The Worst Mistake In The History Of The Human Race,' *Discover,* pp. 64–66.

Dove, M. R. (2006) 'Indigenous People and Environmental Politics,' *Annual Review of Anthropology,* 35: 191–208.

Dove, M.R. and Carpenter, C. (2008) *Environmental Anthropology: A Historical Reader,* Blackwell Anthologies in Social and Cultural Anthropology, Oxford: Blackwell Publishing.

Buttel, F.H., Dickens, P., Dunlap, R., and Gijswijt, A. (2002a) 'Sociological theory and the environment: An overview and introduction,' In R. Dunlap, P. Dickens, F.H. Buttel, and A. Gijswijt (eds) *Sociological Theory and the Environment: Classical Foundations and Contemporary Insights,* Lanham, MD: Rowman and Littlefield.

Dunlap, R. & Catton, W. (1979) Environmental Sociology, *Annual Review of Sociology,* 5: 243–73.

Dunlap, R. and Catton, W. (1983) 'What environmental sociologists have in common (Whether concerned with 'built' or 'natural' environments)' *Sociological Inquiry,* 53: 113–35.

——(1994) 'Struggling with human exemptionalism: The rise, decline and revitalization of environmental sociology,' *The American Sociologist,* 25: 5–30.

Durkheim, E. ([1893] 1984) *The Division of Labor in Society.* London: Macmillan Press.

Ellen, R. F. (1982) *Environment, Subsistence, and System: The Ecology of Small-Scale Social Formations,* Cambridge: Cambridge University Press.

Escobar, A. (1996) 'Constructing Nature: Elements for a Poststructural Political Ecology,' In R. Peet and M. Watts (eds) *Liberation Ecologies: Environment, Development, Social Movements,* pp. 46–68, London: Routledge.

Evans-Pritchard, E. E. (1940) *The Nuer: A Description of the Modes of Livelihood and Political Institutions of a Nilotic People,* New York: Oxford University Press.

Fairhead, J. and Leach, M. (1995) 'False forest history, complicit social analysis: rethinking some West African environmental narratives,' *World Development,* 23(6): 1023–35.

——(1996) 'Misreading the African Landscape: Society and Ecology in a Forest-Savanna mosaic, 1893–1993,' *Environment and History,* 1: 55–91.

Friedman, J. (1974) 'Marxism, structuralism and vulgar materialism,' *Man,* 9(444–69).

Geertz, C. (1959) 'Form and Variation in Balinese Village Structure,' *American Anthropologist,* 61:991–1012.

——(1963) *Agricultural Involution: The Process of Ecological Change in Indonesia,* Berkley: University of California Press, Association of Asian Studies.

Gibson, C.C. and Marks, S.A. (1995) 'Transforming rural hunters into conservationists: an assessment of community-based wildlife management programs in Africa,' *World Development,* 23(6): 941–57.

Haenn, N. (2006) 'The Power of Environmental Knowledge: Ethnoecology and Environmental Conflicts in Mexican Conservation,' in N. Haenn and R. Wilk (eds) *The Environment in Anthropology: A Reader in Ecology, Culture, and Sustainable Living*, pp. 226–37. New York: New York University Press.

Haenn, N. and Wilk, R. (eds) (2006) *The Environment in Anthropology: A Reader in Ecology, Culture, and Sustainable Living*, New York: New York University Press.

Hardesty, D. L. (1977) *Ecological Anthropology*, New York: Wiley.

Harris, M. (1968) *The Rise of Anthropological Theory: A History of Theories of Culture*, New York: Crowell.

Hern, W. M. (1992) 'Family Planning, Amazon Style,' *Natural History*, 101(12); Reprinted in A Podolefsky and P. J. Brown (eds) (1994) *Applying Cultural Anthropology*, pp. 170–74, London: Mayfield Publishing Company.

Herskovits, M. J. (1926) 'The Cattle Complex in East Africa,' *American Anthropologist*, 28: 230–72, 361–88, 494–528.

Hornborg, A. and Crumley, C.L. (eds) (2007) *The World system and the Earth system: global socioenvironmental change and sustainability since the Neolithic*, Walnut Creek, CA: Left Coast Press, Inc.

Infield, M. (1988) 'Attitudes of a rural community towards conservation and a local conservation area in Natal, South Africa' *Biological Conservation*, 45: 21–46.

Ingold, T. (1992) 'Comments,' *Current Anthropology*, 33(1): 208–9.

——(2007) 'The trouble with 'evolutionary biology,'' *Anthropology Today*, 23(2): 13–17.

Johnston, B.R. (ed.) (1994) *Who Pays the Price?: The Sociocultural Context of Environmental Crisis*, Washington, DC: Island.

Johnston, B.R. (1995) 'Human rights and the environment,' *Human Ecology*, 23(2): 111–23.

Johnston, B.R.(ed.) (1996) *Life and death matters: human rights and the environment at the end of the millennium*, Walnut Creek, CA: AltaMira Press.

Kalland, A. (2009) *Unveiling the Whale: Discourses on Whales and Whaling*, New York: Berghahn Books.

Kemf, E. (ed.) (1993) *The Law of the Mother: Protecting Indigenous Peoples in Protected Areas*, San Francisco: Sierra Club Books.

Kidner, D.W. (2000) A Critique of the Social Construction of Nature. In D. Inglis, J. Bone, R. Wilkie (eds) *From Nature to Natures: Contestation and Recontruction*, pp 263–81, London: Routledge.

Kopnina, H. and Keune, H. (eds) (2010) *Health and Environment: Social Science Perspectives*, New York: Nova Science Publishers, Inc.

Kottak, C. P. (1999) 'The New Ecological Anthropology,' *American Anthropologist*, 101: 23–35.

Kroeber, A. L. (1963) *Cultural and Natural Areas of Native North America*, Berkeley: University of California Press.

Kuper, A. (1996) *Anthropology and Anthropologists*, London: Routledge.

Lomborg, B. (2001) *The Skeptical Environmentalist: Measuring the Real State of the World*, Cambridge: Cambridge University Press.

Lomborg, B. (ed) (2010) *Smart Solutions to Climate Change: Comparing Costs and Benefits*. Copenhagen Business School: Copenhagen.

Maffi, L. (ed.) (2001) *On Biocultural Diversity: Linking Language, Knowledge, and the Environment*, Washington, D.C.: Smithsonian Institution Press.

Maffi, L. (2005) 'Linguistic, Cultural, and Biological Diversity,' *Annual Review of Anthropology*, 34: 599–617.

Maffi, L. and Woodley, E. (eds) (2010) *Biocultural Diversity Conservation: A Global Sourcebook*, London: Earthscan.

Maida, C. A. (2007) *Sustainability and Communities of Place*, Studies in Environmental Anthropology and Ethnobiology, New York: Berghahn Books.

Malinowski, B. (1922) *Argonauts of the Western Pacific*, London: Routledge.

Marks, S.A. (1976) *Large Mammals and a Brave People: Subsistence Hunters in Zambia*, Seattle: University of Washington Press.

Marks S.A. (1984) *The Imperial Lion: Human Dimensions of Wildlife Management in Central Africa*, Boulder, CO: Westview.

Mason, P. (1990) *Deconstructing America: Reconstructions of the Other*, London: Routledge.

Merlan F. (1991) 'The limits of cultural constructionism: the case of Coronation Hill, *Oceania* 61: 341–52.

McElroy, A. and Townsend, P. K. (1989) *Medical Anthropology in Ecological Perspective* 2nd edn, Boulder, CO: Westview Press.

Milton, K. (1996) *Environmentalism and Cultural Theory: Exploring the Role of Anthropology in Environmental Discourse*, (Environment and Society), London: Routledge.

Moran, E. F. (1990) 'Ecosystem Ecology in Biology and Anthropology,' in E. Moran (ed.) *Ecosystem Approach in Anthropology*, Ann Arbor: University of Michigan Press.

——(2006) *People and Nature: An Introduction to Human Ecological Relations*, (Primers in Anthropology), Oxford: Blackwell Publishing.

——(2008) *Human Adaptability: An Introduction to Ecological Anthropology*, Boulder, CO: Westview Press.

Moran, K., King, S.R., and Carlson, T.J. (2001) 'Biodiversity Prospecting: Lessons and Prospects,' *Annual Review of Anthropology*, 30: 505–26.

Muhlhausler, P., and Peace, A. (2006) 'Environmental Discourses,' *Annual Review of Anthropology*, 35: 457–79.

Nazarea, V.D. (1999) 'A View from a Point: Ethnoecology as Situated Knowledge,' In V. D. Nazarea (ed.) *Ethnoecology: Situation Knowledge/Local Lives*, Tucson: University of Arizona Press.

Netting, R. M. (1977) *Cultural Ecology*, Menlo Park, CA: Cummings Publishing Co.

——(1981) *Balancing on an Alp: Ecological Change and Continuity in a Swiss Mountain Community*, Cambridge: Cambridge University Press.

——(1993) *Smallholders, Householders: Farm Families and the Ecology of Intensive, Sustainable Agriculture*, Stanford: Stanford University Press.

Oliver-Smith, A. (1996) 'Anthropological Research on Hazards and Disasters,' *Annual Review of Anthropology*, 25: 308–28.

Oliver-Smith, A. and Hoffman, S.M. (eds) (1999) *The Angry Earth: disaster in anthropological perspective*, London: Routledge.

——(2002) *Catastrophe & Culture: the anthropology of disaster*, Santa Fe, N.M: School of American Research Press.

Orlove, B. S. and Brush, S. B. (1996) 'Anthropology and the conservation of Biodiversity,' *Annual Review of Anthropology*, 25: 329–52.

Parker, E. (1993) 'Fact and Fiction in Amazonia: The Case of the Apete,' *American Anthropologist* 94(2): 406–28.

Posey, D. A. (1998) 'Diachronic Ecotones and Anthropogenic Landscapes in Amazonia: Contesting the Consciouness of Conservation,' In W. Balee (ed.) *Advances in Historical Ecology*, pp. 104–18, New York: Columbia University Press.

Rambo, A. T. (1985) 'Primitive Polluters: Semang Impact on the Malaysian Tropical Rain Forest System,' Anthropological Papers 76, Museum of Anthropology, Ann Arbor: University of Michigan.

Rappaport, R. A. (1968) *Pigs for the Ancestors: Ritual in the Ecology of a New Guinea People*, New Haven: Yale University Press.

Reid, W.V., Laird, S.A., Meyer, C., Gámez, R., Sittenfeld, A., Janzen, D.H., Gollin, M.A., and Juma, C. (eds) (1993) *Biodiversity Prospecting: Using Resources for Sustainable Development*, Washington, DC: World Resource Institute.

Rikoon, J.S. and Goedeke, T. (2000) *Anti-Environmentalism and Citizen Opposition to the Ozark Man and the Biosphere Reserve* (Symposium Series, v. 61). New York: Edwin Mellen Press.

Salzman, P.C. and Attwood, D.W. (eds) (1996) *Encyclopedia of Social and Cultural Anthropology*, London: Routledge.

Smith, E. and Wishnie, M. (2000) 'Conservation and Subsistence in Small-Scale Societies,' *Annual Review of Anthropology*, (29): 493–524.

Smith-Cavros, E. (2006) 'Black Churchgoers and Environmental Activism' *Ecological Anthropology*, 10: 33–44.

Sponsel, L (2007) 'Ecological Anthropology,' in S. Sarkar and L. Kalof (eds) *Encyclopedia of Earth*, Washington, D.C.: Environmental Information Coalition, National Council for Science and the Environment. Website: http://www.eoearth.org/article/Ecological_anthropology.

Stearman, A.M. (1984) Yuquí connection: another look at Siriono deculturation, *American Anthropologist*, 86(3): 630–50.

Stearman, A.M., Redford, K.H. (1995) Game management and cultural survival: the Yuquí Ethnodevelopment Project in lowland Bolivia, *Oryx*, 29(1): 29–24.

Steward, J. H. (1949) *Handbook of South American Indians*, vol. 5: Comparative Ethnology of South American Indians, Prepared in cooperation with the U.S. Dept. of State, Washington, DC: Government Printing Office.

——(1955) *Theory of Culture Change: The Methodology of Multilinear Evolution*, Urbana, IL: University of Illinois Press.

——(1968) 'The Concept and Method of Cultural Ecology,' In Jane C. Steward and Robert F. Murphy (eds) *Evolution and Ecology: Essays on Social Transformation*, Urbana: University of Illinois Press.

Stonich, S. (1993) *'I am destroying the land!': the political ecology of poverty and environmental destruction in Honduras*, Boulder, CO: Westview Press.

Strang, V. (1997) *Uncommon Ground: cultural landscapes and environmental values*, (Explorations in Anthropology), London: Berg.

Tsing, A. L. (1999) 'Becoming a Tribal Elder, and Other Green Development Fantasies,' in T.M. Li (ed.) *Transforming Indonesian Uplands: Marginality, Power and Production*, pp. 159–202, OPA, Netherlands: Harwood Academic Publishers.

Townsend, P.K. (2000) *Environmental Anthropology. From Pigs to Policies*, Illinois: Waveland Press.

Turner, T. (1993) 'The role of indigenous peoples in the environmental crisis: the example of the Kayapó of the Brazilian Amazon,' *Perspect. Biol. Med.*, 36(3): 526–47.

Vayda, A. P. (2008) 'Causal explanation as a research goal: a pragmatic view,' In B.B. Walters, B.J. McCay, P. West, and S. Lees (eds) *Against the Grain: the Vayda tradition in human ecology and ecological anthropology*, Lanham, MD and New York: AltaMira Press.

Vayda, A. P and Rappaport, R.A. (1968) 'Ecology: cultural and non-cultural,' in J. A. Chifton (ed.) *Introduction to Cultural Anthropology*, pp. 477–97, Boston, MA: Houghton Mifflin Co.

Vayda, A. P., and Walters, B.B. (1999) 'Against political ecology,' *Human Ecology*, 27(1) 167–79.

Vayda, A. P. and McCay, B.J. (1975) 'New Direction in Ecology and Ecological Anthropology,' *Annual Review of Anthropology*, 4: 293–306.

Vivanco, L. A. (2006) *Green Encounters: Shaping and Contesting Environmentalism in Rural Costa Rica*, Vol. 3 in 'Environmental Anthropology and Ethnobiology' Series, Oxford: Berghahn Books.

Wagley, C. (1976 [1953]) *Amazon Town*, New York: Oxford University Press.

Wells, M.P., Brandon, K., Hannah, L.J. (eds) (1992) *People and Parks: Linking Protected Area Management with Local Communities*, Washington, DC: World Bank/World Wildlife Fund/US Agency International Development.

West, P. (2005) 'Translation, value, and space: theorizing an ethnographic and engaged environmental anthropology,' *American Anthropologist*, 107(4): 632–42.

West, P., Igoe, J. and Brockington, D. (2006) 'Parks and Peoples: The Social Impact of Protected Areas,' *Annual Review of Anthropology*, 35: 251–77.

Williams, M.A. (2002) 'When I can read my title clear: Anti-Environmentalism and Sense of Place in the Great Smoky Mountains,' in B. Howell (ed.) *Culture Environment and Conservation in the Appalachian South*, pp. 87–100, Chicago: University of Illinois Press.

Wolf, E. (1982) *Europe and the People without History*, Berkeley, CA: University of California Press.

Part I
The Theoretical Perspectives

1

THE RELIGION AND ENVIRONMENT INTERFACE

Spiritual Ecology in Ecological Anthropology

Leslie E. Sponsel

Among the most elemental, perennial, and pivotal questions are these: What is nature? What is human nature? What is the place of humans in nature? What should be the place of humans in nature? Historically, ecological anthropology has addressed these questions in various ways and degrees, and continues to do so, especially the third question. The present chapter explores how spiritual ecology can contribute to this pursuit. Basically, spiritual ecology reveals aspects that have tended to be ignored or neglected, but that are increasingly important given the ongoing environmental crisis. First, however, spiritual ecology in general must be outlined.

Spiritual Ecology

What is spiritual ecology? Spiritual ecology is a complex and diverse arena of intellectual and practical activities at the interface of religions and spiritualities on the one hand, and on the other, ecologies, environments, and environmentalisms (Sponsel 2007: 340). The use of the plural in these terms reflects the variation and variability within each category. Some scholars prefer labels such as religion and ecology, or religion and nature, instead of spiritual ecology. However, the qualifier 'spiritual' is more inclusive because many individuals who do not choose to affiliate with any particular religious organization or to identify themselves with some religion in general are nevertheless spiritual, while those who do choose to associate with a religion can also be spiritual. In addition, the term conveniently encompasses the beliefs of many in spiritual beings and forces in nature (Harvey 2006, Sponsel 2001a, 2007a, b). Among academics who have used the label spiritual ecology are Merchant (2005) and S.M. Taylor (2007).

The spiritual and practical aspects of spiritual ecology are very ancient, whereas the intellectual aspects in academia are quite recent. The earliest and most widespread spiritual ecologists are the indigenous adherents to some manifestation of Animism, such as traditional Australian Aborigines (Harvey 2006, Rose 1992). Animism, a generic label, encompasses a belief in spiritual beings and forces in nature, but is not the only religion with such beliefs. Within Western culture, one of the earlier outstanding examples of a spiritual ecologist is the Medieval Catholic monk Saint Francis of Assisi, who was many centuries ahead of his time, among other things, in his deep concern for all beings in nature as sacred (Nothwehr 2002).

Within modern academia in the United States, more than anyone else Lynn White, Jr. (1907–87) initiated scholarship in spiritual ecology. His classic essay published in 1967 in the prestigious journal *Science* is titled 'The Historical Roots of Our Ecological Crisis.' It generated a discussion and debate that continue to this day. Furthermore, it led to the development of ecotheology, which usually focuses on the relationship between Christianity and environment in particular. This field often concentrates on trying to refute White's thesis; namely, that anthropocentrism, utilitarianism, and other elements of the worldview and values toward nature reflected in the predominant interpretation of the Bible are the ultimate cause of the ecocrisis (Santmire 2003). However, the various activities associated with the Forum on Religion and Ecology since the 1990s, developed largely by Mary Evelyn Tucker and John Grim, probably have done more than any other initiative to launch what is here called spiritual ecology as a contemporary field of academic and scientific research, publications, conferences, and teaching (Tucker 1997). Two other truly extraordinary contributors are Bron Taylor (2005, 2010) and Roger S. Gottlieb (2006a, b) as demonstrated by their many publications as well as other work.

In general, each of the three primary components of spiritual ecology – intellectual, spiritual, and practical – can be pursued alone, but often two or all three of them reinforce one another in various degrees and ways (e.g. Tucker and Berling 2003, Taylor 2010). The intellectual one encompasses academic scholarship across the humanities and the natural and social sciences. This interdisciplinary, multi-disciplinary, and transdisciplinary field of study is growing exponentially (Gottlieb 2006b). Indeed, there is sufficient literature on many of the world religions in relation to ecology to launch an entire academic and/or activist career focused on exploring just one of them, such as Buddhist ecology and environmentalism (Tucker and Williams 1997, Kaza and Kraft 2000, Sponsel and Natadecha-Sponsel 2008).

The spiritual aspect may be pursued by an individual or group in nature or through participation in a religious organization. It may involve sacred places, rituals, pilgrimage, and related phenomena. This is the least studied component of spiritual ecology so far, although it is often the most important one. Many environmentalists and conservationists are ultimately motivated by some kind of personal spiritual, mystical, or epiphanic experiences in nature, albeit this is usually implicit in their writings at best (Taylor 2005, 2010).

The practical component of spiritual ecology refers to environmental action on behalf of nature or the environment, and some of this action is explicitly recognized as religious environmentalism (Bassett, et al., 2000, Palmer and Finlay 2003, Dudley, et al., 2005, Gardner 2006, Gottlieb 2006a, b, Sponsel 2007b, c, Taylor 2005, 2010; Alliance for Religions and Conservation 2010). A multitude of diverse specific projects are well underway in this arena, such as Interfaith Power and Light in the USA, and internationally the Alliance of Religions and Conservation, to mention just two.

Since Earth Day on April 22, 1970, the environmental crisis has not only continued, but also it has become progressively worse and more urgent. Organizations such as the Worldwatch Institute, the United Nations Millennium Ecosystem Assessment, and the Intergovernmental Panel on Climate Change have been systematically documenting the worsening ecocrisis from the local to the global levels. This situation has transpired in spite of many secular approaches ranging from the impressive developments in the second half of the twentieth century of the environmental components in education, natural and social sciences, humanities like history, philosophy, and ethics, and law and other professions, not to mention the establishment of numerous natural history, environmental, and conservations organizations since the nineteenth century (Collett and Karakashian 1996, De Steiguer 2006). It should be obvious that *secular approaches, although certainly necessary and important, have proven insufficient in meeting the challenges of the ecocrisis.*

Like White (1967: 28, 30–31), many individuals from diverse backgrounds and persuasions are convinced that the ecocrisis will be resolved, or at least markedly reduced, only if there is *a fundamental rethinking, refeeling, and revisioning of the place of humans in nature.* They believe that religion and spirituality can generate such a profound transformation in many individuals, groups, and societies where secular approaches have proven inadequate (World Wildlife Fund International 1986, Tucker and Berling 2003, Berry and Tucker 2006, 2009, Watling 2009). For instance, The Global Forum (1990) in Moscow in January 1990 concluded: 'The Environmental crisis requires changes not only in public policy, but in individual behavior. The historical record makes clear that religious teaching, example, and leadership are powerfully able to influence personal conduct and commitment. As scientists, many of us have had profound experiences of awe and reverence before the universe. We understand that what is regarded as sacred is more likely to be treated with care and respect. Our planetary home should be so regarded. Efforts to safeguard and cherish the environment need to be infused with a vision of the sacred.' Among the scientific luminaries endorsing this statement were Freeman J. Dyson, Stephen Jay Gould, Peter Raven, Carl Sagan, and Stephen H. Schneider.

No particular religious or spiritual path is designated as the sole solution for the ongoing and worsening ecocrisis. Instead, scientists, scholars, educators, clerics, adherents, politicians, and others are each looking into their own religion or spirituality for elements to help them construct more viable environmental worldviews, attitudes, values, and practices for themselves and like-minded individuals and organizations (World Wildlife Fund International 1986, Tucker and Berling 2003, Gottlieb 2006a,b, Watling 2009). Individuals who are not religious or spiritual pursue their own alternative paths (e.g., Crosby 2002).

Whether or not spiritual ecology becomes a nonviolent revolutionary movement and finally resolves or at least reduces the ecocrisis, it remains a most fascinating and important phenomenon. Religions, spiritualities, ecologies, environments, and environmentalisms are each interesting and significant, and it is even more interesting when one examines their interrelationships (Sponsel 2001a, 2007a, c).

Spiritual ecology has already demonstrated an extraordinary capacity to facilitate constructive dialog and collaboration between disparate and sometimes antagonistic parties, including religions, religion and science, and the humanities and sciences (Carroll and Warner 1998, Conroy and Petersen 2000, Swearer 2009). As argued below, spiritual ecology may even become a catalyst for a theoretical and practical new synthesis in understanding some of the most elemental, perennial, and pivotal questions: What is nature? What is human? What is the place of humans in nature? What should be the place of humans in nature?

At the same time, clearly there are some serious obstacles and limitations facing spiritual ecology. First, there is the powerful establishment which is seriously challenged by spiritual ecology, including hegemonic economic and political interests, religious conservatives, individuals pursuing scientism, Marxists who ignore the significance of religion and spirituality, and so on (Haught 1990: 199–250). Second, there is the hypocritical discrepancy between ideals and behaviors among adherents to various religions as well as the need for transcending rhetoric to pursue practical action. Third, there are tensions and factions within any given religion or religious sect or school. Fourth, far more outreach to the grass roots or community level is sorely needed. (For further discussion of obstacles see Taylor 2010: 177–79).

While spiritual ecology remains in its infancy in many respects, it is likely to mature rapidly within coming decades. Indeed, there is clearly the substantial momentum of the exponential growth of spiritual ecology pursued in numerous and diverse ways in many levels and sectors of society (Taylor 2010: 200–2002, Sponsel 2011). For instance, the subject matter of spiritual ecology, by whatever label, is beginning to gain recognition in textbooks on the anthropology of religion, environmental anthropology, human ecology, radical ecology, and resource management among other subjects (Marten 2001, Merchant 2005, Bowie 2006, Townsend 2009). The focus of the rest of this chapter is on the potential of spiritual ecology to contribute to ecological and environmental anthropology, fields that have tended to ignore the possible relevance of religion. Here environmental anthropology is viewed as the applied dimension of ecological anthropology, the latter a more inclusive rubric (Sponsel 2007b).

Nature

What is nature? In the history of ecological anthropology nature has been studied successively from the main perspectives of geography as a landscape containing natural resources for use, management, and conservation; biology as ecosystem with energy flow and nutrient cycling; and postmodernism as cultural construction such as in ideas like wilderness and biodiversity (Glacken 1967, Coates 1998, Sponsel 2007b). With relatively few exceptions, only fairly recently has nature been studied also from the perspective of religion and spirituality, and particularly in the case of sacred places in nature (Selin 2003, Sponsel 2007c, d). Accordingly, spiritual ecology brings a new perspective to bear on the question of what is nature. The answer, in general and in brief, is that *nature is sacred and has intrinsic value.* Moreover, for many indigenous and other cultures, nature is far more than an exclusively biophysical reality; in addition, it is a spiritual reality. Nature is considered to be permeated with a multitude of diverse and powerful spiritual beings and forces. Accordingly, spiritual ecology attends to the fact that *religion and spirituality can be a significant influence on worldviews, values, attitudes, and behaviors, and that aspects of these may have environmental consequences.* Thereby spiritual ecology complements the other major approaches within ecological anthropology of cultural ecology, historical ecology, and political ecology which, with a few notable exceptions, have usually ignored religion and spirituality (Sponsel 2001a, 2007a, b, c, Townsend 2009). Spiritual ecology should be part of the new trends in ecological and environmental anthropology.

In spite of the customary neglect of the role of religion and spirituality in most research on human-environment interactions (e.g., Kottak 1999, Robbins 2004), an increasing number of cases demonstrate that, indeed, they can be an important factor. For example, Susan M. Darlington (1998, 2003) documents the mobilization of local people by Phrakhru Pitak Nanthakhun, a prominent Buddhist environmentalist monk from the community, to protect the trees in their forest in northern Thailand. Their popular religion is syncretic, a mixture of Animism, Hinduism, and Buddhism. They believe that spirits in the forest, some good and others evil, dwell in the land, trees, and waterways. Consequently, to establish and protect a community forest, villagers first construct a shrine where they request the assistance of the village guardian spirit. Then the monk leads a symbolic ordination ritual wrapping saffron cloths around a giant tree in the forest and some associated trees in its vicinity. The combination of the fear of antagonizing spirits together with the respect for the Buddha and Buddhism is an especially powerful motivator inhibiting potential loggers. In the process, the monk also informs villagers about the urgency and benefits of environmental conservation through community forestry and other measures. Consequently, not only is a portion of the landscape ritually sanctified, but also community identity and solidarity are promoted powerfully as well. According to Darlington, this sense of community is crucial for the successful management and conservation of community forests and other environmental and social projects, and it is achieved through religious ceremony in this and other areas of Thailand.

Another particularly striking case is a study by Bruce A. Byers, Robert N. Cunliffe, and Andrew T. Hudak (2001) with the Shona people who live in the Zambezi Valley of northern Zimbabwe. The Shona consider trees, rivers, pools, mountains, and even whole mountain ranges to be sacred. Their concept of the sacred connotes something that is life sustaining and linked to rain and the fertility of the land. A sacred place is where spirits are present. Associated with it are certain rules of access as well as prohibited behaviors. Moreover, deforestation is at least 50 per cent lower in sacred forests than in their secular counterparts. Some 133 species of native plants occur in these sacred forests, whereas they are variously threatened, endangered, or extirpated elsewhere in Zimbabwe. These authors conclude that strategies for biodiversity conservation that connect nature and culture are more likely to be effective than those imposed from the top down by governmental and/or international agencies that ignore the traditional beliefs, values, institutions, and practices of local societies.

Christopher Hakkenberg (2008) investigated local conservation practices of northwestern Yunnan in China. He observed that mountains and forests that Tibetans consider sacred are higher in biodiversity. A majority of inhabitants adhere to religious values in their relationship with nature and resources. Furthermore, he asserts that the local and global discourses on biological and cultural diversity coincide and coexist in this region, and that their traditional environmental knowledge and Western scientific knowledge are complementary. (Also, see Ramakrishnan, et al., 1998; Posey 1999; Dudley, et al., 2005; and Sponsel 2005a, 2007d).

Sacred groves are stands of trees or patches of forest that local communities conserve primarily because of their religious importance. However, these groves can also serve economic, medicinal, social, and cultural functions. For example, some plant species in sacred groves may provide emergency foods during periods of crop failure and famine through drought. Furthermore, such sacred places can help protect watershed resources like springs, soil fertility and moisture, and ecosystem processes such as nutrient cycling. A variety of factors promote the conservation of biodiversity in sacred groves like general or selective limits on the use of different species.

Sacred groves can be quite extensive. In India, for instance, traditionally they are associated with almost every village and temple (e.g., Kent 2009). Currently there are still some 150,000 sacred groves covering a total of 33,000 hectares (Malhotra 1998, also see Srivastana, et al., 2007). They range in size from a fraction of a hectare to several square kilometers. While each sacred grove may be a relatively small island refuge of biodiversity, they are numerous. Therefore, collectively through space, and cumulatively over time, they are of some ecological and conservation significance. In India and elsewhere, sacred groves appear to be, in effect but not necessarily by design, a very ancient, widespread, and important traditional system of environmental conservation that existed long before the implementation of Western strategies for protected areas such as wildlife sanctuaries and national parks (Sponsel, et al., 1998).

In the case of sacred groves, the Western dichotomies between nature and culture as well as between the natural and supernatural not only may not apply, but also might well be misleading. Sacred groves also demonstrate that beliefs and emotions about nature, including its meaning and significance, can be as important as reason in natural resource use, management, and conservation (Posey, et al., 1999, Milton 2002, Anderson 2010).

Here Roy A. Rappaport's (1979: 97–99) analytical distinction between the cognicized and operational models of the environment is especially pertinent. The cognicized environment refers to those aspects of their habitat that a local community identifies and consciously responds to in adapting. These aspects may be biophysical, sociocultural, or spiritual. The operational environment refers to those aspects that are identifiable by the methods of Western science. The two types of environmental models overlap, but are not isomorphic. Ultimately, it is most useful to consider both the cognicized and operational environments that correspond respectively to the local insider (emic) and the scientific outsider (etic) viewpoints on what is nature (cf. Harris 1979). Rappaport (1979: 97) explained that: 'Nature is seen by humans through a screen of beliefs, knowledge, and purposes, and it is in terms of their images of nature, rather than of the actual structure of nature, that they act. Yet, it is upon nature itself that they do act, and it is nature itself that acts upon them, nurturing or destroying them.'

Human Nature

What is human nature? Ecological anthropologists almost always focus on the ecology and adaptation of particular cultures at the community level and rarely consider human nature in general. Nevertheless, often ideas about human nature are behind their work and reflected in it, even if only implicitly. The generic capacities and attributes that are universal, elemental, and unique to the human species comprise human nature from an anthropological viewpoint. What makes humans different, as well as the difference this makes, are the two pivotal questions in exploring human nature (Adler 1967, Stevenson and Haberman 1998).

Much of human nature is most likely related to the hunter-gatherer mode of existence, although human evolution certainly didn't stop there (Shepard 1973). The religions of hunter-gatherer societies are Animistic. Like hunter-gatherer economies and their associated cultures, Animism is the most ancient and widespread of all world religions (Harvey 2006).

In general, humans are religious and spiritual beings. Religion is an ancient cross-cultural universal; no society is known that does not have one or more religions, although individuals within a society vary in the degree of their religiosity and spirituality if any. Religion can be one of the most important factors influencing the worldviews, values, attitudes, motivations, decisions, and behaviors of individuals, groups, and societies, for better or worse (Rappaport 1999). Religions are alternative ways of affording nature various cultural, moral, and spiritual meanings, and defining the place of humans in nature, including how they should act toward non-human beings and other phenomena.

The Kogi view both nature and human nature as primarily spiritual. They are a relatively traditional indigenous society living in the Sierra Nevada de Santa Marta in Colombia. Through a series of publications, films, and websites by outsiders who have been permitted to visit them to convey their message from what they consider to be the heart of the world, the Kogi express a deep sense of gravity and urgency about how much of humankind is degrading and even destroying nature. They are sounding the alarm to the rest of humanity most of whom they consider to be irrational, helpless, and dangerous younger siblings. The Kogi believe that their spiritual purpose is to safeguard the world from destruction by industrial society.

The Kogi have survived in the isolation of the highest coastal mountains in the world, which range up to 19,000 feet, this in spite of the Spanish conquistadores and other colonial forces that over recent centuries have devastated so many indigenous societies elsewhere. The Kogi have developed a sustainable society that is not only in relative balance with nature, but also thinks about nature and their place in it in a profoundly spiritual way. They can serve as one heuristic model in considering some of the possibilities for transforming industrial society into a more sustainable and greener one based more on respect for nature and fellow humans than the short-sighted, selfish worship of materialism with unbridled consumerism and greed.

The message of the Kogi is not simply another chilling doomsday proclamation from some environmental extremists. They, like most contemporary indigenous peoples, are the descendants of the original spiritual ecologists who cultivated reverence and stewardship for nature over millennia of intimate daily experience interacting with it for their survival and wellbeing. Furthermore, the Kogi reflect much of the concern of many of those who are variously engaged in spiritual ecology as an intellectual and practical arena of environmentalism (e.g., Taylor 2005, 2010). (For more on the Kogi, see Ereira 2009).

Some may view the depiction of the Kogi as merely romantic idealism, an example of the 'ecologically noble savage' myth or syndrome (Redford 1990). The French philosopher Jean-Jacques Rousseau is usually credited, but not always accurately, with the positive view that the 'noble savage' enjoys a life of social and natural harmony. The 'noble savage' encompasses a romantic image of a natural manifestation of humanity that is unsurpassed in innocence, simplicity, generosity, purity, goodness, equity, peacefulness, and freedom. This ideal type of humankind is supposed to reside in a utopian society and natural paradise from some golden age.

By the eighteenth century, this cult of primitivism emphasized self-analysis and self-criticism in scrutinizing European society, morality, and politics by glorifying the 'primitive' in contrast to degenerate European civilization. Some primitivists even went so far as to reject civilization in their narrative, although rarely in practice. Most importantly, such idealistic images offered a set of alternative possibilities for society, identified variously as archetypal communists, ecologists, environmentalists, conservationists, spiritualists, healers, philosophers, and pacifists.

Such societies practice some variant of nature religion or eco-spirituality. Thus, a range of environmental organizations such as the Sierra Club, Worldwatch Institute, and Earth First! often consider traditional indigenous people to be stewards and guardians of nature; this is sometimes referred to as green primitivism. Neo-pagan and New Age religions frequently contain elements of green primitivism. Consequently, implicitly if not explicitly, the societies and religions of civilization are criticized as unnatural and environmentally destructive. The positive role of the so-called primitive is exemplified in anthropology by cultures like the Kogi, Koyukon, Kuna, Mbuti, Penan, San, and Semai.

The opposite of this positive view, the dystopic 'ignoble savage,' is often attributed to English philosopher Thomas Hobbes, even though its roots extend far back into classical antiquity in Western civilization. From this perspective, 'primitive' life is poor, nasty, brutish, and short. It is permeated with disharmony, conflict, and violence, both socially and ecologically. Among the more outstanding anthropological cases of the negative image of the 'primitive' are supposedly the Cuiva, Guayaki, Ik,

Tasmanians, Yahgan, and Yanomami (cf. Sponsel 2010). Moreover, Hobbesian characterizations have often been used by colonial empires along with ideas of racial and cultural superiority as part of their rationalizations to conquer, oppress, and exploit, if not even to exterminate, indigenous societies that become obstacles to their capture of land, resources, and labor in frontier zones (see Bodley 2008).

In considerations of the 'primitive' as the most basic expression of human nature, the general tendency remains to emphasize one or the other of these two polar extremes, often to the point of distortion. That is, either 'primitives' exemplify a life of harmony socially and ecologically far more than any other type of culture, or they are antithetical to sociality and nature. Either extreme – the 'noble savage' or the 'ignoble savage' – is reductionistic, essentializing, and distorting. Such representations need to be critically scrutinized, deconstructed, and demystified. The real world is far more complex, varied, and variable than to sustain such simplistic antithetical postures of either/or, all/none, and always/never. It is much more scientific and scholarly to consider the great diversity in the manifestations of human nature through examining particular cases among some 7,000 extant cultures, rather than to over-generalize in either idealistic or derogatory excess. The diversity of humankind is the practical reality that challenges many attempts at generalizations about human nature as well as about the place of humans in nature (Sponsel 2005b).

Human Niche

What is the place of humans in nature? Ecological anthropology has attended to this question far more than to any of the others addressed in this chapter, but at the level of particular cultures rather than the prehistoric and historic evolutionary trajectories of the human species in general. Indeed, the forte of ecological anthropology has been to document human-environment interactions in particular cultures at the community level generating a substantial archive of ecologically focused ethnographies (Sponsel 2007b). In any case, at both the community and the species levels, the possible influence of religion in human-environment interactions has usually been ignored with only a few notable exceptions until recently.

The most outstanding exception is Roy A. Rappaport (1967, 1968, 1984), who, more than any other ecological anthropologist before him, applied the systems approach to field research on the relationship between religion and environment. He pioneered in the scientific study of the natural functions of the supernatural in his classic study of the role of ritual in regulating the Maring Tsembaga population of Papua New Guinea. His 1968 book is still one of the most widely read ethnographies. He summarized it in a 1967 article, and in 1984 published a second edition of his ethnography with a substantial epilogue in response to critics.

Rappaport's approach to the study of religion and ecology encompasses an elegant application of biological principles in human ecology, systems and cybernetics, ritual regulation of resources and population dynamics, ecological equilibrium (homeostasis), quantitative empirical data, and elements of functionalism, cultural materialism, and mentalism. Thereby his case study achieved a new level of sophistication in theory and method in ecological anthropology. He analyzed Tsembaga ritual and warfare as mechanisms regulating the delicate balance between the local human and pig populations to reduce competition between them and to maintain the human population within carrying capacity (cf. Foin and Davis 1984).

Rappaport (1979, 1999) also explored more generally the relationships between religion and ecology in cultural evolution arguing that religion can influence significantly human ecology and adaptation (Hart and Kottak 1999, Messer and Lambek 2001). As Hart observes, Rappaport's last book reflects ' … his intense concern with the rediscovery of ritual forms capable of addressing the huge challenges humanity faces in the management of society and nature' (Hart and Kottak 1999: 161). Hart also notes that this is a religious book as well as a comprehensive study of religion (Hart and Kottak 1999: 160).

Another pioneer in applying a systems approach in ecological anthropology that encompasses religion is J. Stephen Lansing. He brilliantly documents the practical relationships between water temple rituals and irrigation systems in wet rice fertilization and pest control in Bali, Indonesia. His long-term field research is extraordinary in engaging a multidisciplinary team, systems approach, quantitative and qualitative data, historical and ethnographic information, and computer modeling and simulation. Lansing demonstrates the efficacy of the natural functions of the supernatural; that is, how Balinese religion regulates human-environment interactions in complex ways as part of adaptive processes. The wet rice farming system of Bali has proven sustainable for a thousand years (Lansing 1991, Lansing and Kremer 1993).

The case studies by Rappaport and Lansing demonstrate that religion can contribute significantly to the development and maintenance of a population's niche within the carrying capacity of the ecosystems in its habitat. Nevertheless, the general trend throughout cultural evolution has been toward increasing ecological disequilibrium (Bennett 1976: 123–55). Some of the factors associated with that trend may be hypothesized as follows. Forager or hunter–gatherer societies tend to be in dynamic equilibrium with their environment; have a minimal impact on their environment, although some may modify it over the long-term through the repeated use of fire; consider nonhuman beings and physical features of the landscape to be sacred in various ways; and pursue an ecocentric and biophilic environmental ethic. Biophilia refers to a subconscious affective emotional attraction and bonding with nature (Wilson 1984). Most foragers also pursue a rotational system of land and resource use that moderates their environmental impact.

At the opposite extreme, industrial manufacturing societies with urban centers, market economies, and especially capitalism desacralize and commodify nature; tend toward increasing ecological disequilibrium with conversion, fragmentation, and toxification of their habitat and that of others; and pursue an egocentric and biophobic environmental ethic. Biophobia refers to fear and repulsion toward nature, especially wilderness. Another attribute in the evolution of urban societies is that individuals are progressively alienated from nature as well as from each other, a phenomenon ecopsychologists and others may refer to as nature deficit (Louv 2008).

Farming societies tend to fall along a continuum somewhere in between these two polar extremes, but with the shift from subsistence-based extensive horticulture with polycropping to market-based intensive agriculture with monocropping they increasingly pursue an anthropocentric environmental ethic. The above evolutionary ecological model integrates factors from materialist and mentalist perspectives. In addition, it provides a heuristic conceptual framework for comparing the spiritual ecology of different types of socio-economic systems including forager, horticultural, agricultural, and industrial in terms of multilinear evolution (cf. Hultkrantz 1987, Steward 1955). Incidentally, in many instances, sacred groves may be an attempt to maintain some forest in a landscape otherwise dominated by its conversion and fragmentation for agricultural production to support a growing population and/or economy. (For a broader characterization of the evolutionary trajectory of increasing thresholds of human environmental impact see Redman 1996, Sponsel 2001b, Ponting 2007).

Environmental Ethics

What should be the place of humans in nature? Ecological anthropologists, like anthropologists in general, have afforded relatively little direct attention to the subject of worldviews and values in other cultures. One rare exception is Eugene N. Anderson (1996, 2010), who relates religion and ecology from a theoretical and methodological perspective with ethnographic examples from his fieldwork in British Columbia, Malaysia, Mexico, and elsewhere. Anderson (1996: vii-viii) argues that environmental problems result from human choices, and that choices are based on emotion as well as reason. Sustainable resource and environmental management necessarily involve a moral and ethical code backed by emotional force in which religion can be a powerful influence. Furthermore, he notes that, while natural resource strategies connected with religious beliefs and practices can appear irrational, actually they may be effectively grounded in intimate daily observations of nature over many generations (Grim 2001, Milton 2002; Terhaar 2009).

In spiritual ecology, worldviews and values are among the more important considerations (e.g., Gottlieb 2006b). Some of Gerardo Reichel-Dolmatoff's (1971, 1976, 1996) work is especially pertinent here, particularly his classic research on the cultural ecology of the myths, rituals, and symbols of the Tukano Desana in the Colombian Vaupes region of the northwestern Amazon. The Desana are geographically circumscribed by other groups. If their population pushes carrying capacity and their resources diminish, then they can only expand geographically by resorting to warfare and conquest. Reichel-Dolmatoff argued that the Desana shaman operates like an ecological engineer in monitoring trends in the distribution and abundance of prey populations and in implementing food and sex taboos to regulate the balance between the human predator and its animal prey.

A similar case is provided by Reimar Schefold (1988), who studied the symbolic expression of the perceptions and beliefs regarding nature among the Sakkudai of the Mentawai Islands of Siberut in Indonesia. He asserts that 'The traditional ecological balance on the island did not, in any case, exist in spite of the people. It existed with them. The Mentawaians long ago evolved ritual prescriptions and proscriptions that, expressing their ideology of harmony, prevented any ruthless exploitation of the environment' (p. 212). He notes the respect for spirits in nature through strict taboos that prevent over-hunting. The hunters avoid sex and certain foods. Moreover, any intervention in the environment is considered sinister and disruptive of ecological equilibrium, and, accordingly, certain rituals are performed to restore and maintain.

More generally, by now research and dialog on the environmental relevance of each of the world's major religions have advanced to the point that some attempts have been made to discern parallels or common denominators among them. For instance, in the last chapter of the first textbook on spiritual ecology, David Kinsley (1995: 227–32) identifies these ten basic principles:

1 Many religions consider all of reality, or some of its components, to be an organic whole or a living being.
2 There is an emphasis on cultivating rapport with the local environment through developing intimate knowledge about it and practicing reverence for its beauty, mystery, and power through ritual celebrations of recognition and appreciation.
3 The human and nonhuman realms are directly interrelated, often in the sense of some kind of kinship, and in certain cases, even to the extent of animals being viewed as another form of persons or humans.
4 The appropriate relationship between humans and nature should be reciprocal; that is, humans do not merely recognize interdependence, but also promote mutually beneficial interactions with nature.
5 Ultimately, the dichotomy between humans and their environment is nonexistent; humans are embedded in nature as an integral part of the larger whole or cosmos.
6 This non-dualistic view reflects the ultimate elemental unity of all existence; nature and spirit are inseparable, there is only one reality, and this continuity can be sensed and experienced.
7 This underlying unity is moral as well as physical; humans and nonhumans participate in a shared moral system wherein environmental issues are first and foremost ethical concerns; and nature has intrinsic as well as extrinsic values.
8 Humans should act with restraint in nature by avoiding the anthropocentric arrogance of excessive, wasteful, and destructive use of the land and other resources, and in other ways they should exercise proper behavior toward plants, animals, and other aspects of nature as sacred.
9 Harmony or balance between humans and the rest of nature must be maintained and promoted, and, if it is upset, then it should be restored.
10 Frequently the motivation, commitment, and intensity of ecological concerns are essentially religious or spiritual.

Each of these principles could be formulated as a hypothesis for exploration and testing in investigating other cultures and religions in terms of their relevance for ecology and adaptation (cf., Pedersen 1998, Earth Charter 2010).

Discussion

There is yet one more question to consider here. What are some of the most important concerns for future research in ecological anthropology for those who may elect to pursue the approach of spiritual ecology? There is a need to investigate the contexts as well as texts of religion, actions as well as ideas, and maladaptive as well as adaptive behaviors and consequences. The full range of relevant individuals needs to be studied including religious specialists and adherents. The table of contents in the textbook by Ralph Tanner and Colin Mitchell (2002) provides a convenient inventory of many topics for the study of the interrelationships between religion and environment.

Much more rigorous field research is needed to systematically, empirically, and critically explore the environmental consequences of religious and spiritual beliefs, values, attitudes, and behaviors in particular events, sites, landscapes, and ecosystems. As much as feasible, hard data are required to demonstrate whether or not sacred places and other religious phenomena have any ecological efficacy, especially through testing competing hypotheses. For instance, a multidisciplinary team could collect scientific data for a controlled comparison of biodiversity in a sample of sacred places in nature with their secular counterparts in the same region and the same kind of environment (Ramakrishna et al., 1998, Dudley et al., 2005; Sponsel et al., 1998, Sponsel 2007c, d).

Cultural anthropologists have tended to pursue either a materialist or a mentalist approach to the description and analysis of a particular culture, and to treat these two approaches as mutually exclusive (Harris 1979; Sponsel 2007b). However, such exclusivity is problematic because in reality humans in general are simultaneously biological, economic, political, social, cultural, mental, and religious or spiritual beings (Sponsel 2001a, 2007a). While surely either a materialist or a mentalist approach alone can have some validity and utility, spiritual ecology naturally offers a third approach, namely the integration of material and mental aspects of human interaction with the environment. The contributions of Rappaport, Reichel-Dolmatoff, and Lansing in particular exemplify this integrative potential.

As with new trends in ecological anthropology in general, with spiritual ecology far more attention needs to be given to biological ecology, this encompassing biodiversity, ecosystems, ecological processes, and related natural phenomena (Sponsel 2005a; UN Millennium Ecosystem Assessment 2010). Insufficient incorporation of biological ecology is far too often a weakness of research in human ecology. One way to surmount this weakness is to include biologists and other specialists on teams investigating aspects of the interrelationships between religion and environment (Sponsel, et al., 1998). While important contributions can be generated by lone researchers, the arena of spiritual ecology provides a special opportunity for multi-disciplinary team research and other kinds of collaboration. For instance, the present author is developing a project with a team focused on probing the possible ecological interconnections among sacred caves, Buddhist monks, bats, forests, and biodiversity conservation in northern Thailand (Sponsel and Natadecha-Sponsel 2004).

Religions may generate very different interrelationships between their adherents and nature with varying impacts on biodiversity, ecosystems, ecological processes, and related phenomena (Tanner and Mitchell 2002; Gottlieb 2006a,b; Taylor 2005, 2010; Watling 2009). The spread of a new religion into a region can alter the trajectory of the historical ecology of local societies, a subject that merits far more research. For example, frequently when a world religion enters new areas it suppresses or even destroys previous religions (e.g., Metzner 1994).

Another complexity at the interface of religion and environment is internal contradictions, such as discrepancies between ideals and actions. For instance, Kelly D. Alley (2002) addresses a deeply rooted and very difficult paradox: How can the Ganga River be considered so sacred for ritual purification by Hindus throughout India and at the same time so physically polluted? Alley analyzes the interplay between religious, scientific, and government discourses about the Ganga. In another example from India, Emma Tomalin (2002) distinguishes between nature religion and religious environmentalism. She asserts that nature religion, such as the worship of sacred trees, does not necessarily indicate any inherent environmental awareness. Tomalin cautions that religious environmentalism could be a Western idea that may not be operative where people depend on natural resources for their daily survival and simply cannot afford to pursue it.

In spite of the above and other complexities at the interface of religion and environment, just as the psychological, social, cultural, economic, political, and historic significance of religion cannot be denied a priori, neither can its possible ecological relevance in certain situations as illustrated by the above sampling of the literature. Indeed, it bears repeating that *often religion is the most influential determinant of the worldviews, values, attitudes, motivations, decisions, and behaviors of individuals, groups, and societies, either for better or worse, depending on the specific circumstances, and that this may have significant environmental consequences* (Edwards and Palmer 1997, Gardner 2006; Gottlieb 2006a, b; Selin 2003; Sponsel 2001a, 2007a, c, 2011; Taylor 2005, 2010; Forum on Religion and Ecology 2010).

Conclusions

With a few notable exceptions, until recently ecological anthropologists have usually ignored religion as a possible factor influencing human-environment interactions. However, enough should have been presented here about each of four elemental and pivotal questions to demonstrate some of the potential contributions of the approach of spiritual ecology in advancing ecological anthropology in new directions. Of course, individual researchers have their own personal preferences and may choose to focus on phenomena other than religion in pursuing the study of the ecology of a particular culture. Nevertheless, they should be aware that ignoring religion entirely could be misleading, if it is an important factor in a particular situation.

Human-environmental interactions can involve the supernatural as well as the natural, and emotion as well as reason. Religion can be a powerful influence, but either adaptive or maladaptive. Such phenomena can be researched like any other aspect of culture through standard ethnographic field methods within the framework of cultural relativism and from a cultural materialist, mentalist, or integrative perspective. Spiritual ecology can also serve as a vehicle to integrate some aspects of the natural sciences, social sciences, and humanities for a more holistic understanding of the dynamics of human-environment interactions. However, more attention needs to be paid to complexities such as internal variations and contradictions within a religion. In particular, sacred places in nature offer a special opportunity for research, including when they are contested by different interest groups.

Spiritual ecology can add an exciting and important new component to ecological anthropology. In general, spiritual ecology proceeds through testing the assumptions in particular cases that nature, human nature, the place of humans in nature, and human interactions with nature each may have some religious salience. This may present a radical challenge to orthodox thinking, but for anyone with an open mind it should be provocative in a positive sense. After all, an open mind is supposedly an indispensable attribute of rationality, science, and scholarship.

References

Adler, Mortimer J. (1967) *The Difference of Man and the Difference it Makes*, New York: Holt, Rinehart, and Winston.

Alley, Kelly D. (2002) *On the Banks of the Ganges: When Wastewater Meets a Sacred River*, Ann Arbor: University of Michigan Press.

Alliance of Religions and Conservation/World Wide Fund for Nature (WWF). HTTP: http://www.arcworld.org (accessed July 28, 2010).

Anderson, Eugene N. (1996) *Ecologies of the Heart: Emotion, Belief, and the Environment*, New York: Oxford University Press.

——(2010) *The Pursuit of Ecotopia: Lessons from Indigenous and Traditional Societies for the Human Ecology of Our Modern World*, Santa Barbara: ABC-LIO, LLC/Praeger.

Bassett, Libby, Brinkman, John T., Pedersen, Kusumita, (eds) (2000) *Earth and Faith: A Book of Reflection for Action*, New York: United Nations Environmental Programme Interfaith Partnership for the Environment.

Bennett, John W. (1976) *The Ecological Transition: Cultural Anthropology and Human Adaptation*, New York: Pergamon Press.

Berry, Thomas, and Tucker, Mary Evelyn (2006) *Evening Thoughts: Reflecting on Earth as Sacred Community*, San Francisco: Sierra Club Books.

——, and ——(2009) *The Sacred Universe: Earth Spirituality and Religion in the Twenty-first Century*, New York: Columbia University Press.

Bodley, John H. (2008) *Victims of Progress*, Lanham: AltaMira Press.

Bowie, Fiona (2006) 'Religion, Culture, and Environment', in *The Anthropology of Religion: An Introduction*, Malden, MA: Blackwell Publishing, pp. 107–37.

Byers, Bruce A., Cunliffe, Robert N., and Hudak, Andrew T. (2001) 'Linking the Conservation of Culture and Nature: A Case Study of Sacred Forests in Zimbabwe', *Human Ecology*, 29(2): 187–218.

Carroll, John E., and Warner, Keith (eds) (1998) *Ecology and Religion: Scientists Speak*, Quincy: Franciscan Press.

Coates, Peter (1998) *Nature: Western Attitudes Since Ancient Times*, Berkeley: University of California Press.

Collett, Jonathan, and Karakashian, Stephen (eds) (1996) *Greening the College Curriculum: A Guide to Environmental Teaching in the Liberal Arts*, Washington, D.C.: Island Press.

Conroy, Donald B., and Petersen, Rodney L. (eds) (2000) *Earth at Risk: An Environmental Dialogue between Religion and Science*, Amherst, NY: Humanity Books.

Crosby, Donald A. (2002) *A Religion of Nature*, Albany: State University of New York Press.

Darlington, Susan M. (1998) 'The Ordination of a Tree: The Buddhist Ecology Movement in Thailand', *Ethnology*, 37(1): 1–15.

——(2003) 'The Spirit(s) of Conservation in Buddhist Thailand',' in *Nature Across Cultures: Views of Nature and the Environment in Non-Western Cultures*, Helaine Selin and Kalland, Arne (eds) Dordrecht: Kluwer Academic Publishers, pp. 129–45.

De Steiguer, J.E. (2006) *The Origins of Modern Environmental Thought*, Tucson: University of Arizona Press.

Dudley, Nigel, Higgins-Zogib, Liza, and Mansourian, Stephanie (2005) *Beyond Belief: Linking Faiths and Protected Areas to Support Biodiversity Conservation*. Gland: World Wide Fund for Nature (WWF) and Alliance of Religions and Conservation. HTTS: *http://www.arcworld.org* (accessed July 28, 2010).

Earth Charter. HTTP: *http://www.earthcharter.org* (accessed July 28, 2010).

Edwards, Jo, and Palmer, Martin (eds) (1997) *Holy Ground: The Guide to Faith and Ecology*, Northamptonshire: Pilkington Press Ltd.

Ereira, Alan (2009) *The Elder Brother's Warning*, London: Tairona Heritage Trust.

Foin, Theodore C., and Davis, William G. (1984) 'Ritual and Self-Regulation of the Tsembaga Maring Ecosystem in the New Guinea Highlands', *Human Ecology*, 12(4): 385–412.

Forum on Religion and Ecology (FORE), New Haven:Yale University. HTTP: http//www. religionandecology.org (accessed July 28, 2010).

Gardner, Gary (2006) *Inspiring Progress: Religion's Contributions to Sustainable Development*, New York: W. W. Norton and Company, Inc. (Worldwatch Book).

Glacken, Clarence J. (1967) *Traces on the Rhodian Shore: Nature and Culture in Western Thought from Ancient Times to the End of the Eighteenth Century*, Berkeley: University of California Press.

Global Forum, (1990) 'Preserving and Cherishing the Earth: An Appeal for Joint Commitment in Science and Religion' Moscow: Global Forum.HTTP: http://fore.research.yale. edu/publications/statements/preserve.html (accessed July 28, 2010).

Gottlieb, R. S. (2006a) *A Greener Faith: Religious Environmentalism and Our Planet's Future*, New York: Oxford University Press.

——(ed) (2006b) *The Oxford Handbook of Religion and Ecology*, New York: Oxford University Press.

Grim, J. A. (ed) (2001) *Indigenous Traditions and Ecology: The Interbeing of Cosmology and Community*, Cambridge: Harvard University Press/Harvard Divinity School Center for the Study of World Religions.

Hakkenberg, C. (2008) 'Biodiversity and Sacred Sites: Vernacular Conservation Practices in Northwest Yunnan, China', *Worldviews: Global Religions, Culture, and Ecology*, 12(1): 74–90.

Harris, M. (1979) *Cultural Materialism: The Struggle for a Science of Culture*, New York: Random House.

Hart, K., and Kottak, C. (1999) 'Roy A. 'Skip' Rappaport (1926–97)', *American Anthropologist*, 101(1): 159–61.

Harvey, G. (2006) *Animism: Respecting the Living World*, New York: Columbia University Press.

Haught, J. F. (1990) *What Is Religion? An Introduction*, Mahwah: Paulist Press.

Hultkrantz, A. (1987) 'Ecology', in *The Encyclopedia of Religion*, Mircea Eliade, et al. (eds), New York: Macmillan 4: 581–85.

Interfaith Power and Light Renewal Project, HTTP: http://www.renewalproject.net (accessed July 28, 2010).

Intergovernmental Panel on Climate Change HTTP: http://www.ipcc.ch/ (accessed July 28, 2010).

Kaza, S., and Kraft, K. (eds) (2000) *Dharma Rain: Sources of Buddhist Environmentalism*, Boston: Shambhala Publications, Inc.

Kent, E. F. (2009) 'Sacred Groves and Local Gods: Religion and Environmentalism in South India', *World Views: Global Religions, Culture, and Ecology*,13(1): 1–39.

Kinsely, D. (1995) *Ecology and Religion: Ecological Spirituality in Cross-Cultural Perspective*, Englewood Cliffs: Prentice Hall.

Kottak, C.P. (1999) 'The New Ecological Anthropology', *American Anthropologist*,101(1):23–35.

Lansing, S.J. (1991) *Priests and Programmers: Technologies of Power in the Engineered Landscape of Bali*, Princeton: Princeton University Press.

——, and Kremer, J. N. (1993) 'Emergent Properties of Balinese Water Temples', *American Anthropologist*, 95(1):97–114.

Louv, R. (2008) *Last Child in the Woods: Saving Our Children from Nature-Deficit Disorder*, New York: Algonquin Books.

Malhotra, K.C. (1998) 'Anthropological Dimensions of Sacred Groves in India: An Overview', in *Conserving the Sacred for Biodiversity Management*, P.S. Ramakrishnan, et al., eds., Enfield: Science Publishers, Inc., pp. 423–38.

Marten, G. G. (2001). 'Perceptions of Nature', in *Human Ecology: Basic Concepts for Sustainable Development*, Sterling: Earthscan Publications Ltd., pp. 121–35.

Merchant, C. (2005) 'Spiritual Ecology', in *Radical Ecology: The Search for a Livable World*, New York: Routledge, pp. 117–38.

Messer, E. and Lambek, M. (eds) (2001) *Ecology and the Sacred: Engaging the Anthropology of Roy A. Rappaport*, Ann Arbor: University of Michigan Press.

Metzner, R. (1994) *The Well of Remembrance: Rediscovering the Earth Wisdom Myths of Northern Europe*, Boston: Shambhala Publications, Inc.

Nothwehr, D.M. (ed) (2002) *Franciscan Theology of the Environment: An Introductory Reader*, Quincey: Franciscan Press.

Palmer, M. and Finlay, V. (2003) *Faith in Conservation: New Approaches to Religion and Environment*, Washington, D.C.: World Bank.

Pedersen, K. P. (1998) 'Environmental Ethics in Interreligious Perspective', *Explorations, in Global Ethics: Comparative Religious Ethics and Interreligious Dialogue*, Sumner B. Twiss and Bruce Grelle, eds., Boulder: Westview Press, pp. 253–90.

Ponting, C. (2007) *A New Green History of the World: The Environment and the Collapse of Great Civilizations*, New York: Penguin.

Posey, D.A. (ed.) (1999) *Cultural and Spiritual Values of Biodiversity*, London: Intermediate Technology Publications/UNEP.

Ramakrishnan, P.S., Saenxa, K.G., and Chandrashekara, U.M. (eds) (1998) *Conserving the Sacred for Biodiversity Management*, Enfield: Science Publishers, Inc.

Rappaport, R.A. (1967) 'Ritual Regulation of Environmental Relations among a New Guinea People', *Ethnology*, 6(1):17–30.

——(1968) *Pigs for the Ancestors: Ritual in the Ecology of a New Guinea People*, New Haven: Yale University Press.

——(1979) *Ecology, Meaning, and Religion*, Richmond, CA: North Atlantic Books.

——(1984) *Pigs for the Ancestors: Ritual in the Ecology of a New Guinea People*, 2nd edn, New Haven: Yale University Press.

——(1999) *Ritual and Religion in the Making of Humanity*, New York: Cambridge University Press.

Redford, K.H. (1990) 'The Ecologically Noble Savage', *Orion Nature Quarterly*, 15(1):46–48.

Redman, C. L. (1999) *Human Impact on Ancient Environments*, Tucson: University of Arizona Press.

Reichel-Dolmatoff, G. (1971) *Amazonian Cosmos: The Sexual and Religious Symbolism of the Desana Indians*, Chicago: University of Chicago Press.

——(1976) 'Cosmology as Ecological Analysis', *Man*, 11(3):307–18.

——(1996) *The Forest Within: The Worldview of the Tukano Amazonian Indians*, Totnes, Devon: Themis.

Robbins, P. (2004) *Political Ecology: A Critical Introduction*, Malden: Blackwell Publishing.

Rose, D.B. (1992) *Dingo Makes Us Human: Life and Land in an Australian Aboriginal Culture*, New York: Cambridge University Press.

Santmire, H.P. (2003) 'Ecotheology', in *Encyclopedia of Science and Religion*, J. Wentzel Vrede van Huyssteen (ed), New York: Thomson Gale 1:247–51.

Schefold, R. (1988) 'The Mentawai Equilibrium and the Modern World', in *The Real and the Imagined Role of Culture in Development: Case Studies from Indonesia*, M. R. Dove (ed) Honolulu: University of Hawai'i Press, pp. 201–15.

Selin, H. (ed) (2003) *Nature Across Cultures: Views of Nature and the Environment in Non-Western Cultures*, Boston: Kluwer Academic Publishers.

Shepard, P. (1973) *The Tender Carnivore and the Sacred Game*, New York: Scribners.

Sponsel, L.E. (2001a) 'Do Anthropologists Need Religion, and Vice Versa?: Adventures and Dangers in Spiritual Ecology' in *New Directions in Anthropology and Environment: Intersections*, C. Crumley (ed) Walnut Creek: AltaMira Press, pp. 177–200.

——(2001b) 'Human Impact on Biodiversity, Overview' in *Encyclopedia of Biodiversity*, Simon Asher Levin (editor-in-chief) San Diego: Academic Press 3:395–409.

——(2005a) 'Biodiversity', in *The Encyclopedia of Religion and Nature*, B. Taylor (editor-in-chief), London: Thoemmes Continuum 1:179–82.

——(2005b) 'Noble Savage and the Ecologically Noble Savage', in *The Encyclopedia of Religion and Nature*, B. Taylor (editor-in-chief), London: Thoemmes Continuum 2:1210–12.

——(2007a) 'Spiritual Ecology: One Anthropologist's Reflections', *Journal for the Study of Religion, Nature and Culture*, 1(3):340–49.

——(2007b) 'Ecological Anthropology', in *Encyclopedia of Earth*, S. Sarkar and L. Kalof (eds) Washington, D.C.: Environmental Information Coalition, National Council for Science and the Environment. HTTP: http://www.eoearth.org/article/Ecological_anthropology *(accessed July 28, 2010)*.

——(2007c) 'Religion, Nature and Environmentalism', in *Encyclopedia of Earth*, S. Sarkar and Linda K. (eds) Washington, D.C.: Environmental Information Coalition, National Council for Science and the Environment. HTTP: http://www.eoearth.org/article/ Religion,_nature_and_environmentalism (accessed July 28, 2010).

——(2007d) 'Sacred Places and Biodiversity Conservation', in *Encyclopedia of Earth*, S. Sarkar and L. Kalof (eds) Washington, D.C.: Environmental Information Coalition, National Council for Science and the Environment. HTTP: http://www.eoearth.org/article/ sacred_places_and_biodiversity_conservation (accessed July 28, 2010).

——(2010) 'Into the Heart of Darkness: Rethinking the Canonical Ethnography of the Yanomamo,' in *Nonkilling Societies*, J. E Pim (ed) Honolulu, HI: Center for Global Nonkilling Chapter 6, pp. 197–242. HTTP: http://www.nonkilling.org/pdf/nksocieties.pdf.

——(2011) *Spiritual Ecology: A Quiet Revolution*, Westport: Praeger (forthcoming).

——, and Natadecha-Sponsel, P. (2004) 'Illuminating Darkness: The Monk-Cave-Bat-Ecosystem Complex in Thailand', in *This Sacred Earth: Religion, Nature, Environment*, Roger S. Gottlieb (ed) 2nd edn New York: Routledge, pp. 134–44.

——, and ——(2008) 'Buddhism: Environment and Nature', in *Encyclopedia of the History of Science, Technology, and Medicine in Non-Western Cultures*, H. Selin, (ed) 2nd edn Dordrecht: 2nd edn New York:Springer 1:768–76.

——, Natadecha-Sponsel, Poranee, Ruttanadakul, Nukul, and Juntadach, Somporn (1998) 'Sacred and/or Secular Approaches to Biodiversity Conservation in Thailand,' *Worldviews: Environment, Culture, Religion*, 2.1:155–67.

Srivastana, S., Chatterjee, S., Gokhale, Y., and Malhotra, K. C. (2007) *Sacred Groves of India: An Overview*, New Delhi: Aryan Books International.

Stevenson, L. and Haberman, D.L. (1998) *Ten Theories of Human Nature*, New York: Oxford University Press.

Steward, J.H. (1955) *Theory of Culture Change: The Methodology of Multilinear Evolution*, Urbana: University of Illinois Press.

Swearer, D.K (ed) (2009) *Ecology and Environment: Perspectives from the Humanities*, Cambridge: Harvard Divinity School Center for the Study of World Religions.

Tanner, R. and Mitchell, C. (2002) *Religion and the Environment*, New York: Palgrave.

Taylor, B. (editor-in-chief) (2005) *The Encyclopedia of Religion and Nature*, London: Thoemmes Continuum.

——(2010) *Dark Green Religion: Nature, Spirituality, and the Planetary Future*, Berkeley: University of California Press.

Taylor, S.M. (2007) *Green Sisters: A Spiritual Ecology*, Cambridge: Harvard University Press.

Terhaar, T.L. (2009) 'Evolutionary Advantages of Intense Spiritual Experience in Nature', *Journal for the Study of Religion, Nature and Culture*, 3(3): 303–39.

Tomalin, E. (2002) 'The Limitations of Religious Environmentalism for India', *Worldviews: Environment, Culture, Religion*, 6(1): 12–30.

Townsend, P.K. (2009) 'Holy Ground', in *Environmental Anthropology: From Pigs to Policies*, Prospect Heights: Waveland Press, pp. 61–68.

Tucker, M. Evelyn (1997) 'The Emerging Alliance of Religion and Ecology', *Worldviews: Environment, Culture and Religion*, 1(1): 3–24.

——, with Judith A. Berling (2003) *Worldly Wonder: Religions Enter Their Ecological Phase*, LaSalle: Open Court.

——, and Duncan Ryuken Williams (eds) (1997) *Buddhism and Ecology: The Interconnection of Dharma and Deeds*, Cambridge: Harvard University Press.

United Nations Millennium Ecosystem Assessment. HTTP: http://www.millenniumassessment.org (accessed July 28, 2010).

Watling, Tony (2009) *Ecological Imaginations in the World Religions: An Ethnographic Analysis*, New York: Continuum International Publishing Group.

White, Lynn, Jr., (1967) 'The Historical Roots of Our Ecologic Crisis', *Science*, 155: 1203–7.

Wilson, Edward O. (1984) *Biophilia: The Human Bond with Other Species*, Cambridge: Harvard University Press.

WorldWatch Institute. HTTP: http://www.worldwatch.org (accessed July 28, 2010).

World Wildlife Fund International (WWF) (1986) *The Assisi Declarations: Messages on Man and Nature from Buddhism, Christianity, Hinduism, Islam, and Judaism*, Gland: World Wildlife Fund International.

2

DRAWING FROM TRADITIONAL AND 'INDIGENOUS' SOCIOECOLOGICAL THEORIES

Eugene N. Anderson

I will concern myself here with a possible future for environmental anthropology.

Traditional and local people have managed, in most cases, to conserve environments and manage resources sustainably. These wider systems of consciousness and ideology have, however, been usually ignored as sources of ideas for anthropology and environment—partly because many are founded on beliefs in 'spirits' or 'supernaturals' that 'rational' social scientists do not accept. Yet, quite apart from the highly debatable meanings of the words in scare quotes, most of the actual moral and ethical teachings involved do not necessarily depend on the 'supernatural' material. Traditional Chinese, as well as indigenous peoples of Mexico and the Northwest Coast of North America, have developed various worldviews that parallel the New Ecological Paradigm in seeing 'people in nature' rather than 'people vs. nature,' and thus working with nature rather than trying to destroy the natural and create a purely humanized setting. Traditional views present opportunities for using traditional cultural materials to motivate conservation and sustainable management. They also provide some knotty problems for philosophers. Our universities have quite literal walls between 'ontology,' 'epistemology,' 'religion,' 'social science,' and 'art.' Indeed, they are often in different buildings. We need an environmental anthropology that takes traditional cultures seriously, including their philosophies of knowledge and emotion. This would extend the New Ecological Paradigm in potentially interesting ways. Such an anthropology could significantly inform policy and advocacy in regard to conservation and environment.

Learning from Others

The contemporary human world has acquired its crops, as well as countless medical techniques, songs, technological inventions, agricultural methods, and philosophical and religious concepts from traditional societies. This has recently become a serious problem, when individuals or corporations try to patent indigenous or traditional crops and medicines for personal gain (Shiva 1997, 2001; Vogel 1994, 2000). Such 'biopiracy' is deplorable when it cheats people of their rightful due, but in the more general context of cultural flow, ideas and methods have circulated around the world since the beginning of humanity. We are hardly in a position to find and compensate the modern descendents of the inventors of bread, pottery, or the wheel. Moreover, we now live in a world where—for instance—indigenous artists expect and can receive some appropriate form of proper credit and compensation for their medicines, recipes, and works of art.

One odd exception to the universal flux of culture is anthropology itself. Anthropologists have generally depended on Western philosophy and social science for theories. Yet, unlike the situation in (say) nuclear physics, where what we can learn from small-scale societies may be limited, all humans have opportunities and incentives to observe and theorize about society and about human-environment relationships.

Admittedly, anthropologists borrow more than they let on from the societies they study. It is fairly obvious that the famous (or infamous) anthropological obsession with kinship is due to the great importance of kinship, and consequent elaboration and systematization of kinship relations, in traditional societies (see Trautman 1987). Almost all of us of my anthropological generation share the same experience of being bored with kinship in the classroom, then discovering that it was all-important when we went to the field.

After doing research in Malayo-Polynesian societies from Malaysia to Tahiti, I am convinced that it is no accident that the field of 'ethnoscience' was developed by people studying societies in that group: Ward Goodenough (1953), Charles Frake (1980), Harold Conklin (1957, 1981, 2007), Thomas Gladwin (1970), and others. Malayo-Polynesian people seem to share, widely, a culture trait of loving to talk about their classification systems and folk sciences. They revel in telling visiting anthropologists about the proper names for fish, diseases, flowers, stars, and rice varieties.

Athapaskan theories of landscape and place have influenced anthropological thinking via the work of such exceptionally sensitive and attentive ethnographers as Keith Basso (1996) and Robin Ridington (1988, 1990). In sharp contrast with the Malayo-Polynesians, Athapaskans live in a quiet, physically engaged world, where totalizing experience is far more important than talking. Basso's and Ridington's sensitive phenomenological approaches are influenced by this. My own studies of Chinese food (Anderson 1988) were done not because I went out to study food, but because I often could not get my consultants to talk about anything else.

In the current case, traditional theories of environment and traditional anthropologies are particularly useful because they often come close to the New Ecological Paradigm described in the Introduction to the present volume. Compared to the West, most cultures, worldwide, have been notably less prone to cut themselves off from the rest of the world.

Expanding Human Ecology to Include Other Cultural Views

All societies and cultures have to theorize the human/environment interface enough to deal with today's and tomorrow's problems. Thus, one feels surprised that so little has been done with traditional theories.

In spite of the best efforts of many human ecologists, most cultural and political ecology has not perfectly overcome a characteristic pattern in modern European thought: the idea that people are motivated by rational individual self-interest. The classic, simplest form, seen in microeconomic theory, holds that people act for their rational individual material or financial interest: they want to maximize personal wealth. At least since the work of Sahlins (1972, 1976), anthropologists know this is too simplistic to be fully adequate for explaining human-environment interactions. However, derivative theories still hold wide credibility. Among these are the naïve adaptationism of much early cultural ecology; the calory maximization and protein maximization approach in optimal foraging theory (Winterhalder and Smith 1981); and a number of economic theories of development, intensification, and household economics (e.g. Boserup 1965).

Humans do not usually maximize individual wealth or calories. They maximize social connectedness and personal satisfaction; usually the personal satisfaction comes largely from the social connectedness. Wealth, calories, and such are means to those ends (Anderson 2010; Sahlins 1976). Modern 'consumer' societies consume to maximize social conformity and connection rather than to consume actual calories. Worldwide, research shows that the first things people buy when they get money are TV sets, cellphones, and other communications devices. 'Luxury' consumption, from lawns to name-brand clothing, is typically to show social status, not to provide actual comfort or material benefits. Lawns and McMansions require enormous amounts of annoying work; name-brand items differ in no essential respect from cheap knock-offs; people buy these things for conspicuous consumption.

A great deal of political ecology is based on the same inadequate microfunctionalist theory, with 'power' substituted for 'money' or 'calories.' This idea of political ecology views the field as human ecology with power relations foregrounded, or sometimes considered exclusively. (See devastatingly funny critique in Sahlins 1993; also Vayda 2009 and Vayda and Walters 1999. Classic definitions of political ecology are more sophisticated; see Robbins 2004: 6–7).

In this case, the problems are even greater, because, unlike money or calories, 'power' is an extremely difficult and slippery concept. Sometimes, it is assumed that people act solely or largely to take and maintain personal control over other people. This is a Nietzschean assumption that is simply wrong, as anyone knows who has tried to find administrators or even committee members for academic or community programs. Most people will do anything to avoid getting in a position of power over others (outside of, perhaps, their own children). Moreover, too many of the exceptions—the 'power-mad' people—are deeply troubled individuals, far outside the norm.

On the other hand, especially in the Foucaultian tradition that has been so important in political ecology, 'power' is a more diffuse cluster of relationships that is maintained by governments over their subjects or victims. It is impossible to understand, from Foucault or his many followers, whether this power (or governmentality, or hegemonic discourse) is maintained by individuals for themselves, or by individuals acting together in a government, or by some abstract 'government' or 'hegemonic' group that somehow acts as if it were a thinking individual. It somehow seems that Power is a force on its own (Sahlins 1993), like a supernatural being. 'Power' and 'government' become things, but are not defined and have no physical instantiation. They are Platonic ideals without the ideal type. Foucaultians do not break out the Weberian methods for maintaining power: force, legitimacy, charisma, persuasion, etc.

This sort of reification of abstract entities is a classic problem in social science (see e.g. Mills 1959). Even reifying 'social' is problematic enough (Latour 2005). The most naïve political ecology gives us abstract entities—colonialism, neoliberalism, globalization, the modernist program, and so on—that somehow think, have agency, and do things (Vayda 2009). Colonialism was real and colonialists did assert naked power. Globalization originally labeled the very real phenomena of worldwide economic integration and the related worldwide spread of American culture (some might say the worst of American culture), but today 'globalization' is often used loosely, without specific referent. 'Neoliberalism' is a label without a membership; nobody calls himself or herself a 'neoliberal.' The 'power' that, say, neoliberalism wants to maximize and tries to assert over its victims is not power in any normal sense of the word. Neoliberalism has been defined in countless ways, most of which lump vague economic policies. Sometimes these policies are actually mutually exclusive, such as 'free market' and multinational-firm domination. (This paragraph has benefited from reading Stuart Kirsch's *Reverse Ethnography* [2006] and especially Arturo Escobar's great work *Territories of Difference* [2008] and the recent writings of Bruno Latour [2004, 2005].)

All of this may make little difference when one is looking at the common subject of political ecology: cases in which one group of people quite openly moves in to dominate another, for the purpose of looting them, exploiting their labor (as slaves or underpaid workers), or dumping toxic wastes on them. Here, power is naked and is exerted in all its forms, so one can simply study how it plays out on the ground and what happens to the victims. Even here, one runs the risk of ignoring their agency and ability to resist (cf. Scott 1990, 1998), but most authors are now aware of this problem.

However, such works still run the risk of degenerating into morality plays: yet one more case of the innocent, virtuous indigenes betrayed and brutalized by the villainous alien rulers. Arturo Escobar, in his recent book *Territories of Difference* (2008), has critiqued such simple and disempowering narratives, and has dealt at length with the diversity and multilocality of power and the many and active forms of resistance to it. Escobar, like others, does not deny the villainy of power or the real suffering of the indigenous people; the difference is that he focuses on their agency and on what they are doing about it all, rather than merely portraying them as victims with nothing to offer. His detailed discussion of the difference this makes defies summary and should be read with care.

Overattention to power keeps us from examining a quite different question: why some people have succeeded for thousands of years in living at fairly high densities, in fairly complex and materially elaborate cultures, without wiping out their subsistence base. Given the world's current inability to manage even the most necessary and most easily managed resources (such as water; Anderson 2008), the success of the Maya or the Northwest Coast Native peoples to manage whole environments seems nothing short of incredible. They are technologically quite capable of wiping out their resource base; the Maya may have done so in the 900s AD (Diamond 2005; but see Gill 2000, Webster 2002, and McAnany and Gallareta 2010 for other views). But they restrain themselves by a series of complex mechanisms. Indeed, so good are traditional people at preventing 'eco-catastrophe' that Diamond (2005) could find only a few cases of 'collapse' due to ecological overshoot—and now all those cases have been challenged (McAnany and Yoffee 2010). Clearly, we have some learning to do.

Rational individual maximizing is a recent European invention, dating to the microeconomics of the late nineteenth century. Other societies do not limit their motivation theories this radically. Not only non-Western societies, but also the folk and traditional sides of modern Western societies, are aware that, in practice, humans integrate emotion, mood, cognition, impulse, and embodied knowledge, and are motivated by love, generosity, foolishness, sociability, irrational hate, and above all group conformity, as well as individual material advantage. I have been working, therefore, with phenomenological ideas of humans as emotional and social, and concerned with experience rather than with rational calculus. (Kay Milton's book *Loving Nature*, 2002, is the best statement of this view so far in political ecology.) This seems to supply the orientation necessary to understand conservation and management mechanisms in traditional societies where neither government (and governmentality) nor the 'discipline of the market' do the job.

The Maya View

I have now done research in three regions that have very elaborate knowledge of human/environment relationships: China, the Northwest Coast of Canada, and the Yucatec Maya region of Mexico. All these have a wealth of what is, in reality, human ecology.

I will begin with the Maya, because their view of human/environment relationships is clear and explicit and is extremely different from that typical of the European tradition. Since the Maya are confronted with the latter in the form of Hispanic-Mexican resource use, they are, to varying degrees, aware of the differences. Most of the views discussed here are quite general among Yucatec Maya (see e.g. Anderson 2005; Anderson and Medina Tzuc 2005; Faust 1998; Haenn 2005; Redfield and Villa Rojas 1934;), but the specific details apply to the Yucatec of the Zona Maya of central Quintana Roo.

The Maya have no concept corresponding to the opposition of 'nature' and 'people' or the 'human' realm in Western philosophy and folk cosmology. (This opposition seems to have entered the world via Greek philosophers around the fourth to fifth centuries BC; Lloyd 2007.) There is also no real concept of 'wild' or 'wilderness.' The Maya recognize that there is a difference between things people make and things people do not make, but they regard this as a rather minor difference. Humans influence the entire environment. The forests of Quintana Roo, including the most remote old-growth, have all been cleared for agriculture at some point, and all show traces of earlier occupation, often in the ancient Maya period (see Sharer and Traxler 2006). Contemporary Maya are always working on the forest—renewing trails, harvesting wild fruit, clearing small firebreaks around valuable trees, planning future fields, hunting game, watching birds, or harvesting wild medicinals. There is a constant, inconspicuous presence, influencing every square inch of forest land.

The opposition between wilder and tamer landscapes is expressed in the opposition of *k'aax* 'forest,' *k'ool* 'field,' and *kaah* 'community.' Old-growth forest, the nearest to 'wild,' is *kaanal k'aax* 'tall forest.' Wild animals are *k'aaxih* 'of the forest,' tame ones are *alakbih* 'raised [by people].' Maya farms and gardens include many tolerated weeds, game animals, insects, and other life forms that people did not deliberately introduce. The line between wild and domesticated plants is often impossible to draw, because so many plants are encouraged though not planted. These include many medicinal plants, and also such exotic items as the cycad *Zamia lodigesii*, tolerated because its roots provide the only good rat poison available in the rural Maya world.

Maya environmental ethics are premised on a general idea of using everything but not taking too much of anything. Any sizable animal, down to the large gophers, is fair game. Almost every plant is used, many of them for several purposes (Anderson 2003). Some 350 plants are used medicinally, and well over 100 for food. No one species is heavily used, with the vitally important exception of maize, the sacred staple. It still provides 75 per cent of calories in the more traditional households.

Overuse is considered bad behavior, conducive to supernatural punishment. The general rule is to use whatever is there and usable, but not take so much that others would be deprived. Conversely, anyone can take what is seriously and immediately needed—not only from the wild, but from neighbors' fields—without asking. Self-regulation is remarkably strong and successful, though in today's world of high population and rifle and shotgun availability, large game animals are seriously depleted (Anderson and Medina Tzuc 2005). A general sense that everyone is in the community together, dependent on all available resources and needing them frequently, leads people to be responsible and to use resources fairly responsibly.

Particularly notable is the preservation of forest through management. Fields are cut, burned, abandoned after two years, and allowed to regrow for varying lengths of time, depending on soil. This leads to a 'managed mosaic' (Fedick 1996) of forest and field types, and to preservation of all sorts of ecologies.

The world is also ordered by usually-invisible beings, of whom there are many. Belief in *Dios*, the Christian God, is universal. Traditional people also believe in a large range of more directly important and influential beings: the storm gods (*chaak*, which also means the storms themselves), spirits of the fields (usually called something like *yumihk'ool*, Lords of the Fields), spirits of the forests (*yumihk'aax*), protective spirits or masters of game animals, and other protective spirits. There are also minor occasionally-visible beings like elves, ghosts, and witches in animal form. Disembodied, nonpersonal evils are *ik'* 'winds,' and often all spirits are called *ik'* also. There is an obvious problem telling these from actual physical winds, especially when people are discussing someone who is ill, since illness is generally due to *ik'* that can be either ordinary cold draughts or bad spiritual forces. People are often unsure what kind of *ik'* made someone sick.

Dealing with the spirit world involves ceremonies, including the famous *ch'a chaak* 'praying for rain,' which is now rare, and the many *loh* 'ceremonies' that are given to ask or thank the spirits for good harvests, successful hunting, and other good things. Curing and divining ceremonies also occur. A complex, active balance must be maintained between the many spirits and the human world (the best account is still that in Redfied and Villa Rojas 1934, which after 80 years remains broadly descriptive of the more traditional individuals and communities). There is a strong awareness that ceremonies serve to bring the commuity together, and the *ch'a chaak* I attended was arranged specifically for that purpose (more than for the rain).

Conservation and sustainable practices are mediated this way. One cannot take too many animals, because the spirits guarding and protecting the game and the forests will cause trouble. A *loh ts'oon* 'ceremony of the gun' must occur when a certain, rather small number of animals has been killed by it; its luck has to be renewed. This ceremony involves some effort and expense, and makes one think about hunting and overhunting. Similarly, the *yumihk'ool* make sure that people do not burn carelessly, cut too much, or otherwise abuse the environment.

These traditions are fading, as more widespread, mainstream forms of Christianity grow in importance. Protestants and Catholics are both numerous in the area, and both broken up into many types—various Protestant sects and various forms or movements within Catholicism. As these wax in importance, the old conservation and management teachings tend to fade, but they are proving fairly resilient, because many people recognize their value and redefine them in mainstream Christian terms. Such people are often quite aware of the value of conservation and the need to tie it to religious morality, and also of the value of religion as a community-building and community-consolidating mechanism. (One of the many things that makes me follow Durkheim [1995] in seeing religion as the collective representation of community, basically about social solidarity, is the fact that my Maya and also my Chinese friends have so often said so themselves—another case of folk social science influencing the anthropologist.)

Thus the sense is that the various rules for managing plant and animal resources have some divine or spiritual origin and force, but are useful, pragmatic, and grounded in the social community. The rules thus can—and, for many, should—carry over into whatever new forms of religiosity become prevalent. Rain ceremonies may die out, but not the more general ideas of thanksgiving, of careful cultivation, and of not taking too much.

The contrast with Hispanic Mexicans is quite striking (cf. Haenn 2005). New small-farming migrants to the area tend to learn Maya norms, but large landowners, as well as farmers outside the Maya settlement areas, simply clear the forest and plant monocrops (most commonly introduced pasture grasses for cattle, but also food and fibre crops). They see *naturaleza* as something to eliminate. Some enjoy it aesthetically, more find it annoying and unpleasant, but all see it as necessarily destroyed for 'progress' and 'development.' The idea of a nature separate from humans and in competition therewith, and the corollary that anything artificial is better than anything natural, is an ancient part of Hispanic culture, going back to the Roman Empire. This idea is changing fast, and many Hispanic Mexicans now respect the Maya and their culture, but (sadly and ironically) the last place to change is the South Mexican rural sector. Thus, ironically, when Maya acculturate to Hispanic Mexican norms, they often pick up ways that the Hispanics themselves are learning to discard as pernicious.

However, Maya ways are gaining ground, as the wider society realizes their benefits. Within my research experience in Mexico (almost four decades now), the country has shifted dramatically from the attitude summarized in the last paragraph to a far more environmentally sensitive one. The problem is that the new attitudes are spreading from the cities and the centers of education, and remote indigenous towns are the last to be reached—though there have been some astonishingly successful efforts in Maya villages, when biologists, concerned citizens, and the Maya have been able to work together. Francisco Rosado May, a Maya trained at the University of California, has started a university in my field area to train local Maya in both academic and traditional ways. There have also been failures (see e.g. Faust et al. 2005; Haenn 2005) but at least the models and possibilities are out there for dialogue.

Northwest Coast Views

The Northwest Coast Native peoples have a view that is broadly similar, because they share a common (if distant) North American Native heritage with the Yucatec. Northwest Coast management of resources is now well documented (Deur and Turner 2005; Turner 2005). Societies of the Northwest Coast of North America construct personhood to include all beings, and their societies include local trees, bears, and mountains. They therefore treat all these beings with care and respect. These moral messages are in turn propagated through oral traditions and through spectacular and aesthetically compelling visual arts.

Most sources report that Native Americans did not separate humans from nature, but detailed ones sometimes present a somewhat inconsistent view. The discrepancy is real. Native Americans see themselves as completely incorporated in the world. Animals and plants are 'other-than-human persons,' as classically discussed by A. Irving Hallowell (1955, 1960). However, the world existed before people came. In our terms, there was a purely natural world before there were people-in-nature.

To prepare for humans, transformer beings progressively changed this earlier world from a sliding, formless, fluid cosmos into the familiar world we know. These origin myths probably represent interpretations of the actual history of Ice Age hunters coming into a formless and self-organizing late-glacial environment. Before, animals were human-like, though with their current distinctive traits. They still live like humans in their own worlds. Transformer beings had to change them into their current furry, feathery or scaly forms for human use.

These transformers were usually, but not always, animal powers. On the Northwest Coast, transformers included Raven, Coyote, and others. In any case, the myths portray humans are both incorporated into and basically separate from the rest of the cosmos. This is quite different from the Maya case; the Maya may never have had such myths, and have now long accepted the Biblical Christian story, which they interpret as saying that humans were created in a garden environment at essentially the same time as the rest of life.

One spectacular result of the Northwest Coast view is the spectacular artistic tradition. Not only the famed 'totem poles' and masks, but the houses, the rituals held therein, the dances, and the stories, poems, and songs draw on the power of animal and nature spirits. An inspired artist has received power from Master Carver or an equivalent spirit being. The powerful effect of his or her work on the viewers is proof that real spirit power is being communicated directly. Art themes, stories, and songs are frequently owned by particular descent groups, and anyone from another group must pay a fee for using them, as in European copyright law. Art is thus a key mode of expression and communication of myth, religion, emotion, and social place.

Northwest people have a similar sense of individuals in society. Each individual is a fully distinctive person, but each is a full member of the social circle—family, community, tribal entity. ('Tribes' in the modern sense were not recognized; the unit was the group that wintered together in an established winter village.) Society was responsive to individual needs, and made up of persons each of whom had a special rank, name, lifeway, and task. Spirit power gained through a vision quest at puberty provided a calling, in the old sense of the term. The spirits or divine beings had actually called the individual to be a hunter, or boatbuilder, or artist, or shaman, or other task. This had the function of validating the individual's life choice. Parents who wanted their son to be a doctor could hardly complain if the spirits—rather than the wilful son—chose a hunting career instead. (This account is synthesized from dozens of sources, but particularly useful for readers might be Collins 1974 and Jilek 1982).

Thus, the model was individual-in-society, and society did not stop at the edge of the human species; it included all beings nearby. (Cf. Cajete 1994 for discussion of Native American ideals). Within this framework, sustainability is motivated by considerations of both human and other-than-human society. (The following draws on many accounts, including Atleo 2004 and George 2003 for the Nuu-chah-nulth; Frey 2001 and Reyes 2002 for the Interior Salish; Nadasdy 2004 for the Kluane; Ridington 1981, 1988, 1990 for the Dunne-Za; Willerslev 2007 for the culturally related Yukaghir of Siberia.) The rules are the same as those of the Maya, but they are enforced by the animals themselves. The animals have spirits and can have humanoid forms, and these can capture humans and punish them. All groups have important mythic stories of disrespectful treatment of animals in the past, and of the punishment it received.

Typically, one child or pair of children refrained from the bad treatment, and were spared; in other stories, a disrespecter of animals might be captured by the animals and given a stern warning (tales of this sort are common among the Maya also). Either way, the individual is taken to the animal world and told how to act properly. Overhunting, wasting, and unnecessary or wanton killing are the worst of sins and the most punished. However, animal powers as well as ordinary humans recognize that feasting is necessary to make alliances with neighbors, and some waste of meat is inevitable then, so feasts provide a very partial exception to the rules. However, vain or flagrantly unnecessary consumption even in a feast is unacceptable.

Stories of overhunting punished by lack of game are obviously circumstantial, recalling real events. The explanation that sheer overhunting was the sole cause is not considered adequate, however, because the animals are intelligent, social beings that present themselves to humans more or less voluntarily; if they are withholding themselves, it is to punish an offense rather than because they were simply killed out. This has the effect of making overhunting truly immoral and abhorrent, but also the effect of making it seem reasonable, because the animals are not really exterminated; they survive out there somewhere, at least as souls that can reincarnate.

Leaving aside the question of whether spirits are 'real' or not (some hard-headed Anglophone ethnographers have come to believe in them; and see Nadasdy 2007), we have several philosophical insights that are useful to the modern world. As with the Maya, the parallel ideas of people-in-nature and individuals-in-society are basic, and contrast sharply with the people-vs.-nature and individual-vs.-society basis of much of Euro-American civilization—the ideas called the 'Human Exceptionalist Paradigm' in the current volume. Animals and plants are persons who deserve consideration and respect just as human persons do. This is shown by taking as little as possible and never overusing. On the other hand, animals present themselves as game, plants present themselves as useful, and absolute preservation is immoral; it too is disrespectful to the other-than-humans. The Northwest Coast people have reservations about a world that gives over some areas to lock-down preservation (no indigenous traditional uses allowed) while throwing other areas open to total destruction of forests or game for frivolous purposes such as making toilet paper or having a rack of antlers on the wall.

In spite of the full impact of Euro-American society and culture, Northwest Coast views of the world are anything but dead. In fact, a large number of Native intellectuals, such as Richard Atleo (2004), Earl George (2003), and Lawney Reyes (2002), now define themselves in part through opposing their views to Euro-American ones. They are not self-consciously reviving the past, either; my research (and many others') has disclosed widespread continuing belief in the old system, in spite of and in reaction to Western views. This parallels Escobar's findings in Colombia, noted above, on the surprising strength of local agency and resistance.

For the indigenous people, animals and plants are people too, and part of our society; we must therefore treat them with respect; and we must maintain a social

community, involving them as well as ourselves, through an intense ritual and cere-
monial life that involves emotions, moods, aesthetic feelings, and moral sentiments as
well as cognitive knowledge. The cited Native intellectuals believe this is a more
accurate and predictive way to look at human–environment relationships than are the
'rational choice' and 'humans vs. nature' perspectives usual in the modern world, and
see it as a basis for a new and improved way of conserving and managing resources;
this fits very well with the New Ecological Paradigm described in the present
volume. Many Euro-American scholars would agree (Anderson 2010; Deur and
Turner 2005; Turner 2005). Native efforts have, in fact, been a major and often
decisive force in delaying the destruction of forests, fisheries, wildlife, and other natural resources in the Northwest. They have also been major inspirations for the work
of the Suzuki Foundation and other Northwest-based ecological research and conservation
organizations.

Chinese Views

What has caused neglect of these theories up till now has been the Human Exceptionalist Paradigm, and also the Western stereotyping of the traditional views as
'religion.' This term has been a thoroughly dismissive label—first because it was used
by Christian missionaries who fought all non-Christian spirituality, then because it
was used by social and biological scientists who regarded 'religion' as, at best, unex-
amined and unverified belief, and, at worst, mere nonsense and foolishness (see e.g.
Dawkins 2006). Northwest Coast and Maya belief remained strictly within the 'religion' or 'cosmovision' orbit in most ethnographies. Until recently, it was pigeonholed as 'primitive religion' with all that that implies (see e.g. Redfield and Villa
Rojas 1934 for the Maya).

The long-civilized, highly literate Chinese could not be dismissed that way. But
since Chinese philosophy lacks the appearance of formal syllogistic logic and other
markers of sophisticated philosophy in Europe, it was consigned to a rather lowly
status until recently. Current rehabilitation by leading Sinologists (e.g. Graham 1989;
Harbsmeier 1998; Lloyd 2002) teaches us that Chinese social thought was intended to
be useful for managing one's life and for governing people, not to be an exercise in
rigorous systematicization. In any case, recent environmental histories of China have
not even bothered to take Chinese thought seriously—though in fact it could have
helped the distinctly preliminary theorizing in that field (Elvin 2004; Elvin and Liu
1998; Marks 1998). Fortunately, not all Westerners are so limited, and there are now
excellent compendia on Chinese environmental thought—though, again, largely
within the tradition that sees it as religious (Girardot et al. 2001; Tucker and Berthrong
1998).

In China, social theory is an old and self-conscious enterprise, and Chinese social
theories are sophisticated and much debated. Nothing quite like human ecology
developed in dynastic China, because of a focus on humanity and human social
relationships (Elvin and Liu 1998). However, the obvious fact that people live in and
depend on a wider environment led to thinking on the subject.

One early and rather extreme Daoist position held that the human realm is insignificant, and humans have no higher goal than to let themselves be absorbed in nature (Zhuang Zi in Graham 1981). Another extreme sees nature more or less as the Western world usually does: merely a mine of resources to exploit. However, the vast majority of Chinese thinkers see humans as firmly and fully embedded in the environment, but an environment humanized by cultivation. The wild was a rare commodity in old China. It was usually seen by sages as a place to meditate and restore oneself, but by more practical people as something to be used.

In either case, harmony (*he*) and balance (*bing*) with nature and with the environment was desired. The Chinese almost universally believed that working with nature was necessary, and that following the natural 'way' (*dao*) and 'principles' (*li*) of things was the only way to succeed in any endeavor. Except for the radical Daoists, this did not mean inaction; it meant—proverbially—'not pulling up the crops to see how they were growing,' 'keeping the dykes low and the channels deep,' and otherwise doing what would make maximal use of nature's own devices in making them work for the benefit of humans.

This led to a strong conservationist view, but one that in Western terms could be said to be devoted to 'wise use' rather than 'preservation.' Chinese protected sacred but highly useful groves around villages and temples, and also had forest plantations; but they logged off most forests. Their failure to save forests is probably the worst blot on their ecological escutcheon, as they themselves knew, and as outsiders have confirmed (Elvin 2004; Marks 1998). However, it was not the only blot. They overgrazed grasslands, filled wetlands, and polluted waters. Again, this was not universal, and religion or local custom preserved much. They protected game animals in hunting parks, and protected insect-eating birds and other useful fauna, but did not save wildlife for itself. On the other hand, the strong Buddhist and Daoist influences on Chinese culture did work to prevent unnecessary killing, and even to a strong ideology of protecting any living thing from wanton abuse. India's cult of cows spread with Buddhism, and traditional Chinese rarely killed cattle or ate beef (though they would do it; in traditional Japan, by contrast, cattle were as safe as in India.)

Saving resources, whether wise use or preservation, necessarily involves motivating individuals to defer consumption, often at considerable personal cost. Motivation can be moral or religious or financial. Social pressure is necessary, and usually government authority is inadequate, since the police cannot always be there. This is where social thought necessarily enters (see chapter by Eleanor Shoreman-Ouimet, this volume). The Chinese motivated conservation through religion and through folk-scientific knowledge, involving clear knowledge of the consequences of bad actions.

More to the point, however, is their assumption of the innate moral nature of people, and their consequent appeal to morality as well as any other factors. Confucius began serious discussion of these issues in the sixth century BC. Early philosophers, writing about both human-human and human-environment interactions, usually held that humans are innately 'good,' meaning 'eusocial.' The most famous name in this regard, and the most convincing and psychologically astute, was Mencius (Mencius 1970). He argued that just as a deforested mountain's nature is to bear trees, a bad person would naturally be good but has been badly educated or subjected to a bad environment. Xunzi, in contrast, argued that people's inborn nature (*ben xing*) is prone to foreground self-interest above society (Xunzi 1999). This view was downplayed over time, but was never lost; it tempered the optimism of Mencian views. The resolution was a belief that humans are basically social and well-meaning, but all too prone to fall into selfishness and meanness. Strong environmental influences are needed to keep them on the right path. The one thing everyone agreed on was that people are basically social and moral. They want and need society and sociability, and are emotionally involved in their communities. They naturally feel moral impulses, though these need to be trained and reinforced by society. No one assumed the cold rationality and complete self-centeredness assumed by microeconomic theory.

This led to an environmentalism based on both moral and economic appeals. The economic ones transcended. Forests, fish, rice terraces, insectivorous birds, and marshes were conserved because they were productive. But in preventing tragedies of the commons, moral appeals were necessary. Confucius and the early Confucians stressed wise management of biotic resources. Both Mencius and Xunzi were very strong conservationists (see e.g. Mencius 1970: 164; Xunzi 1999: 241, 245, 283). They saw the need to add moral, political, and religious/spiritual appeals to pragmatic ones. It is interesting to see the foundational texts of Chinese thought provide explicit, comprehensive, holistic, and ecologically sophisticated conservation advice. These sages made it clear that conservation depended on a holistic moral vision and on precept and example by the Emperor and other high-level figures. Buddhist and Daoist sources were less specific about conservation measures, but taught a deep love and devotion toward the wide world and a deep sensitivity to nature. Local folk religion also revered trees, birds, rocks, mountains, wild animals, and other natural features, and lies behind the exquisite landscape and flower-and-bird art of China and neighboring countries.

These views were broadly confirmed in practice, at the village and farm level as well as at higher governmental levels. Quotes from the sages—including Mencius' forest story—were widely known, even by illiterate farm workers. The broad worldview, whether in social thought, medicine, or environmental management, stressed working with nature, harmony and balance with the cosmos in so far as possible, and personal responsibility within a mutually supportive community framework. Of course, nothing could completely save resources over two millennia of wars, famines, economic and demographic expansion, and the sheer human greed that Xunzi deplored. What is astonishing is that anything survived.

The resources that were saved into the twentieth century were saved largely for reasons that westerners call 'religious' or 'magical,' but that the Chinese do not necessarily see that way. The Chinese knew or believed that general disaster would follow from certain procedures, not only because of practical problems, but also because the gods and spirits would disapprove. This was certainly true in the case of the rice terraces, river dykes, and marshes (which absorbed floodwaters). Cutting sacred groves led to real disasters (erosion, exposure to wind, lack of firewood and timber) but also to supernatural retribution.

However, in the end they were not enough. Mencius was too optimistic. Not only did the environment slowly deteriorate over time, but in the mid-twentieth century the traditional Chinese ways of thought were abandoned, and total destruction became a political mission. Mao Zidong's slogan 'struggle against nature' was a radical new idea in the 1950s, and not a popular one. It has done incalculable harm.

Conclusion: Lessons

We have here three very different views from very different societies: the Maya manage and care for all their environment as if it were one big garden; the Northwest Coast people work as hunters among other species of hunters, respecting all and honoring all; the traditional Chinese saw humans as enormously and necessarily impacting nature but necessarily working in harmony with it and with its basic principles (*li*). The modes of livelihood involved vary from swidden farming to fishing to intensive agriculture. The societies range across the entire spectrum of sociocultural integration.

All these ideas could well serve as foundation for a new cultural and political ecology. They are all perfectly consonant with the New Ecological Paradigm emphasized in the present book. They all see humans as firmly embedded in nature; they see nonhuman lives as important and part of the greater picture, not to be dismissed or neglected. They all see working with nature as necessary, and working against nature as a fool's errand.

The holders of these views managed natural resource intensively yet more or less sustainably. Not all traditional societies were so sustainable. Many had no concept of sustainable management, others tried and failed, and some collapsed outright (Diamond 2005; Hames 2007). Even the three considered here were not perfect in their treatment both of nature and of other people. The Northwest Coast communities were prone to protect their own fish while making savage war on more distant humans. The Maya have overcut and overburned forests in the past and in the present. The Chinese in old times overused the resource base in far too many places. However, none of the three groups shared the Western idea that it is worth sacrificing an entire ecosystem for the profit of a handful of rich humans, or the even more extreme idea that 'development' is a good even if it brings *no* profits, simply because destroying nature is desirable in itself (on which see Glacken 1967).

The three considered here must therefore have shared some useful approaches. By comparison to the Euro-American ('western') cultural world, these three traditions share a much less pronounced differentiation of people from 'nature.' They share a strongly spiritual view of the world, with protection of resources religiously enjoined. They share a respect for the nonhuman world and for nonhuman lives as Kantian subjects, not mere stuff to use or waste according to whim. They share a concept of mutualism: humans and nonhumans depend on each other, or at least need to accommodate to each other. They see community in terms of 'we're all in this together,' and they include nonhuman lives in this assessment, however much they may use and overuse those lives in practice.

All three groups see humans as integrating emotion and cognition, and see society as depending on ceremonies that involve intense aesthetic experiences as well as religious feelings. They thus apply all aspects of human mentation—from 'rational' to aesthetic—to representing and managing the environment. They thus see humans as living within society, but as retaining individuality therein. They do not share the 'rational individual choice' model. Choices are emotional, social, and directed toward goals set emotionally and socially.

All three also share a high respect for the word, but not an extreme privileging of it. All three areas have traditions of powerful verbal spells, charms, songs, and incantations that are believed to affect the world. On the other hand, the people themselves are not highly verbal. This ranges; at one extreme are the interior Northwest Coast Athapaskans, who save words for real need (see e.g. Nadasdy 2004), while at the other the Chinese can be very verbal.

Indigenous traditions lead us away from separation of art, philosophy, social science, and biology. Anthropologists often work with political scientists and geographers, but rarely with psychologists, artists, or philosophers.

The classic model in the Euro-American world—the model on which the globalized economy and worldwide culture are based—involves not only an opposition of people vs. nature, but an opposition of individual vs. society. The mythic form, seen in the careers of Socrates and Jesus, and countless religious and political martyrs since, is of the courageous loner standing up against Society and being killed for his (or, rarely, her) trouble. Individualism is seen at its best in philosophies of human and civil rights, but has a very dark side in the social irresponsibility of many. The converse in Euro-American tradition is the triumph of Society over the individual, as in fascism, doctrinaire conservative Christianity, communitarian philosophy, and the abject conformity that characterizes so much of American life (Riesman 1953). There seems to be no way to reconcile these within Western thought—no way to have a socialized but distinctive individual in a responsive, tolerant, but rule-based society.

This leads, among other things, to the Human Exceptionalist Paradigm described in the Introduction to the present volume. It also gives us the 'rational individual choice' model, so common in human ecology, but so hopelessly wrong for it. Michael Taylor (2006) found that Native American groups who 'irrationally' saved their communal lands eventually did better economically and socially than those that 'rationally' sold them off for individual profit maximization. One of the reasons for the survival of 'rat choice' is that it fairly well explains failure to conserve (e.g. via Tragedy of the Commons models; Hardin 1968). Political ecologists tend to look at failure stories, or what they consider to be failure stories, in which local people are mere victims, not agents (Escobar 2008). Where rational choice fails is in explaining successes. As the three cultural traditions show, success in sustainable management depends on involving community, morality, and emotion in one package.

Political ecology in the last 20 years has been dominated by the ideas of a tiny handful of people, largely Europeans of two to three generations ago: Gramsci, Foucault, Bourdieu, Derrida, Deleuze and Guattari, and a few others (as well as the 'rat choice' model). However brilliant some of these men may have been, they share to an extreme degree the Western paradigm and its Human Exceptionalist version. This has embedded that paradigm in political ecology. In extreme cases, political ecologists have even recycled the right-wing 'jobs vs. owls' rhetoric, sometimes almost word-for-word from corporate press releases. Often, political ecologists consider local and indigenous people, but not the nonhuman lives or the wider human society. Thus the work of international conservation agencies can appear purely malevolent.

Political ecology from the European philosophical tradition also privileges the word above physical reality; indeed, some political ecologists appear to believe words are real and reality isn't. Continental Platonic discourse has led to regarding ideas as somehow more real than reality (as Plato himself apparently did). This has led, in political ecology, to the above-noted privileging of abstractions. These now resemble animist spirits; they are no more real, and they appear to the present writer to have less beneficial effects on theory and action.

It is possible to revive the ideas of more ecologically grounded Continental thinkers, such as Maurice Merleau-Ponty and Claude Lévi-Strauss. It seems at least as worthwhile to take the ideas of our indigenous friends and consultants seriously, as social and ecological theory.

On to Globalization

In regard to globalization, however defined, these examples show that local cultures do survive and can make a difference. 'Globalization' is not a thing and is not an irresistible process. It is partly a cover term for economic changes that basically involve the extension of the corporate-governmental interests of the strongest nations to the entire world; in this sense it is merely a new term for the mercantilism so memorably attacked by Adam Smith. It is also a cover term for the spread of American popular culture and, to some extent, a few other popular cultures that have managed to 'swim against the stream' and spread in spite of the Hollywood tsunami. The implications of the three worldviews considered above—and the thousands of other local, traditional, and indigenous cultural views in the world—for this system should be obvious. Globalization threatens them, because its economic agenda is fatal to their way of managing, but it also provides channels of communication and political action that allow them a worldwide hearing and a chance for world action. At worldwide fora, indigenous people from many groups are now regularly meeting with each other and with biologists and social scientists of all origins. Whatever problems such fora may have, they provide the best and perhaps the only chance for saving the planet.

Acknowledgements

I am deeply grateful to Helen Kopnina and Elle Ouimet for valuable editorial commentary.

References

Anderson, E. N. (1988) *The Food of China*, New Haven: Yale University Press.

Anderson, E. N., with José Cauich Canul, Aurora Dzib, Salvador Flores Guido, Gerald Islebe, Felix Medina Tzuc, Odilón Sánchez Sánchez, and Pastor Valdez Chale (2003) *Those Who Bring the Flowers: Maya Ethnobotany in Quintana Roo, Mexico*, Chetumal, Quintana Roo: ECOSUR.

Anderson, E. N (2005) *Political Ecology in a Yucatec Maya Community*, Tucson: University of Arizona Press.

Anderson, E. N. (2008) 'Water,' lecture, Sharlot Hall Museum, Prescott, AZ, October.

Anderson, E. N., and Tzuc, F.M. (2005) *Animals and the Maya in Southeast Mexico*, Tucson: University of Arizona Press.

Anderson, E. N. (2010) *The Pursuit of Ecotopia*, Santa Barbara, CA: Praeger.

Atleo, E. R. (Umeek) (2004) *Tsawalk: A Nuu-chah-nulth Worldview*, Vancouver: University of British Columbia Press.

Basso, K. (1996) *Wisdom Sits in Places: Landscape and Language among the Western Apache*, Albuquerque: University of New Mexico Press.

Boserup, E. (1965) *The Conditions of Agricultural Growth: The Economics of Agrarian Change under Population Pressure*, Chicago: Aldine.

Cajete, G. (1994) *Look to the Mountain: An Ecology of Indigenous Education*, Skyland, NC: Kivaki Press.

Collins, J.M. (1974) *Valley of the Spirits: The Upper Skagit Indians of Western Washington*, Seattle: University of British Columbia Press.

Conklin, H.C. (1957) *Hanunoo Agriculture*, Rome: FAO.

——(1981) *Ethnographic Atlas of Ifugao: A Study of Environment, Culture, and Society in Northern Luzon*, New Haven: Yale University Press.

——(2007) *Fine Description*, Joel Kuipers and Ray McDermott, eds, New Haven: Yale University Southeast Asian Series, Monograph 56.

Dawkins, R. (2006) *The God Delusion*, Boston: Houghton Mifflin.

Deur, D.; Turner, N. (eds.) (2005) *Keeping It Living: Traditions of Plant Use and Cultivation on the Northwest Coast of North America*, Seattle: University of Washington Press; Vancouver: University of British Columbia Press.

Diamond, J. (2005) *Collapse: How Societies Choose to Fail or Succeed*, Viking.

Durkheim, E. (1995 [1912]) *The Elementary Forms of Religious Life*, Tr. Karen E. Fields. New York: Free Press.

Elvin, M. (2004) *The Retreat of the Elephants: An Environmental History of China*, New Haven: Yale University Press.

Elvin, M.; and Ts'ui-Jung, L. (eds.) (1998) *Sediments of Time: Environment and Society in Chinese History*, New Haven: Yale University Press.

Escobar, A. (2008) *Territories of Difference: Place, Movements, Life, Redes*, Durham: Duke University Press.

Faust, B.B. (1998) *Mexican Rural Development and the Plumed Serpent*, Westport, CT: Greenwood.

Fedick, S. (ed.) (1996) *The Managed Mosaic: Ancient Maya Agriculture and Resource Use*, Salt Lake City: University of Utah Press.

Frake, C. O. (1962) 'Cultural Ecology and Ethnography,' *American Anthropologist* 64:53–59.

——(1980) *Language and Cultural Description*, Anwar S. Dil, ed., Stanford, CA: Stanford University Press.

Frey, R. (2001) *Landscape Traveled by Coyote and Crane: The World of the Schitsu'umsh (Coeur d'Alene) Indians*, Seattle: University of Washington Press.

George, E.M. (2003) *Living On the Edge: Nuu-Chah-Nulth History from an Ahousaht Chief's Perspective*, Winlaw, BC: Sono Nis Press.

Gill, R. (2000) *The Great Maya Droughts*, Albuquerque: University of New Mexico Press.

Girardot, N. J.; Miller, J.; Xiaogan, L. (eds.) (2001) *Daoism and Ecology: Ways within a Cosmic Landscape*, Cambridge, MA: Harvard University Press.

Glacken, C.J. (1967) *Traces on the Rhodian Shore: Nature and Culture in Western Thought from Ancient Times to the End of the Eighteenth Century*, Berkeley: University of California Press.

Gladwin, T. (1970) *East Is a Big Bird: Navigation and Logic on Puluwat Atoll*, Cambridge, MA: Harvard University Press.

Goodenough, W. (1953) *Native Astronomy in the Central Carolines*, Philadelphia: University Museum, University of Pennsylvania.

Graham, A. C. (1981) *Chuang Tzu: The Inner Chapters*, London: George Allen & Unwin.

——(1989) *Disputers of the Tao*, La Salle, IL: Open Court.

Haenn, N. (2005) *Fields of Power, Forests of Discontent: Culture, Conservation, and the State in Mexico*, Tucson: University of Arizona Press.

Hallowell, A. I. (1955) *Culture and Experience*, Philadelphia: University of Pennsylvania Press.

——(1960) 'Ojibwa Ontology, Behavior, and World-View,' in *Culture in History: Essays in Honor of Paul Radin*, Stanley Diamond, ed. New York: Columbia University Press. Pp. 19–52.

Hames, R. (2007) 'The Ecologically Noble Savage Debate,'\' *Annual Review of Anthropology* 36: 177–90.

Harbsmeier, C. (1998) *Science and Civilisation in China, Vol. 7, part 1, Language and Logic*, Cambridge: Cambridge University Press.

Hardin, G. (1968) 'The Tragedy of the Commons,' *Science* 162: 1243–48

Jilek, W. (1982) *Indian Healing: Shamanic Ceremonialism in the Pacific Northwest Today*, Surrey, BC: Hancock House.

Kirsch, Stuart (2006) *Reverse Anthropology: Indigenous Analysis of Social and Environmental Relations in New Guinea*, Stanford, CA: Stanford University Press.

Latour, B. (2004) *Politics of Nature: How to Bring the Sciences into Democracy*, translated by Catherine Porter. Cambridge, MA: Harvard University Press.

——(2005) *Reassembling the Social*, New York: Oxford University Press.

Lloyd, G. (2002) *The Ambitions of Curiosity: Understanding the World in Ancient Greece and China*, Cambridge: Cambridge University Press.

——(2007) *Cognitive Variations: Reflections on the Unity and Diversity of the Human Mind*, Oxford: Oxford University Press.

McAnany, P., and T. G. Negrón (2010) 'Collapse in Ancient Mesopotamia: What Happened, What Didn't,' in *Questioning Collapse: Human Resilience, Ecological Vulnerability, and the Aftermath of Empire*, Patricia A. McAnany and Norman Yoffee, eds. Cambridge: Cambridge University Press. Pp. 142–75.

McAnany, P.; and Yoffee, N. (eds.) (2010) *Questioning Collapse: Human Resilience, Ecological Vulnerability, and the Aftermath of Empire*, Cambridge: Cambridge University Press.

Marks, R.B. (1998) *Tigers, Rice, Silk, and Silt: Environment and Economy in Late Imperial South China*, New York: Cambridge University Press.

Mencius (1970) *Mencius*, translated by D. C. Lau, Harmondsworth, Sussex: Penguin.

Mills, C. W. (1959) *The Sociological Imagination*, New York: Grove Press.

Milton, K. (2002) *Loving Nature: Towards an Ecology of Emotion*, London: Routledge.

Nadasdy, P. (2004) *Hunters and Bureaucrats*, Vancouver: University of British Columbia Press.

——(2007) 'The Gift of the Animals: The Ontology of Hunting and Human-Animal Sociality,' *American Ethnologist* 34: 25–47.

Redfield, R.; Rojas, A.V. (1934) *Chan Kom, A Maya Village*, Washington, DC: Carnegie Institution of Washington.

Reyes, L. L.(2002) *White Grizzly Bear's Legacy: Learning to be Indian*, Seattle: University of Washington Press.

Ridington, R. (1981) 'Technology, World View, and Adaptive Strategy in a Northern Hunting Society,' *Canadian Review of Sociology and Anthropology*, l9:4:469–48l.

——(1988) *Trail to Heaven: Knowledge and Narrative in a Northern Native Community*, Iowa City: University of Iowa Press.

——(1990) *Little Bit Know Something, Stories in a Language of Anthropology*, Vancouver and Toronto: Douglas & McIntyre.

Riesman, D.; Glazer, N. (1953) *The Lonely Crowd: A Study of the Changing American Character*, New Haven: Yale University Press.

Robbins, P. (2004) *Political Ecology*, Oxford: Blackwell.

Sahlins, M. (1972) *Stone Age Economics*, Chicago: Aldine.

——(1976) *Culture and Practical Reason*, Chicago: University of Chicago Press.

——(1993) *Waiting for Foucault, Still*, Chicago: Prickly Paradigm Press.

Scott, J.C. (1990) *Domination and the Arts of Resistance: Hidden Transcripts*, New Haven: Yale University Press.

——(1998) *Seeing Like a State*, New Haven: Yale University Press.

Sharer, R.J.; Traxler, L. (2005) *The Ancient Maya*, 6th edn, Stanford: Stanford University Press.

Shiva, V. (1997) *Biopiracy: The Plunder of Nature and Knowledge*, Boston: South End Press.

——(2001) *Protect or Plunder? Understanding Intellectual Property Rights*, London: Zed Books.

Taylor, M. (2006) *Rationality and the Ideology of Disconnection*, New York: Cambridge University Press.

Trautman, T. (1987) *Lewis Henry Morgan and the Invention of Kinship*, Berkeley: University of California Press.

Tucker, M.E.; Berthrong, J. (1998) *Confucianism and Ecology: The Interrelation of Heaven, Earth, and Humans*, Cambridge, MA: Harvard University Press for Harvard University Center for the Study of World Religions.

Turner, N.J. (2005) *The Earth's Blanket*, Vancouver: Douglas and MacIntyre; Seattle: University of Washington Press.

Vayda, A.P., and Walters, B. (1999) 'Against Political Ecology,' *Human Ecology* 27: 167–79.

Vogel, J.H. (1994) *Genes for Sale: Privatization as a Conservation Policy*, Oxford: Oxford University Press.

——(2000) *The Biodiversity Cartel: Transformation of Traditional Knowledge into Trade Secrets* (CD), Quito, Ecuador: CARE.

Webster, D. (2002) *The Fall of the Ancient Maya*, New York: Thames and Hudson.

Willerslev, R. (2007) *Soul Hunter: Hunting, Animism, and Personhood among the Siberian Yukaghirs*, Berkeley: University of California Press.

Winterhalder, B.; Smith, E.A. (eds.) (1981) *Hunter-Gatherer Foraging Strategies: Ethnographic and Archeological Analyses*, Chicago: University of Chicago Press.

Xunzi (1999) *Xunzi*, trans. John Knoblock, Changsha and Beijing, China: Hunan People's Publishing House and Foreign Language Press.

3

ENVIRONMENTAL POLITICS AND POLICY AMBIGUITIES IN ENVIRONMENTAL ANTHROPOLOGY

Peter Bille Larsen

As environmental policy matters have gained unprecedented attention at both global and local levels, where does environmental anthropology position itself? Rarely protagonists in policy-making, should anthropologists rethink ethnographies, produce more data and engage more directly in 'policy relevant' work? This chapter argues that anthropological engagement is, and needs to remain, ambiguous in approaching environmental policy. As environmental policy language has become omnipresent, while imploding as a self-evident master narrative, analytical ambiguity is not only a natural consequence, but also an anthropological necessity. This chapter compares different strands of anthropology and argues for a renewed engagement with environmental policy matters grounded in current methodological multiplicity. The chapter compares three different ways of approaching environmental policy. Efforts to explain environmental change and inform policy are analyzed according to their epistemological underpinnings and contrasted with political ecologies grounded in post-structural theory. Subsequently, phenomenological approaches questioning human-nature dichotomies and the modernist assumptions of policy making are debated. The question, I argue, is not whether, but how, to situate and understand the politics and policy aspects of human environment relationships. The relevance of anthropology is not merely about its ability to inform policy makers, but grounded in its capacity to critically address how policy matters intersect with human environment relationships. This entails addressing the multiple levels, effects and intersections of policy in everyday relations, an agenda requiring multiple theoretical frameworks and empirical detail. In particular, it entails the consolidation of environment as a relational category.

Anthropology in Times of Policy Implosion

Environmental politics have gained omnipresence in the public sphere unthinkable forty years ago. The environment is a standard element of political campaigns, party programs and national elections. Environmental policy, in turn, has emerged as a favored political technology, not only of state structures, but equally among private corporations and NGOs. Yet, the centrality of environmental politics reveals a fundamental paradox resulting from the simultaneous process of environmental policy explosion and implosion. The explosive character of environmental policy making has indeed secured it a naturalized place in the institutional landscape. Municipal by-laws in the most remote corners, national environmental policies, and global agreements illustrate the intensity of policy proliferation at stake. Such policies are now so common that something must be presumed to have gone wrong if a state or business does not yet have one. Simultaneously, environmental policy as a naturalized response to problems has imploded. Growing anthropogenic pressures, the watering out of omnipresent sustainability language or disarmed state machineries, have led to the inward bursting of environmental policy self-evidence. In the latest 'Global Biodiversity Outlook', UN Secretary General Ban Ki-moon recognized the 'collective failure' of halting biodiversity loss, 'conflicting policies' and the need for a 'new vision' (SCBD 2010). Despite policy proliferation and some 170 national biodiversity strategies and action plans, species extinction, habitat degradation and human ecological footprints have accelerated. Beyond initial waves of environmentalism, the contradictions and constraints of environmental policy are just as evident as their immediate necessity and functionalities. Take, for instance, the proliferation of policy language on green economies, climate neutrality and biodiversity conservation side-by-side with policies to encourage further consumption, production and global trade to fight economic recession. Whereas Rappaport hypothesized regulation through ritual creating feedback in a context of institutional absence, we are, conversely, now faced with maladaptation in a context of ritualized environmental institutionality and policy proliferation. Such proliferation has prompted anthropological attention to move beyond definitions of policy merely as neutral problem-solving devices. Such contradictions also confront us as we try to determine how to reconfigure anthropology in a context of ecological constraints (Catton and Dunlap 1980).

Is there a distinctive anthropological contribution to such policy realities and failures? 'From pigs to policies', the subtitle of Patricia Townsend's introduction to environmental anthropology (2009), summarizes the growing importance of policy matters as both a societal concern and object of study. Much ethnography today deals as much with state agencies, policy fields and green movements as with kinship, symbols and ritual. Environmentalisms have penetrated the farthest and most intimate corners and lives of ethnographic interest, often in ways far more dramatic than in the environment discourse producing centers. Take, for example, anthropological encounters with conservation-induced displacement and dispossession (Oliver-Smith 2009). The human ecologies of hunter-gatherers, pastoralists or farmers are no longer merely portrayed as local adaptation issues, but increasingly contrasted or juxtaposed with national, even global, policy prescriptions and their underlying assumptions.

The shift from the study of localized forms of adaptation and equilibrium towards politically situated situations of change, disequilibrium and context is clear, yet adherence to political context is far from unequivocal (Walters and Vayda 2009).

Whereas ecological adaptation was read into cultural systems and human ecologies (Rappaport 1984), the growth of environmentalism has since then made (mal)adaptation an explicit, and global, policy concern. Human-environment relationships are no longer (only) debated along terms of questions of culture, adaptation and ecology, but equally bound up in global, national and local green politics. While policy matters and the state have thus entered much ethnographic description, their significance remains unsettled.

This reflects long-standing debates about anthropological engagement, particular epistemological debates and the diversity of objects of study. Ranging from hands-on involvement, silence to critical distance, environmental anthropology hosts a range of different positions towards policy involvement. This chapter is structured around three sections describing the variety of perspectives. The first section portrays anthropology engaged in explaining environmental change and informing policy decisions. The second dwells on political ecology analysis interrogating the politics of policy making. The third section explores phenomenological approaches and the uneasiness of approaching policy matters. The final section discusses and compares their differences. Rather than privileging one form of environmental anthropology over others, the article argues that all three approaches described offer complementary contributions. It is by reasserting the environment as a relational concept that such seemingly divergent anthropologies, and epistemological contradictions, can and need to be brought into play.

Explaining Environmental Change, Science and Policy Engagement

There is, arguably, a longstanding inclusion of policy dynamics in ecological anthropology (McCay 2008). Yet, even where anthropology has been linked to policy questions, funding and international cooperation, delivery has not been straightforward. Cristina Eghenter, for example, deemed the amount of analysis remaining on shelves as 'staggering' calling for a less 'assertive' and more methodologically aware anthropology (Eghenter 2008). Informing policy inevitably raises long-debated questions of historical legacies, countered, however, by a vibrant field of engaged theory-cum-problem solving anthropology (Rylko-Bauer et al. 2008). For many, there is a clear-cut need for contributing to the formulation and improvement of environmental policy. Anthropologists have joined policy decision-making tables, as they have engaged in debates on environmental change, resource management and property systems. Science, from this perspective, has a natural, even constitutive, role in relation to environmental policy. Take Harrison and Bryner noting how: 'Science *and* politics define environmental policy making. Environmental problems *invite* scientific research' (Harrison and Bryner 2004:1, italics added). Their goal is one of synergies allowing scientists to 'infuse policy with good science' (ibid:2). Such intimate relations between science and policy are particularly evident in relation to solving environmental problems such as biodiversity loss. Engaging with policy from this perspective becomes a legitimate form of providing explanation in a contested field, where decisions with socio-environmental outcomes are naturally formed by scientific description and data. Anthropologists have increasingly claimed particular contributions in terms of describing, explaining and resolving environmental problems. Take, for instance, calls to 'strengthen the links among anthropology, policy, and sustainable environmental management' (Haenn and Casagrande 2007) and a 'persistent desire that anthropology's relevance be translated into governmental action' arguing that 'anthropological skills in delineating and negotiating across identity differences would place the discipline at the heart of environmental policy-making' (ibid: 9). From this angle, social science contributions form part of the knowledge, competencies and data basis for environmental decision-making considered to have privileged knowledge about social aspects, distant places, 'cultural' aspects or social process. Approaches closest to the epistemological foundations of natural science and objective description through problem analysis and documentation of human ecologies have arguably been more readily mobilized. The empiricism of some ecological anthropologists and the search for causal explanations (Vayda 2008; Walters and Vayda 2009) resonates with the internal logic of policies in the emphasis on scientific fact as something independent from theoretical (and political) frameworks. Ethnobotany or indigenous knowledge studies, paralleling scientific classificatory systems, are, for example, used more frequently in site-based planning compared to studies questioning Western knowledge categories altogether. It is thus not surprising that a recent article in *American Anthropologist* urges to 'bring back' quantitative and environmental data into anthropological work in order to effectively contribute to policy (Charnley and Durham 2010).

Anthropologists have made critical contributions in fields as diverse as site-based planning, environmental change analysis, ethnobotany and impact assessments. Much work in human ecology has sought to translate anthropological insights about socio-ecological realities into new forms of policy action. This has often involved closer connections between ecological data, energy flows and human ecology questions. Grounded knowledge about communities, foraging, fishing or agricultural practices in particular ecosystems formed natural starting points to inform policy and solve 'post-Rio' policy problems as deforestation and biodiversity loss. Anthropologists emphasized use rationalities, customary management and local knowledge, where others saw deforestation and ignorance of ecological processes. This has involved building alternative models of environmental degradation, reframing questions such as population pressure and poverty. Cultural ecologies, in places like the Amazon basin, were in the 1970s and 1980s mobilized alongside environmentalisms to counter state incorporation and internal colonization. Anthropology described domestication and organization where others saw diminishing wilderness (Posey 1985). The anthropological rebuttal of the 'tragedy of the commons' and an empirical-cum-policy emphasis on common property rights systems is a good example (McCay and Acheson 1987). Ethnographies, often written in opposition to privatization or enclosure, depicted community institutions and management, where decision-makers saw open access.

While some 'political ecologists perceive policy as a kind of uncouth cousin to be kept at a distance' (Walker 2006: 382), others have researched distribution, access and marginalization issues with fairly explicit policy intentions often couched in environmental justice, rights and equity language (Paulson et al. 2003). Such approaches not only seek to provide information for supposedly data-hungry decision-makers, but also attempt to politically contextualize and question the problem assumptions, categories and constructions employed. What is questioned is not just the accuracy and relevance of policy, but the underlying political ecology. Such analysis has, by some, been viewed as a theory-driven attempt to explain everything through the political economy (Vayda 2008; Vayda and Walters 1999; Walters 2008). These authors questioned the explanatory value of rendering explicit the political economies of policy, resource access and decision-making. Political ecology, they argue, risks overgeneralization by failing to provide the ecological evidence for the relative importance of political and economic factors. Take James Scott's recent analysis of cropping patterns in highland Southeast Asia as 'escape agriculture' to evade tax collectors and the state (2009: 195pp). While his emphasis on politics to explain human environmental relationships is thought provoking, the risk is that other key variables, notably, the particular ecology of highland environments, are underestimated. The alternative, proposed by Vayda and Walters, involves empirically analyzing events, questions and problem-driven research to prime over theoretical propositions. Yet, can we afford to drop theoretical questioning altogether? While the empirical vigor is laudable, Vayda's rejection of 'theory deploying' (Vayda 2008:n.37) seems overstated. Political ecologists have responded maintaining a focus on 'knowledge, power and practice' and 'justice, governance and ecological democracy' (Watts and Peet 2004: 20). On another level, it would seem that the insistence on the empirical establishment of environment change causalities underestimates the importance of multiple theoretical frameworks to illuminate different aspects of a given environmental change complex. Jonathan Friedman in an earlier critique of functionalist underpinnings of ecological anthropology and cultural materialism emphasized the importance of contradictions, autonomy of different subsystems and the interaction of relatively independent structures (Friedman 1974, 1979). If we assume human environment relationships as the confluence of interlinked social and ecological systems with independent, yet mutually impacting, dynamics (Hornborg 2006), multiple causalities can hardly be apprehended only through theory-free fieldwork. If we acknowledge that human environment dynamics entail constantly changing states of disequilibrium involving a range of co-existing and intersecting processes, rather than a particular logic, theoretical concepts are necessary. Whether speaking of commodity flows, fiscal incentives, carbon credits or power, theoretical insights are fundamental to ask the right questions, work at appropriate scales and consider what is relevant data in the first place. The question is not whether, but how, to situate and understand the politics and policy aspects of environmental change. This is not merely about deconstructing policy logics,[1] but recognizing the multiple levels, effects and intersections of policy. While this certainly requires ethnographic openness, it also entails tackling the presence of politics head-on. This is not the same as taking either policy language or theoretical frameworks for granted. As Rappaport noted:

> It may be an epistemological mistake to give our troubles substantive names, for to do so is to reify them and to set them up for the corrective approach dear to American hearts called 'problem-solving,' which is likely to set more problems than it solves by ripping aspects of complex systems out of their contexts.
>
> *(Rappaport 1993: 297)*

Policy remains external to socio-environmental realities as the empirical starting point, but may 'lose touch' with reality. A frequent argument from the ecological perspective is thus one of policy engagement risking scientific compromise (Rappaport 1993; Harris 2001: 220; Vayda 2008). Take Rappaport's assessment of the fundamental life processes being subordinated by the contingent and instrumental (1993: 299). He argued how economic instrumentalities priming in policy logics neglect fundamental biological-ecological systems. For Rappaport this produced social injustices, degradation, and reduced the ability of social systems to respond. Yet, beyond the diluted politics of 'problem solving,' politico-economic dynamics and policy effects are more fundamentally a constitutive part of human environmental relationships. Approaching such intersections necessarily requires theoretical sensitivity to allow for a comprehensive empirical understanding. Rappaport thus noted how different values were 'not free-floating', but 'held and promulgated by particular institutions, interest groups, sectors, classes, and individuals, all of which are differentially powerful' (ibid: 300). Anthropologists seeking to inform policy have exactly been confronted with such power realities. As Carol Colfer notes, much anthropological engagement has come from inaccurate assumptions that more information about localities would improve policy decisions (Colfer 2008: 273–75). Policy makers rarely have the time to read and environmental change often requires rapid decisions. Colfer notes how 'we did not adequately account for the powerful economic and political forces at play keeping policy makers from acting on our findings' (ibid). Her response is one of engaging policy makers more directly in the research process taking into account their institutional, social and time realities. Interestingly, this joins critical studies of the centrality of bureaucracies, policy makers and an understanding of the political economy of environmental decision-making.

Politics of Policy and the Skeptical Anthropologist

The emergence of environmentalism and policies banning DDT following the publication of *Silent Spring* (Carson 2002 (1962)), marked an often-cited environmental turn, yet without fundamentally putting into question 'overproduction' identified by Rachel Carson as 'our real problem' (ibid:9). The immediate policy fix was one thing, changing the wider political economy of growth another. Just as Rappaport was criticized for assuming implicit regulatory functions, based on negative feedback, in cultural systems (Friedman 1979), a critical appraisal of the functionalist assumptions of explicit regulatory policy is today warranted. Whereas managerial approaches to environmental governance, for example, may speak of the 'necessity' of environmental institutions, the role of policy measures as rational problem-solving feedback mechanisms is increasingly questioned. At stake are not merely poorly designed or ineffective policy thermostats, but the conditions and political contexts of regulating environmental affairs. On the one hand, environmentalist policy and agency is no longer the monopoly of governments, but widely distributed among state bureaucracies, business operations and civil society actors. On the other hand, the contradictions of green policy making are increasingly evident. Peter Brosius has, for example, shown the political displacement taking place when Malaysian authorities succeeded in transforming a Northern anti-logging campaign into managerial questions of 'sustainable forest management' and certification (Brosius 1999). Political ecologists have increasingly underscored the political economy underpinnings of policy making. Growing anthropological uneasiness with green truths, environmental narratives and policy action has generated critical literature on environmental discourses. More recent post-structural or post-Marxist political ecologies (Biersack 2006) have rejected the presumed innocence, linearity and moral high grounds of environmental managerialism and replaced it with detailed descriptions of discourse, power and politics. Where Bjørn Lomborg questioned the numbers of environmental litanies (2001), skeptical anthropologists question the underlying distribution of power, inequities and discursive authority.

What is emerging is, however, not a blind application of political economy, nor the transformation of environmental anthropology into political science. Firstly, anthropologists are less likely to assume the nature of a will to power, *libido dominandi*. Secondly, the focus on social categories, discourses and conflict has generated empirical attention to questions of social movements, ideology and cultural politics as inherent aspects of ecological relations. Take Arturo Escobar's critique of managerial solutions and biodiversity discourse produced by dominant institutions (Escobar 1998), and his plea for bringing social movements, progressive academics and NGOs into the debate (ibid: 76). Resurfacing the politics of environment, often drowned in the technicalities of policy, is a salient aspect of much contemporary ethnography (Zerner 2000). As Brosius asked 'who is listened to, ignored, or regarded as disruptive, and in which contexts?' (1999: 50) in what he saw as 'institutional envelopment' and 'environmental surveillance'. What and who is behind technical policy solutions? Shore and Wright have argued for specific attention to policy as a 'central concept and instrument in the organization of contemporary society' (1997: 4). In a Foucauldian vein, they emphasize policy as language and power, policy as cultural agent and policy as political technology. From that perspective, power dimensions are easily masked in the 'objective, legal-rational idioms' of policy (Shore and Wright 1997: 8). Confronted with the limitations of managerialism and policy failure, the construction of scientific facts and contributions to policymaking has been rendered problematic. Fairhead and Leach argued how the employment of social science language and analysis is easily complicit in the reproduction of flawed environmental narratives. Their point was exactly that policy narratives on deforestation disregarded local realities (Fairhead and Leach 1995). Without questioning environmental problems altogether, they questioned the instrumentalization of social science for the sake of dominant representations in turn generating particular effects. With the empirical shift from human ecology and the biophysical environment to public policy as an object of analysis (Wedel et al. 2005), the risk is, as others in this volume stress, distance to the effects and actual ramifications of environmental policy 'on the ground.' Furthermore, while the uneasiness or upfront critique of environmental policy and bureaucratization (Brosius 1999) may have dampened interest or ability to directly engage in policy formulation, the focus on policy agency and discourse also offer alternative entry-points. Rather than dooming policy and bureaucratic engagement to failure and surveillance, other anthropologists have engaged in the playing field of the politics of policy. Assessments of agency, interest groups and discourse have, for example, been employed through advocacy or participatory processes to actively promote more just and locally relevant forms of policy (Keeley and Scoones 1999). Research agendas of political ecologies stressing the agencies, discourses and politics at stake provide complementary knowledge to such policy engagement (Paulson et al. 2003; Biersack 2006) seeking simultaneously to inform and render problematic the ecologies at stake.

Beyond Dichotomies and the Ontological Irrelevance of Policy

At first sight, certain anthropologies seeking to display the variety of ways in which human environment relationships are conceived, ontologically constituted and lived out seem somewhat distant from the policy debates discussed above. Couched in the language of ontology, cosmology and perspectivism, anthropologists have argued vehemently against dichotomies such as society/culture and subject-object (Descola and Pálsson 1996; Viveiros de Castro 1998; Descola 2006). Stressing the diversity of embedded experiences, policy and politics have remained either in the background or radically questioned in depictions of other ontologies. The move beyond the nature-culture dichotomy has maintained such anthropology in epistemological rupture with the underlying separation of humanity from the 'global environment' (Ingold 1993). Philippe Descola thus assumes that if we acknowledge 'an unproblematic natural world' then there 'can be no escape from the epistemological privilege granted to western culture' (Descola 1996: 85). Policy from this perspective illustrates the radical 'other' state, NGO or science projects incommensurable with local realities. The ontological underpinnings of modernist policy action, whether by NGOs or scientists, are contrasted with different ontologies and experiences of the ethnographic interlocutors. Mario Blaser, based on his work among the Yshiro, e.g., speaks of the 'inherent coloniality of the modern ontology' and that the modern constitution would collapse 'if Indigenous worlds and ontologies were taken seriously' (2009: 18). Tim Ingold in seeking to recover 'the reality of life process' in ecology notes resistance to 'transmission in an authorized textual form' (2000: 16). Paige West has questioned the assumptions implicit in political ecology reducing 'local socio-ecological lives' to Western categories of self and agency (West 2005). Certainly, anthropologists have been at the forefront of contrasting imposed forms of regulations and policy categories with localized forms of environmental relations (Ellen 1996: 28;

Campbell 2005). Gísli Pálsson expresses concerns about the postmodernist emphasis on embeddedness, monism and the absence of certainty hampering 'effective politics' (2006:76). Whereas Pálsson's conclusion is the necessity of narratives to maintain earth integrity and avoid ecological bankruptcy, the dilemma encountered is clear. In arguing against society-nature dichotomies, the basis for societal, not to even mention global, management is considered a modern pretension; both ontologically flawed and averse to other realities. Pálsson suggests a democratic process combining theoretical expertise and practical knowledge (2006: 76). Something similar could arguably be considered in the case of the Yshiro, although Blaser sees indigenous knowledge efforts as co-opted under modern ontologies. Yet, can we assume that policy logics and institutional operations operate at another level ontologically in opposition to and distinct from local ontologies? There continues to be an awkward separation between studies of indigenous perception, experience and cosmology and the day-to-day experience of living in and engaging with 'policyfied' environments. Does this divide, formulated through an emphasis on ontological difference, not risk implying radical essentialized alterity rendering the possibility of building new shared understanding of environmental problems almost impossible? Is it ethnographically pertinent to maintain a sharp ethnographic divide? While constructed as phenomenological, is there not a risk that the separation of local ontologies from wider policy concerns and language reflects more of a methodological bias than the social and cultural fabric as lived out? Is there not a risk that shared understandings of phenomena, such as declining food stocks, biodiversity loss or contamination, are put in the background in the eagerness to demonstrate ontological difference? While rejection of modernist dominance and power is warranted, is the insistence of ontological difference not in risk of reproducing the very dichotomy it sought to break away from in the first place? By presenting control, management, and clumsy ways to acknowledge indigenous knowledge, as inherently 'modern' is there not a danger of reiterating the existence of non-modern, non-managerial and apolitical ontologies? In prolongation, is it not necessary, ethnographically speaking, to include intersections with the policy field as part of human environment relationships and their ontological underpinnings? How do we theoretically come to terms with the people with supposedly radically different ontologies themselves who do policy work, propose management and use science? Is this 'buy-in', radical change or do we perhaps need to revisit how politics and policy are conceived in the first place? Can we, in response, conceptualize different subjectivities, forms of agency and ways of relating without being caught up in modernist limitations? Additionally, rather than remaining stuck in ontological alterity, need we not move towards a far more fluid notion of human environment relationships, where dialogue and new ways of communicating and understanding environmental problems across ontological boundaries, although often on very unequal terms, is part of the everyday lives of our interlocutors? I believe it is imperative to do so, just as it is imperative to recognize the ontological diversity at stake within modernist forms. Indigenous peoples and their organizations have now for at least a couple of decades, I would argue, amply proven the point. Frequently cited as practitioners employing different ontologies of nature, indigenous representatives have with remarkable effectiveness engaged heavily in both global and national environmental policy processes confirming their proximity to policy effects as well as an interest in reformulating policy premises. Universal thinking and understanding policy interconnections is not a Western monopoly, albeit universalities at stake may differ. Rather than dismissing indigenous engagement in policy processes on contamination in the Arctic, tropical forest policy or climate change as potentially ontologically different,[2] such engagement reveals the centrality of transversal environmental policy concerns to very localized and diverse realities. This prompts attention to policy intersections and contradictions in ethnography rendered possible through a more open-ended understanding of human-environment relationships.

As Ingold noted, what for the anthropologist is a cosmology, is a lifeworld for the people themselves (Ingold 2000: 14). Such lifeworlds, the study of them and ethnographic representation, are obviously political, just as concepts of nature are inherently political (Ingold 2005: 503). Rather than situating policy concerns 'outside' experience, they are often in intricate ways part of the environmental relationship. However dramatically technocratic language may seem in opposition to 'direct' experience, sharp boundaries cannot be assumed. Ways of walking, experiencing and living environmental relations are often intertwined with resource use restrictions, trade regimes and use policies (Ingold and Vergunst 2009). Whereas anthropologists frequently have stressed the ontological distance between political constructions and other human environmental relationships, far more needs to be explored regarding their proximity, co-existence and intersections. To move beyond the dilemmas presumed by certain ontology studies, Tim Ingold's emphasis on environment as relational, historical and never complete offers a way out (2000:20). It is exactly in the interface through different ways of environing rather than aggregated cultural models or ontologies in opposition, where the real life politics and human environment relationships take form. From this perspective, environment is not merely what surrounds, but a dynamic process of agency-centred *environing*, intimately interlinked and emergent within *surrounding* processes reproducing or transforming the very human ecologies at stake. I use environing here to illustrate open-ended processes of relationship building and regular interaction. 'Environing' captures processes such as forest domestication, engagement with spirit worlds or non-humans transforming landscapes. Surrounding, on the contrary, implies dynamics driven from the outside. It is about human environmental relationships being redefined through broader flows of energy, material, meaning and agency beyond immediate control. The distinction is, of course, analytical. Both processes in practice are intertwined. Whether in the form of dog agency in the Ecuadorian Amazon (Kohn 2007), flows of PCB toxins to Inuit breast milk, wildlife trade or agricultural subsidies, ecological relationships are deeply entangled between processes of environing and surrounding. Policy intersections arguably thus form part of local ontologies, even if their prescriptions and effects may be articulated very differently. Blaser's 'political ontology' of asymmetrical clashes between Yshiro hunting practice and project attempts to install 'modern' regulation illustrates such intersections (2009). He theoretically employs multinaturalism[3] and 'many kinds of nature' to describe indigenous ontologies and question the limitations of reductionist multiculturalism. However, from the perspective of addressing environmental problems, the analytical emphasis on 'different worlds' becomes problematic. Whereas much policy-making, not least proposed by indigenous organizations, entails national, transboundary and global measures, anthropological emphasis on the multiplicity of worlds tends to radicalize difference rather than theorize real-world interaction. Rather than insisting on ontological difference in opposition, Blaser's analysis reveals how different environmental relations intersect, relate and contradict each other. We need to move beyond the analytical impasse of being pigeonholed as relativists, and sharpen ways to explore how the so-called modern forms part of environmental relations as lived out. Beyond depicting the arrogance and limitations of policy, anthropology needs to rethink how issues and differences are dealt with across ontological models at stake. Consider, for example, how indigenous efforts take up 'modern ontology' in the Amazon by formulating environmental policy, reworking ways of doing management or collaborating with government agencies. If we were simply to assume that this implied the imposition of modern categories on Amazonian worlds epitomizing the ontological other, we would likely not only risk essentialisms, but also rule out indigenous agency, shared ways of formulating environmental problems and appropriations of managerial institutions as inauthentic. More fundamentally, we would reify human environment relationships having separate existences, rather than emphasize their relational characteristic in movement. I therefore find the attempts to speak of multiple worlds problematic.[4] We need to maintain the 'environment' as relational category in all its diversity without losing touch with their interconnected nature and potentialities. I thus prefer the terminology 'plurality of environments' over 'plurality of ontologies.' This does not rule out ontological friction, but allows for far more agency and ethnographic attention to realms of interaction and particular flows at stake. Søren Hvalkof's work, for example, juxtaposing *colono* ideologies and Ashéninka cosmologies within a historical political ecology of development in the Peruvian Amazon (Hvalkof 2006) reveals the importance of ethnographic attention to ontological friction and vitality in understanding forest change. One is not more real than the other, nor can we assume ontological 'clashes of civilization' taking place. Rather different forms of environmental relations intersect and co-evolve. Of importance is not only ontological difference *per se*, but their internal logics, social reproduction and *surrounding* dynamics in terms of how they co-exist, intersect or potentially enter into conflict.

If we revisit a relational understanding of environment, it does not exclude *other* politics and policy, nor the possibility of reconfiguring shared understandings of problems or possible solutions. The answer is not sticking to flawed narratives for the lack of better ones, but working through different narratives and how they currently, as well as potentially, relate to each other. Human nature dichotomies are not merely to be rejected as flawed, but form part of the diverse repertoires employed to communicate environmental change. Anthropology clearly has a role in continuously juxtaposing categories and revealing the inequities in thinking about – and acting on – human environment relationships. Paige West's call for attention to 'the politics of translation and theories of value and spatial production' (West 2005) goes in this direction. Translation is feasible, she argues, yet often misses the 'fact that human relations with the natural world are aesthetic, poetic, social, and moral' (ibid: 633). Ethnographic attention to the diverse environmental relations, and the vocabularies of translation, are fundamental to policy-oriented anthropology. Rather than accepting the premises of sterile state categories and policy rationalities, there is a continued need for ethnography to portray complexity where simplicity prevails, but also to reshuffle the very arenas, language and power premises for policy formulation and action. Such work should, however, not fall in the trap of radical ontological difference, but rather portray intersections and friction, and potentially radically different ways of communicating and crafting policy. Poststructuralist political ecology offers analytical openings to explore such avenues by questioning how environments are discursively produced and grounded in power dynamics in the first place. If we take environing as relational in process, the question of policy and politics does not involve a choice between ontologies, nor necessarily the idea of hybridity.[5] This is not a question of hybridization of natures (Escobar 1998: 13), arguably always in working, but of paying ethnographic attention to the particular articulations of meaning creation, production and forms of interaction. Rather than hybridity, what is at play here is the very relational or contextual nature of environment *per se* being redefined in motion. This entails ethnographic attention to how policy prescriptions and consequences intersect with the wider web of human environment relationships. In summary, anthropology has not only put into question human ecologies grounded in equilibrium, but increasingly questioned the very social categories, 'interest groups', ontological basis and ways of environing that constitute a given human-environment relationship. Yet, in insisting on difference, policy measures have tended to be discarded as outside constructions, rather than firmly part of the environmental relationship. This carries the risk a relativist *impasse* unarmed to address policy implications in ethnographic description of historically situated environmental relationships as well as a somewhat unproductive epistemological distance to environmental change and policy engagement. I here propose recuperating the relational dimension as a necessary way out.

Ambiguities and Complementarities

Is seeking to reconsolidate politics in environmental anthropology like opening a Pandora's box of longstanding debates and epistemological differences on determinism, adaptation and symbolism such as those found in Amazonian anthropology (Viveiros de Castro 1996: 184,194)? Is there a need for an integrative approach bridging ecological anthropologies with phenomenological and political ecologies? What is to gain from it? Do differences in terms of epistemology, methodology and objects of study not make the exercise futile in the first place? Put more positively, isn't the variety of approaches exactly valuable due to their separate trajectories?

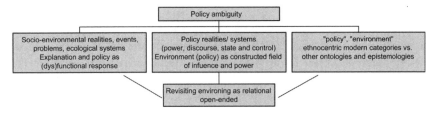

FIGURE 3.1 Policy ambiguity.

Clearly, the objects of study and their underlying epistemologies are multiple (see Figure 3.1). Yet, in tracing some of the ambiguities present in terms of addressing policy and politics, there are more commonalities than might be apparent at first sight. Where conventional wisdom would situate the environment as the non-human, the biophysical and natural, different strands of environmental anthropology have firmly and repeatedly made the point of its embeddedness in social, cultural and political fields. In addition to socio-cultural complexity, anthropologists emphasize environmental *relationships*, albeit with different theoretical underpinnings. A number of issues could be singled out in this respect.

Firstly, policy ambiguity is a shared tenet as different anthropologies compel us to look beneath policy. Ecological anthropologists may interrogate the validity of problem analysis and socio-ecological relevance of policy measures, whereas the political ecology perspective includes a stronger emphasis on the powers, discourses and political economy behind policy making in the first place. For realist-grounded political ecology, it is a question of political compromise, where policy reflects the given political economy of distributed claims, entitlements and resources. Poststructuralist political ecologies, in turn, emphasize policy as political device and instrument of power, favoring particular constructions of nature; the environment becoming one of several fields of policy making, social construction and control. Policy engagement, from this perspective, thus not only risks misrepresentation, but reproducing power imbalances, by aligning anthropological production with the dominant actors, discourse and knowledge categories.

In prolongation, phenomenological environmental anthropologists have questioned the very ontological contradictions between policy making and ethnographically described human environmental relationships. We are compelled to look beyond policy to understand lived out realities. All reveal uneasiness with master narratives and the simplifications of policy prescriptions, and their underlying premises, albeit for quite different reasons. They thus share a concern for what Joan Vincent called 'infrapolitics' as anthropology looks beneath surface realities (2004). Such ethnographic digging may take different trajectories, which are not as mutually incompatible as current divisions would indicate.

Secondly, the different lines of questioning retain relevance for a renewed anthropological engagement with the environmental policy field. Grounded data about human environmental relationships remain absolutely essential to counter desk-based policy prescriptions with limited understanding of actual dynamics and social effects. Such 'data production' need, however, not be limited to standard socio-environmental data categories. Political ecology has, for example, equipped anthropology with a research agenda and set of tools fine-tuned to both engage with and question political economies of policy-making. Anthropology is today more than ever attentive to the consequences of (un)environmental politics and environmental (in)action whether resulting from trade agreements, consumption patterns or national policy-making. Finally, broader questioning of human-nature dichotomies forces us to question, more profoundly, the categories and representations of environmental matters. Such rethinking could very well be at the heart of environmental policy making fundamentally concerned with environmental perceptions, behavior and interaction.

Thirdly, dialogue between different traditions has not only been productive, but remains indispensable. Longstanding debates about function and adaptation, politics or concepts of culture continuously allow for a reframing of human environment relationships. Critique of political ecology, at times, considered to reduce ecological and cultural complexity has helped sharpen approaches, just as I believe far more needs to be done in terms of bridging political ecologies, problem analysis and more phenomenological approaches.

Fourthly, anthropologists share a common perspective on the environment as a fundamentally relational category of processes and interaction rather than something 'out there'. This may be formulated as relations within socio-ecological systems, politically situated relations or ontologically grounded relationships of experience and exchange. Debates about the relational nature of the environment is not merely of academic interest, but more fundamentally relevant in rethinking how environmental policy is being reconfigured to address the ecosystem degradation both in terms of its underlying drivers and its socio-environmental effects.

Fifthly, human – environment relationships can no longer be maintained in isolation from wider policy dynamics, nor are politics merely another 'factor' in understanding environmental degradation. Nor need we limit politics, even policy, to state formations and instruments paraphrasing Clastres (1974). Politics and policy are, I believe, not merely possible theoretical lenses or particular objects, but part of constitutive processes of everyday human environmental relationships. Local environmental relations are in direct or indirect ways intertwined with global and national policy dynamics. The importance of such intersections is widely acknowledged (Walters and Vayda 2009: 538). Its relative importance may be debated, but the question is one of degree. The ethnographic challenge is one of exploring distinct policy articulations and implications, rather than embracing a constrained policy perspective *per se*.

Whether addressing hegemonic forces, intimate power realities, non-human agency or necessary means for environmental change, environmental anthropology offers multiple avenues for empirical investigation and policy engagement of such relations. Michael Herzfeld has argued against 'political anthropology' as a separate domain as 'all anthropology is fundamentally political' (Herzfeld 2001: 131). We might similarly retain various environmental anthropologies as fundamentally political, and thus policy relevant, albeit in distinct ways and equipped differently to study it.[6]

Between Politics and Policy: Concluding Remarks

The discussion of these five features brings me to a last point about policy engagement. Anthropological policy engagement can roughly be divided between efforts that seek to inform policy through data or problem analysis, critical analysis at a distance and more proactive forms of advocacy activism, facilitation and brokering. While there is certainly an argument for more timely and rapid research to keep up with the pace of policy makers, organizations and the perceived speed of environmental change, this should not diminish the importance of long haul thinking in catalyzing change. Four decades of intensive environmental policy-making has not delivered magic bullets, but are revealing the complexity of environmental matters at the intersection between social, economic, cultural and biophysical processes. The limitations, ambiguities and politics of environmental discourse and policy decisions are at the heart of the matter. Current climate change canopies or oil spills have, for example, cast shadows over other environmental matters such as biodiversity loss, which despite having 2010 dedicated to its cause, has largely disappeared from the public radar screen. Environmentalist tropes of rapid change and urgency often disguise far more systemic changes and lengthy time frames, which need to be unraveled. There is no escaping from such politics of representation, however apolitical research may define itself. Renegotiating human environmental relationships is at the core of contemporary politics and policy formulation, and multiple anthropologies have much to offer in this respect. We need to get beyond 'dichotomizing critiques' of anthropological advocacy (Rylko-Bauer et al. 2008: 184), recognizing the shifting terrains of environmental policy and action, in dire need for both theoretical distance, advocacy and practical engagement. This ambiguity in relation to environmental movements, policies and projects may lead to occasional *malaise*, but remains an important feature and source of innovation not just for environmental anthropology itself, but society at large.

Whereas some anthropologists have moved away from environmentalist action and policy engagement, others continue to promote environmental justice, question development agendas and dialogue with policy makers. Differences are not likely to disappear right away, nor should they. As environmental policy language has gained omnipresence, while imploding as a self-evident master narrative, policy ambiguity is not only natural consequence, but also imperative for a critical anthropology. This raises doubts about recent calls for more quantitative approaches to make policy-oriented environmental anthropology effective. Fears that environmental anthropology is 'becoming anthropology without environment' (Charnley and Durham 2010: 411) may be exaggerated. While the integration of quantitative and environmental data is certainly important, it should hardly be a prerequisite 'whatever its focus' (ibid). Policy relevance is not only about immediate inputs to policy processes and associated data needs, but fundamentally about our disciplinary ability to think through, beneath and beyond existing environmental policy. This may take the form of numbers and hard data, as it may involve softer qualitative approaches. The question is not simply one of making anthropology more policy compatible, but acknowledging the multiplicity of approaches necessary to illuminate a whole range of policy aspects of human environment relationships. Rather than only privileging data density and problem solving, this chapter equally emphasizes the policy relevance of debates within political ecology and more phenomenological approaches. Policy contradictions between growth ambitions and environmental constraint abound, and are hardly resolved by language on green economies, payment for ecosystem services or economic incentives. Keith Hart has on several occasions cracked the joke about the optimist falling off a skyscraper.[7] As he passed the 35th floor on the way down, he goes 'So far so good'. Optimistic biodiversity policy thinking is not much different, as biodiversity degradation continues at alarming rates. While we have abandoned previous ivory towers of state planning and protection, optimism continues around new towers in the making founded on market-based models and greening economies. These are bound to yet again reconfigure human environmental relationships, yet not necessarily in the ways hoped for. My point here is not to discredit environment policymaking, nor the admirable optimism of environmentalist circles. On the contrary, it is a call for far more attention to real-life policy intersections building on decades of global experimentation in creating awareness, regulatory measures and incentives to address sustainability concerns. Anthropological insights are critical to counter one-size-fits all policy quick fixes and display how policy intersects with human environmental relationships whether among urban consumers, global policy making ideologists or forest dwellers. This places ethnography not in a reactive mode of retrieving Western fantasies of ecological harmony in the jungle, but as a discipline committed to human environmental relationships grounded in real-life diversity. Take Descola's call, echoing longstanding anthropological principles, for a 'new universality' open to individual conciliation and respectful of particularities (2006: 552). Perhaps rather than yet another universality, a first step would be recognizing the reality of different universalities and how they currently intersect.

It is only by exploiting our niche betwixt and between that anthropology maintains a constructive critique of environmental challenges and their solutions. This not only requires reaching out to other disciplines and policy makers, but equally bringing our own disciplinary diversity into play. It is exactly anthropology's continuous emphasis on the environment as a relational category, which can allow it to bridge such approaches and reinvigorate disciplinary contributions to the field of environmental policy.

Notes

1 Vayda e.g. questions the utility of forest discourse analysis, seeing evidence limited to 'its own domain' (2008: 333).
2 Blaser, following Viveiros de Castro, speaks of 'uncontrolled equivocation' to make the point that interlocutors in policy interfaces may not be speaking of the same thing (2009: 11).

3 According to Blaser, building on the work of Viveiros de Castro (1998), 'a 'multi-naturalist' approach focuses on what kinds of worlds are there and how they come into being (an ontological concern).' (2009: 11).

4 Take attempts to pluralize ontologies and worlds such as Blaser's emphasis 'that there exist multiple ontologies–worlds and the idea that these ontologies–worlds are not pregiven entities but rather the product of historically situated practices, including their mutual interactions' (2009: 11). Rather than speaking of them as entities, we need to see them as relational categories, something his inclusion of 'mutual interaction' alludes to.

5 Arturo Escobar emphasizes the contemporary rupture of nature ceasing 'to be essentially anything for most people' (1998: 15). Crisis of nature being a crisis of identity, except as he (foot)notes native peoples explaining essential connections to nature (n.27). Relations previously defined by essence are flowing in change. Could this new situation allow for hybridization, 'new ways of living' and 'new grounds for existence'? Escobar asks in a post-modern vein. He, for example, speaks of hybrid natures when 'groups attempt to incorporate multiple constructions of nature in order to negotiate with translocal forces' (1999: 13), albeit later acknowledges that 'all natures are hybrid' (ibid: 14).

6 We might for that matter also state that all anthropology is fundamentally environmental, challenging environmental anthropology to continuously explore how work on identity, kinships, consumption, world system and economics interlink with work on human environment relationships.

7 http://blog.theasa.org/?p=132, accessed 21/10/2010.

References

Biersack, A. (2006) 'Reimagining political ecology: culture/power/history/nature' In A. Biersack and James B. Greenberg (eds.) *Reimagining political ecology*, Durham and London: Duke University Press.

Blaser, M. (2009) 'The Threat of the Yrmo: The Political Ontology of a Sustainable Hunting Program,' *American Anthropologist*, 111(1):10–20.

Brosius, P. (1999) 'Green Dots, Pink Hearts: Displacing Politics from the Malaysian Rain Forest,' *American Anthropologist*, 101(1):36–57.

Campbell, B. (2005) 'Changing Protection Policies and Ethnographies of Environmental Engagement', *Conservation and Society*, 3(2).

Carson, R. (1962, 2002 edition). *Silent Spring*. New York: First Mariner Books.

Catton, W. and R. Dunlap. (1980) 'A new ecological paradigm for post-exuberant sociology', *American Behavioral Scientist*, 24(1).

Charnley, S. and W. H. Durham (2010) 'Anthropology and Environmental Policy: What Counts?', *American Anthropologist*, 112:397–415.

Clastres, P. (1974) *La societé contre l'état; recherches d'anthropologie politique*, Les éditions de minuit.

Colfer, C.J. (2008) 'From understanding to action: building an anthropological approaches to influence policy making', in B. Walters, B.J. McCay, P. West and S. Lees (eds.), *Against the grain: the Vayda tradition in human ecology and ecological anthropology*, Lanham and New York: AltaMira Press.

Descola, P. (1996) 'Constructing natures: symbolic ecology and social practice' In P. Descola and G. Pálsson (eds.) *Nature and society: anthropological perspectives*, London: Routledge.

——(2006) *Par-delà nature et culture*, Paris: Gallimard.

Descola, P. and G. Pálsson (1996) *Nature and society: anthropological perspectives*, London: Routledge.

Eghenter, C. (2008) 'What kind of anthropology for successful conservation management and development?' in B. Walters, B. McCay, P. West and S. Lees (eds.), *Against the grain: the Vayda tradition in human ecology and ecological anthropology*, Lanham and New York: AltaMira Press.

Ellen, R. (1996) 'Introduction', in R. Ellen and K. Fukui (eds.) *Redefining nature: ecology, culture and domestication*, Oxford and Washington D.C.: Berg.

Escobar, A. (1998) 'Whose Knowledge, Whose nature? Biodiversity, Conservation, and the Political Ecology of Social Movements', *Journal of Political Ecology*, 5.

Fairhead, J. and M. Leach (1995) 'False forest history, complicit social analysis: rethinking some West African environmental narratives', *World Development*, 23(6):1023–35.

Friedman, J. (1974) 'Marxism, structuralism and vulgar materialism', *Man*, 9(3).

——(1979) 'Hegelian ecology: between Rousseau and the world spirit' In P.C. Burnham and R. Ellen (eds.), *Social and ecological systems*, London, New York and San Francisco: Academic Press.

Haenn, N. and D. G. Casagrande (2007) 'Citizens, experts and anthropologists; finding paths in environmental policy', *Human Organization*, 66(2).

Harris, M. (2001) *The rise of anthropological theory: a history of theories of culture*, Walnut Creek: AltaMira Press.

Harrison, N. E. and G. Bryner (2004) 'Thinking about science and politics', in N. E. Harrison and G. Bryner (eds.), *Science and politics in the International environment*, Lanham, Boulder and New York: Rowman and Littlefield Publishers.

Herzfeld, M. (2001) *Anthropology: theoretical practice in culture and society*, Malden and Oxford: Blackwell Publishing.

Hornborg, A. (2006) 'Conceptualizing Socioecological Systems', in A. Hornborg and C. Crumley (eds.), *The world system and the earth system; global socioenvironmental change and sustainability since the Neolithic*, Left Coast Press.

Hvalkof, S. (2006) 'Progress of the victims: political ecology in the Peruvian Amazon' in A. Biersack and J.B. Greenberg (eds.), *Reimagining political ecology*, Durham and London: Duke University Press.

Ingold, T. (1993) 'Globes and spheres: the topology of environmentalism', in K. Milton (ed.) *Environmentalism: the view from anthropology*, London: Routledge.

——(2000) *The perception of the environment: essays in livelihood, dwelling and skill*, London: Routledge.

——(2005) 'Epilogue: towards a politics of dwelling', *Conservation and Society*, 3(2).

Ingold, T. and J.L. Vergunst (2009) *Ways of walking: ethnography and practice on foot*. Aldershot, Hampshire: Ashgate.

Keeley, J. and I. Scoones (1999) *Understanding environmental policy processes: a review*, IDS Working Paper, Sussex: Institute of Development Studies.

Kohn, E. (2007) 'How dogs dream: Amazonian natures and the politics of transspecies engagement,' *American Ethnologist*, 34(1).

Lomborg, B. (2001) *The skeptical environmentalist: measuring the real state of the world*, Cambridge: Cambridge University Press.

McCay, B.J. (2008) 'An intellectual history of ecological anthropology', in B. Walters, B. McCay, P. West and S. Lees (eds.), *Against the grain: the Vayda tradition in human ecology and ecological anthropology*, Lanham and New York: AltaMira Press.

McCay, B. and J. Acheson. (1987) *The question of the commons: the culture and ecology of communal resources*. Tucson: University of Arizona Press.

Oliver-Smith, A. (2009) 'Conservation and the displacement of indigenous and traditional peoples', in A., Oliver-Smith (ed.) *Development & dispossession: the crisis of forced displacement and resettlement*, Santa Fe: School for Advanced Research Press.

Pálsson, G. (2006) 'Nature and society in the age of post-modernity', in A. Biersack and J. Greenberg (eds.), *Reimagining political ecology*, Durham and London: Duke University Press.

Paulson, S., L. Gezon and M. Watts (2003), 'Locating the Political in Political Ecology: An Introduction', *Human Organization*, 62(3).

Posey, D. (1985) 'Indigenous management of tropical forest ecosystems: the case of the Kayapó Indians of the Brazilian Amazon', *Agroforestry Systems*, 3:139–58.

Rappaport, R. (1984) *Pigs for the Ancestors: Ritual in the ecology of a New Guinea People*, (with epilogue), Long Grove: Waveland Press, Inc.

——(1993) 'Distinguished Lecture in General Anthropology: The Anthropology of Trouble', *American Anthropologist*, 95(2).

Rylko-Bauer, B., M. Singer and J. van Willigen (2008) 'Reclaiming Applied Anthropology: Its Past, Present, and Future,' *American Anthropologist,* 108(1):178–90.

SCBD (2010) *Global Biodiversity Outlook 3*, Montréal: Secretariat of the Convention on Biological Diversity.

Scott, J. (2009) *The art of not being governed: an anarchist history of upland Southeast Asia.* New Haven and London: Yale University Press.

Shore, C. and S. Wright (1997) 'Policy: a new field of anthropology' in C. Shore and S. Wright (eds.) *Anthropology of policy: critical perspectives on governance and power*, London and New York: Routledge.

Townsend, P. (2009) *Environmental anthropology: from pigs to policies*, 2nd edition, Long Grove: Waveland Press, Inc.

Vayda, A. P. (2008) 'Causal explanation as a research goal: a pragmatic view' in B. Walters, B. McCay, P. West and S. Lees (eds.) *Against the grain: the Vayda tradition in human ecology and ecological anthropology*, Lanham and New York: AltaMira Press.

Vayda, A. and B. Walters (1999), 'Against political ecology'. *Human Ecology*, 27(1).

Vincent, J. (2004) 'Introduction' in D. Nugent and J. Vincent (eds.) *A companion to the anthropology of politics*, Malden and Oxford: Blackwell Publishing.

Viveiros de Castro, E. (1996) 'Images of nature and society in Amazonian ethnology. Annual Review of Anthropology', *Annual Review of Anthropology*, 25:179–200.

——(1998), 'Cosmological Deixis and Amerindian Perspectivism.' *Journal of the Royal Anthropological Institute*, 4(3).

Walker, P. A. 2006. 'Political ecology: where is the policy?', *Progress in Human Geography*, 30(3).

Walters, B. (2008), 'Events, politics, and environmental change', in B. Walters, B. McCay, P. West and S. Lees (eds.), *Against the grain: the Vayda tradition in human ecology and ecological anthropology*, Lanham and New York: AltaMira Press.

Walters, B. and A. Vayda (2009) 'Event ecology, causal historical analysis and human–environment research', *Annals of the Association of American Geographers*, 99(3).

Watts, M. and R. Peet (2004) 'Liberating political ecology', in R. Peet and M. Watts (eds.) *Liberation ecologies: environment, development, social movements*, London and New York: Routledge.

Wedel, J., C. Shore, G. Feldman and S. Lathrop (2005) 'Toward an Anthropology of Public Policy' *Annals of the American Academy of Political and Social Science,* 600.

West, P. (2005) 'Translation, Value, and Space: Theorizing an Ethnographic and Engaged Environmental Anthropology', *American Anthropologist*, 107(4).

Zerner, C. (2000) 'Toward a broader vision of justice and nature conservation', in C. Zerner (ed.) *People, plants and justice: the politics of nature conservation*, New York: Columbia University Press.

Part II
Methodological Challenges

4

ENVIRONMENTAL ANTHROPOLOGY AS ONE OF THE SPATIAL SCIENCES

Emilio F. Moran

The growth of anthropological engagement with the importance of 'place' has roots in archeological approaches, and the use of aerial photography by some cultural ecologists. Spatial approaches exploded since the 1990s as more anthropologists saw advantages to using Geographic Information Systems (GIS) and satellite remote sensing data and spatial analysis in their environmental research. This increased use of spatial analysis has also led the field to be more interdisciplinary, more team-based in its field research, and more integrative than in the past. These are directions that an engaged environmental anthropology must take if it hopes to be a part of addressing the challenges of climate change and environmental change. All along anthropology has borrowed from other disciplines to achieve this interdisciplinarity in spatial approaches, borrowing from ecology, geography and other disciplines.

One of the key elements in the practice of anthropology has always been its attention to the ethnographic detail present in a village or community. More than simply a favored form of doing research, this became the only way we expected anthropological research to be carried out. This preference fitted well with a desire to provide a holistic picture of human society, and it helped ecologically-oriented anthropologists measure the relevant variables with some degree of completeness. This preference has become increasingly questionable as we have become more aware that the single village fails to adequately represent the range of variation present within even a limited region. Localized studies provide insights into family structure, subsistence strategies, labor inputs, health and nutritional status, flow of energy, socialization, and cultural institutions. Studies at this level, however, cannot address issues of origin and social evolution, economic development, demography, history, or political economy. They also neglect more current concerns with the long-term and/or larger scale impact of environmental damage done by local communities (whether they be industrial or non-industrial societies). These issues require a different type of research method emphasizing historical, geographic, economic, and political change over time and space (Moran 1990: 286; Moran and Ostrom 2005). This increased aerial coverage also means that it is difficult to carry out such studies without resorting to some new methods that allow greater spatial coverage with an economy of effort.

Studies based on a single village should not be expected to represent the range present in any population and the construction of theory is set back by generalizing from single-site data. While some anthropologists have expanded to include regional analysis, many still are trained in single village approaches. Even the most isolated human population and its immediate environment maintains a fluid set of relationships with other communities—opening it up to demographic, economic, and cultural exchange that over time changes the constitution of those same communities. Ellen demonstrated how this works itself out in the Moluccas (1990). Earlier, Rappaport (1968: 226) had commented how, in retrospect, he had found the Maring local populations to be ephemeral through time and that the regional population would have been a more appropriate unit of study. A growing number of scholars have begun to consider local case studies in a regional context (Foster and Aber 2004; Turner 2005; Moran and Ostrom 2005), and to do so they have turned to spatial technologies such as GIS and remote sensing.

Regional Analysis and the Human Dimensions Agenda

This trend toward regional analysis gained further focus with the development of what has come to be known as human dimensions research (cf. NRC 1992, 1994, 1998; Moran and Ostrom 2005). What was new in this approach was a concern for the cumulative impact of human action. Research in this new multidisciplinary field concerns human activities that alter the earth's environment, the driving forces or causes of these activities, the consequences of environmental change for human societies, and human responses to global change. Such research takes place at scales from local to global. It began with trying to understand causes, consequences, and responses to climate change events (for example, sea level rise, El Niño forecasts). It has also focused on the impacts of climate change; impacts of land use and land cover change on biodiversity, and on issues such as urban sustainability and globally significant resources such as water and energy (NRC 1992, 1994, 1998, 1999a,b; Tillman 1999). The NRC Committee on Human Dimensions of Global Change led the way in this area, and provided early syntheses of work done by the scholarly community.

Human dimensions research has already made a significant contribution to global change research by convincing the physical scientists (Lambin and Geist 2006) that research on global issues must address regionally-scaled processes. What is most evident to environmental anthropologists (cf. Moran 2006, 2007, 2010; Brondizio 2008; Brondizio and Moran 2008; Tucker 2008) is that human communities vary greatly in how they use resources. Less industrialized countries show even more variability in resource use. Tropical deforestation may be driven by population growth in Indonesia, but in Brazil it is more a product of tax breaks and subsidies given to cattle ranchers.

These environmental changes (i.e. deforestation, a global water crisis, pollution of air and water, erosion of coastal areas, sea level rise) will only continue in the twenty-first century. Major climate change cannot be safely relegated to the future (for example, carbon dioxide in the atmosphere had doubled already by 2003 from its 400,000 year geologic record as found in the Vostok ice core (Steffen et al. 2004)). The general scientific consensus is that climate change is here, it is real, and we are experiencing its impact. The demands of an additional 3–5 billion people by 2050 will alter land cover, water availability and quality, and social systems beyond what we can imagine. Environmental anthropology, environmental geography, human ecology, and environmental social science have a lot to contribute to addressing these challenges (cf. Moran 2010 for a discussion of the emerging metadiscipline of environmental social science). This will require new technologies and new ways of conceptualizing communities and how they interact with the environment.

The attention that the physical sciences' research community and policy circles are giving to the human dimensions of global environmental change offers a rare opportunity to environmental anthropologists and other environmental social scientists (Peck 1990; Vitousek et al. 1997; Moran 2010). Solutions to contemporary environmental problems will require the integration of experimental and theoretical approaches at a variety of levels of analysis, from local to global (Levin 1998). For participation in the contemporary debates over human impact on global environments, ecosystem models and ecosystem theory are fundamental (cf. Moran 1990 for a discussion of ecosystem approaches). This does not mean abiding by notions of equilibrium, fixation on calories, energy flow models, and functionalism (cf. Moran 1990, chapter 1, for a full discussion). Rather, it means understanding the nature of complex systems that link the atmosphere to the geosphere and to the living components of our planet (the biosphere). These systems are tied by complex cycles of matter, energy, and information. An environmental anthropology lacking the ecosystem approach would be largely irrelevant to the debates over the processes of global environmental change – possibly the most important research agenda for the twenty-first century (Lubchenco 1998).

The Challenge Before Us: Space, Time, and Scale

Contemporary environmental anthropology builds on the past experience of scholars who studied human interaction with the environment, but it must go beyond those approaches. Human-environment research for the twenty-first century must add refined approaches that permit analysis of global environmental changes and their underlying local and regional dynamics (Moran and Ostrom 2005). This poses a major challenge to research methods, as all researchers must employ generally agreed-on ways of selecting sample communities or sites and collecting data across highly variable sites, despite significant differences in environment, culture, economy, and history (Moran and Brondizio 2001; Moran and Ostrom 2005).

No single approach will be adequate to the complex tasks ahead. Past approaches that emphasized equilibrium and predictability and were necessary to test hypotheses, do not serve this research agenda well because they hide the dynamic processes of ecosystems. Dynamic, stochastic ecosystem models are necessary to address global environmental change (Xu and Li 2002; Walker et al. 2006). Environmental anthropologists need to use such approaches to engage, for example, ecosystem restoration (Pietsch and Hasenauer 2002; Mitsch and Day 2004), biodiversity (Tillman 1999; Nagendra 2001; Wätzold et al. 2006), agroecology (Vandermeer 2003; Wojtkowski 2004), and deforestation (Skole and Tucker 1993; Kaimowitz and Angelsenn 1998; Lambin and Geist 2006).

A tool ecological anthropologists and other human-environment scientists will need to use is geographic information systems (GIS) and the techniques of satellite remote sensing. Remote sensing from satellite platforms such as the National Oceanographic and Atmospheric Administration (NOAA)'s AVHRR sensor, the National Aeronautics and Space Administration (NASA)'s Landsat thematic mapper (TM) sensor, and the French SPOT satellite provide information of considerable environmental richness for local, regional, and global analysis (Conant 1978, 1990; NRC 1998; Moran and Brondizio 1998; Brondizio 2008). For analyzing global processes of large continental areas such as the entire Amazon basin, NOAA's AVHRR is the most appropriate satellite sensor. Its resolution is coarser, but it offers daily coverage. More recently, MODIS, a midrange resolution satellite with 250 meter spatial resolution that provides daily coverage, has been used and connected to satellites capable of finer resolution (Hansen et al. 2002 a,b; Wessels et al. 2004; Anderson et al. 2005; Morton et al. 2005). Although designed primarily for meteorology, it has been profitably employed to monitor vegetation patterns over very large areas. Because of its coarse scale, social scientists to date have made little use of this data. Engagement with the use of these tools requires retooling and study on the part of social scientists just as acquiring a new set of tools (such as demographic ones) would require us to do. While one is likely not to be a stand alone specialist, one can learn enough to effectively think and participate alongside physical scientists in this work (NRC 1998 for an example of how social scientists engaged with remote sensing in the 1990s). Funding has been available at the National Science Foundation, NASA, NOAA and NIH since the mid-1990s to engage in this sort of work linking spatial technologies with social science.

Available since 1972, data from Landsat's multispectral scanner (MSS) is relatively inexpensive and has been used by a number of anthropologists. The pioneering work of anthropologists Francis Conant (1978) and Priscilla Reining (1973) depended on this data. Use of MSS data is still valuable for studying relatively dichotomous phenomena such as forest/non-forest cover and establishing a historical account of land cover change in a particular region. Before 1972, remotely sensed data came from aerial photographs (Vogt 1974).

A significant advance took place in 1984 with the launch of the Landsat thematic mapper (TM) sensor that improved the spatial resolution from the 80 meters of MSS to 30 meters. It also included three visible spectrum channels and four infrared spectrum channels. This satellite has allowed anthropologists to make detailed studies of land cover changes in some of the most difficult landscapes known: the Amazon basin and the Ituri forest of central Africa (Wilkie 1994; Moran et al. 1994, 2002; Brondizio 1996, 2008; Moran and Brondizio 2001). Discriminating between age classes of secondary growth vegetation was achieved for the first time using satellite data (Moran et al. 1994, 1996), as well as discrimination between subtle palm-based agroforestry management and flooded forest in the Amazon estuary (Brondizio et al. 1994, 1996), erosion in Madagascar (Sussman et al. 1994), and intensification in indigenous systems (Guyer and Lambin 1993; Behrens et al. 1994).

Appreciation for scaling issues has increased as the challenge of integrating data and models from different disciplines and different temporal and spatial scales becomes necessary with the growth of global environmental change studies (Wessman 1992: 175; Walsh et al.1999). Bioecological data, coming as it often does from the study of individual organisms, must be connected to regional and global scales. Complex spatial variations and nonlinearities across landscapes occur which challenge facile extrapolations from the local scale to more inclusive scales (Green et al. 2005a). The points of articulation between different scales of analysis challenge our narrow disciplinary approaches and require new strategies for acquiring and interpreting data (Wessman 1992: 175; Walsh et al. 1999).

The precision of regional analysis depends on the quality of the sampling at the local level. Detailed local-level sampling is far from common in traditional remote sensing. Much of what goes for 'ground truthing' is visual observation of classes such as dense forest or cropland, without detailed examination of land use history, vegetation structure, and composition. The long-standing anthropological bias for understanding local-level processes, when combined with the use of analytical tools capable of scaling up and down, helps advance land use/land cover change research and articulation between differently scaled processes.

In order to advance the current state of knowledge, there is a need to engage all of the social sciences in multidisciplinary research, jointly with each other and with the biophysical sciences. In this enterprise, environmental anthropology has much to offer. Anthropologists and geographers bring two main contributions to the analysis of global change. First, both are committed to understanding local differences. When looking at a satellite image, for instance, they search for land use patterns associated with socioeconomic and cultural processes coming from local populations. Consequently they strive to find the driving forces behind land use differences and come up with land use classifications that are meaningful in socioeconomic and cultural terms.

A second important contribution is related to data collection and methods. Anthropologists, sociologists, and human geographers using satellite images want to reveal the living human reality behind land cover classes. Such a perspective requires methods that link local environmental differences to human behavior and geography (Moran and Brondizio 1998, 2001; Rindfuss et al. 2003). Environmental social scientists take pride in their fieldwork, and they can harness this interest to make important contributions to advancing the state of spatially-explicit social science (Walsh and Crews-Meyer 2002; Moran and Ostrom 2005; Moran 2010).

The Use of Remote Sensing and GIS

It is hard to imagine trying to address global environmental change research challenges without the availability of earth-orbiting satellites capable of providing time-series data on features such as soils, vegetation, moisture, urban sprawl, and water-covered areas (Campbell 1987; NRC 1998; 2005; Lillesand et al. 2004; McCoy 2005; Jensen 2005, 2007), or studying impacts of climatic variability on populations (Gutmann 2000; Galvin et al. 2001; Moran et al. 2006). Environmental social scientists have enjoyed increasing opportunities since the launch of most recently a new generation of commercial satellites such as IKONOS with 1–5 meter resolution (see Figure 4.1 for a comparison of other satellites and resolutions available) (Batistella et al. 2004).

The use of GIS to overlay data layers in spatially-explicit ways added to this powerful set of techniques (Campbell and Sayer 2003; Goodchild 2003; Goodchild

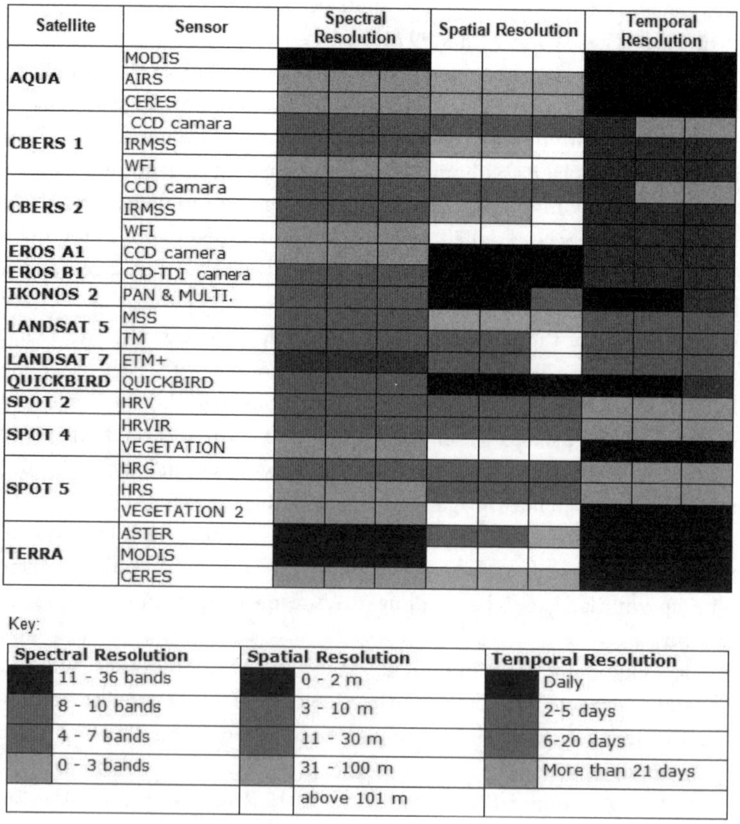

Satellite	Sensor	Spectral Resolution	Spatial Resolution	Temporal Resolution
AQUA	MODIS			
	AIRS			
	CERES			
CBERS 1	CCD camara			
	IRMSS			
	WFI			
CBERS 2	CCD camara			
	IRMSS			
	WFI			
EROS A1	CCD camera			
EROS B1	CCD-TDI camera			
IKONOS 2	PAN & MULTI.			
LANDSAT 5	MSS			
	TM			
LANDSAT 7	ETM+			
QUICKBIRD	QUICKBIRD			
SPOT 2	HRV			
SPOT 4	HRVIR			
	VEGETATION			
SPOT 5	HRG			
	HRS			
	VEGETATION 2			
TERRA	ASTER			
	MODIS			
	CERES			

Key:

Spectral Resolution	Spatial Resolution	Temporal Resolution
11 - 36 bands	0 - 2 m	Daily
8 - 10 bands	3 - 10 m	2-5 days
4 - 7 bands	11 - 30 m	6-20 days
0 - 3 bands	31 - 100 m	More than 21 days
	above 101 m	

FIGURE 4.1 Comparison of spatial, spectral and temporal resolution of main sensors used in environmental applications.
Source: Adapted from Batistella et al. 2004; updates available at www.sat.cnpm.embrapa.br.

and Janelle 2004; Aronoff 2005; Okabe 2006; Steinberg and Steinberg 2006). GIS is an essential tool in the environmental analysis tool kit, and is also widely used by environmental NGOs, urban planners, and scientists in the natural and social sciences (Evans et al. 2005a; Hesse-Biber and Leavy 2006; Greene and Pick 2006).

Remote sensing techniques have elicited interest among environmental anthropologists. For example, Conklin (1980) used aerial photography in his *Ethnographic Atlas of Ifugao*. He integrated ethnographic and ecological data to show land use zones from the perspective of the local population (compare the review of aerial photo usage in anthropology in Lyons et al. 1972; Vogt 1974). The use of satellite remote sensing in anthropology started in the 1970s, with Reining (1973) studying Landsat's MSS images to locate individual Mali villages in Africa and Conant (1978) examining Pokot population distribution. After spatial resolution was improved in 1984 with the Landsat TM sensor, more researchers began using this tool (see Conant 1990 for an overview).

Analysis of land use intensification is one of the most promising topics addressed by anthropologists using remote sensing and GIS tools (Behrens 1990). In Nigeria, Guyer and Lambin (1993) used remote sensing combined with ethnographic research to study agricultural intensification, demonstrating the potential of remote sensing to address site-specific ethnographic issues within a larger land use perspective. A special issue of *Human Ecology*, September 1994, was dedicated to regional analysis and land use in anthropology. There was substantial agreement among the articles about the importance of local-level research to inform land use analysis at the regional scale. This conclusion was reinforced in an issue of *Cultural Survival Quarterly* (1995) dedicated to showing the connection between local knowledge and remote sensing, GIS, and mapping tools. The growing use of remote sensing in the social sciences is addressed in *People and Pixels: Linking Remote Sensing and Social Science* (NRC 1998), including the work of environmental anthropologists (Moran and Brondizio 1998; Sever 1998).

The use of spatial data in analysis presents a number of challenges. Scale persists as a problem, even at the basic level of terminology (Green et al. 2005b). In cartography the term 'large scale' refers to detailed resolution, while in anthropology 'large scale' refers to a large study area and loss of ethnographic detail. Another basic problem is the interplay between absolute and relative scales, which can result in confusion in modeling ecological processes. This challenge is being addressed by landscape ecology. Many scholars are using landscape ecology methods to better understand land use dynamics, and spectral analysis is being refined to work at the local level with more detailed requirements. In order to continue solving the challenges posed by multiscalar research on global change, social scientists must develop research methods that are explicitly multiscale and capable of nesting data and sampling strategy in such a way that scaling up or down is feasible and integral to the research strategy (see part 3 in Moran and Ostrom 2005: 127–214, for a discussion of methods linking remote sensing, GIS, and social science; also NRC 1998). Evans and colleagues (2005b) provide a detailed and user-friendly introduction to the handling of spatially-explicit data.

Methods for Multilevel Analysis

Multilevel research can start at any scale of analysis; hence, sampling at one level may need to be aggregated to a higher level or disaggregated to lower levels.[1] This requires paying attention to levels of analysis without subordinating scales. Land use/cover analysis provides us with a setting for the study of levels of analysis that connects human behavior in relation to economic forces and management strategies with ecological aspects of land cover.

We can conceptualize multilevel analysis of land use/cover change as built on a structure of four integrated levels of research: landscape/regional level; vegetation class level; farm/household level; and soil level (Figure 4.2). The conceptual model relies on a nested sampling procedure that produces data that can be scaled up and down independently or in an integrated fashion. The integration of multitemporal, high-resolution satellite data with local data on economy, management, land use history, and site-specific vegetation/soil inventories aims to make it possible to understand ecological and social dimensions of land use at the local scale, and link them to regional and global scales of land use.

Household/Farm or Local Level of Analysis

Data collection at the farm/household level can include a variety of internal and external aspects of this unit of analysis (Netting et al. 1995; Moran 1995). It is important to collect local data so that it can be aggregated with that of larger populations in which households are nested. For instance, demographic data on household

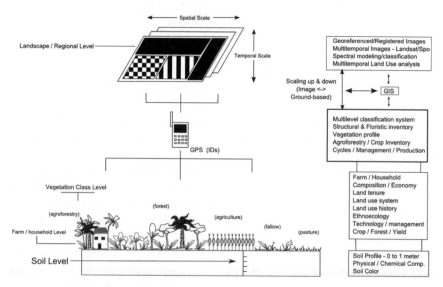

FIGURE 4.2 Multiscale analysis of land use and land cover change, showing examples of data collected at each scale and how to nest the data.
Source: Adapted from E.S. Brondizio, 1994.

composition (including sex and age) can be aggregated to the population level to construct a demographic profile of the population, but only if the data is collected in such a way that standard intervals of five years are used (Moran 1995). Another important set of data that is collected at this level and can be aggregated at higher levels is related to subsistence economy. It is fundamental for the analysis of land use to understand resource use, economic strategies, market relationships, labor arrangements, and time allocation in productive and nonproductive activities. At this level, it is important to cover the basic dimensions of social organization, such as settlement pattern, labor distribution, resource use, and kinship (cf. Netting et al. 1995 for a three-level approach to collecting social organization data relevant to land use).

Current concern with global change means that data collection at the local level must be capable of aggregation to higher levels of analysis, both in geographical and database formats. Georeferencing the household, farm boundaries, and agriculture and fallow fields (i.e. providing precise coordinates) may be achieved through the use of global positioning system (GPS) devices. These are small units that permit locating any point on the planet within a few meters. The level of precision will vary depending on a number of factors, such as the quality of the GPS receiver.

Vegetation mapping has implications for understanding the impact of land use practices on land cover. Basic vegetation parameters need to be included so they can inform mapping at the landscape level. In general, vegetation structure, including height, ground cover, basal area, density of individuals, DBH (diameter at breast height), and floristic composition are important data to be collected. These data inform the interpretation of satellite digital data, provide clues to the characteristics of vegetation following specific types of disturbance, and take into account the spatial arrangement of vegetation cover. Remote sensing has considerable potential in vegetation analysis because it enables wide-area, nondestructive, real-time data acquisition (Inoue 2003; Loris and Damiano 2006). The applications are also important in estimating aboveground carbon stocks, relevant to effective reports on Kyoto Protocol requirements (Patenaude et al. 2005) to reduce human-induced emissions of carbon dioxide by at least 5 percent below levels of 1990 by 2012 (most EU countries have failed to meet their targets, and some like the USA did not even try to set targets). To do so, countries must estimate carbon stocks in 1990 and any changes since that date, whether through afforestation, reforestation, or deforestation (Patenaude et al. 2005). The applications to monitoring and predicting severe drought also have grown in sophistication (Boken et al. 2005).

In terms of satellite data interpretation, the definition of structural parameters to differentiate vegetation types and environmental characteristics, such as temperature and humidity, is particularly important. Structural differences provide information that can be linked to the image's spectral data. Floristic composition, although important, is less directly useful in interpreting spectral responses, but it may have to be considered depending on research questions. Environmental factors, such as soil humidity, soil color, and topographic characteristics, also are associated with spectral responses of vegetation cover. For example, at the farm level, vegetation structure is the main parameter used to evaluate the impact of human management practices, though floristic composition can be relevant. Some plant species are excellent indicators of soil type which are, in turn, associated with given management practices. Farmers commonly use the presence of given species to site crops. For instance, the presence of *Imperata brasiliensis* may be a sign of low soil pH in parts of the Amazon estuary (Brondizio et al. 1994). This kind of ethnoecological knowledge is site specific, and such local knowledge does not extrapolate well to landscape, regional, or global analysis. To incorporate this data it is essential that the data be precisely georeferenced and that the sampling be transparent as one goes to higher levels of aggregation in analysis.

To determine representative sampling sites of a study area's land cover, four types of information need to be aggregated: vegetation classification, ethnoecological information of resource use, composite satellite images, and classified image/land use/ cover maps of the area. Based on the analysis of these data, one can decide how sampling can best be distributed in the area to inform both the image classification (land use/cover map) and the structural-floristic variability of vegetation classes. In selecting a site to be a representative sample of a vegetation type or class, one needs to consider the size of the area and its spatial location on the image. The spatial distribution of the vegetation class must also be taken into account to avoid clustering of the samples and biased information about the vegetation structure and floristic composition. With the use of a GPS device, geographical coordinates of the sampled area are obtained as part of the inventory. If possible, the area should be located on a hard copy of the georeferenced image at the site, to avoid confusion and ensure precision of the GPS information. However, it is in the laboratory, using more precise methods of georeferencing, that the site will be definitively incorporated into the image file. A nested data set on land use history and vegetation inventory can be related through GPS-derived coordinates to a multitemporal image, allowing complex analysis of land use trajectories and re-growth history at site, local, and landscape levels.

Information on land use history is important not only in defining sampling areas of anthropogenic vegetation (for example, fallow and managed forest), but also in verifying that natural vegetation has not been affected or used in the past. For instance, it is important to know whether a savanna has been burned, and if so, with what frequency; or if a particular forest plot has been logged, which species were taken and when the clearing event took place. Land use and management history are more detailed in areas directly subjected to management (for example, agroforestry), since management and technology determine the structure and composition of the site. In these areas, estimates and actual measurements of production are critical for analyzing the importance of the activity on a broader land use and economic context. More importance should be given to the spatial arrangements of planted species and their life cycles as part of the inventory. This area has been neglected in past environmental anthropology research and needs to be addressed by working closely with spatially oriented scientists such as environmental geographers and ecologists.

Vegetation re-growth and agricultural production analyses are limited in their usefulness without information about soil characteristics. Soil analysis should always be associated with vegetation cover analysis; soils should be collected at inventoried vegetation, agroforestry, and crop sites of known land use history and management and georeferenced to the image through a GPS device (Moran et al. 2002). Ethnoecological interviews can elucidate many soil characteristics. Taxonomic classification of soil types based on color, granulometry, and fertility help identify the major soil types and their distribution with relative reliability. Folk classification can then be cross-checked and compared with systematic soil analyses. Soil analyses should include both chemical (pH, P, K, Ca, etc.) and textural (sand, clay, silt) analyses and permit the aggregation of data to regional levels (Nicholaides and Moran 1995).

Landscape and Regional Level of Analysis

The landscape/regional level provides a more aggregated picture of management practices and driving forces shaping a particular land use/cover at sub-regional scale. At this level, long-term environmental problems can be more easily identified and predicted than at farm or household scales (Booth 1989; Skole and Tucker 1993; Brondizio and Moran 2008). This level integrates information from vegetation class, soil, and farm/household levels (Adams and Gillespie 2006). However, landscape level data also informs important characteristics of local-level phenomena that are not measurable at the site-specific scale. For instance, information about the heterogeneity and patchiness of the vegetation is an important parameter to include in site-specific secondary succession analysis, but it can only be observed at the landscape level.

There are four major steps in landscape-level research: (1) understanding the ecological and socioeconomic nature of the features of interest in land use/cover analysis, (2) identifying the extent and frequency of features of interest that can inform the appropriate spatial and temporal scales of analysis, (3) progressively increasing sampling, depending on the emergence of important variables, a process that landscape ecologists call using an adaptive approach (Turner et al. 1989) and that bears some resemblance to what Vayda calls 'progressive contextualization' (1983), and (4) considering the empirical methods needed for checking map accuracy, change detection, and projections and/or predictions, especially when associated with land use planning.

Satellite data are the most important for analysis at the landscape/regional level. However, it is always associated with other sources, such as radar images, aerial photography, and thematic and topographic maps. Anthropologists in the past left this kind of work to others, but today a growing number of anthropologists are developing these skills and making useful contributions to the analysis of satellite images (Behrens 1994, 1990; Moran et al. 1994, 2002; Brondizio et al. 1994, 1996, 2002; Moran and Brondizio 1998, 2001; Nyerges and Green 2000; Tucker and Southworth 2005). The digital analysis of satellite images may be divided in four parts: preprocessing, spectral analysis, classification, and post-processing. During preprocessing one needs to define an image subset, georeference it to available maps and coordinate systems, and register it to other images available if multi-temporal analysis is desired. The georeferencing accuracy depends on the quality of the maps, availability of georeferenced coordinates collected during fieldwork, and the statistical procedure used during georeferencing (Jensen 1996). A georeferenced image has a grid of geographical coordinates and is crucial for relating landscape data to site-specific data. When multitemporal analysis is desired, images from different dates need to be registered pixel to pixel, creating a composite image that provides a temporal change dimension at the pixel level, thus allowing the analysis of spectral trajectories related to change in land use. For instance, in a two-date image (for example, two images that are five years apart), one can quantify the change during regrowth of secondary vegetation or a shift in crops grown in that five-year period with considerable accuracy, including statistics for the change in area for each vegetation type or class.

Digital analysis provides the flexibility to use a variety of scales to analyze parameters and to define sampling procedures, depending on the land use/cover pattern and extent of the study area. In general, one can work at the landscape or regional scale (for example, the whole Landsat or SPOT image, 185 by 185 kilometer areas for Landsat images) while staying in close association with local scale processes (for example, image subsets of a watershed) to help the selection of sampling areas that will inform the image about specific spectral and spatial characteristics of land use/cover classes. By taking a hybrid approach during image classification and processing, one can integrate unsupervised and supervised classification procedures. A hybrid approach allows one to develop an analysis of spectral patterns present in the image, in conjunction with ground information, and to arrive at spectral signature patterns which account for detailed differentiation of land use/cover features. In this fashion, a conceptual spectral model can be developed in which the features of interest can be incorporated. The model considers the reflection and absorption characteristics of the physical components that comprise each feature. For instance, in a Landsat TM image, the model attempts to account for chlorophyll absorption in the visible bands of the spectrum, for mesophyll reflectance in the near-infrared band, and for both plant and soil water absorption in the mid-infrared bands (Mausel et al. 1993; Brondizio et al. 1996). The integration of those spectral features with field data on vegetation height, basal area, density, and dominance of species can be used to differentiate stages of secondary re-growth (Moran et al. 1994). The analysis of spectral statistics derived from unsupervised clustering and from areas of known features and land use history allows the development of representative statistics for supervised classification of land use/cover.

Classification accuracy analysis requires close association with fieldwork. Accuracy may decrease as spatial variability increases. Thus ground-truth sampling needs to increase in the same proportion. In this case, the use of a GPS device is necessary to provide reliable ground-truth information, whereas in areas with low spatial heterogeneity visual spot-checking may be enough. Accuracy check of a time series of satellite images for an area requires the analysis of vegetation characteristics and interviews about the history of a specific site with local people, so it is possible to accurately relate past events with present aspects of land cover (Mausel et al. 1993; Brondizio 2005, 2008).

Integration of data at these scales is an interactive process during laboratory analysis of images and field data, and during fieldwork (Meyer and Turner 1994; Moran and

Brondizio 1998). Advanced data integration and analysis is achieved using GIS procedures that integrate layers of spatial information with georeferenced databases of socioeconomic and ecological information. Georeferencing of the database to maps and images must be a consideration from the very beginning of the research so that appropriate integration and site-specific identification are compatible. Data on household/farm and vegetation/soil inventory need to be associated with specific identification numbers that georeference it to images and maps so that integrated associations can be derived. For instance, the boundaries of a farm property may compose a land tenure layer that overlaps with a land use/cover map. These two layers may be overlapped with another layer that contains the spatial distribution of households. Each household has a specific identification that relates it to a database with socioeconomic, demographic, and other information. In another layer, all the sites used for vegetation and soil inventory can be associated with a database containing information on floristic composition, structural characteristics, and soil fertility, which will also relate to land use history.

Global Level of Analysis

The 1990s saw the rapid development of approaches variously called integrated assessment modeling, GCMs (global circulation models), and other approaches at a biosphere level of analysis. Some of these have even managed to focus on the human impacts on the earth system (compare Weyant et al. 1996). GCMs were developed first and lacked a human dimension. They were largely concerned with climate and atmospheric processes, using a very aggregated scale of analysis that made even large-scale units, such as national boundaries, not always relevant to understanding differences, say, in rates of energy consumption. However, a new generation of models has emerged in the past few years that have relevance for environmental anthropologists. These are a vast improvement from the pioneering work of the Club of Rome models that appeared in the early 1970s in *Limits to Growth* (Meadows et al. 1972). Despite the many problems with this early effort, it introduced important concepts like feedback, overshoot, and resource limits to everyday discourse and scientific debate. The next attempt came from the International Institute of Applied Systems Analysis (IIASA) in Austria, with its Finite World model examining global energy flows (Häfele 1980). This attempt was broadly criticized in the scientific community and little happened until the first Intergovernmental Panel on Climate Change (IPCC) published its initial assessment in 1990. New generation models benefited from the progress made by GCMs, growing evidence of the global nature of environmental problems, and the democratization of computer technology through its wide availability (Alcamo et al. 1998: 262). The next step was clear: both social and physical aspects of the world system had to be coupled in so-called integrated assessment models. Most global modeling groups today acknowledge that progress on the accuracy and predictability of modeling efforts at this scale will require a simultaneous effort to link them to regionally scaled models that can improve the quality of the spatial resolution, and the role of human drivers in global change.

One of the more sophisticated models to date is known as IMAGE 2 (Alcamo et al. 1998). It was the first global integrated model with geographic resolution, an important feature that permits improved representation of global dynamic processes, including feedback and rapid, efficient testing against new data. It is composed of two fully linked systems of models: a socioeconomic system model, and an earth system model. The socioeconomic model is elaborated for twenty-four regions of the world, whereas the earth system (or ecosystem/atmospheric) model is spatially explicit on a 0.5 degree grid scale. The terrestrial environmental model simulates changes in global land cover on a grid scale based on climatic and economic factors. The atmosphere-ocean model computes the build-up of greenhouse gases and aerosols and the resulting impact on average temperature and precipitation. Factors such as population change, economic change, and technical change are particularly important in the terrestrial model, and the ones most in need of good-quality regional data to inform the grid-based model. To date, few environmental anthropologists have engaged this community of global modelers' efforts, forcing the modelers to make estimates based on very coarse national-scale statistics rather than derived from more refined regional studies. This is an important new direction for environmental anthropologists, given the importance of global simulation models on policies such as carbon trading, setting emission ceilings for carbon dioxide by the beginning of the twenty-first century, and debt-for-nature swaps. The main participants in these exercises have been economists who rely on the use of optimizing utility functions, rather than the less than optimal, more realistic behavior of human populations, whether in the so-called developed and developing countries. Without the informed participation of anthropologists and geographers these exercises can lack adequate attention to the behavior of human populations and thus fail to deal with why people drive the system the way they do and how to benefit from new policies that encourage carbon sequestration.

The relevance of regionally informed approaches to global models becomes evident when we begin to design a classification system of vegetation types and of land use classes as a first step toward a classification of land use/cover. This can be achieved through bibliographies and databases of the study area, analysis of satellite images, fieldwork observation, and ethnoecological interviews with local inhabitants. Different levels of organization are required to define a vegetation cover of a region. In general, levels are organized to fit a specific scale of analysis into the phytogeographical arrangement and into the land use types present in the area. In other words, one starts with a more aggregated level of major dominant classes (first) adequate to a regional scale and proceeds with increased detail at the next sublevel (second) to inform more detailed scales. For instance, the first level may include major vegetation covers such as forest, secondary succession, and savanna. In the second, more detailed level, forest is subdivided into open forest and closed forest, secondary succession into old secondary succession and young secondary succession, and savanna into grassland savanna and woodland savanna. At the third level of this classification system, still more detailed information needs to be included to account for the variability of vegetation required at this local scale. So, a new subdivision of the forest class may include a third structural variation of the former two and/or a floristic variation of them, such as a forest with a dominant tree species. The importance of developing a detailed classification key is crucial to inform the land use/cover analysis at the landscape level, as well as the sampling distribution at the site-specific level.

Conclusions

Conklin, Reining, and Conant were early pioneers in anthropology in the use of spatial analysis. Anthropologists, and even those in environmental anthropology were slow to enter this area of research. This has now begun to change. Since the early 1990s a slow but steady stream of contributions have been made and a small cadre of anthropologists have participated in integrative research on human dimensions of global environmental change. Netting provided encouragement for this within the National Academy of Science's Committee on the Human Dimensions; this was followed by contributions from Behrens et al. (1994), Moran et al. (1994, and other papers cited in the bibliography), Wilkie (1994), Brondizio et al. (1994), and others discussed in this chapter.

The end result is that the presence of environmental anthropologists in major expert committees on global environmental change, and in NGOs and other settings, is now seen as crucial. But this is a role that we should not take for granted. It must be earned every day through collaborative, integrative, and cutting-edge methods and insights. It is not enough to contribute ethnographic insight, but it is necessary that we lead in the rapidly changing field of human-environmental science and sustainability science (Moran 2010). Not everyone in environmental anthropology needs to use spatial analytic methods in their work, but this array of tools of research is destined to grow and become as important a tool as the ethnographic interview, or survey research. It is a set of tools which facilitates dialogue with other disciplines since all behavior occurs in time and space. We now have the tools to georeference not only the physical environment but the dynamic movement of people in space and across time, to connect their histories through spatial analysis, and to understand commodity chains and other economic choices in close to real-time. There are many ethical challenges that this emphasis on spatial analysis brings but we must contribute to how best to protect human subjects without crippling the many advantages that these technologies offer to understand human behavior and social organization (among them how to report data that is precisely known from space and acquired without the subject's permission; it is customary to publish this data in aggregated form so that individual confidentiality is protected). We need all these tools to address the many questions that are generated by the many challenges that the contemporary environmental crises pose to our very survival and well-being.

Acknowledgements

I want to thank Eduardo Brondizio, with whom many of these ideas were developed over several years of collaboration. I am grateful to the National Science Foundation, the National Institute of Child Health and Human Development, the National Aeronautics and Space Administration, and Indiana University for support over two decades that permitted the development of these ideas. None of these funding sources or colleagues should be held responsible for the views espoused herein. They are the sole responsibility of the author.

Note

1 I am grateful to Eduardo Brondizio for his substantial contribution to this discussion, based on two earlier joint papers (cf. Moran and Brondizio 1998, 2001).

References

Adams, J. B. & Gillespie, A. R. (2006) *Remote Sensing of Landscapes with Spectral Images: A Physical Modeling Approach*, New York: Cambridge University Press.

Alcamo, J. R., Leemans, R. & Kreileman, E. (1998) *Global Change Scenarios of the 21st Century: Results from IMAGE 2.1 Model*, Oxford: Elsevier.

Anderson, L. O., Shimabukuro, Y. E., DeFries, R.S. & Morton, D. (2005) 'Assessment of land cover and land use changes in the Brazilian Amazon using multitemporal fraction images derived from Terra MODIS: Examples from the state of Mato Grosso,' *IEEE Geoscience and Remote Sensing Letters,* 2(3): 315–18.

Aronoff, S. (2005) *Remote Sensing for GIS Managers*, Redlands, CA: ESRI Press.

Batistella, M. (2001) *Landscape Change and Land Use/Land Cover Dynamics in Rondonia, Brazilian Amazon*, CIPEC Dissertation Series, no. 7, Center for the Study of Institutions, Population and Environmental Change, Bloomington: Indiana University.

Batistella, M., Criscuolo, C., de Miranda, E. E. & Filardi A. L. (2004) *Satélites de Monitoramento*, Embrapa Monitoramento por Satélite, Campinas. Available at: http://www.sat.cnpm.embrapa.br.

Behrens, C. (1990) *Applications of Satellite Image Processing to the Analysis of Amazonian Cultural Ecology*, Proceedings of the Applications of Space Age Technology in Anthropology, John C. Stennis Space Center, MS: NASA.

——(1994) 'Recent advances in the regional analysis of indigenous land use and tropical Deforestation,' *Human Ecology*, 22(3): 243–47.

Behrens, C., Baksh, M., and Mothes, M. (1994) 'A regional analysis of Bari land use intensification and its impact on landscape heterogeneity,' *Human Ecology*, 22: 279–316.

Boken, V. K., Cracknell, A. P., and Heathcoate, R. L. (2005) *Monitoring and Predicting Agricultural Drought: A Global Study*, New York: Oxford University Press.

Bolstad, P. (2005) *GIS Fundamentals: A First Text of Geographic Information Systems*, 2nd edn, White Beak Lake, MN: Eider Press.

Booth, W. (1989) 'Monitoring the fate of forests from space', *Science,* 243: 1428–29.

Brondizio, E. S. (1996) *Forest Farmers: Human and Landscape Ecology of Caboclo Populations in the Amazon Estuary*. Ph.D. diss. Environmental Science Program, School of Public and Environmental Affairs, Indiana University.

——(2005) 'Intraregional analysis of land-use change in the Amazon' in E.F. Moran and E. Ostrom (eds) *Seeing the Forest and the Trees*, Cambridge, MA: MIT Press.

——(2008) *The Amazonian Caboclo and the Açaí Palm: Forest Farmers in the Global Market*, New York: New York Botanical Garden Press.

Brondizio, E. S. & Moran, E. F. (2008) 'Human dimensions of climate change: The vulnerability of small farmers in the Amazon,' *Philosophical Transactions of the Royal Society B*, 363(1498): 1803–9.

Brondizio, E. S., McCracken, S., Moran, E. F., Siqueira, A., Nelson, D. & Rodriguez-Pedraza, C. (2002) 'The colonist footprint: Towards a conceptual framework of deforestation trajectories among small farmers in frontier Amazonia' in C.H Wood and R. Porro (eds) *Patterns and Processes of Land Use and Forest Change in the Amazon*, Gainesville: University of Florida Press.

Brondizio, E. S., Moran, E. F., Mausel, P. & Wu, Y. (1994) 'Land use change in the Amazon estuary: Patterns of caboclo settlement and landscape management,' *Human Ecology*, 22(3): 249–78.

Brondízio E. S., Moran, E. F., Mausel, P. & Wu, Y. (1996) 'Land cover in the Amazon estuary: Linking of thematic with historical and botanical data,' *Photogrammetric Engineering and Remote Sensing*, 62(8): 921–29.

Campbell, J. B. (1987) *Introduction to Remote Sensing*, New York: Guilford Press.

Campbell, B. M. & Sayer, J. (2003) *Integrated Natural Resource Management: Linking Productivity, the Environment, and Development*, Wallingford, UK: CABI Publishers/CIFOR. UK.

Conant, F. (1978) 'The use of Landsat data in studies of human ecology', *Current Anthropology*, 19: 382–84.

——(1990) '1990 and beyond: Satellite remote sensing and ecological anthropology' in E. F. Moran (ed.) *The Ecosystem Approach in Anthropology*, Ann Arbor: University of Michigan Press.

Conklin, H. C. (1980) *Ethnographic Atlas of Ifugao*, New Haven, CT: Yale University Press.

Cultural Survival Quarterly (1995) Geomatics (Special Issue), *Cultural Survival Quarterly*. Winter.

Ellen, R. (1990) 'Trade, environment and the reproduction of local systems in the Moluccas' in E.F. Moran (ed.) *The Ecosystem Approach in Anthropology*, Ann Arbor: University of Michigan Press.

Evans, T., Munroe, D. K., and Parker, D.C. (2005a) 'Modeling land-use/land-cover change: Exploring the dynamics of human–environment relationships' in E. Moran & E. Ostrom (eds) *Seeing the Forest and the Trees: Human-Environment Interactions in Forest Ecosystems*, Cambridge, MA: MIT Press.

Evans, T., VanWey, L., and Moran, E. F. (2005b) 'Human-environment research, spatially-explicit data analysis, and geographic information systems' in E. Moran & E. Ostrom (eds) *Seeing the Forest and the Trees: Human-Environment Interactions in Forest Ecosystems*, Cambridge, MA: MIT Press.

Forsberg, M. C. (1999) *Protecting an Urban Forest Reserve in the Amazon: A Multi-scale Analysis of Edge Effects Population Pressure, and Institutions*, Ph.D. dissertation, Environmental Science Program, School of Public and Environmental Affairs, Indiana University.

Foster, D. & Aber, J. (eds) (2004) *Forests in Time: The Environmental Consequences of 1000 Years of Change in New England*, New Haven, CT: Yale University Press.

Futemma, C. (2000) *Collective Action and Assurance of Property Rights to Natural Resources: A Case Study from the Lower Amazon Region, Santarem, Brazil*, CIPEC Dissertation Series, no. 6. Bloomington: Center for the Study of Institutions, Population, and Environmental Change, Indiana University.

Galvin, K. A., Thornton, P. K., Boone, R. B. & Sunderland, J. (2001) 'Impacts of climate variability on East African pastoralists: Linking social science and remote sensing,' *Climate Research*, 19(2): 161–72.

Goodchild, M. (2003) 'Geographic information science and systems for environmental management', *Annual Review of Environment and Resources*, 28: 493–519.

Goodchild, M. & Janelle, D. (eds) (2004) *Spatially-integrated Social Science*, Oxford: Oxford University Press.

Green, G. M., Schweik, C. M. & Randolph, J. C. (2005a) 'Linking disciplines across space and time: Useful concepts and approaches for land cover change studies' in E. Moran & E. Ostrom (eds) *Seeing the Forest and the Trees: Human-Environment Interactions in Forest Ecosystems*, Cambridge, MA: MIT Press.

——(2005b) 'Retrieving land cover change information from Landsat satellite images by minimizing other sources of reflectance variability,' in E. Moran & E. Ostrom (eds) *Seeing the Forest and the Trees: Human-Environment Interactions in Forest Ecosystems*, Cambridge, MA: MIT Press.

Greene, R. P. & Pick, J. B. (2006) *Exploring the Urban Community: A GIS Approach*, Upper Saddle River, NJ: Pearson-Prentice Hall.

Gutmann, M. P. (2000) 'Scaling and demographic issues in global change research,' *Climatic Change*, 44: 377–91.

Guyer, J. & Lambin, E. (1993) 'Land use in an urban hinterland: Ethnography and remote sensing in the study of African intensification,' *American Ethnologist*, 95: 836–59.

Häfele, W. (1980) *Energy in a Finite World*, Cambridge, MA: Ballinger.

Hansen, M., DeFries, R., Townshend, J. R. G., Marufu, L. & Sohlberg, R. (2002a) 'Development of a MODIS tree cover validation data set for Western Province, Zambia,' *Remote Sensing of Environment*, 83(1–2): 320–35.

Hansen, M. C., DeFries, R. S., Townshend, J. R. G., Sohlberg, R., DiMiceli, C. & Carroll, M. (2002b) 'Towards an operational MODIS continuous field of percent tree cover algorithm: Examples using AVHRR and MODIS data', *Remote Sensing of Environment*, 83 (1–2): 303–19.

Hesse-Biber, S. N. & Leavy, P. (2006) *Emergent Methods in Social Research*, Thousand Oaks: Sage Publications.

Human Ecology (1994) Recent Advances in the Regional Analysis of Indigenous Land Use and Tropical Deforestation, *Human Ecology*, September.

Inoue, Y. (2003) 'Synergy of remote sensing and modeling for estimating ecophysiological processes in plant production', *Plant Production Science*, 6(1): 3–16.

Jensen, J. (1996) *Introductory Digital Image Analysis: A Remote Sensing Perspective*, Upper Saddle River, NJ: Pearson-Prentice Hall Press.

——(2005) *Introductory Digital Image Analysis: A Remote Sensing Perspective*, Revised edn, Upper Saddle River, NJ: Pearson-Prentice Hall Press

——(2007) *Remote Sensing of the Environment: An Earth Resource Perspective*, Upper Saddle River, NJ: Pearson-Prentice Hall.

Johnson, C. D., Kohler, T. A. & Cowan, J. A. (2005) 'Modeling historical ecology, thinking about contemporary systems', *American Anthropologist*, 107(1): 96–108.

Kaimowitz, D. & Angelssenn, A. (1998) *Economic Models of Tropical Deforestation: A Review*, Bogor, Indonesia: Center for International Forestry Research (CIFOR).

Lambin, E. F. & Geist, H. J. (eds) (2006) *Land Use and Land Cover Change: Local Processes and Global Impacts*, IGBP Springer Book Series, no. 9. Heidelberg: Springer-Verlag.

Levin, S. (1998) 'Ecosystem and the biosphere as a complex adaptive system', *Ecosystems*, 1(5): 431–36.

Lillesand, T. M., Kiefer, R. W. & Chapman, J. W. (2004) *Remote Sensing and Image Interpretation*, 5th edn, New York: John Wiley & Sons.

Lo, C. P. & Yeung, A. K. W. (2002) *Concepts and Techniques in Geographic Information Systems*, Upper Saddle River, NJ: Pearson Prentice Hall.

Loris, V. & Damiano, G. (2006) 'Mapping the green herbage ratio of grasslands using both aerial and satellite derived spectral reflectance,' *Agriculture, Ecosystems and Environment*, 115 (1–4): 141–49.

Lubchenco, J. (1998) 'Entering the century of the environment: A new social contract for science', *Science*, 279: 491–97.

Lyons, T., Inglis, M. & Hitchcock, R. (1972) 'The application of space imagery to anthropology' in *Proceedings of the Third Annual Conference on Remote Sensing in Arid Lands*, Tucson, AZ: University of Arizona, Office of Arid Land Studies.

Mausel, P., Wu, Y., Li, Y., Moran, E. F. & Brondizio, E. S. (1993) 'Spectral identification of successional stages following deforestation in the Amazon', *Geocarto International*, 8: 61–71.

McCoy, R. M. (2005) *Field Methods in Remote Sensing*, New York: Guilford Press.

Meadows, D. H., Meadows, D. L., Randers, J. & Behrens III, W. (1972) *The Limits to Growth*, New York: Universe Books.

Meyer, W. & Turner II, B. L. (1994) *Changes in Land Use and Land Cover: A Global Perspective*, Cambridge, UK: Cambridge University Press.

Mitsch, W. & Day, J. (2004) 'Thinking big with whole ecosystem studies and ecosystem restoration: A legacy of H.T. Odum', *Ecological Modelling*, 178(1–2): 133–55.

Moran, E. F. (2006) *People and Nature*, Malden, MA: Blackwell Publishing.

——(2007) *Human Adaptability: An Introduction to Ecological Anthropology*, 3rd edn, Boulder, CO: Westview Press/Perseus Books.

——(2010) *Environmental Social Science: Human-Environment Interactions and Sustainability*, Malden, MA: Wiley-Blackwell Publishing.

Moran, E. F. (ed) (1990) *The Ecosystem Approach in Anthropology: From Concept to Practice*, Ann Arbor: University of Michigan Press.

——(1995) *The Comparative Analysis of Human Societies: Toward Common Standards for Data Collection and Reporting*, Boulder, CO: L. Rienner.

Moran, E. F. & Brondizio, E. S. (1998) 'Land-use change after deforestation in Amazonia' in *NRC, People and Pixels: Linking Remote Sensing and Social Science*, Washington, D.C.: National Academy Press.

——(2001) 'Human ecology from space: Ecological anthropology engages the study of global environmental change' in E. Messer and M. Lambeck (eds) *Ecology and the Sacred: Engaging the Anthropology of Roy A. Rappaport*, Ann Arbor: University of Michigan Press.

Moran, E. F. & Ostrom, E. (eds) (2005) *Seeing the Forest and the Trees: Human-Environment Interactions in Forest Ecosystems*, Cambridge, MA: MIT Press.

Moran, E. F., Adams, R. T., Bakoyema, B., Fiorini, S. & Boucek, B. (2006) 'Human strategies for coping with El Niño related drought in Amazônia,' *Climatic Change*, 77: 343–61.

Moran, E. F., Brondizio, E. S., Mausel, P. & Wu, Y. (1994) 'Integration of Amazonian vegetation, land use and satellite data,' *BioScience*, 44: 329–38.

Moran, E. F., Brondizio, E. S. & McCracken, S. (2002) 'Trajectories of land use: Soils, succession and crop choice' in C. Wood and R. Porro (eds) *Deforestation and Land Use in the Amazon*, Gainesville: University Press of Florida.

Moran, E. F., Packer, A., Brondizio, E. & Tucker, J. (1996) 'Restoration of vegetation cover in the eastern Amazon', *Ecological Economics*, 18: 41–54.

Morton, D., DeFries, R., Shimabukuro, Y., Anderson, L., Espirito-Santo, F., Hansen, M. & Carroll, M. (2005) 'Rapid assessment of annual deforestation in the Brazilian Amazon using MODIS data,' *Earth Interactions*, 9(8): 1–22.

Nagendra, H. (2001) 'Using remote sensing to assess biodiversity', *International Journal of Remote Sensing*, 22(12): 2377–2400.

Netting, R., Stone, G. & Stone, P. (1995) 'The social organization of agrarian labor' in E. F. Moran and L. Rienner (eds) *The Comparative Analysis of Human Societies*, Boulder: Westview Press/Perseus Books.

Nicholaides, J. J., III & Moran, E. F. (1995) 'Soil indices for comparative analysis of agrarian systems' in in E.F. Moran and L. Rienner (eds) *The Comparative Analysis of Human Societies*, Boulder: Westview Press/Perseus Books.

NRC (National Research Council) (1992) *Global Environmental Change: Understanding the Human Dimensions*, Washington, D.C.: National Academy Press.

NRC (1994) *Science Priorities for the Human Dimensions of Global Change*, Committee on the Human Dimensions of Global Change, Washington, D.C.: National Academy Press.

——(1998) *People and Pixels: Linking Remote Sensing and Social Science*, Committee on the Human Dimensions of Global Change, Washington, D.C.: National Academy Press.

——(1999a) *A Global Environmental Change: Research Pathways for the Next Decade*, Committee on Global Change Research, Washington, D.C.: National Academy Press.

——(1999b) *Making Climate Forecasts Matter*, Washington, D.C.: National Academy Press.

——(2005) *Valuing Ecosystem Services: Toward Better Environmental Decision-Making*, Washington, D.C.: National Academy Press.

Nyerges, A. & Green, G. (2000) 'The ethnography of landscape: GIS and remote sensing in the study of forest change in West African Guinea Savanna', *American Anthropologist*, 102 (2): 271–89.

Okabe, A. (2006) *GIS-Based Studies in the Humanities and Social Sciences*, Boca Raton, FL: CRC/Taylor & Francis.

Patenaude, G., Milne, R. & Dawson, T. P. (2005) 'Synthesis of remote sensing approaches for forest carbon estimation: Reporting to the Kyoto Protocol', *Environmental Science and Policy*, 8(2): 161–78.

Peck, D. L. (1990) *Our Changing Planet: The FY 1991 U.S. Global Change Research Program*, Washington, DC: Office of Science and Technology Policy, Committee on Earth Sciences.

Pietsch, S. & Hasenauer, H. (2002) 'Using mechanistic modeling within forest ecosystem restoration', *Forest Ecology and Management*, 159(1–2): 111–31.

Rappaport, R. (1968) *Pigs for the Ancestors*, New Haven, CT: Yale University Press.

Reining, P. (1973) *ERTS Image Analysis of a Site North of Segon, Mali, W. Africa*, Springfield, VA: NTIS.

Rindfuss, R., Walsh, S., Mishra, V., Fox, J. & Dolcemascolo, G. (2003) 'Linking household and remotely sensed data: Methodological and practical problems' in J. Fox, S. Walsh & V. Mishra (eds) *People and the Environment: Approaches for Linking Household and Community Surveys to Remote Sensing and GIS*, Dordrecht: Kluwer.

Sever, T. (1998) 'Validating prehistoric and current social phenomena upon the landscape of the Peten, Guatemala' in *People and Pixels: Linking Remote Sensing and Social Science*, National Research Council, Washington, DC: National Academy Press.

Skole, D. & Tucker, C. (1993) 'Tropical deforestation and habitat fragmentation in the Amazon: Satellite data from 1978 to 1988', *Science*, 260: 1905–10.

Steffen, W., Sanderson, A., Tyson, P., Jager, J., Matson, P., Moore III, B., Oldfield, F., Richardson, K., Schellnhuber, J. K., Turner II, B. L. & Wasson, R., (eds) (2004) *Global Change and the Earth System: A Planet Under Pressure*, IGBP Synthesis Volume, Berlin: Springer-Verlag.

Steinberg, S. J. & Steinberg, S. L. (2006) *GIS: Geographic Information Systems for the Social Sciences: Investigating Space and Place*, SAGE Publications, Thousand Oaks, CA.

Sussman, R., Green, G. M. & Sussman, L. (1994) 'Satellite imagery, human ecology, anthropology and deforestation in Madagascar,' *Human Ecology*, 22(3): 333–54.

Tillman, D. (1999) 'Ecological consequences of biodiversity: A search for general principles,' *Ecology*, 80: 1455–74.

Toniolo, M. A. (2004) *The Role of Land Tenure in the Occurrence of Accidental Fires in the Amazon Region: Case Studies from the National Forest of Tapajós, Pará, Brazil*, Ph.D. dissertation, Joint Program in Public Policy, Department of Political Science and School of Public and Environmental Affairs, Indiana University.

Tucker, C. (2008) *Changing Forests: Collective Action, Common Property, and Coffee in Honduras*, Berlin: Springer Publishers.

Tucker, C. & Southworth, J. (2005) 'Processes of forest change at the local and landscape levels in Honduras and Guatemala' in E. Moran and E. Ostrom (eds) *Seeing the Forest and the Trees*, Cambridge, MA: MIT Press.

Turner, M. G. (2005) 'Landscape ecology: What is the state of the science?' *Annual Review of Ecology, Evolution and Systematics*, 36: 319–44.

Turner, M. G., Dale, V. H. and Gardner, R. H. (1989) 'Predicting across the scales: Theory development and testing', *Landscape Ecology*, 3: 245–52.

Vandermeer, J. H. (2003) *Tropical Agroecosystems*, Boca Raton, FL: CRC Press.

Vayda, A. P. (1983) 'Progressive contextualization: Methods for research in human ecology,'- *Human Ecology*, 11(3): 265–81.

Vitousek, P., Mooney, H., Lubchenco, J. and Melillo, J. (1997) 'Human domination of Earth's ecosystems', *Science*, 277: 494–99.

Vogt, E. (ed) (1974) *Aerial Photography in Anthropological Field Research*, Cambridge, MA: Harvard University Press.

Walker, D. M., Perez-Barberia, F. J. and Marion, G. (2006) 'Stochastic modelling of ecological processes using hybrid Gibbs samplers', *Ecological Modeling*, 198: 40–52.

Walsh, S. & Crews-Meyer, K. (eds) (2002) *Linking People, Place and Policy: A GIScience Approach*, Boston: Kluwer.

Walsh, S., Evans, T., Welsh, W., Entwisle, B. & Rindfuss, R. (1999) 'Scale dependent relationships between population and environment in Northeastern Thailand,' *Photogrammetric Engineering and Remote Sensing*, 65(1): 97–105.

Wätzold, F., Drechsler, M., Armstrong, C. W., Baumgärtner, S., Grimm, V., Huth, A., Perrings, C., Possingham, H. P., Shogren, J. F., Skonhoft, A., Verboom-Vasiljev, J. and C. Wissel (2006) 'Ecological-economic modeling for biodiversity management: Potential, pitfalls, and prospects,' *Conservation Biology*, 20(4): 1034–41.

Wessels, K. J., Moran, E. F., DeFries, R. S., Dempewolf, J., Anderson, L. O., Hansen, A. J. and Powell, S. L. (2004) 'Mapping regional land cover with MODIS data for biological conservation: Examples from the greater Yellowstone ecosystem, USA and Para State, Brazil', *Remote Sensing of Environment*, 92: 67–83.

Wessman, C. (1992) 'Spatial scales and global change: Bridging the gap from plots to GCM grid cells', *Annual Review of Ecology and Systematics*, 23: 175–200.

Weyant, J., Cline, W., Frankhauser, S., Davidson, O., Dowlatabadi, H., Edmonds, J., Grubb, M., Richels, R., Rotmans, J., Shukla, P. & Tol, R. (1996) 'Integrated assessment of climate change: An overview and comparison of approaches and results' in J. P. Bruce, H. Lee & E. F. Haites (eds) *Climate Changes, 1995: Economic and Social Dimensions of Climate Change*, Contribution of Working Group III to the Second Assessment Report of the Intergovernmental Panel on Climate Change, New York: Cambridge University Press.

Wilkie, D. (1994) 'Remote sensing imagery for resource inventories in Central Africa: The importance of detailed data,' *Human Ecology*, 22: 379–404.

Wojtkowski, P. A. (2004) *Landscape Agroecology*, Food Products Press, New York.

Xu, C. L. & Li, Z. Z. (2002) 'Stochastic ecosystem resilience and productivity: Seeking a Relationship,' *Ecological Modeling*, 156(2–3): 143–52.

5

WHAT ABOUT THAT WRAPPER? USING CONSUMPTION DIARIES IN GREEN EDUCATION

Helen Kopnina

Date: April 2010. Setting: classroom of elementary school in Amsterdam. Participants: Four children aged 8, five parents, one teacher (as an observer).

FOCUS GROUP MODERATOR (FGM): Today we are going to talk about consumption – that is what we eat, drink and use, and what we throw away. I hasten to say I know as much as you do about consumption, and probably less [...] I have your consumption diaries in front of me ... First, I want to ask the kids: what is consumption?

ANGELA: It's that diary ... that we had to like ... make. Right?

JAN: It's what we eat and drink.

FMG [TO THE OTHER TWO CHILDREN]: What do you think?

ANNEKE: Same as [Angela].

DIRK: Consumption is when you consume things.

DIRK'S FATHER: [Laughs] And what is consume?

DIRK: [shyly] Eating stuff ...

JAN [EXCITEDLY]: That's what I said!

FMG [READING FROM JAN'S DIARY]: 'Mum wants me to have sandwiches for breakfast. So I have to have at least one before going to school'. So, can you say you 'consume a sandwich?'

JAN [READILY]: Yeah!

FMG: What about drinks, is that also consumption?

[ALL CHILDREN NOD, THEIR PARENTS LOOK ENCOURAGING. JAN SLYLY PRODUCES A WRAPPED SANDWICH FROM HIS SCHOOL BAG AND BITES INTO IT; HIS MOTHER SHAKES HER HEAD DISAPPROVINGLY, AUDIBLY REMINDING HIM THAT HE 'SHOULDN'T EAT IN CLASS'].

FMG: So, Jan has a sandwich! What shall we call it?

DIRK'S FATHER: Consumption item?

[EVERYBODY NODS ENTHUSIASTICALLY]

JAN'S MOTHER: For all it takes me to convince him to eat it in the morning ...

[General enlivened discussion on the part of parents about the difficulty of feeding their children in the morning, till FMG's interruption]:

FMG: What about that wrapper? […] The sandwich wrapper?

[Confused whispering, shrugging on the part of the children, careful consideration and suspicious glances from the parents]

FMG: Is this a consumption item?
DIRK'S FATHER: Yes.
FMG: Let's ask the children first. What do you think?
ANGELA: Mmmm … I don't know.
JAN: You cannot eat it!
FMG: So, it's not a consumption item? What do you think, Anneke?
ANNEKE: I think … I think it is …
ANNEKE'S MOTHER [DEFENSIVELY]: Are you going to say now that this is bad?
FMG: Why? Why do you say that – that it is bad?

[General uncomfortable silence. Anneke looks perplexed, Jan, Dirk and Angela look at their parents, Anneke's mother turns pink, Jan's and Dirk's fathers look from FMG to Anneke's mother, the observant teacher reaches out for her notepad and taps it with her pen, Angela's mother smiles soothingly into space].

(Recorded, transcribed and translated from Dutch by the author)

Introduction

Environmental or 'green' education is an important driving force behind the 'greening' of society as it plays a critical role in raising environmental awareness and preparing students for green jobs. None of the existing environmental attitudes and behavior measures is focused on evaluation of green education, especially in relation to consumption. To date no longitudinal studies of children and students' attitudes towards consumption influenced by education exist. Also, little has been done to explore the socio-cultural context in which attitudes toward consumption are being formed and to explain the cross-cultural differences in environmental attitudes. This pilot study is designed to take the first step towards developing methods complementing existing quantitative measurements with qualitative strategies, such as consumption diaries, focus groups and concept mapping. While this research is just a first attempt to tackle children's knowledge and attitudes towards consumption, preliminary results of the research on which this chapter is based and enthusiasm of the research participants encourage the author to stress the importance of consumption studies as part of green education for educational program developers. As a chapter of this volume, the author hopes that this study will add to the anthropological depository of research on the cultural variants in perception of environment in children.

This chapter draws upon the consumption diaries collected from the upper-elementary school children in Amsterdam, The Netherlands, between September 2009 and May

2010. Consumption diaries are chronological documents recording purchase, use and waste of materials, which can be used both as analytical tools and the means to stimulate environmental awareness. The four main methodological steps involved in this research were as follows. Children were asked to complete the consumption diary, paying specific attention to use and waste materials. Consequently, focus group meetings were held with parents and their children to discuss the diaries. Finally, interviews with the children were conducted in order to generate statements that supplement those generated by focus groups for carrying out the concept mapping analysis. The concept mapping analysis was then conducted to organize order and analyze the ideas expressed in focus group and interview sessions.

Pluralistic research combining different methodological tools might be beneficial for the study of EE at schools, especially in relation to the topic of 'consumption'. The driving questions of this research were: 1. How aware are the children of their consumption patterns? (see Figure 5.1) 2. How important are the opinions of the children's

FIGURE 5.1 *What about the wrapper?* © Engelbert Fellinger, www.engelbert.org.

peers, parents, and teachers in their conceptions of consumption? (Socio-cultural influences). 3. How can consumption be translated into green education? (Conversion of social scientific data into pedagogical practice). 4. How can green education be assessed? (Evaluation).

In order to answer the first question, environmental values of the children need to be addressed. This chapter reviews some of the available methodological tools used by sociologists and social psychologists for measuring children's environmental awareness and proposes alternatives combining traditional anthropological methods with those developed within other disciplines. In order to address the second question, the influence on the children's consumption patterns and perceptions thereof of their peer group, parents, teachers and other stakeholders needs to be examined. To this end, the discussion of consumption diaries through focus group sessions and open interviews are employed to unravel the children's and their parents' perceptions and awareness of their consumption patterns. The more ethnographic approach to perceptions of consumption suggests the answer to the third question, by providing rich qualitative data on the basis of which a comprehensive consumption-oriented program, integrated into regular school curriculum can be developed. In order to be effective, such a course should be a product of collaborative effort between the children, their peers, their parents, their teachers and other stakeholders (such as educational managers, local policy-makers and the researchers themselves). The program will also need to involve information not necessarily generated by present methodology, such as 'responsible' or 'sustainable' or 'Cradle to Cradle' consumption, which will be briefly discussed at the end of this chapter.

In order to address the last question, referring to the assessment of the program about consumption, the same methodology can be used to assess the possible changes in attitudes and behavior of children who have completed the program on consumption. Changes in actual consumption patterns could be deduced from the consumption diaries, changes in social dynamics can be observed on the basis of focus group session analysis, and changes in children's perceptions could be assessed through repeated in-depth interviews. This pilot study particularly addressed the first question, aiming to build a foundation for answering the other three, for which a wider methodological framework needs to be developed.

Green Education and Studies of Environmental Attitudes

Studies addressing green education were quite rare until recent years (for an overview, see Beard 2009). The topics of learning and sustainability start to appear more frequently in interdisciplinary books and journals since the turn of the century (Louv 2005; Wals 2007; Reid et al. 2008; Andrezejewski et al. 2009). Studies measuring environmental awareness by school and college students are still limited to sociological, pedagogical or social psychological studies (Miller 1975; Kahn 1999; Eagles and Demare 1999). To date, social psychologists interested in environmental sustainability have applied knowledge from the research literatures on attitudes (Kellert 1993; Rauwald and Moore 2002), conversion of environmental intentions to environmental behaviors (Gardner and Stern 2002; Kaiser 2004; Evans et al. 2007), participation and environmental learning (Barratt Hacking et al. 2009), responsible environmental behavior (Hines et al. 1987), the barriers to environmental behavior (Kollmuss and Agyeman 2002), behavioral change in environmental education (Heimlich and Ardoin 2008), behavior-based environmental attitudes (Kaiser, Oerke and Bogner 2007), moral reasoning and persuasion (Gonzales et al. 1988; Davis 1995; Kellert 1995), reasoning about environmental dilemmas (Kahn and Kellert 2002), commitment (Pallak et al. 1980; Werner et al. 1995), normative influence (Aronson and O'Leary 1982; Cialdini et al. 1990), and incentives (Levitt and Leventhal 1986). Based on Maloney et al. (1975) item sampling domains to measure adult environmental attitudes, Williams and McCrorie (1990) and Leeming and Dwyer (1995) developed the scale for measuring first to seventh graders' behavioral commitments, affective states and knowledge about the environment.

Since the 1980s, there was a marked interest in environmental education as a tool of infusion of ecological worldviews among the younger generations. Environmental education—both formal and informal from the elementary to university levels—has continued to help expand ecological worldview among students (Dunlap 2008:15). Even short educational programs can stimulate environmental awareness in children (Sanera and Shaw 1996; Manoli et al. 2007) and college students (Rideout 2005). More recent efforts have moved away from local approaches to a broader conception of our relationship to nature, including cultural values (Stern and Dietz 1994; Stern 2000), how concern for nature can be increased through empathy (Schultz 2000 and 2001), and how our identity is shaped by the natural environment (Clayton and Opotow 2003). Various techniques have been used for the study of green values in children and adolescents, such as a behavior-based attitude scale, which is based on people's recall of their past behavior (Kaiser et al. 2007).

One of the most popular measures of ecological beliefs or worldview in studies that use theoretical models predicting environmental attitudes and behaviors is the New Ecological Paradigm (NEP) Scale. The scale is a widely used measure of people's shifting worldviews from a human dominant view to an ecological one, with humans as part of nature. The original NEP scale consisted of three dimensions: the balance of nature, anthropocentrism, and limits to growth (Dunlap and Liere 1978). Later, additional elements were added to the scale, including human exemptionalism (the idea that human beings are exempt from constraints of nature), and ecocrisis (concerns about the occurrence of potentially catastrophic environmental changes) (Dunlap 2008). The NEP Scale for children was developed, using a standard Likert-type format with wording changes to make it suitable for use with upper elementary school-aged children (Manoli et al. 2007) and the other using a highly innovative adaptation of key themes of the NEP into games appropriate for first- and second-grade children (Evans et al. 2007). NEP scale was successfully applied internationally (Van Petegem and Blieck 2006). However, the author found the NEP scale inapplicable to the case of consumption as the study of this topic required consideration of the specifications of social and cultural contexts in which consumption study can serve as a starting point of integrating green education within European society.

As Efird notes in his contribution to this volume, despite societal and interdisciplinary interest in environmental learning, anthropological research on environmental learning has been very limited. While detailed ethnographic studies might add very valuable insights to the existing body of literature on environmental learning, anthropologists might also profit from incorporating interdisciplinary methodology into their toolkit.

Consumption in Anthropology

In his review of consumption studies in anthropology, Daniel Miller finds links to consumption in different subjects of anthropology, such as spheres of exchange, gifting, the study of prestige goods, sumptuary laws, cargo cults and so forth (Miller 1995: 264). Sometimes all these subjects are linked through the study of material culture through archeology, but none of them amount to a recognized category of consumption studies. The publication of Mary Douglas and Baron Isherwood's *The World of Goods* (1978) and Pierre Bourdieu's *Distinction* (1984) lie at the root of the anthropology of consumption (Miller 1995: 265).

According to the review of Mayer and McPherson (2004), early research in the field of consumption addressed energy use in the home (Pallak et al., 1980), littering (Cialdini et al., 1990) and the re-use of materials (Burn 1991; Heckler 1994; Oskamp 2000). Broader studies included cross-cultural consumption (Howes 1996), culture of capitalism (Robbins 2007), consumer culture (Slater 1997; Wilk 2002, 2006, 2009, 2010), material culture (Miller 1998), consumption and everyday life (Mackay 1997), consumption and environmentalism (Miller 1995; Lilienfeld 1998; Shepherd 2002), and political ecology and consumption (Bryant and Goodman 2004). Ethnographic studies addressed barriers that consumers face in their attempts to reduce their environmental impacts (Isenhour 2010), myths of sustainable consumption (Wilk 2004), and consumption and garbage (Wilk 1982; Ritenbaugh 1984; Reilly and Hughes 1985; Radhje and Murphy 1992). However, none of these studies linked consumption to attitudes and learning. Neither did literature on responsible or ethical consumption, such as third party certification, e.g. Fair Trade (Bacon et al. 2008, Jaffe et al. 2004) or 'green consumption' (Connolly and Prothero 2008) link the environmental education to responsible consumption.

Green Education in Schools in the Netherlands

Innovation in green education that takes consumption into account is necessary to address the 'sustainability', both in terms of recognizing global and historical forces that lead to environmental degradation and local – and in this case – Western patterns of consumption. The author argues that anthropologists could adapt some of the existing tools and measuring techniques for studies of environmental attitudes (such as the New Ecological Paradigm scale discussed in the following section) and combine them with their own ethnographic approach to produce rich contextual data necessary for innovation in green education.

Green education in The Netherlands has been developing in tune with the recent interest, expressed by the Dutch ministries of Education and Social Affairs, in 'preparing the new generation for green jobs of the future.' A number of organizations sponsored by these Dutch ministries have developed green education programs for school and college students. One organization coordinating such programs is the platform for Nature and Environment Education (NME). NME, together with the Dutch testing and assessment company CITO, has developed guidelines for the development of green education in elementary schools, such as Nature Education for Elementary Schools (Thijssen 2002) and Sustainable Development for the Elementary Schools (Wagenaar 2007). The point of departure is integrating socially and environmentally relevant knowledge into existing curriculum for subjects such as geography, botany, biology and history. The Dutch Ministry of Education also supports Sustainable Teacher's Colleges Foundation (DHO), 'working on sustainable development in education; either through separate modules or by means of an incorporated view.' DHO developed an on-line forum called (Plado), in which professionals involved in environmental education can contact each other and share knowledge on issues of sustainable development in education. One of the themes developed by Plado is consumption and Cradle to Cradle principle. However, Cradle to Cradle is not (yet) discussed in relation to school curriculum.

There are no consistent studies on either content or success of green programs at schools. A lot of what may be characterized as 'green education', including lessons on environmental awareness, alongside regular biology or geology lessons, is offered to school children without specific assessment of their 'green' values. Field trips to parks to study local plants and insects, tending 'school gardens' ('schooltuinen'), or lessons about poverty and pollution in the developing world are examples of activities that by broader definition could be characterized as green education. While, in accordance with the combined statistics from the United Nations Statistics Division, Economic Commission for Europe and Economic Commission for Africa, Dutch consumption of, for example, energy per capita is hundreds of times higher than that of most citizens of the Sub-Saharan Africa, green education in the Netherlands includes no information on (domestic) consumption.

Two Elementary Schools in Amsterdam

For this study, the sample consisted of school children aged between 7 and 10 from two Dutch elementary schools in the Amsterdam area (see Table 5.1). The sample also included parents of selected children and teachers for the second stage of research (focus groups). The children were contacted through their parents. One (Montessori) school contained the population of 79 children aged between 7 and 10, and another (regular public) school contained the population of 122 children of the same age. Both schools selected for this study were located in the predominantly 'white' (ethnically Dutch), well-to-do areas of Amsterdam. The majority of the teachers expressed interest in the results of the study. Ten of the teachers from the first school (out of a total of seventeen) and six from the second school (out of ten) expressed their interest

TABLE 5.1 Sample and methodology.

Methodology	No of participants School 1		No of participants School 2	
	Children	Parents	Children	Parents
Consumption diary	31		60	
Focus group	15	9	19	12
Interview	5		12	
Concept mapping	31	20	60	39

in working together on developing a new program based on consumption education. Both directors and administrators expressed interest in research results and indicated that they would be willing to consider amendments to the curriculum.

The children were selected by contacting their parents through the class mailing lists. Parents and children received separate introductory letters. Invitation letters to parents contained basic information about the aim of the research and provided rationale for allowing their children to participate in this study. The letter specified that the consumption items were not to be perceived as 'good' or 'bad' but needed to be listed to open up a focus group discussion. Children received a simplified version of this letter, inviting them to complete the diary.

The sample consisted of the elementary school children aged between 7 and 10 from two Dutch elementary schools in the Amsterdam area. The sample also included parents of selected children and teachers for the second stage of research (focus groups). The total of 59 adult family members (20 from the first school, 39 from the second school) participated and will be henceforth referred to as 'parents', including grandparents, older siblings and other guardians. Thus, a total of 97 children, adult family members and teachers participated in the focus group sessions, organized at respective school's locations.

Obvious sample limitations can be noted, including a self-selection bias (the fact that children and parents more interested in environmental issues volunteered to participate) and characteristic of the sample itself having to do with the fact that both schools were located in the predominantly 'white' (ethnically Dutch), well-to-do areas of Amsterdam. Another limitation has to do with the intergenerational differences and influences of parents over their children's knowledge and opinions, which will be discussed in the reflection of this chapter. It needs to be noted that the Dutch parents and their children might examine different patterns of behavior than the other ethnic groups, which were not included in this sample. Studies of migrant groups in the Netherlands reveal large inter-generational behavioral differences between, for example, the Turks and the Moroccans (Stevens et al. 2003). Some studies showed Dutch parents to be less authoritative and hierarchical than, for example, the Russians (Kopnina 2005). Cross-cultural studies on children's consumption patterns and attitudes in more ethnically heterogeneous schools might offer very divergent data and valuable insights.

Another feature of the sample is that not all participants took part in all four steps of methodological procedure. The parents' and children's opinions were sometimes measured separately, sometimes together as the author did not establish clear participation criteria for focus groups. Since the author was interested primarily in qualitative detailed investigation of a small sample, issues associated with the peculiarity of a sample and low response rates are partially justified for this study, but need to be addressed in case more vigorous study of this kind is undertaken. All these shortcomings are due to the fact that the present research constitutes a pilot study that lays a foundation for a more ambitious research of green education with special focus on consumption.

Methodological Steps

The author finds herself in an emic position, as apparent from the segment from the group session quoted above. The researcher does not position herself as an authoritative or objective 'expert' while interacting with the group of participants, paying tribute to the self-reflective, subjectivist tradition of postmodern anthropology. Especially in the case of the focus group sessions, the researcher's own 'involved' approach attempts to deploy both the Platonian dialectic and personal activist position at eliciting participants' responses. This activist position refers to the ultimate goal of this research, namely measuring and simultaneously increasing the children's (and incidentally their parents') awareness of their own consumption patterns – something that will be discussed in the 'next step' section of this chapter. While 'traditional' anthropologists rarely conduct research with the intention of swaying the minds of their 'informants', the environmental anthropologists, some of whom have contributed to this volume, are increasingly using this type of 'involved' ethnography.

This study employed the four-step methodology procedure to elicit information about the children and their parents' awareness of their consumption patterns. This procedure involved the use of consumption diaries by the children, which were consequently discussed in mixed children-parents' focus groups, followed by in-depth interviews with the children. These procedures were used to generate statements on the subject of consumption. Qualitative data resulting from these sessions was organized through concept mapping analysis.

In contrast to the anthropological methodological tradition, the present methodology may strike the reader as a 'hybrid' between sociological, social psychological and pedagogical approaches. As discussed in the Introduction to this volume, (environmental) anthropology can no longer be defined in terms of clear methodological domains. Adding ethnographic skills to the existing methodological toolkit would be valuable for deeper understanding of green education. Such skills comprise participant observation, discourse analysis, in-depth interviews; giving specific attention to the individual's worldview; group-generated dynamics in collaborative generation of knowledge; as well as subjective probing of socio-cultural and inter-generational factors comprising such knowledge. Standard evaluation procedures used for developing and assessing success of educational programs (such as CITO in The Netherlands) rarely involve ethnographic studies. A greater reliance on ethnographic methodology could aid examination of intergenerational processes and dynamics involved in the discussion of consumption between the children and their peers, or the children and their parents or teachers.

Consumption Diaries

The simplest consumption diary (administered to the youngest segment of the children, between 7 and 8 years of age) consists of the following matrix: time of day (starting with 'when you wake up' to 'when you go to bed'), food and drink consumed, and waste products (specified as 'for example, packaging'). Multiple items could be entered in one time slot, but no room for clarifications or comments was allowed. Parents were asked to assist their children in completing this diary. The more advanced consumption diary (administered to the older segment of the children, between 8 and 9) consists of the same matrix, with addition of 'energy' as separate categories. Finally, the age group between 9 and 10 years old is given an open-ended diary in which the children are asked to enter all consumed and disposed items, specifying in the introduction to the diary that they should consider food, drink, utilities use (such as water and electricity) and disposed items (including sanitary items). Other consumption items, such as objects (clothes, furniture, etc.), cultural (cinema, theatre, etc.), transportation were excluded from the analysis.

Consumption diaries alone, however, cannot fulfill an anthropological study of consumption, but are helpful in conjunction with more qualitative study of behavior and attitudes, which focus groups and interviews provide. Consumption diaries completed by children with the assistance of their parents are neither objective nor concise as they only indicate the simplest types of consumed products (such as 'food' or 'drink') without quantifying these items (children are not asked, for example how big or heavy their sandwich was) or specifying 'quality', such as composition or origin (such as what type of bread was used for the sandwich and whether the tomato in it was locally grown). Rather, the entries in the diary serve as a starting point for opening a discussion about consumption items, as well as quantity, composition and origin of the products consumed. Children were asked to reflect on their diaries together with their parents during the focus-group sessions and individual interviews.

Focus Group Sessions

At each school, the concept mapping meetings were held, led by a facilitator. Parents, teachers and children were invited to participate in the focus-group sessions to discuss the consumption diaries as well as ways to make consumption more 'responsible' and 'sustainable'. The term 'sustainability' was explained using the Brundladt definition in the case of parents and the formula 'good for health and nature' for the children. During the focus group sessions, this term was discussed in greater detail, bridging the gap between parents' and children's ideas about 'sustainability'.

The extract from a group discussion at the beginning of this section was used as an 'opener' for a discussion guided by the focal question: '*healthy and environmentally-friendly consumption should include the following.* ... '. At the first school, the meeting started with a 50 minute brainstorm session during which participants were asked to formulate statements to complete the focal question. It needs to be noted that initially the author conceived the focal question without evoking 'health', since the author believes that health and environment are not necessarily complementary to each other (Kopnina and Keune 2010). During the process of collaborative inquiry during the initial and largest focus group session involving 7 children of different ages, 9 parents and 1 teacher, the majority of participants have evoked the topic of 'health' in relation to consumption. Participants felt that the discussion of the environmental impact of consumption needs to be strengthened by its relation to health, thus convincing the researcher to include 'health' in the focus question. The following summary of the focus group discussion provides a clue as to why such a connection might indeed be significant (as well as why the author was reluctant to include it in the first place). Themes discussed in the two-hour session included questions of what consumption is, what 'healthy consumption' is and what 'environmentally-friendly consumption' is. These themes were largely organized under the 'food', 'drink', 'waste', and 'utility/energy' items.

In regard to food, while the ideas about healthy and environmentally-friendly items often overlapped (as in the case of 'organic', 'biological', or 'home-grown' foods), other items seemed to be either good for health but not 'environmentally-friendly' (such as peeling fruit for the fear of chemicals in the peel – thus reducing perceived risk of 'poisoning' but simultaneously wasting part of the fruit), or good for the environment but not necessarily healthy (veganism). A number of adult participants stressed ambiguity of presumed 'goodness' of biological (organic) food as, one of the participants remarked 'it requires more space to grow' ('environmentally bad'), and as another adult reflected, 'might not be all that healthy'.

As far as 'drink' is concerned, similar overlaps occurred as with food (for example, drinks without chemical additives such as taste enhancers were both viewed as 'healthy' and 'good for the environment'). Drinking tap water constituted a significant theme that divided the groups along the lines of beliefs in health safety and risks associated with factors such as 'treatment chemicals', 'chloral substance', 'fluoride additive level' (all factors, without exception, named by the parents). Drinking bottled water was seen as less 'risky' than tap water by less than half of the parents, who evoked added 'minerals', 'vitamins', and particularly the 'purity' as greatest health advantages. During two focus groups, the opinions among parents clashed significantly over the advantages and disadvantages of tap versus bottled water. In the rare case when an 8-year-old girl joined the parent-dominated discussion, the subject of bottles was raised as the most problematic in the 'environmentally friendly' items. Another item discussed was 'packaged juice'. Whereas some parents pointed out that the color additives or sweeteners were 'not healthy', the children tended to think that juice was healthy (because, ironically, their parents told them so). When asked to elaborate on what the children perceived as healthy, a few younger children issued that the healthiness is due to 'the vitamins' and 'stuff that makes your bones and hair stronger' and, as a 7-year-old boy put it, 'natural and good for nature'. When asked to elaborate on that, the boy said that 'juice is made of apples ... and oranges' and that those 'grow on trees ... so it's good'.

Packaging was sometimes seen as 'healthy' (protecting food from germs and other contaminants and keeping it fresh) or 'unhealthy' (when packaging was thought to contain dangerous substances). In most cases, packaging was seen as 'bad for the environment', although some parents named the benefits of 'biodegradable' or 'eco-friendly' packaging. As to the 'packaging' of the juice, one parent came up with the statement: 'Nutritional and health information contained on [packages] helps us make informed choices'. An 8-year-old boy issued that packaging 'lets us see where the juice comes from', and while he could not elaborate on this point, his father supplied 'so we can choose not to buy juice that is flown from far away'. This statement unlocked the discussion about the information on the packaging that could be either 'good for health' (nutritional values) or environment (whether the product needs to be transported from afar). A 7-year-old girl supplied that if the juice needs to be 'flown from afar' it is good that the package 'protects it from spilling'. Transportation discussion sparked one parent's memory of the 'milk farmer' who used to collect milk bottles from the villagers and bring them back refilled with milk. Older parents who were born outside of Amsterdam recalled the same event, one of them reflecting: 'This way you didn't have to throw away [the bottle]'. A 9-year-old boy asked: 'But cannot the packages be recycled?' which initiated the discussion on what is packaging made of, how it can be recycled or reused.

Groups with older children participated in the discussion of 'utilities', including water and electricity. The parents approximated the amount of water use to be much higher than the children, especially being aware of the water used for 'flushing the toilet', 'taking a shower', 'washing hands', and 'cooking' – some naming water that was used for growing food or producing drinks they consumed. Children, however, seemed equally aware as their parents of the electricity use, especially 'the lights' and 'the use of electrical items', such as TV and computers and even 'electrical cars' (which none of the adults had). Consumption was also discussed in terms of 'good or bad for others' as sustainable development was mentioned. Issues like 'fair payment to poor farmers in developing countries for their produce' and 'using other country's land to produce food we eat' were mentioned.

As the session was video-recorded and analyzed, group's processes and dynamics were examined. The author observed the power shifts and information gaps between parents and their children, including situations when parents became defensive of their children's consumptive behavior (as can be seen from the extract from a session quoted at the beginning of this chapter) or when the children were corrected by their parents about their consumption. Other curious shifts were noted, such as the children actually 'educating' their parents about – in one case – more efficient use of utilities, or, in another case, about the more 'environmentally friendly' consumption of meat substitutes. The effects of intergenerational group dynamics and power shifts should be examined in greater detail in consequent research. These would also be of anthropological interest in regard to analyzing where, when and from whom children learn about and develop environmental consciences.

In-depth interviews

In the course of the focus-group sessions, the researcher has noted that children's opinions were under-represented in mixed groups. Insufficient amount of children's statements in parents'–dominated groups necessitated the follow–up in–depth interviews with children in order to generate usable statements for concept mapping analysis. Interviews were held with seventeen children on the subjects raised during the focus group sessions.

Children were asked to reflect upon their consumption diaries as well as upon discussions raised by their parents and peers. The interview topics included the topic of consumption (what children understood it to be); consumption in general (with the interviewer specifying that consumption in itself is neither 'good' not 'bad', but also introducing the idea of 'global consumption' and 'country differences'); the quantity and quality of consumed items (how much of what is being consumed, composition and origin of consumed items); health effects of consumed items (which products are 'good for one'); environmental effects (what implications can there be for 'nature' and how 'nature' is being understood in relation to consumption). The interviewer has consciously allowed children to take the discussion in any direction as long as it stayed anchored in these broad topics. Perceiving potential ethical difficulties, connected with possible value judgments about the harmful effects of consumption or the possibility of evoking guilt or denial, the interviewer attempted to only elicit opinions already present among the children rather than 'educating' them about consumption. As in the case of focus group discussions, the researcher stressed her own lack of knowledge or judgment on what is 'good or bad' and her interest in what the children themselves thought about consumption. Interviews were recorded, transcribed and analyzed using the Qualitative analysis software program MAXQDA. This program helped to generate a number of statements from both the focus group and interview transcripts that enabled the researcher to undertake the concept mapping analysis.

Concept mapping

Focus group sessions were conducted simultaneously with the concept mapping, which is commonly used to elicit ideas about complex issues in small groups, and to map those ideas in a structured way at group level (Trochim 1987). The concept mapping method requires that statements are clear and do not contain multiple ideas. Therefore, the facilitator encouraged participants to clarify jargon, and helped to edit the statements. Statements expressing similar ideas could be submitted only once. All statements were typed out on the computer and printed on a card. After a break, the participants received a complete set of cards. They were first asked to rate how important they considered each statement, using a five point Likert scale: 1 (not important); 5 (extremely important). They were then asked to sort the statements logically according to themes or clusters and to provide a name for each cluster. These tasks were performed individually, with a group facilitator (but not the parents) helping the children. Subsequently scoring forms were entered into the computer and preliminary results generated by the concept mapping software (concept maps) were discussed in the group.

The statements generated at the first meeting were also the basis of the concept mapping at the second school. Here, participants were only invited to rate and sort the statements generated at the first school and to discuss the preliminary results.

Following this procedure, the mean priority and standard deviations (SD) of the ratings the participants assigned to each statement were calculated at group level. This resulted in a rating list of statements for younger and older children and their parents. Multi-dimensional scaling techniques and cluster analysis were used to calculate how often statements were grouped into the same cluster. This resulted in a two-dimensional point map for each group. On these maps statements that were more often placed under the same theme by the group members are located closer to each other. The researcher selected the final number of clusters, based on the proximity and the content of the statements. To identify similarities and differences between the children and their parents, the clusters they produced were compared by content analysis (see Table 5.2 and Table 5.3).

Results: The children

TABLE 5.2 Clustered statements and their ratings: children.

Cluster 1. Food should not damage nature (7 statements)	Food should be made without killing animals (5)
	Food should be made without using too many plants (5)
	Over-fishing is bad for nature (5)
	I want to be a vegetarian (4)
	Meat is important for my health but bad for nature (3)
	I may become a vegetarian some time (2)
	I am a vegetarian (1)
Cluster 2. 'Packaging is not good for nature' (3)	Packaging is dirty (as it pollutes nature) (4)
	Packaging uses too much space (4)
	It's too bad packaging goes in the garbage (3)
Cluster 3 'Things I do and how they affect the world (5)	I should not eat or drink too much (3)
	Eating too much is bad for nature (3)
	Eating other animals is not good (2)
	Eating 'vegetables' [plants] is not good (1)
	If I eat all plants there will be nothing left for animals to eat (1)
Cluster 4. 'Things that are (not) good for others or yourself' (5)	I should not eat or drink too much (3)
	Eating too much is bad for nature (3)
	Eating other animals is not good (2)
	Eating 'vegetables' [plants] is not good (1)
	If I eat all plants there will be nothing left for animals to eat (1)
Cluster 5. Trade-offs (3)	My parents never use their car, so we can sometimes take an airplane – and that saves energy (1)
	We pack our car full [of groceries], this way dad says we know what we need per week... and don't buy too much (1)
	If you use less electricity you can do other things (1)
Cluster 6. 'Consumption and health' (2)	If you are fat it's unhealthy (1)
	Eating meat is unhealthy (1)

Results: The parents

TABLE 5.3 Clustered statements and their ratings: parents.

Cluster 1. General awareness of consumption (6 statements)	Knowledge of health benefits and risks of consumed items (6) Children and parents should know more about consumption (6) Children should have nutritional knowledge (5) Nutritional knowledge should be passed from parents to children (3) Product developers have responsibility to report facts (3) Producers need to report facts (2)
Cluster 2. 'Social responsibility' (4)	Consumers should use fair trade products (10) Consumers should pay more for Max Havelaar products (6) Distribution of food in the world needs to be fair (3) Rich and poor should be able to consume the same (1)
Cluster 3 'Environmental awareness of consumed items' (8)	Fish consumption is good for health (6) Consumer should know whether the product is locally grown or imported (5) Consumer should know whether the pesticides were used (4) We are considering vegetarianism (4) We are vegetarians because meat consumption is bad (2) We are suggesting vegetarianism to our children (2) Over-fishing is bad for environment (2) Increased population in The Netherlands leads to increased land use for food production (1)
Cluster 4. 'Awareness of energy and water use' (5)	More 'clean', 'green' or 'renewable' energy is needed (combined statements (8). Energy consumption influences climate change (3) We need to limit energy use (3) Our energy use should be more efficient (3) House insulation is needed to protect the house from cooling (1)
Cluster 5. 'Environmental responsibility in regard to waste' (7)	We need to do more to reduce the amount of waste (8) We need to limit packaging materials (5) Recycling is important (4) (Eco)-efficiency needs to be developed (4) Human waste can be used (3) Sewage systems should not be chemically treated (1) Human waste could be better used for fertilization (1)
Cluster 6. Left-over statements (3)	Over-consumption is related to tragedy of the commons (1) Children need to be educated about consumption (1) Talking about consumption makes us feel bad (1)

Reflection

Comparison of the clusters shows that parents and children identified common thematic clusters referring to social and environmental responsibility. Social responsibility was linked to both health (of the consumers) and conditions of people who produce food. In cases like meat consumption and packaging being seen as 'bad for the environment' and 'chemical additives in food and drink' as 'bad for health' parents and children's opinions overlapped. Some clusters, such as 'trade-offs' were present only in (older) children's groups. In the case of parents, greater importance was placed on health and social responsibility aspects of consumption, while children formed more 'environmental awareness' clusters. Children generally formed more clusters than their parents, with many semantic overlaps (as with 'if you eat too much you become too fat and it's unhealthy', related to both personal responsibility, social responsibility, health and other possible cluster categories), each cluster containing fewer items (statements). This could be due to the fact that fewer children participated in the interviews than parents in the focus group sessions. Surprisingly, children placed low priority on health issues. This could be due to the nature of interviewing (rather than group sessions that generated parents' statements). It is also possible that there is evidence of children's lower awareness of or stress over health concerns or an 'immortality' mindset – all these hypotheses need to be expanded in consequent research.

Based on the preliminary results, the author hopes that the data produced through this interactive collaborative inquiry will aid in the development of new elementary school programs addressing alternative modes of consumption. Much more vigorous research is needed to separate behavior (actual consumption patterns), intentions and perceptions of the children. This pilot study leaves us with many questions and calls for in-depth reflection on the place of consumption in our society in general and in the green education in particular. Reflecting on how much of 'green education' is really 'lifestyle education' we may wonder how much of it is culturally and socio-economically biased? How explicit is the connection between consumption and the knowledge the children are gaining of the processes of environmental protection and appreciation of the environment? While the parents seem to have a general idea of what can be 'good' for health and environment, it is hard to tell how the children perceive their own potentially positive role in 'responsible consumption'. Intergenerational differences in perceptions of (health and environmental) risk, as well as own agency and influence over consumption choices and their consequences of such choices need to be addressed in consequent research. Opinions of parents and their children, and the influence of one on the other also need to be studied in greater detail.

In the evaluative meeting with the children, parents and teachers discussing the concept mapping results, the research participants expressed their interest in the development of the pilot program on consumption in their schools. Findings from this research need yet to be incorporated into the larger framework of educational program, incorporating the Cradle to Cradle principle into the 'sustainable consumption' program.

Next Step: Alternative Modes of Consumption: Cradle to Cradle Principle

The Cradle to Cradle principle refers to the concept developed by the American architect William McDonough and the German chemist Michael Braungart in their influential book *Cradle to Cradle: Remaking the way we make things* (2002). The authors made the case that an industrial system that 'takes, makes and wastes' can become a creator of goods and services that generate ecological, social and economic value. Arguing that the products and materials used for consumption do not necessarily have to be produced 'cradle to grave' and discarded through waste incinerators or in landfills, but can be retained for infinite use. The authors argued that consumption items could be designed to be retained in either a biological or technical cycle. Resulting products will not be wasted but returned into either 'nature' or a technical domain where they could be infinitely reproduced, rather than merely reused, recycled and actually down-cycled. Making a point of the fact that recycling is actually down-cycling, and that efficiency in a faulty system only makes consumption 'less bad', McDonogh and Braungart produced a set of new ideas about consumption. The authors succeeded in producing a number of designs, ranging from construction to textiles (often based on pre-industrial knowledge of 'natural' building materials or 'organic' clothing) that not only brought them commercial success and recognition, but also established Cradle to Cradle (C2C) practices and organizations across the globe. McDonough's and Braungart's responsible consumption can be very appealing to the course aimed at critical and yet positive learning about consumption. Ethical considerations, implicit in the research presented in this chapter, such as the need to avoid guilt feelings about consumption in favor of positive learning, may be addressed through the application of the Cradle to Cradle principle.

Conclusion

This research was conducted as a pilot study only on the basis of which proposed methodology could be tested and fine-tuned in order to conduct a more ambitious research of green education with special focus on consumption. Although the scope of this chapter does not allow for it, this research could be embedded into the scholarship of the risk society – particularly environmental and health risk perceptions (Beck 1992; Giddens 2009) and consumption (Sahlins 1976; Baudrillard 1981; Carrier and Heyman 1997). In line with the work of two other contributors to this volume, Anderson (1996) and Efird (in this volume), the author finds anthropology of environmental learning to be of paramount importance in the environmental anthropologists' ambition to contribute to the understanding of societal influences on environmental change and to the development of solutions to environmental problems. While many techniques for measuring environmental attitudes, values and behaviors have been developed by sociologists and social psychologists, anthropologists seem to have left this area to other disciplines. While anthropologists may be reluctant to 'measure' knowledge and attitudes, they could, however, contribute to the applied studies of children's understanding of the environment and how to protect it, as well as studies of green education, and studies of our own, Western cultures' conceptions of and attitudes about nature and consumption. They could also be aided in these studies by the supplemental use of measuring devices such as the ones discussed. The ethnographic data on children's consumptive practices and perceptions is lacking, and more vigorous research is needed to provide a foundation for incorporating consumption into green education. Ethnographic methodology could be very useful in gaining insights into the consumption patterns and perceptions of children in their socio-cultural context. This research, aimed at integrating various methodological strategies, did not try to exhaust but rather to open up some of the possibilities available to anthropologists for studying existing beliefs, values, perceptions and attitudes of children towards consumption. In order to find out whether the educational program addressing consumption is working, the same methodology used for the baseline measurement of consumptive patterns and attitudes can also be used to measure the success of educational program on consumption.

The study of the social influences of children's peers, parents and teachers in their consumption choices requires further investigation, involving a diversified methodological toolkit. It is the author's hope that the results of this study will be relevant for teachers as well as policy makers as they can form a foundation for translating the existing knowledge on consumption into green education. The concept mapping data can be used as a foundation for the development of a new curriculum, augmenting children's knowledge by providing a framework for responsible consumption, as suggested by the Cradle to Cradle principle.

The study of EE from a methodologically mixed perspective may lead us to propose a new Post-NEP model, informed by anthropological attention to ethnographic detail and cultural context, more nuanced and context-dependent than the current NEP theory. The state-of-the-art in environmental education research is dominated by quantitative studies characterized by uniform, standardized models, which, according to their critiques, fail to emphasize socio-cultural dimension of the new phenomenon of green education. Through the new Post-NEP model, the appropriateness and socio-cultural sensitivity of disparate components of EE could be assessed in terms of the particularities of national contexts and integrated into the design of the successful green education programs. Appropriating sociology's concern for social patterning and anthropological expertise in cultural comparison, as well as combining methodological strengths of both disciplines, consequent research promises not only an innovative account of the national differences in green education, but a positive policy output that could supplant the generic environmental policy approach that is proving more and more problematic in increasingly diversified national settings.

Harnessing both sociological methodological focus on conceptualization and modeling as well as anthropology's specialization in in-depth ethnographic study, consequent research may open new opportunities for embedding green education within socio-cultural processes through proposing the Post-NEP model based on the insights from the environmental social science. Much scholarship in the area of national appropriation of environmental policy has been over-determined either by instrumental, practical approaches that fail to take account of socio-cultural contexts in which generically formulated policy occurs, or by purely 'socio-cultural' descriptions of how such policies are received at the grass roots level. Whereas current studies of green education focus on either societal benefits determined by instrumental needs (such as the necessity for long term sustainable solutions to the current environmental crisis), or by particularistic pedagogical prescriptions, consequent research may bridge that divide. Follow-up research drawn from this pilot study may do so by invoking two distinct strategies of enquiry: interdisciplinary methods (combining measuring scales and ethnographic approaches), twinned with the employment of focus group and concept mapping approaches as methods of enquiry. Consequent research may also address the explanatory theories of the formation of environmental attitudes in general and in relation to consumption in particular and to test a hypothesis that social, political and the institutional context – particularly environmental education – can be reliably assessed and shown to play an important role in shaping children's and adolescents' environmental perspectives.

References

Anderson, E. N. (1996) *Ecologies of the Heart*, Oxford: Oxford University Press.

Andrezejewski, J., Baltodano, M. P., Symcox, L. (2009) *Social justice, peace, and environmental education: transformative standards*, New York: Routledge.

Aronson, E. and O'Leary, M. (1982) 'The relative effectiveness of models and prompts on energy conservation: A field experiment in a shower room,' *Journal of Experimental Systems*, 12: 219–24.

Bacon, C. M., Mendez, V.E., Gliessman, S.R., Goodman, D., and Fox, J.A.(eds) (2008) *Confronting the Coffee Crisis: Fair Trade, Sustainable Livelihoods and Ecosystems in Mexico and Central America*, Cambridge: The MIT Press.

Barratt Hacking, E., R. Barratt, Scott, W. (2007) 'Engaging children: research issues around participation and environmental learning,' *Environmental Education Research*, 13 (4): 529 – 544.

Baudrillard, J. (1981) 'For a critique of the political economy of the sign,' St Louis: Telos Press.

Beck, U. (1992) *Risk Society: Towards a new modernity*, London: Sage.

Bourdieu, P. (1984) *Distinction: a social critique of the judgement of taste*, London: Routledge and Kegan Paul.

Bryant, R. L., and Goodman, M.K. (2004) 'Consuming Narratives: the Political Ecology of 'Alternative' Consumption,' *Transactions of the Institute of British Geographers* 29 (3):344 – 366.

Burn, S.M. (1991) 'Social psychology and the stimulation of recycling behaviors: The block leader approach,' *Journal of Applied Social Psychology*, 21:611–29.

Carrier, J. G., and McHeyman, C. (1997) 'Consumption and political economy,' *Journal of the Royal Anthropological Institute*, 2: 355–73.

Cialdini, R.B., Reno, R.R. and Kallgren, C.A. (1990) 'A focus theory of normative conduct: Recycling the concept of norms to reduce littering in public places,' *Journal of Personality and Social Psychology*, 58:1015–26.

Clayton, S. and Opotow, S. (2003) *Identity and the natural environment: The psychological significance of nature*, Cambridge: MIT Press.

Connolly, J. and Prothero, A. (2008) 'Green Consumption: Life-politics, risk and contradictions,' *Journal of Consumer Culture*, 8: 117.

Davis, J.J. (1995) 'The effects of message framing on response to environmental communications,' *Journalism and Mass Communication Quarterly*, 72: 285–99.

Douglas, M. and Isherwood, B. (1978) *The world of goods*, Harmondsworth: Penguin.

Dunlap, R. E. (2008) 'The New Environmental Paradigm Scale: From Marginality to Worldwide Use,' *The Journal of Environmental Education*, 40 (1): 3–18.

Dunlap, R. E. and Van Liere, K. D. (1978) 'The New Environmental Paradigm: A Proposed Measuring Instrument and preliminary results,' *The Journal of Environmental Education*, 9 (4): 10–19.

Eagles, P. F. J., & Demare, R. (1999) 'Factors influencing children's environmental attitudes,' *The Journal of Environmental Education*, 3: 33–37.

Evans, G. W., Brauchle, G., Haq, A., Stecker, R., Wong, K., & Shapiro, E. (2007) 'Young children's environmental attitudes and behaviors,' *Environment and Behavior*, 39: 645–59.

Gardner, G., & Stern, P. C. (2002) *Environmental problems and human behavior* (2nd ed.), Boston: Allyn & Bacon.

Giddens, A. (2009) *Global Politics and Climate Change*, Cambridge: Polity Press.

Gonzales, M.H., Aronson, E. and Costanzo, M.A. (1988) 'Using social cognition and persuasion to promote energy conservation: A quasi-experiment,' *Journal of Applied Social Psychology*, 18: 1049–66.

Heckler, S. E. (1994) 'The role of memory in understanding and encouraging recycling behavior. Special Issue: Psychology, marketing, and recycling,' *Psychology and Marketing* 11, pp. 375–92.

Heimlich, J.E., & Ardoin, N.M. (2008) 'Understanding Behavior to Understand Behavior Change: A Literature Review,' *Environmental Education Research*, 14 (3): 215–37.

Hines, J. M., Hungerford, H., & Tomera, A. (1987) 'Analysis and synthesis of research on responsible environmental behavior: A meta analysis,' *The Journal of Environmental Education*, 18 (2): 1–8.

Howes, D. (1996) *Cross Cultural Consumption: Global Markets Local Realities*, London: Routledge.

Isenhour, C. (2010) 'On Conflicted Swedish Consumers, the Effort to "Stop Shopping" and Neoliberal Environmental Governance,' *Journal of Consumer Behavior* Special Issue on Anti-Consumption and Sustainability 9(6), pp. 454–69.

Jaffe, D., Kloppenburg, J. and Monroy, M. (2004) 'Bringing the 'moral charge' home: fair trade within the North and within the South,' *Rural Sociology* 169–96.

Kahn, P. H., Jr. (1999) *The human relationship with nature*, Cambridge, MA: MIT Press.

Kahn, P. H., & Kellert, S. R. (2002) *Children and nature*, Cambridge MA: MIT Press.

Kahn, R. and Nocella, A. J. II. (2009) *Greening the Academy: Environmental Studies in the Liberal Arts*, Syracuse University Press.

Kaiser, F. G. (2004) 'Conservation behavior,' In C. Spielberger (Ed.) *Encyclopedia of applied psychology* (Vol. 1:473–77), New York: Academic Press.

Kaiser, F.G., Oerke, B., Bogner, F.X. (2007) Behavior-based environmental attitude: Development of an instrument for adolescents. *Journal of Environmental Psychology*. 27(3): 242–51.

Kellert, S.R. (1993) 'Attitudes, knowledge, and behavior toward wildlife among the industrial superpowers: United States, Japan, and Germany,' *Journal of Social Issues* 49: 53–69.

——(1995) *The value of life*, Washington, DC: Island Press.

Kollmuss, A. and Agyeman, J. (2002) 'Mind the Gap: Why do people act environmentally and what are the barriers to pro-environmental behavior?' *Environmental Education Research*, 8(3): 239–260.

Kopnina, H. (2005) *East to West Migration: Russian Migrants in Western Europe*. Aldershot Ashgate.

Kopnina, H. and Keune, H. (2010) 'Introduction'. In H. Kopnina and H. Keune (eds) *Health and Environment: Social Science perspectives*, New York: Nova Science Publishers.

Leeming, F. C., & Dwyer, W. (1995) Children's environmental attitude and knowledge scale: Construction and evaluation, *The Journal of Environmental Education*, 26, 22–31.

Levitt, L. and Leventhal, G. (1986) Litter Reduction: How Effective is the New York State Bottle Bill? *Environment and Behavior*, 18: 467–79.

Lilienfeld, R. M. (1998) *Use Less Stuff: Environmentalism for Who We Really Are*, New York: Ballantine Publishing Group.

Louv, R. (2005) Last Child in the Woods: Saving Our Children From Nature-Deficit Disorder, North Carolina: Algonquin Books of Chapel Hill.

Maloney, M. P., Ward, M., & Braucht, G. (1975) 'A revised scale for the measurement of ecological attitudes and knowledge' *American Psychologist*, 30, 787–90.

Manoli, C. C., Johnson, B., & Dunlap, R. E. (2007) Assessing children's environmental worldviews: Modifying and validating the New Ecological Paradigm Scale for use with children, *The Journal of Environmental Education, 38*(4): 3–13.

Mayer, S. F. and McPherson F. C. (2004) 'The connectedness to nature scale: A measure of individuals' feeling in community with nature,' *Journal of Environmental Psychology* 24, 503–15.

Mackay, H. (ed) (1997) *Consumption and Everyday Life*, London: Sage.

McDonough, W. and M. Braungart (2002) *Cradle to Cradle, Remaking the way we make things*, North Point Press, New York.

Miller, D. (1995) 'Consumption studies as the transformation of anthropology'. In D. Miller (ed.) *Acknowledging consumption: a review of new studies*, London: Routledge.

Miller, D. (ed.) (1998) *Material Cultures: Why Some Things Matter*, University of Chicago Press.

Miller, J. D. (1975) The development of pre-adult attitudes toward environmental conservation and pollution, *School Science and Mathematics*, 27: 729–37.

Oskamp, S. (2000) Psychological contributions to achieving an ecologically sustainable future for humanity, *Journal of Social Issues*, 56: 373–90.

Pallak, M. S., Cook, D.A. and Sullivan, J.J. (1980) Commitment and energy conservation. In L. Bickman, (ed.), *Applied social psychology annual*, Beverly Hills, CA: Sage, pp. 235–53.

Radhje, W. and Murphy, C. (1992) *Rubbish! The Archeology of Garbage*, New York: HarperCollins Publishers, Inc.

Rauwald, K.S. and Moore, C.F. (2002) Environmental attitudes as predictors of policy support across three countries, *Environment and Behavior*, 34: 709–39.

Reilly, M. D. and Hughes, W.W. (1985) *Household Garbage and the Role of Packaging: the United States/Mexico City household refuse comparison*, Tucson: Solid Waste Council of the Paper Industry.

Reid, A., Jansen, B., Nikel, J. and Simovska, V. [eds] (2008) *Participation and Learning: perspectives on education and the environment, health and sustainability*, New York: Springer.

Rideout, B. E. (2005) The effect of a brief environmental problems module on endorsement of the New Ecological Paradigm in college students, *The Journal of Environmental Education, 37*(1): 3–11.

Ritenbaugh, K. (1984) *Household Refuse Analysis: theory, method, and applications in social science*, Beverly Hills, California: Sage Publications.

Robbins, R. (2007) *Global Problems and the Culture of Capitalism*. Prentice Hall: Pearson Education.

Sahlins, M. (1976) *Culture and practical reason*, Chicago: University of Chicago Press.

Sanera, M. and Shaw, J. (1996) *Facts, not fear: Teaching children about the environment*. Washington, DC: Regnery.

Schultz, P.W. (2000) 'Empathizing with nature: The effects of perspective taking on concern for environmental issues', *Journal of Social Issues*, 56: 391–406.

——(2001) 'Assessing the structure of environmental concern: Concern for self, other people, and the biosphere', *Journal of Environmental Psychology*, 21: 327–39.

Shepherd, N. (2002) 'Anarcho-Environmentalists: Ascetics of Late Modernity', *Journal of Contemporary Ethnography*, 31: 135.

Slater, D. (1997) *Consumer Culture and Modernity*. Cambridge, UK: Polity Press.

Stern, P. C. (2000) 'Toward a coherent theory of environmentally significant behavior', *Journal of Social Issues*, 36: 407–24.

Stern, P. C. and Dietz, T. (1994) 'The value basis of environmental concern', *Journal of Social Issues*, 50: 65–84.

Stevens, G. W. J. M., Pels, T., Bengi-Arslan, L.,Verhulst, F. C., Vollebergh, W. A. M. and Crijnen, A. A. M. (2003) Parent, teacher and self-reported problem behavior in The Netherlands: Comparing Moroccan immigrant with Dutch and with Turkish immigrant children and adolescents, *Social Psychiatry and Psychiatric Epidemiology*, 38(10): 576–85.

Thijssen, J. (2002) *Nature education for elementary schools [Natuuronderwijs voor de basisschool]*, Cito, Arnhem.

Trochim, W.M.K. (1989) *An introduction to concept mapping for planning and evaluation.* Evaluation Program Planning; 12:1–16.

Van Petegem, P. and Blieck, A. (2006) 'The environmental worldview of children: a cross-cultural perspective', *Environmental Education Research*, 12(5): 625 – 635.

Wagenaar, H. (2007) *Sustainable Development for the Elementary Schools: Domain description and lesson examples [Duurzame Ontwikkeling voor de basisschool: Domeinbeschrijving en voorbeeldlessen]*, Cito, Arnhem.

Wals, A. E. J. (2007) *Social Learning: towards a sustainable world: principles, perspectives and praxis*, Wageningen: Wageningen Academic Publishers.

Werner, C. M., Turner, J. Shipman, K. and Twitchell, F. S. et al. (1995) 'Commitment, behavior, and attitude change: An analysis of voluntary recycling. Special issue: green psychology', *Journal of Environmental Psychology*, 15: 197–208.

Wilk, R. W. (1982) 'Household Archaeology,' *American Behavioral Scientist*, 25(6): 617–39.

——(2002) Culture and Energy Consumption, In R. Bent, L. Orr, and R. Baker (eds) *Energy: Science, Policy and the Pursuit of Sustainability*, edited by Island Press: Washington. Pp. 109–30.

——(2004) 'Questionable Assumptions about Sustainable Consumption,' In L. Reisch and I. Røpke (eds.) *The Ecological Economics of Consumption*, Edward Elgar (Cheltenham UK). Pp. 17–22.

——(2006) 'Consumer Culture and Extractive Industry on the Margins of the World System,' In J. Brewer and F. Trentmann (eds) *Consumer Cultures: Global Perspectives*, Oxford: Berg Publishers. pp. 123–44.

——(2009) 'Consuming Ourselves to Death,' In S. Crate (ed.) *Anthropology and Climate Change: from Encounters to Actions*, Durham: Duke University Press.

——(2010) 'Consumption Embedded in Culture and Language: Implications for Finding Sustainability,' *Sustainability: Science, Practice and Policy*, 6(2): 1–11.

Williams, S. M., and McCrorie, R. (1990) 'The analysis of ecological attitudes in town and country,' *Journal of Environmental Management*, 31: 157–62.

6

TIME AND POPULATION VULNERABILITY TO NATURAL HAZARDS

The Pre-Katrina Primacy of Experience

Daniel H. de Vries

The Objective Gaze of the New Environmental Paradigm

In their 1978 paper outlining their critique on the culturally dominant Human Exceptionalist Paradigm (HEP), Catton and Dunlap pointed out that 'most Americans (until recently) ardently believed that the present was better than the past and the future would improve up on the present' (Catton & Dunlap 1978: 43) and argued that sociologists analyzing human societies easily followed this same technologically optimist worldview. Central to Catton and Dunlap's critique was the commonly held assumption that human cultural evolution would outpace biological change, and cultural adaptivity and associated technological innovations would be able to continue progress without limit, 'making all social problems ultimately soluble.' A tantalizing proposition for sociologists, as this superiority of human innovation elevated humans above nature in a society where there are no known limits to improvements of technology and organization, the relationship between a growing population and its earthly habitat could be sustained.

Catton and Dunlap's impetus for an environmental sociology came as a critique on this shared anthropocentrism that was historically based on two mainstream currents of thoughts in sociology. First, the Durkheimian tradition argued that social facts can only be explained by linking them to other social facts, in an effort to claim space for the social sciences to be equally as disciplinary and authoritative as the natural sciences, requiring its own set of dynamic understandings. A second (Weberian) stream of thought emphasized that the ways in which people define their situations to explain their actions was primarily explainable by surrounding actors and not by the situation's physical characteristics. Emphasizing the actor's definition, the 'environment' came to be relevant only relative to how it was perceived and defined in this 'constructivist' approach. Physical conditions never themselves produce awareness of an environmental problem, but this is always socially attributed through a human interpretative framework (Douglas and Wildavsky 1983).

The *New Environmental Paradigm* (NEP) challenged these sociological currents. Humans were placed back into nature and the limits of ecological resources were acknowledged to influence human societies with a vengeance, as 'intricate linkages of cause and effect and feedback in the web of nature produce many unintended consequences from purposive human action' (Catton & Dunlap, 1978: 45). The alternative which Catton and Dunlap brought to sociology was a liberation of the anthropocentric perspective through an admittance of the relevance of dynamics at other levels—the physical, biological, neurological—to explain social facts in their own right. In defense of the HEP, critics stressed that the NEP missed the main point of environmental sociological analysis, which was to explain which social processes and mechanisms cause something to appear as an environmental problem (Lidskog 1998). Further, critics pointed out that the assumption made by Catton and Dunlap that somehow 'objective' environmental problems forced themselves into public consciousness, thereby promoting a realist, almost environmental deterministic, position and ignoring the social mediation proposed by constructivists was untenable. As sociology grappled with the constructivist versus realist debate, Dunlap and Marshall (2007) eventually concluded that both constructivist-relativist and realist proponents could find common ground in 'critical realist' or 'contextual construcitivist' positions.

But while common ground was found, this also illustrated the limits of the New Environmental Paradigm proposed. While the NEP repositioned the position of humanity from above nature (anthropocentric) into nature (ecocentric), it did not reorient environmental sociology's methodological emphasis from an objectified, anthropocentric gaze favoring positivist, human observer's interpretation of a modeled (reductionist) reality into an ethnographic perspective in which ecocentric vision and evaluation is embedded in the landscape, the people therein, and the flow of events. What the NEP did not do is move sociology closer to its ethnomethodological (under)current, which postulates that interpretation and significance can only be obtained by immersion and embeddedness *inside* the environment of study. In cultural anthropology, Rappaport distinguished this cultural model as 'the model of the environment conceived by the people who act in it' from the more objective, scientific quantifiable depiction of the 'physical world'—the operational model—adhered to in environmental sociology (Rappaport 1968; Biersack 1999). This difference originally was referred to as 'emic' versus 'etic.' In an emic approach local knowledge and ethno-semantic taxonomies are central. In etic approaches, objective and scientifically 'true' representations of an objective reality are expressed, represented by measures of perceived reality in quantitative models. While the NEP broke up the conversation about the relationship of humans in nature, the inclusion of ecological relationships in sociology remained controlled by this objectivist, etic gaze, wherein a sociological reality interprets a pre-given biophysical reality. The argument made in this chapter is that this paradigmatic emphasis on objective seeing core to the empirical sciences limits the applicability of the NEP. In particular when it comes to temporality, the etic emphasis on time as chronological disfavors emic relationships to biophysical reality common to a true ecological vision. The question surfaces if, temporally speaking, environmental sociology ever left the Human Exemptionalist Paradigm. Unable to emerge within environmental sociology, it is argued that this compromised vision limits understanding of the complete temporal experience that explains risk behavior and underlies population vulnerability to natural and man-made disasters. It is argued that this missed opportunity of using the New Environmental Paradigm to reclaim an ecological, emic phenomenological perspective in sociology can literally have disastrous consequences, because environmental sociology tends to miss a crucial dimension of system vulnerability to hazards and disturbances which emerges from the human embeddedness inside complex, *temporal* ecological relationships, or the position that humans are *in* time.

Disaster and Chronological Temporality

Vulnerability to hazard events is the potential for loss (Cutter 1996), the degree to which a system or subsystem is likely to experience harm due to exposure to a hazard, either as a perturbation or stressor (Turner *et al.* 2003), or the inverse of the local capacity to anticipate, cope with, resist, and recover from the impact of a natural hazard, or resilience (Blaikie *et al.* 1994). Socially vulnerable populations are typically seen as those who live in a marginalized state of permanent emergency as a result of negative power relationships (Wisner 1993). From a sociological point of view, this swiftly leads to the integration of census and survey variables, such as poverty, into vulnerability indices for specific administrative geographies in an effort to estimate a population's proneness to loss when faced with a hazard at a certain point in time. To account for the temporal in this exercise, more time periods are added through standardized (measurable) time-intervals, creating historical patterns of changing levels of vulnerability 'through time', complemented with historical descriptions of the causes for these dynamics. In this view of temporality, time remains seen as from the outside, in an objective, etic view. This way of understanding time is firmly rooted in the Human Exemptionalist Paradigm. Western, rationalist or Cartesian tradition of thought has long promoted a de-situated understanding of people and things relying on the merits of detachment; a mode of being which allows a distanced view that enables us to obtain a wider view because we extract ourselves from the immediate pressures and passions of the moment (Spinosa *et al.* 1997). The disciplinary approach to the study of social movements through time follows this detached perspective as it privileges an absolute, true and mathematical time, which of itself, and from its own nature, flows equably without regard to anything external. Sociology's objective gaze presupposes and is built upon this notion of external, linear time as it allows for standardization of time intervals needed to measure speeds of change. How else can a social movement, such as environmentalism, be objectively traced 'through' time? Statistical and spatial modeling and simulations use chronological time-series to predict future systemic scenarios and states. In this sociological reality, change is predicated on the standardization of time in measureable order, allowing for movements of 'levels' of environmentalist attitudes to be traced.

The modernist view on temporality still provides the major philosophical grounding for most of the definitions of temporality that underlie environmental sociological analysis, including studies of social vulnerability to disasters. Since the Western, commonsensical way of thinking depends on non-historical detachment (or non-historical improvisation in the post-modernist case), researchers and theorists dealing with temporality in disaster research are ill prepared to describe or even notice how 'history making' is embedded in practices, activities, and the skills of people themselves. The field as a whole tends to undervalue the contribution which the situatedness of a floodplain population *in* time makes to its vulnerability (or resiliency). This is a serious error with a long history that is seemingly taken for granted and follows the temporal assumption central to the Human Exceptionalist Paradigm that humans have control over nature. As Catton and Dunlap's proposal was largely focused on empirically detecting, measuring, and monitoring a new, sociologically shared public attitude, namely that of environmentalism, the NEP critique did not problematize the sociological paradigm of objective time inherent to empiricism.

Social Time

In the early twentieth century, philosophical critique gave rise to a sociology of time in which the concept of 'social time' came to be emphasized (Heidegger 1927; Durkheim 1915; Elias 1991). The opening up of the time concept allowed a plethora of notions of time to be identified (Ma 2000). Time shrinks when it passes, and as such eventually disappears, ceases to take place (Derrida 1995). Time is a fluid, a space, a sheet or field that percolates (from 'passoir' or 'sieve') and as such passes and does not pass (Serres & Latour 1995). A task- or event-orientated time is shaped by the onset, duration, and completion of daily, weekly or seasonal tasks. For example, for the nomadic Nuer in Ethiopia 'the daily timepiece is the cattle clock, the round of pastoral tasks, and the time of day and the passage of time through a day are to Nuer primarily the succession of these tasks and their relation to one another' (Evans-Pritchard 1940). Body time is an organic form of time which 'squirms and wiggles like a bluefish in a bay, making its mind as it goes along' (Couclelis 1998). What all these ways of understanding time have in common is the way in which time is not seen as an external, 'natural' category out there, independent of social life, but instead intrinsically connected to the rhythms of the social. Or, that temporality has been made relative to human ecological experience; the point of view of the observer in their historical ecological system.

In the world of disaster studies, social time was recently introduced by the United States National Resource Council (2006), who called for a complementary treatment of social and chronological time in the 'Societal Response to Disasters.' Social time is argued to be nonlinear and multidirectional and experienced differently by individuals. Three ontological claims are made. First, within social time, the past may be reconstructed from the present. Second, the present may be reconstructed from the past. Third, the future is linked to the present and past in social time. Decisions to build in a floodplain are based on prior disaster experience and future disaster expectations as both relate to assessment of hazard vulnerability. According to the council, this ties disaster mitigation and preparedness to emergency response and recovery. Chronological time compresses and expands in social time as individuals and social systems create, define, and adapt to environmental hazards, the risks associated with them, and the disasters that occur for them.

Since the temporality which is relevant to those living and dwelling within hazardscapes is not chronological but experiential, it is sensible to identify research approaches which fit within this profoundly social context. Grounded in the everyday existence of populations in their 'lifeworld,' such a perspective is identified as dealing with social time. Few researchers appear to have identified the emic connection between vulnerability and populations situated in social time. Forrest (1993) uses a social time framework to explore how six communities acknowledged the first and second anniversaries of Hurricane Hugo and as such built a process for collective remembering:

> Disaster anniversaries entail an interactive process in which people share personal experiences. Public officials make declarative comments while the press and electronic media reconstruct the disaster experience by recording current thoughts and reflections. In short, the disaster anniversary is a process of collective remembering.
>
> *(Forrest 1993: 448)*

Bankoff (2004) has taken this collective remembrance a step further, by arguing that historians have systematically seen disasters as non-sequential historical 'events' instead of social-historical processes, a position strongly brought forward in anthropology by Hoffman and Oliver Smith (2002). Based on this, he proposes a temporally produced state of vulnerability that underlies other forms of vulnerability, yet remains often implicit as a factor:

> First, of course, there is the particular sequence of events that situate people in time and place; then there are the historical processes that determine their condition and their capacity to withstand its effects. But individuals also 'construct' disasters as both a function of their prior experience of hazards as well as from their particular 'class' or social group's perception of what is happening around them. Moreover, disasters are not so much objective events as subjective ones that can be privileged or erased according to a sense of selective memory or collective amnesia. Only when the study of a hazardous event is linked to its specific perceptual, social and cultural historical context can it really reveal the processes at work in creating a disaster. Thus, in a real sense, time itself is as much a factor that needs consideration in how disasters are created, as are politics, society, the economy, culture and the environment. Few historians, however, have approached disasters from this perspective.
>
> *(Bankoff 2004: 34–35)*

A Dwelling Methodology

An ecocentric vision suggests that people and the environment are mutually constitutive components of the same world. Phenomenology has motivated such vision by proposing that in both perception and consumption, meaning embodied in environmental objects is drawn into the experience of subjects by being in a world and trying to decipher how this being informs our behavior. This perspective proposes an enactive cognition; it is not the representation of a pre-given world by a pre-given mind, but rather the enactment of a world and a mind on the basis of a history of the variety of actions that a being in the world performs (Ingold 1992). This enactive approach is a radical philosophical critique of the idea that the mind is a mirror of nature (Varela *et al.* 1991). Instead, our life-world exists relative to the extent to which a 'world-out-there' is actually appropriated, acted upon, crafted, and transformed, foremost through interactions. Such action in the world is the practitioner's way of knowing it: the acquisition of environmental knowledge is inseparable from being part of it, engaging with it. This emic perspective as such can be seen as the scientific study of experience (Jackson 1996). Ingold (1993) has called this a 'dwelling perspective' in which humans experience the world through active engagement with their environments. He suggested that the landscape is constituted as an enduring record of, and testimony to, the lives and works of past generations who have dwelt within it, and in so doing have left there something of themselves. From this dwelling perspective, the presumed continuity between mind and world 'privileges the understandings that people derive from their lived, everyday involvement in the world' (Ingold 1993: 152). In other words, the landscape through which vulnerability develops not only tells, but *is* a story. As Ingold puts it: 'to perceive the landscape is therefore to carry out an act of remembrance, and remembering is not so much a matter of calling up an internal image, stored in the mind, as of engaging perceptually with an environment that is itself pregnant with the past' (Ingold 1993: 153).

This dwelling perspective was used as a foundation for the ethnohistorical case study of Jefferson Parish, located in the New Orleans Metropolitan Area, with the aim of uncovering how past experiences of hazard events had influenced current situational evaluations of risk and potential collective surprise (as a proxy for emergency unpreparedness). The case study was part of larger ethnographic research conducted in U.S. urban floodplain neighborhoods conducted from 2004 – 2008 (De Vries 2007, 2008). Field visits for the Jefferson Parish case study included open-ended formal interviews with key informants, including disaster mitigation officials (n = 4) and floodplain residents (n = 15), analysis of materials and documents (including a number of videos as part of flood prevention education strategies), and informal conversations and observations. Fieldwork was conducted intermittently during the two years before Hurricane Katrina struck the area (2003 and 2004 visits). The research aim was to find out what particular historical series of events would explain current behavior of the dwelling population. Experiential information about dwelling was obtained by paying attention to how dwellers referenced past events, and how this *temporal referentiality* influenced their expectations into the future, giving attention to surprise events and the timing of their impacts (De Vries 2010). Research analyzed the extent to which the actual historical timing of events—captured in experiential knowledge—mattered to risk behavior, how knowledge about the complex hazardscape of Metropolitan New Orleans depended on the specifics of that narrative history, the extent to which this history was obscured, and what elements of risk hidden in the landscape remained potent but only incompletely or indirectly revealed from view. The following case study evaluates to what extent this dwelling perspective differs from the objective gaze of sociological linear time in its approach to vulnerability and how this difference impacts the local capacity to anticipate, cope with, resist, and recover from the impact of a natural hazard, or resilience.

The Socio-Historical Vulnerability of New Orleans Metropolitan Area

> Just as there is variation in the physical landscape, the landscape of social inequity has increased the division between rich and poor in this country and has led to the increasing social vulnerability of our residents, especially to coastal hazards. Strained race relations and the seeming differential response to the disaster suggest that in planning for future catastrophes, we need to not only look at the natural environment in the development of mitigation programs, but the social environment as well. It is the interaction between nature and society that produces the vulnerability of places.
>
> *(Cutter 2006)*

This quote from one of the leading social vulnerability researchers and creator of the Social Vulnerability Index, now widely reproduced in many hazard mitigation and disaster management fields of practice, follows the NEP as it places the social back into nature emphasizing vulnerability is the interaction of both. The underlying Social Vulnerability Index technique, trademarked as SOVI^{TM}, illustrates this intention by integrating key metrics of demographic census taking—core instrument of sociological empiricism—to use as vulnerability background to the geographically specific impact of natural (or man-made) hazards (Cutter *et al.* 2003). SOVI^{TM} measures the social vulnerability of U.S. counties to environmental hazards using socioeconomic variables 'which the research literature suggests contributes to reduction in a community's ability to prepare for, respond to, and recover from hazards' (HVRI 2010). For example, in the SOVI^{TM} 2000 social vulnerability map distributed on their website, nine significant components are integrated which explain 76 per cent of the variance in the data: socioeconomic status, elderly and children, rural agriculture, housing density, African American female-headed households, gender, service industry employment, unemployed Native Americans, and infrastructure employment. As census surveys are conducted every ten years, the social vulnerability technique can be used to show historical patterns. A paper published in the National Academy of Sciences entitled 'Temporal and spatial changes in social vulnerability to natural hazards' (Cutter & Finch 2008) illustrates this conception of temporality by showing a chronological succession of maps that are based on the mix of census measures mapped through ten year intervals in the United States from 1960 to the present, shown in Figure 6.1.

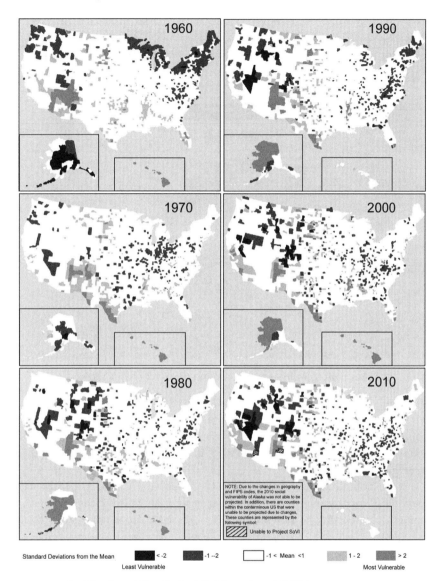

FIGURE 6.1 Social vulnerability 1960–2010 based on SOVI™.

Based on this exercise it is concluded that components consistently increasing social vulnerability for all time periods were density (urban), race/ethnicity, and socio-economic status, and that there is a dispersion of spatial patterning of social vulner-ability. The authors conclude that based on this historic assessment, future preparedness, response, recovery, and mitigation planning, may need to be more responsive to flexible approaches that nest place-specific local variability within broader federal policy guidelines and frameworks. What this 'variability in scale' means is to focus on the historical peculiarities of local U.S. counties, the 'geographic

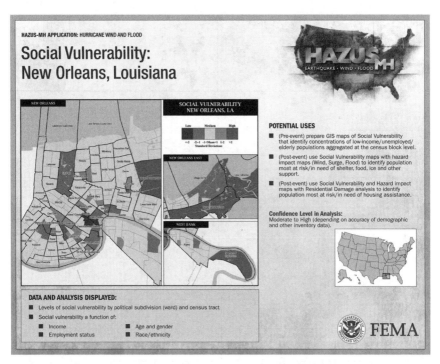

FIGURE 6.2 FEMA's HAZUS-MH application using the SOVI™ approach.

consideration' of variability, and to pay attention to the temporal scale of analysis (e.g. the number of years in the analysis), the 'temporal consideration'. Figure 6.2 shows an example of geographic specificity in the case of the City of New Orleans, simultaneously illustrating the influence of SOVI™ in FEMA's HAZUS-MH vulnerability mapping application.

The emphasis on mapping keeps this social vulnerability analysis temporally static. Figure 6.3 shows the typical temporal consideration, in this case for a number of counties (Parishes) affected by Hurricane Katrina's storm surge using SOVI™ data from 1960 through 2000. Doing this, the conclusion emerges that a remarkable lack of change in social vulnerability for the City can be seen: 'In 1960 Orleans Parish ranked in the top three percent of the most socially vulnerable counties nationally, the same percentile ranking it had in 2000' (Cutter *et al.* 2006: 11).

This differential vulnerability of counties is of course of crucial importance to sociological analysis. The authors conclude:

> What this suggests is that while New Orleans may have seen some incremental improvements in its overall social vulnerability during the past four decades, it is no better off today than it was in 1960. In fact, the dominant indicators of social vulnerability in 1960 in Orleans Parish—race and gender—are the same ones that are driving the production of social vulnerability today.
>
> *(Cutter* et al. *2006: 11)*

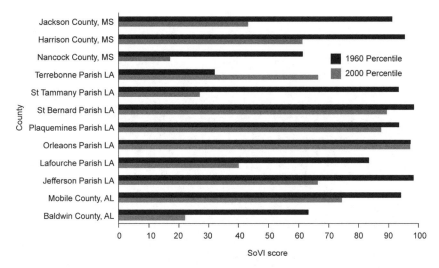

FIGURE 6.3 Comparison of change in SOVI of counties affected by Katrina's storm surge.

But does this historical social vulnerability analysis truly represent the temporal in the vulnerability equation? If vulnerability is the potential for loss, the conclusion that New Orleans was equally socially vulnerable in 1960 as in 2000 bypasses forty (or more) years of dynamic embeddedness of human decision making moments in cultural and experiential realities calibrating hazard events to stories and narratives, references of flooding to disaster, that may or may not influence how prepared this same 'social' actually is in the face of recurrent disaster risk. In the next section I will illustrate this type of vulnerability.

The Temporal Vulnerability of the New Orleans Metropolitan Area

Post-Katrina, social vulnerability analyses pointed at power discrepancies in race, class, and poverty as stated reasons why many residents stayed behind to ride out the storm (Dreier 2006; Burgess 2006; Kellner 2007). Issues related to historical referencing have received much less attention, even though they complicated the evacuation scenario. During the pre-Katrina years, it was publically known that the 'Big One' was possible, likely, and impactful. It was also known that the public was generally complacent on this issue. As a result, evacuation behavior was a major emergency management concern. This is easily illustrated by numerous efforts to have the public understand the reality and necessity of possible evacuation. For example, Jefferson Parish released a public education video in 2003 called 'The Cries of a Hurricane,' in which computer simulations were used to try to visualize to the public the meaning of evacuation messages: 'For those who have been lulled into a false sense of security by false alarms, you are gambling with your lives and those of your family' (The Cries of a Hurricane 2003). The video is dramatic, showing dramatic pictures of the City submerged, as shown in Figures 6.4a and 6.4b.

FIGURE 6.4 a&b Screenshots from the public education video 'Cries of a Hurricane.'

Another example is a public broadcast program produced by Total Community Action in 2005 called 'Preparing for the Big One.' In one of the episodes, the likely possibility of a complete, mandatory evacuation is explained by City of New Orleans Mayor, Mr. Ray Nagin:

> I want to remind everyone we live in a bowl. Everything above a category 2 hurricane has real possibility of flooding. Historically, people think that if they

go to a school site, they're safe. Our experts are now telling us that the school sites might not be strong enough, and the superdome is only a shelter of last resort. People need to have their own plan.

(Preparing for the Big One 2005)

In the video, Oliver Thomas, City Council President, mentions that there has been a significant increase in the number of hurricanes and uses the 1964 Hurricane Betsy baseline event to bring the point home:

Both my sets of families have experience. With Betsy being stuck on the roof of a house waiting for people to come rescue us. I experienced it as a child. I understand how important it is. Every family needs to have an idea of what they will do when a hurricane comes this way. ... People are inclined to do what they've always done, or what their parents or grandparents always did. And it is really hard to convince people that things have changed.

(Preparing for the Big One 2005)

The urgency of the evacuation message is revealed in the notion of change quoted above. During the past generation, Betsy had been the only major hurricane that had flooded part of the City of New Orleans. Betsy brought a 14 feet storm surge through the Industrial Canal, which breached the levee at the dominantly lower-income, minority district called the '9th Ward'. Just as with Katrina, this impact confirms the social vulnerability thesis of class impacts. However, Betsy's storm surge did not match the 27 feet surge that resulted from Hurricane Katrina in 2006 and the potential impacts which Hurricanes Camille (1969), George (1994) and Ivan (2004) *could* have had had their paths been different. What was not reflected in the cultural Betsy risk baseline, was the impact of the rapid disappearing wetlands on surge heights. Canals dug by oil and gas companies in the mid-1960s broke-up the wetlands and increased saltwater saturation from the Gulf of Mexico, while runoff, subsidence and pollution from exploration and extraction compounded the problem (Hecht 1990; Morton *et al.* 2002; Burley *et al.* 2007, Tidwell 2003). Since the 1940s, every kilometer wetland lost increased storm surge wave height by 1 meter. According to the USGS, coastal Louisiana has lost an average of 34 square miles of primarily marshlands per year from 1932 to 2000, totaling 1,900 square miles (United States Geological Survey 2003). During the 1990s, this Louisiana loss accounted for an estimated 90 percent of the coastal marsh loss in the lower 48 states. During this period of wetland loss, a number of hurricanes missed the City after 1964, which did not weaken or challenge Betsy as the only experiential impact baseline scenario. Instead, the opposite happened. Betsy alarmed the U.S. Army Corps of Engineers to problems of channelization and lead to the South Lake Pontchartrain flood protection authorization by the U.S. Congress. This new levee system was supposed to protect the area from the kind of storm that would come only once in two centuries, or with a recurrence interval of 200–300 years (General Accounting Office 1982). The main tool used to design the levee system was a hypothetical storm referred to as the 'Standard Project Hurricane'. However, not until after Katrina did it become clear that calculations for this hypothetical storm did not include the extreme storms of Betsy and Camille (which had by then already occurred), and was instead based on Weather Bureau data on hurricanes which approached the coastal area from 1900 until 1956 (Davis *et al.* 2006). Even later levee reinforcements after 1979 did not use updated Weather Bureau data (Anderson *et al.* 2007:20). What investigative committees concluded was that the Standard Project Hurricane was in fact equivalent to a hurricane with category 2 winds, category 3 storm surge, and category 4 barometric pressure; not nearly as intense as Betsy.

Betsy was also likely strengthened as baseline scenario through another pathway in the dwelling realm: Betsy was the best fitting impact scenario in a reality which brought with it cognitive dissonance as a result of high emotional costs of false evacuation alarms. Many study informants described the evacuations as 'horrendous', 'scaring the living hell out of everybody', and 'They took people out of hospitals. It was the most chaotic thing.' An older couple I interviewed called the Ivan evacuation a '20 hour nightmare,' and told me that their neighbor 'started to evacuate, but the traffic was so terrible he turned around and stayed.' In their assessment, the Ivan experience made a lot of people less inclined to evacuate the next time, which unfortunately was Katrina. In her testimony to Congress, Governor Blanco of Louisiana presented the chaos which Ivan spurred as 'not very pretty' (Babineaux Blanco 2005).

Betsy changed the hazard landscape into a dwelled experience of relatively false security, while the near misses kept Betsy socially active as the baseline reference of 'how bad things could get,' despite overwhelmingly changed environmental conditions which would overwhelm Betsy as historical analog. An example comes from one of the informants related to the emergency management division:

INFORMANT: They had George, Hurricane George. For years the theory was to take residents from low-lying areas that had never been flooded and put them in superdome and high buildings. Then the Government said these high rise buildings were not safe, and then they got the idea to evacuate the entire city.

INTERVIEWER: When did this shift happen?

INFORMANT: In the 90s. We evacuated with George. It was coming in a week or two. We did not know what to do. We did not want to go on a highway.

INTERVIEWER: George was the one before Ivan.

INFORMANT: It kind of veered off. No problem whatsoever. But at the time it was a class 5 hurricane. Theoretically, it could have come here and wiped New Orleans off the map. If you could see what Betsy did. Furniture on the street. Twenty feet water. Days and weeks with trucks. You can imagine the smell.

(Personal Communication 2004)

Describing an unnecessary evacuation—as George eventually veered off—pre-Katrina in 2004, this informant both imagined disaster yet returned to Betsy as the cognitive baseline against which to evaluate and visualize the real impact scenarios of George and Ivan, as he had experienced Betsy as a child. Despite its ill-fitting analogy to current conditions, this miscalibration grew stronger with every missed impact. Not only were those without the lived-experience of a major storm event at risk of complacency, but those who had experienced Betsy seemed to have taken this event not as a warning, but instead as evidence that the 'Big One' could be weathered as well. Particularly the elderly, who stayed at home during Betsy in the past and for whom the decision to evacuate came with substantial additional costs, used this baseline to argue against leaving the area up to Katrina. In 'Act I' of his movie 'When the Levees Broke,' Director Spike Lee interviews a number of residents who decided to stay during Hurricane Katrina. When reasons for staying put are mentioned in these interviews, one item Lee highlights is the Betsy baseline. For example, Donald Harrison, musician and resident of Broadmoor, tells the film director:

> I was here during Hurricane Katrina. Because my mother-in-law decided, as many New Orleanians did, that they could weather the storm. We had not had a major hurricane since 1965. That was Hurricane Betsy. I remember when I was 5-years-old, the water coming up then and driving through it, surviving it. So, I have always been afraid of hurricanes.
>
> *(When the Levees Broke 2006)*

Data from evacuation polls confirm this perception. For example, a survey conducted in 1995 by the Louisiana Population Data Center at Louisiana State University collected information on the experiences of respondents living in affected parishes in Southwestern Louisiana when Hurricane Andrew struck in August 1992 (Irwin & Hurlbert 1995). Counter intuitively, it was found that households with hurricane experience were less likely to evacuate (38.7 per cent) than those without hurricane experience (49.6 per cent) (Mei 2002).

In the face of this misguided dwelling-based referencing, dramatic media campaigns voicing disaster were to some extent met with disbelief, as the intention to evacuate increased only marginally over time according to polls done by the University of New Orleans Survey Research Center (Howell *et al.* 2007). Evacuation polls conducted after Hurricanes Andrew (1989), George (1998), a public hypothetical impact exercise scenario (2004), and after Hurricane Katrina (2007), suggested that before Katrina struck, evacuation warnings were often unheeded, shown in Table 6.1. After the 1998 poll, *The Times-Picayune* reported that the polls offer 'sobering statistics,' showing many residents evacuate too late (*The Times Picayune* 1998). In 2004, this situation was still severe enough for *The Times* to report that 'officials need to do a better job of educating the public about the risk posed by catastrophic storms' (*The Times Picayune* 2004). Despite the monstrous theoretical impacts George or Ivan could have had, historical experience continued to determined behavior up to that point. As Shirley Laska at the Center for Hazards

TABLE 6.1 Hurricane evacuation poll data.

Event	Jefferson	New Orleans	Both	Source
1992 Evacuated after Hurricane Andrew			15%	The Times Picayune 1998
1998 Evacuated after Hurricane George	45%	27%		Howell et al. 1998
2004 Percent likely to evacuate when recommended. Hypothetical Scenario Poll June 2004 (before Hurricane Ivan)	27% definitely 43% probably	30% definitely 40% probably		Howell et al. 2007
2007 Percent likely to evacuate when recommended.	55% definitely 22% probably	75% definitely 14% probably		Howell et al. 2007

Assessment, Response and Technology, at the University of New Orleans wrote in November 2004 as a response to Ivan:

> Recent evacuation surveys show that two thirds of non-evacuees with the means to evacuate chose not to leave because they felt safe in their homes. Other non-evacuees with means relied on cultural traditions of not leaving or were discouraged by negative experiences with past evacuations.
>
> *(Laska 2004)*

After the 2004 evacuation polling, University of New Orleans researchers concluded that people believed that their homes were safe being protected by levees or situated on high ground. This exactly is what Howell et al. reported in 2005 as a result of a study in which they compared willingness to evacuate across southern Louisiana (Howell *et al.* 2005). The most remarkable finding in this study was the low perception of risk felt by most residents in southeast Louisiana:

> In nine of the twelve parishes, 60% or more of the respondents said they felt safe in their homes if a Category 3 hurricane came near. Far fewer residents believe they would be safe in a Category 4 storm, indicating that the difference between Category 3 and Category 4 is the border at which most people believe they are at risk (Table 1). However, based on predictions about flooding from federal agencies, disaster officials in all of these parishes consider nearly everyone in the areas surveyed to be at risk in their home in a Category 3 hurricane.
>
> *(Howell et al. 2005: 3)*

Even more interesting is how the study emphasized two particular factors as to why people felt safe in their homes during a Category 3 hurricane. The first of these included beliefs about the strength or location of their house, and the second was their *past experiences*. The results suggest that having lived in south Louisiana more than thirty years, and having never lived in a home damaged by a hurricane significantly *decreased* residents' likelihood of evacuation. As the researchers wrote:

> People naturally rely on their past experiences to assess how safe they are. Many residents of southeast Louisiana have lived here all of their lives and never experienced hurricane damage to their home. In fact, an average of 40 per cent of residents in these parishes have both lived in southern Louisiana more than thirty years *and* have never had hurricane damage to their home. It is difficult for some of these longtime residents to realize that the environment is much different today, and that past experiences are probably not relevant.
>
> *(Howell* et al. *2005: 3)*

The data from Table 6.2 below illustrate these findings.

The authors note that in six of the twelve parishes, *people who have lived in a home damaged by a hurricane* are more likely to heed the official recommendation to evacuate. They are more likely to feel they are at risk. In six of the twelve parishes, *people who have lived in southern Louisiana more than thirty years* are less likely to evacuate.[1] The authors argue that long-term residents have lived through many hurricane threats and since most of those hurricanes have not directly hit southern Louisiana, these residents are less likely to feel that they should leave their homes. An average of 74 per cent of

TABLE 6.2 Percentage evacuating in last recommended evacuation by type of people.

Parish	Having Lived in a Damaged Home	Never Having Lived in a Damaged Home	Living in Southern Louisiana	Living in Southern Louisiana more than 30 Years
Assumption	46	31	59	31
Jefferson	50	52	60	47
Lafourche	40	24	34	30
Orleans	44	42	47	40
Plaquemines	58	54	67	51
St. Bernard	55	43	43	51
St. James (half)	30	19	29	20
So. St. Tammany	15	14	13	16
Terrebonne (south)	53	30	51	40
St. Charles	74	70	80	68
St. James (half)	30	33	36	31
St. John	52	39	45	41
So. Tangipahoa	20	17	26	15
Overall	**44**	**36**	**45**	**37**

Source: Adapted from Howell et al. 2005.

the residents in these six parishes have lived in southern Louisiana more than thirty years. In no parish were long-term residents significantly more likely to evacuate:

> In some ways southern Louisiana is now a victim of its past good luck; most residents have not experienced damage, and lack of prior hurricane experience promotes a feeling of safety and thus resistance to evacuation.
>
> *(Howell* et al. *2005: 5)*

What these messages address is a false sense of security that is rooted in historical experience, in dwelling. A perception which came to be fatal to anyone who did not take the early warnings seriously and stayed in the City based on their knowledge of the past. In a National Geographic video on Katrina, Dr. Walter Maestri, Jefferson Parish Emergency Management Director, summarizes how this sentiment is directly linked to experiential knowledge of historical ecology:

> They will tell you 'oh we have been here through Betsy, or Camille, or any of the other hurricanes. There have been all kinds of hurricanes which have come through here, none of them could truly devastate the area.'
>
> *(National Geographic Video 2005)*

Conclusion

Contrasting the two narratives on temporality, quite different stories emerge which both depict a vulnerability that has temporal dimensions, but arrive at different conclusions. Looking at the period from 1960 through 2000, the historical Social Vulnerability Index approach shows that vulnerability in the metropolitan area of New Orleans remained equal over time, despite the decrease in social vulnerability of surrounding counties and at national level. The narrative as such points at a social criticism of underlying reasons why the impact of the Katrina event might have been exacerbated by pre-existing socio-demographic trends, in particular the discriminatory impacts of race and gender. While of significance to disaster mitigation and prevention, this vulnerability analysis does not reflect the vulnerability that emerged as a result of the temporal situatedness of the local population relative to previous hazard events. This *temporal vulnerability* emerged as a result of floodplain dwelling and risk behaviors which were relative to inhabitation, learning, cultural and institutional memory, and the stochastic timing of previous events. Hurricane Betsy, a much smaller impact event than Katrina, became the reference baseline, while misguided levee protections and hurricane misses made the City, temporally speaking, more vulnerable each time evacuation was in vain and the actual reality of a real impact came to be transformed into visions of wasted time in chaotic traffic jams. What an analysis of this type of vulnerability shows, is that temporal vulnerability increases the more distant the experiential impact of the last hurricane is, in particular for residents who had not experienced Betsy and only relied on stories and narratives of others. While Katrina was temporally so close, those dwelling in the floodplain experienced its likelihood as somehow removed and normalized as irrelevant. What it also showed was that in the practice of emergency management, concern about the impact of this emergency complacency among the general public was real and growing. Public outreach videos and mayoral speeches were needed to rectify this situation. At the same time, narratives surrounding evacuation behavior remained focused on analyzing social-demographic indicators in the city: inequality, race, and transportation logistics. The growing impact of the temporal distance to the last, (barely) comparable event, Hurricane Betsy, or the length of time a resident had lived in the area, did not translate into emic analyses of vulnerability.

In an effort to account for the proposed temporal vulnerability, more attention should be placed on the mutually constitutive lived-reality of dwelling in population-environment dynamics. The stochastic timing of hazard events, the not-needed evacuations, the relative distance in time to previous historical analogs, landscape levee protections providing a false sense of security, and the quality of referential memories thereof combine to influence dwelling behavior and may as such imply a dimension of vulnerability that is uniquely temporal. For floodplain dwellers, decisions, evaluations, and evacuation plans are not based on forward looking rational projections, but on backward looking referential chains of temporality connecting the timing and occurrence of past events to cultural models of the environment in the present. This co-evolution of the hazard disturbance regime and the experiences and contaminant behaviors of those dwelling inside it is inherently obscure and difficult to measure, as it is entirely dependent on local, cultural variabilities related to social time. Yet, this temporality within the dwelling perspective may produce its own form of vulnerability if not well maintained. When the quality of temporal referencing back to past events is compromised, complacency sets in, and the ability of a population to recover from disturbance is reduced as emergency preparedness is lowered and the potential for collective surprise is enhanced. This surprise, however predictable, is real, human, and anthropological. Without emic knowledge about this systemic, dwelling history, sociological knowledge about vulnerability and change remains limited.

What this case study illustrates is that the dominance of objective time can arguably be seen as one of the final frontiers of the paradigm of environmental control, which underlies the Dominant Social Paradigm. While the New Environmental Paradigm imposed a new conceptualization between culture relative to nature, one which pointed at the ecological equality and interrelationship of both, this has not changed the disciplinary foundation of separating nature and culture through the imposition of an objectified temporality. Environmental sociology as such remains stuck in an anthropocentric environmental paradigm to the extent that it envisions temporality as abstract, linear time, to be mastered by imposing the objectified gaze.

Note

1 Parishes are Assumption, Jefferson, Plaquemines, St. Charles, Terrebonne, and Tangipahoa.

References

Andersen, C.F., Battjes, J.A., Daniel, D.E., Edge, B., Espey, W., Gilbert, R.B., Jackson, T. L., Kennedy, D., Mileti, D.S., Mitchell, J.K., Nicholson, P. Pugh, A.A., Tamaro, G. & Traver, R. (2007) *The New Orleans hurricane protection system: what went wrong and why: a report by the American Society of Civil Engineers*, Hurricane Katrina External Review Panel, Reston, V.A.: American Society of Civil Engineers.

Babineaux Blanco, K. (2005) *Testimony before the U.S. house Select Committee to investigate the preparations for and response to Hurricane Katrina*, U.S. House of Representatives Select Committee to Investigate the Preparation for and Response to Hurricane Katrina, December 14.

Bankoff, G. (2004) 'Time is of the Essence: Disasters, Vulnerability, and History,'. *International Journal of Mass Emergencies and Disasters*. 22: 23–42.

Blaikie, P. Cannon, T. Davis, I, & Wisner, B. (1994) *At Risk: Natural Hazards, People's Vulnerability, and Disasters*, London: Routledge.

Biersack, A. (2008) 'Introduction: From the 'New Ecology' to the New Ecologies,' *American Anthropologist*, 101(1):5–18.

Burgess, A. (2006) 'The Shock of a Social Disaster in an Age of (Nonsocial) Risk,' *Space and Culture*, 9:74.

Burley, D. Jenkins, P., Laska, S. & Traber, D. (2007) 'Place Attachment and Environmental Change in Coastal Louisiana,' *Organization Environment*, 20: 347.

Catton, W. R., Jr., & Dunlap, R. E. (1978) 'Environmental sociology: a new paradigm,' *The American Sociologist*, 13: 41–49.

Couclelis, H. (1998) 'Aristotelian Spatial Dynamics in the Age of Geographic Information Systems,' in Egenhofer, M. J. & Golledge, R.G. (Eds.), *Spatial and Temporal Reasoning in Geographic Information Systems*, Oxford: Oxford University Press.

Cutter, S.L. (1996) 'Vulnerability to environmental hazards,' *Progress in Human Geography*, 20 (4):529–39.

Cutter, S. (2006) 'The Geography of Social Vulnerability: Race, Class, and Catastrophe,' *Understanding Katrina, Perspectives from the Social Sciences*, Social Science Research Council, Accessed June 11: http://understandingkatrina.ssrc.org/Cutter/

Cutter, S.L., Boruff, B.J. & Shirley, W.L. (2003) 'Social Vulnerability to Environmental Hazards,' *Social Science Quarterly* 84 (2): 242–61.

Cutter, S.L. & Finch, C. (2008) 'Temporal and spatial changes in social vulnerability to natural hazards,' *Proceedings of the National Academy of Sciences*, 105(7): 2301–6.

Cutter, S.L., Emrich, C.T., Mitchell, J.T., Boruff, B.J., Gall, M., Schmidtlein, M.C., Burton, C.G. and Melton, G. (2006) 'The Long Road Home: Race, Class, and Recovery from Hurricane Katrina'. *Environment: Science and Policy for Sustainable Development*, Vol. 48(2):8–20.

Davis, T., Rogers H., Shays, C., Bonilla, H., Buyer, S., Myrick, S., Thornberry, M., Granger, K., Pickering, C.W., Shuster, B., & Miller, J. (2006) *Congressional Reports: H. Rpt. 109–396 – A Failure of Initiative: Supplementary Report and Document Annex by the Select Bipartisan Committee to Investigate the Preparation for and Response to Hurricane Katrina*, Select Bipartisan Committee to Investigate the Preparation for and Response to Hurricane Katrina, February 15, Washington, D.C.: House of Representatives.

De Vries, D. H., (2007) 'Being Temporal and Vulnerability to Natural Disasters,' in Warner, K. (ed.), *Perspectives on Social Vulnerability. Studies of the University: Research, Counsel, Education, No. 6/2007*, Bonn: United Nations University Press.

——(2008) *Temporal Vulnerability: Historical Ecologies of Monitoring, Memory, and Meaning in Changing United States Floodplain Landscapes*, Chapel Hill, N.C.: University of North Carolina at Chapel Hill.

De Vries, D.H. (2011) 'Temporal vulnerability in hazardscapes: Flood memory-networks and referentiality along the North Carolina Neuse River (USA),' *Global Environmental Change*, 21(1): 154–164.

Derrida, J. (1995) 'The Time Is Out of Joint,' in Haverkamp, A. (ed.), *Deconstruction Is/in America: A New Sense of the Political*, New York: New York University Press.

Douglas, M. & Wildavsky, A. (1983) *Risk and Culture: An Essay on the Selection of Technical and Environmental Dangers*, Berkeley: University of California Press.

Dreier, P. (2006) 'Katrina and Power in America,' *Urban Affairs Review*, 41: 528.

Dunlap, R. E., Van Liere, K. D., Mertig, A. G., & Jones, R. E. (2000) 'Measuring endorsement of the New Ecological Paradigm: A revised NEP scale,' *Journal of Social Issues* 56: 425–42.

Durkheim, E. (1915) *The Elementary Forms of Religious Life*, London: Allen & Unwin.

Elias, N. (1991) *Time. An Essay*, Oxford: Blackwell.

Evans-Pritchard, E.E. (1940) *The Nuer: A Description of the Modes of Livelihood and Political Institutions of a Nilotic People*, Oxford: Clarendon Press.

Federal Emergency Management Agency (2010) *HAZUS-MH Application: Social Vulnerability: New Orleans, Louisiana*. Accessed January: http://www.fema.gov/library/view-Record.do?id=3144.

Forrest, T. (1993) 'Disaster Anniversary: A Social Reconstruction of Time,' *Sociological Inquiry*, 63(4): 444–56.

General Accounting Office (1982) *Report to the Secretary of the Army: Improved Planning Needed By the Corps of Engineers To Resolve Environmental, Technical, And Financial Issues On The Lake Pontchartrain Hurricane Protection Project*, Washington D.C.: U.S. Army Corps of Engineers.

Hazards and Vulnerability Research Institute (2010) 'Social Vulnerability Index for the United States', University of South Carolina, Accessed November 2010. http://webra.cas.sc.edu/hvri/products/sovi.aspx

Hecht, J. (1990) 'The incredible shrinking Mississippi Delta,' *New Scientist*, 14: 1–13.

Heidegger, M. (1927) *Sein und Zeit*, Halle: Max Niemeyer.

Howell, S.E., McLean, W., & Haysley, V. (1998) *Evacuation Behavior in Orleans and Jefferson Parishes: Hurricane George, New Orleans*, L.A.: University of New Orleans Survey Research Center.

Howell, S.E. & Bonner, Dean E. (2005) *Citizen Hurricane Evacuation Behavior in Southeastern Louisiana: A Twelve Parish Survey*. Released by Survey Research Center In Collaboration with the Center for Hazards Assessment, Response and Technology (CHART) and the Department of Geography. The Southeast Louisiana Hurricane Taskforce. New Orleans: University of New Orleans.

Howell, S. E., Burchard, S. & Hubbard, M. (2005) *The 2004 Quality of Life Survey in Orleans and Jefferson Parishes*, New Orleans, L.A.: University of New Orleans Survey Research Center.

Howell, S.E., Shaw, C.J. & Jencik, A. (2007) 'Keeping People': The 2007 Quality of Life Survey in Orleans and Jefferson Parishes*, New Orleans, L.A.: University of New Orleans Survey Research Center.

Hoffman, S.M. & Oliver-Smith, A. (eds.) (2002) *Catastrophe and Culture: The Anthropology of Disaster*, Santa Fe: School of American Research Press.

Ingold, T. (1993) 'The temporality of landscape,' *World Archaeology*, 25(2): 152–74.

Irwin, M.D., and J.S. Hurlbert (1995) *A Behavioral Analysis of Hurricane Preparedness and Evacuation in Southwestern Louisiana*, Louisiana Population Data Center.

Jefferson Parish (2003) *The Cries of a Hurricane*, Video, Marrero, L.A.: Jefferson Parish Department of Emergency Management.

Jackson, M. (1996) *Things as they are. New Directions in Phenomenological Anthropology*, Bloomington: Indiana University Press.

Kellner, D. (2007) 'The Katrina Hurricane Spectacle and Crisis of the Bush Presidency,' *Cultural Studies < = > Critical Methodologies*, 7: 222.

Laska, Shirley (2004) 'What if Hurricane Ivan Had Not Missed New Orleans?' *Natural Hazards Observer*, XXIX (2):5–6.

Lidskog, R. (1998) 'Society, space and environment. Towards a sociological re conceptualization of nature,' *Housing, Theory and Society*, 15(1): 19–35.

Ingold, T. (1992) 'Culture and the perception of the environment,' in D. Parkin and E. Croll (eds) *Bush Base, Forest Farm: culture, environment and development*, London: Routledge.

Ma, Ming-Qian (2000) 'The Past is No Longer Out-of-Date,' *Configurations*, 8(2): 235–44.

Mei, B. (2002) *Development of Trip Generation Models of Hurricane Evacuation.* Thesis submitted to the Graduate Faculty of the Louisiana State University and Agriculture and Mechanical College, Department of Civil and Environmental Engineering.

Morton, R. A., Buster, N. A., & Krohn, M. D. (2002) 'Subsurface controls on historical subsidence rates and associated wetland loss in Southcentral Louisiana,' *Transactions*, 52:767–78.

National Research Council (2006) *Facing Hazards and Disasters: Understanding Human Dimensions*, Division on Earth and Life Studies, Washington DC: National Academies Press.

Rappaport, R. (1968) *Pigs for the Ancestors: Ritual in the Ecology of a New Guinea People*, New Haven. C.T.: Yale University Press.

Serres, M. & Latour, B. (1995) *Conversations on Science, Culture, and Time*, Ann Arbor: University of Michigan Press.

Spinosa, C., Flores, F. & Dreyfus, H. L. (1997) *Disclosing New Worlds: Entrepreneurship, Democratic Action, and the Cultivation of Solidarity*, Cambridge, M.A.: MIT Press.

The Times-Picayune (1998) 'Evacuation reporting' *The Times-Picayune*, November 16.

The Times-Picayune (2004) 'Have Evacuation Plan, Will Travel: Survey offers insight in locals' attitudes,' *The Times-Picayune*, December 1.

Tidwell, Mike (2003) *Bayou Farewell: The Rich Life and Tragic Death of Louisiana's Cajun Coast*, New York: Vintage Books.

Total Community Action (2005) *Preparing for the Big One*, Video, New Orleans: Total Community Action.

Turner, B. L., Kasperson, R. E., Matson, P. A., McCarthy, J. J., Corell, R. W., Christensen, L., Eckley, N., Kasperson, J. X., Luers, A., Martello, M. L., Polsky, C., Pulsipher, A. & Schiller, A. (2003) 'A framework for vulnerability analysis in sustainability science,' *Proceedings of the National Academy of Sciences,* 10: 1073, June 5.

United States Geological Survey (2003) *Without Restoration, Coastal Land Loss to Continue.* Press Release. National Wetlands Research Center, Lafayette, LA.

Varela, F. J., Thompson, E. & Rosch, E. (1991) *The embodied mind: Cognitive science and human experience*, Cambridge, M.A.: MIT Press.

Wisner, B. (1993) 'Disaster vulnerability: scale, power and daily life,' *Geojournal* 30(32): 127–40.

7

PARTICIPATORY ACTION RESEARCH AND URBAN ENVIRONMENTAL JUSTICE

The Pacoima CARE Project

Carl A. Maida

Introduction

Participatory action research formed the basis of long-term ethnographic fieldwork in Pacoima, an urban community confronting toxics, such as household lead, toxic dumping, and diesel pollution, through resident coalition-building on behalf of community action to mitigate these toxic threats to their homes and neighbourhoods. Pacoima, a working class community in the northeast San Fernando Valley in the City of Los Angeles, has endured multiple crises, including deindustrialization, transnational migration, and environmental degradation, compounded by natural hazards, including the 1994 Northridge Earthquake. A largely African-American community until the mid-1990s, Pacoima is now approximately 85 per cent Latino. The trauma of the earthquake forced residents to acknowledge that their community's built and natural environments had become progressively degraded well before the earthquake. The shared experience of the disaster helped to establish a place-centered community identity among neighbours, many recently migrated into the area, as they began to reconstruct after the temblor. As neighbours set out to repair their homes and to clean up their blocks, they also extended their helping resources to people in adjacent neighbourhoods. A grassroots organization, called Pacoima Beautiful, which was initially formed to help residents clean up but then grew to promote environmental health and justice education, leadership development, and advocacy skills to residents, has an agenda of civic engagement on behalf of environmental awareness and community building. An action research approach designed to enhance the quality of life in the community, together with the cultivation of an aesthetic sensibility, informed the various projects undertaken by Pacoima Beautiful. My fieldwork focused on the tension between lay and professional knowledge among stakeholders as they set priorities and develop strategies to carry out a broad-based action research agenda on behalf of identifying toxic substances, understanding the health implications of potential toxic risks, and ameliorating those risks. The process of community-based participatory action research, together with ethnography, describes how the Pacoima-based environmental justice project followed a strategy that resulted in long-term community capacity to improve the local environment.

Public Anthropology and Community-Based Participatory Action Research

A 'public anthropology', with its mix of critical ethnographic and participatory action research approaches, can help to understand and even frame the ongoing dialogue between practitioners of professional and lay knowledge concerning quality of life in global cities. Anthropological methods for understanding situational conflict, such as the extended-case method of Max Gluckman and the Manchester School (Evens and Handelman 2006), can bring ethnographic analysis and praxis to the various debates about quality of life issues, such as housing, education, health care and the environment, currently taking place in policy arenas in the more engaged communities, worldwide. Within these arenas, experts and laypersons have begun to resolve disputes over competing claims about the definition of an issue, and for equity and greater access to common resources, or public goods. However, there are vast disparities in knowledge as a result of perspectives, both professional and lay, that the various stakeholders in these arenas bring to the table. These disparate viewpoints can result in conflicts, and more often than not, 'bottlenecks' in carrying out stakeholders' plans on behalf of change. Those sitting around the table will hold professional or lay perspectives shaped by divergent occupational techniques, habits of mind and world images. Making sense of the ensuing conflicts, as social processes emerging between and among the various stakeholders in a community, will require an institutional analysis that derives from long-term fieldwork – one that takes into consideration the multiple experiences and cross-cutting ties of the participants in the policy arena.

This was my own experience over the past decade as a co-investigator on action research grants from the U.S. Environmental Protection Agency (US EPA) on behalf of improving the environmental health of residents in Pacoima. Employing principles of community-based participatory action research, I partnered with various community stakeholders to design and evaluate action research projects on toxic dumping, pollution prevention, childhood lead poisoning, and on understanding and reducing toxic risks. As a medical anthropologist experienced in community-based research and evaluation, I led a cross-disciplinary evaluation team that worked together for over a decade, designing a participatory evaluation approach, which combines the conventions of participant-observation with the ethos of community-based participatory action research. Based upon these principles, the evaluation team provided a framework for reporting progress; developed guidelines for the report; and provided both critical readings of preliminary and final reports with suggestions for revision and editorial help to shape each report as a whole. For each project, rather than taking the lead in summarizing a community-based action research team's findings and conclusions, the intent was always to not only maintain the integrity of each team's unique approach to carrying out the overall goals of the project and its own specific objectives and course of action, but also its own unique 'voice' in explaining the study results and their meaning.

The Community

Pacoima is a low-income, working-class community located in the Northeast San Fernando Valley in the City of Los Angeles; it covers six square miles at the base of the San Gabriel Mountains. Located just north of thirty landfills, the community is surrounded by three major freeways with a high volume of diesel truck traffic, bisected by a railroad line, home to a small commuter plane airport, and is subject to emissions from numerous toxic risks. Of the 81,000 residents (the official Los Angeles Department of City Planning estimate, although the population is significantly greater, but 'undercounted' as a result of low participation rates of Pacoima residents in the federal census), 85 per cent are Latino and 7 per cent African American. Thirty-two percent of the population has less than a high school education. The median household income level in 2008 was $49,066 a year. Twenty percent of the population lives below the federal poverty level. Of the 22,000 housing units, 80 per cent are single-family homes. Approximately one-fifth of Pacoima residents live in garages, or rent rooms in single-family homes and many live in extremely over-crowded conditions. There are more than 300 industrial sites in Pacoima, many of which appear to be operating without business licenses or proper permits, or are not regulated in any way; hence there are: improper storage of chemicals, contaminated runoff, harmful emissions, and hazardous working conditions. In several areas in the community, residences are adjacent to industrial facilities.

Pacoima was established as a rail side stop for Southern Pacific Railroad passengers in 1887 (Pitt & Pitt 1997: 375). From the beginning of the twentieth century to World War II, the area remained a community of small farms, vineyards, and orchards. During and following World War II, aircraft and other assembly plants turned mostly inexpensive property into land valuable both for residential and commercial purposes. During the war, restrictions were relaxed to permit African-Americans to purchase homes in Pacoima in order to provide a workforce for the industry in the Northeast San Fernando Valley. After the war, the area became a blue-collar community of mostly single-family homes with a predominantly African-American population. Low-income black families also began moving to Pacoima in the early 1950s, with the completion of public housing projects.

Jobs were plentiful for both low-income factory workers and middle class working families; however change came during the 1980s and 1990s in southern California's economy as aerospace-related and automobile manufacturing, and consumer product light manufacturing left the Northeast San Fernando Valley. These changes had an enormous impact on local employment in Pacoima and surrounding communities. It is estimated that half of minimum wage and lower wage manufacturing and warehousing jobs moved from the area since the signing of the 1994

North American Free Trade Agreement (NAFTA), which removed most barriers to trade and investment among the United States, Canada, and Mexico. A large number of good paying jobs with benefits left the area with the closure of the General Motors assembly plant in Van Nuys, Lockheed's aircraft plant in Burbank, and the Price Pfister plumbing fixture plant in Pacoima. Lack of jobs eventually led to the displacement of African-American families from Pacoima. Because of newly available inexpensive housing, Pacoima attracted recent Latino immigrants, many of whom pooled their earnings to rent or buy a house.

Pacoima sits at the edge of the San Fernando Valley where it rises toward the San Gabriel Mountains. Pacoima, which means 'rushing waters,' was a name given to the area by the San Gabrielino Indians who helped farm the extensive mission gardens after the founding of Mission San Fernando Rey in 1771. A stream of water flows into the area from the nearby mountain canyons. True to its name, Pacoima experienced extensive flooding twice in the last century, during the Great Flood of 1891 and again in 1938 when 29 inches of rainfall swept away homes and took the lives of residents. Flooding has been controlled somewhat by an extensive flood plain managed by the Army Corps of Engineers at nearby Hansen Dam. However, inadequate storm drainage causes water to back up on many streets during light rains.

The area's natural environment, particularly the brush and grass covered foothills to the north and east, block and modify winds. They 'capture' Los Angeles basin smog and other air pollutants during most of the spring, summer and early autumn. In the late autumn and winter months the winds reverse, blowing dust, plant particulate, and manmade pollutants off of the hills and onto the neighbourhoods below. A flood basin, nearly three miles in circumference, comprises much of the area. Fall and winter winds blow across the flat terrain of mostly dirt and rocks, bringing dust and sand into residential neighbourhoods. Several large operating and abandoned open pit gravel processing/cement works proximate to the flood basin also contribute airborne particulates. The foothills are a natural barrier to residential building, however, the visual screening of the hills also makes the small valleys and gullies behind them ideal locations for landfills. Their proximity to greater Los Angeles makes these sites, immediately above Pacoima neighbourhoods, locations of choice for lower cost industrial, residential, and petrochemical waste disposal. Over the years millions of tons have been dumped. Two of the largest urban landfills in the nation were located near Pacoima as are thirty smaller dump sites. In addition, one of the City of Los Angeles' primary asphalt recycling centers is located at the edge of a residential area. Hundreds of diesel powered dump and disposal trucks thread their way twenty-four hours a day through Pacoima's neighbourhoods.

Pacoima Beautiful

Pacoima Beautiful, a community-based environmental health and justice organization, is dedicated to the creation of a healthy environmentally safe, prosperous and sustainable community. It began in 1996 and became a non-profit 501(c) 3 in

December 1999. Since its beginnings, Pacoima Beautiful has evolved from a volunteer beautification committee comprised of five individuals to an environmental justice and environmental health, community-based organization that operates through the support of a policy board consisting of residents as well as professional advisors. Pacoima Beautiful has an eleven-person staff and a budget of $700,000 for the fiscal year 2006–7 (at the inception of the project discussed in this chapter); the organization's mission is 'to empower the Pacoima community through programs that provide environmental education, advocacy and local leadership in order to foster a healthy and safe environment.' The mission is carried out through three programs. The *Community Inspectors Program* teaches residents how to identify the sources of toxics and pollution in the community, to understand the potential risks to health and to find simple solutions to reduce the risks in the community. The *Youth Environmentalists Program* engages approximately 150 local high-school youth, annually, through environmental education projects, leadership development, skills training and college readiness activities. The *Safer Homes for a Healthy Community Program* helps residents to create healthy homes for their families in order to reduce and prevent environmentally related health problems, including lead poisoning and asthma triggers, such as mold and moisture.

Beginning in 1998, Pacoima Beautiful brought together residents, university environmental health scientists, environmental and other organizations, university service-learning classes, and representatives from governmental agencies to address environmental issues in the community. Being able to partner with experts in various fields served to expand the capacity of Pacoima Beautiful and build a valuable knowledge bank. As environmental health and environmental justice became a more prominent part of the work of Pacoima Beautiful it was necessary to enlist the support of those who knew how to address the issues. Pacoima has long suffered from environmental neglect that can likely be blamed for the high rates of environmental health risks in the community and the numerous sources of pollution throughout the area. In addition to freeways, the airport, and a railway line, the more than 300 industrial sites (large and small point sources) have left contaminants behind or continue to pollute the air, soil and water. Pacoima is home to five US EPA Comprehensive Environmental Response, Compensation, and Liability Act (CERCLA) toxic release sites (commonly known as Superfund sites), two of which are currently being remediated. Community concerns focus on the cumulative impacts from contaminants, such as lead in paint and in the soil, emissions from freeways, commuter planes, diesel from trucks and equipment, older 'gross emitting' cars, landfills, and the widespread use of toxic chemicals throughout the community.

Teaming scientists with community residents and youth, the organization created a network that has gathered data in order to understand the effects of environmental hazards on health. The data collection has been coupled with surveys of more than 2,000 residents and merchants. The approach is community-based and community-driven information gathering, following principles of community-based participatory action research (Field Museum 2006). Much like Dutch 'science shops', Pacoima Beautiful's research agenda on environmental quality of life is based upon concerns posed by community residents and carried out with support from local universities (Sclove 1995, 1996). The organization has sought funding, with the assistance of university scientists, from foundations and public agencies often with their own agendas. For example, Pacoima secured a grant from the US EPA through the CARE (Community Action for a Renewed Environment) program (Hansell, Hollander, DeWitt 2009). While the EPA had expectations, at no time did Pacoima Beautiful deviate from its own agenda. This was because from its beginning, the organization engaged in careful planning and set out a 'roadmap' for itself so that, as funding and project opportunities came about, the organization was ready to take advantage of them. Strategic planning was an important part of the work of Pacoima Beautiful dating back to its beginning in 1996. The prospect of partnerships with local non-profit organizations, including universities, and patronage from public agencies and foundations has inspired dialogues around planning Pacoima Beautiful's future as a 'sustainable' organization in a transmigrant community during its early years—a time when the American environmental movement was facing a national debate on issues of population and immigration (Zuckerman 1999).

In 1998, US EPA Environmental Justice Office provided a grant to Pacoima Beautiful in partnership with university-based researchers, which focused on increasing residents' awareness of the consequences of toxic dumping within their community and also moved Pacoima Beautiful's staff members and volunteers toward understanding their role in the environmental justice movement (Faber 1998, Gottlieb 2001, Bullard et al. 2007). Specifically the grant was used to expand the partners' efforts in monitoring pollution, to educate residents through a newsletter distributed through neighbourhood schools, and to focus on the widespread illegal dumping practices of local residents, businesses, and others who view Pacoima as a dumping ground. In 2003, Pacoima Beautiful and its partners hosted an 'Environmental Health Roundtable' for forty community stakeholders, including non-profit and public health agencies, legal services, and university scientists, to share what was learned about environmental health issues. A primary focus of the roundtable was lead and lead poisoning. The roundtable produced a partnership to address lead issues in Pacoima. The first activity of the partnership was to apply for and eventually receive a US EPA Collaborative Problem Solving Grant, which focused on efforts to increase lead blood screening rates of children aged six and under. The project sought to integrate lead hazard control with other community efforts and also to clearly identify lead hazards in high-risk neighbourhoods and present workable solutions to reduce the lead burden. This would be done by analyzing and synthesizing current data, and then convening a stakeholder forum regarding lead poisoning and community development. The partners not only reached consensus on the nature of the problems to be addressed, but took on specific tasks toward the solution of these problems, albeit remaining aligned with their respective organizational missions. Pacoima Beautiful and its partners would participate in efforts to effectively train the Los Angeles City Building and Safety Department to enforce lead-safe work repair practices to pre-1978 housing and to educate contractors, workers, landlords and homeowners in lead-safe work practices, and work with city government to develop a housing registry for lead free homes and apartments. The partnership remained together through a US EPA CARE Program Level 1 grant to identify toxics in the community, to address specific issues, such as the monitoring of all diesel sources in the community, and to extend the childhood lead poisoning prevention and abatement work into other communities. The partnership—of public and non-profit organizations, and of professional experts and lay advocates—thus expanded its work beyond lead to include other toxic risks in the community, such as facilities listed in the US EPA Toxic Release Inventory and was poised to identify potential toxic sites through site screenings in order to develop an understanding of the impact of toxics on the health of Pacoima residents.

The Pacoima CARE Project

The work undertaken through the initial CARE grant arose out of the need by Pacoima Beautiful and its partners to identify sources of toxic substances and their health risks in the community and prioritize remediation of the sources. Historically, few research projects have been conducted in Pacoima, with even fewer involving environmental conditions. This changed as partnerships were formed and resources from the US EPA and other federal agencies were made available to Pacoima. The grant provided an opportunity to organize ideas, concepts, reports and community knowledge into a cohesive set of risks, which could then be prioritized for future action. The goals were set in order to identify all sources of toxic substances in Pacoima that may have negative health or environmental impacts; work with community stakeholders, namely residents, community-based organizations, businesses, and elected officials, to understand the health implications of potential sources of risks; assist stakeholders in setting priorities for amelioration of those risks; and create self-sustaining community-based partnerships that will continue to reduce risks and improve the local environment. Since 1996, Pacoima Beautiful has successfully served as a resident-driven, community-based center for innovative ideas, data, statistics and expertise focused on environmental issues and hazards affecting the residents of Pacoima. As an integral part of the community, the organization has taken the time to build and nurture collaborative partnerships and consensus-building relationships with residents and over 150 organizations, agencies and institutions, inside and outside the community. These relationships served as the basis for the broad-based stakeholders group working together on the CARE project. The stakeholder groups in the project consisted of residents and business owners who attended workshops facilitated by Pacoima Beautiful staff, and included local high school students participating in learning workshops on toxics; community organizations, regulatory agencies and elected officials or their representatives. The involvement of residents, including youth, and of business owners was therefore key in the identification of specific sources of toxics. However, to catalyze diverse stakeholder constituencies within Pacoima and to motivate their ongoing involvement with the CARE project, Pacoima Beautiful would need to plan and stage events specifically targeted to their interests and needs.

Since 2002, high school students have been involved in three month-long 'Environmental Justice Institutes' through which they researched specific environmental issues and concerns, and developed community-wide solutions. Through the CARE project, students were invited to see their community in a new light by engaging in participatory action research, including testing and documenting storm water contamination; exploring and documenting toxic sites; and identifying potential toxic risks and their health impacts. In one project, students tested storm and wastewater coming from businesses in an area of Pacoima dominated by auto dismantlers and similar uses. Exceedingly high levels of fecal coliform bacteria were found in the water, and further investigation was conducted on the water, looking specifically for heavy metals as well as other contaminants. Bilingual and monolingual parents from three schools participated in sixty interactive community environmental education and leadership development workshops entitled *Familias, Comunidad y Salud* ('Families, Community and Health'). These workshops provided parents with information on how to identify and articulate personal and specific environmental risks and concerns, and how to build mutual trust in order to reach consensus in setting priorities for future action. Residents also participated in five *Recorridos de la Comunidad* ('Tours of Our Community'). Participants were encouraged to 'see again, for the first time' those risks that potentially endanger the health of their family, neighbourhood, and community. Prior to the tours, residents participated in an assessment process, through which they defined the environmental strengths and weaknesses in their homes and community. The residents then participated in the tour to identify specific risks, photograph and document specific problem locations, and reflect on their experience. Residents came away from the tours with a new understanding of their roles as change agents.

Pacoima Beautiful then brought together more than 300 community residents, partners, and stakeholders to review data and information on toxic sources that the organization had gathered over a ten-year period. An intern helped to collate much of this information into a usable format to which new information could be added as it was collected. Pacoima Beautiful developed and implemented curriculum, which was shared with community residents to inform them about what was known about the various toxic sources in the community and to solicit their input and concerns. Participating residents came from the programs conducted at local parent centers at three elementary schools where Pacoima Beautiful has a long history of reaching out to parents of school-aged children. The three schools were selected for specific outreach because of their location in what the partners in the project refer to as the 'Pacoima Toxic Belt'. The toxic belt is a swatch down the middle of the community, which is densely populated with multiple families living in single-family residences; residences adjacent to industries, freeways, the railroad, and Whiteman Airport; the toxic belt is outlined by two heavy diesel truck traffic corridors. Altogether, sixty-four resident meetings and workshops were held that involved more than 300 youth and adult residents. As a result of these consensus-building meetings and workshops in the community, Pacoima Beautiful generated a list of toxic risks. Students in an urban studies class at a local public university and a group of students conducting independent research then set out to document and map the approximately 300 businesses in Pacoima. Of these, 200 were determined to be potential problem sites because many are unregulated and/or lack any city permits. In order to address the sites in a systematic way, US EPA helped the partners identify a *pro bono* attorney to create a list of all the permits and regulations that were required for business operation. Of the 200 sites, interns studying environmental and occupational health sciences at the public university conducted a site analysis on ten of these sites; the US EPA Brownfield Division conducted a Phase I site investigation on ten to twenty-five of the sites; and the California Department of Toxic Substances Control conducted a site analysis on five sites. Pacoima Beautiful then gathered together an experienced group of stakeholders and experts to share what was learned from various sources, including residents, on toxic sources and health risks in Pacoima. Ten 'partners meetings' were held; participants included representatives from US EPA and the California EPA, other regulatory agencies and partnering community organizations to collect, discuss and collate data and information on toxic risks in the community. There were also two joint meetings between stakeholders and experts. The first meeting brought together residents, businesses, and staff from regulatory agencies, as well as elected officials and their representatives, to discuss and identify toxic risks in the community. The second meeting was organized with the assistance of US EPA staff, and included partners, stakeholders, and two residents to identify and rank the risks. Another meeting was held at which thirty residents gathered together with Pacoima Beautiful staff members to learn what had transpired at the previous meetings and to discuss the risk ranking and set community priorities. From the various group meetings with parents at the schools, meetings with partners and, ultimately a meeting held with a larger stakeholder group, a consensus-building process was put into place, which led to the identification of eighteen risk categories in Pacoima. There was much overlap in the process of identifying the risks. Individual stakeholders, university faculty members, elected officials and their representatives, staff from regulatory agencies, community-based organizations and residents, including students, were engaged and involved in identifying, documenting and gaining an understanding of the various risks. Finally, under the guidance and skill of an EPA scientist, risk categories were consolidated and ranked (See Table 7.1), based upon the EPA's guidance documents and tools for community-based cumulative risk assessments (US EPA 2007; Zartarian and Shultz 2009).

Of these eighteen risks, residents consistently selected five as high priorities for action. The first were industries (small-point and large); of particular concern to residents is the potential future toxic damage from two industrial sites: Price Pfister, a manufacturer of plumbing fixtures, and Holchem/Chase Chemical Company; both were being remediated at the time of the project. Also of concern to the residents is how to clean up the small point sources, namely auto dismantlers and wood chip type factories. A second priority included diesel emissions from community and freeway truck and bus traffic, and diesel equipment. A third priority focused on bulky items and hazardous waste. A fourth priority was related to indoor hazards, including lead, mold, pesticides, and cleaning solutions. A fifth priority

TABLE 7.1 Categorizing and prioritising risks in Pacoima.

High	Medium-High	Medium	Medium-Low	Low
Diesel	Super emitters	Indoor – Mold	Waste – Hazardous Waste	Radon
Whiteman Airport	Lead	Indoor – Cleaners	Soil – Underground Storage Tanks & Brownfields	Large Point Industrial Sources (Other Than Landfills)
Small-Point Sources	Secondhand Smoke	Storm Water	Indoor Environment – Vapor Intrusion	Soil – Sumps
Highway & Major Arterials		Waste – Bulky Items Landfills		

focused on the Whiteman Airport and the multi-faceted problems associated with it. Of these five prioritized risks, residents, partners and experts agreed upon three as being high priorities, namely industrial facilities/stationary air pollution sources, specifically smaller point sources, such as auto dismantlers; diesel from trucks, buses and equipment; and air transportation hazards, namely, Whiteman Airport, with specific concerns about air toxics emissions including lead, and safety and land uses.

This consensus-building process resulted in a community-based partnership of experts committed to sustain risk reduction efforts, and brought about an expert panel consisting of university- and agency-based scientists from the US EPA, California EPA, and Los Angeles Environmental Affairs Department, who agreed to continue to provide resources and share their expertise. At the lay level, Pacoima Beautiful helped residents build a knowledge base to raise awareness of their surroundings and the environment. The organization served as a bridge between the primarily Spanish-speaking residents, both to communicate lessons learned and resources available to them, and to facilitate ongoing dialogues and decision-making with the partners. Pacoima Beautiful thus served as a catalyst, allowing the community's 'voice' to be heard and placed at the forefront of socio-environmental change.

The CARE I grant provided a clear opportunity for Pacoima Beautiful and its partners to organize ideas, concepts, reports, and community knowledge into a cohesive set of risks, which could then be prioritized for future action. The grant also provided opportunities for Pacoima residents to work with scientists and administrators from the US EPA to monitor local environmental issues and take action on their behalf. For example, the partners and the larger group of community stakeholders and residents were able to address the issue of toxic sources and to consolidate the lessons learned into a set of 18 risks. It was the first time that such an effort had been undertaken in Pacoima. Through the extensive research provided by US EPA scientists, there are now concrete and specific data to justify the need to address the toxic issues in Pacoima. Moreover, during the course of the project, opportunities presented themselves, which permitted the mobilization of federal resources to address identified risks. For example, of the approximately 300 businesses identified in Pacoima, 200 were noted to be potential problem sites. Focusing specifically in the area of the 'toxic belt' and more specifically on the area in which a large number of auto dismantlers are located, the partners contacted the US EPA Brownfield Division, whose staff met with the partners on two occasions to determine which businesses should be investigated as the most problematic sites. Within the national arena, the US EPA's annual training workshop—a 'crossroads event' that convenes representatives from the various CARE projects—served as a forum for grantees, such as Pacoima Beautiful, to discuss common concerns and strategies for the reduction of high-risk toxics and pollutants, and to disseminate 'best practices' across the emerging network of federally supported environmental justice organizations engaged in action research.

In the end, the partnership stayed together through a CARE II grant, 'Reducing Toxic Risks in Pacoima, California,' to specifically address two of the priority concerns identified in the first grant: small-point sources in a specific targeted area of Pacoima and diesel emissions from trucks throughout the community. The partners broadened their base to include more residents and businesses, community and government partners, technical experts and regulatory agencies, to identify and implement risk reduction strategies, and set about to educate and mobilize local residents and businesses to voluntarily reduce toxic risks. They also developed indicators to track progress, measure results, and communicate lessons learned to the Pacoima community as well as other communities facing similar circumstances.

Bridging Expert and Lay Knowledge in Community-Based Participatory Action Research

The case example of Pacoima Beautiful's collaborative efforts on behalf of reducing toxic exposures in the community illustrates how local-level coalitions have allied business, government, non-profits and universities to implement planned change. Each aspect of the initiative was publicly discussed in meetings of Pacoima Beautiful's leadership and community advisory board, and among neighbourhood residents. Outside experts who participated in these environmental health initiatives have had to be sensitive to the autonomy and leadership issues involved in the community-based and resident-driven model embraced by Pacoima Beautiful.

In the above case, early identification of the issue by a community-based organization helped to engage others to address the issue and sustain the effort and make it grow. Pacoima Beautiful identified and worked closely with all stakeholders to reach consensus on the three project goals, which allowed them to collaborate on an effective strategy that integrated the unique contributions that were available from the numerous partner organizations. Following this was the need to identify appropriate partners. Each of the partners has different constituencies so that the work done to come up with an agenda for change was spread in many different venues throughout the community. In addition, the partners had the benefit of university-based evaluators who continued to evaluate the project during the process of planning and implementation.

Once identified, considerable attention was given to the clarification of each partner's role. Pacoima Beautiful took it upon itself to communicate actively and clearly with the partners at the outset of the project, in order to eliminate any potential misunderstandings with respect to the project goals and other data that each partner might want to collect during the project to satisfy their specific needs. During these early communications, the organization's staff maintained its role as the key decision-makers with regard to project scope and direction. Throughout there was a need for frequent clarification of the issue and potential resolutions. Pacoima Beautiful served as the clearinghouse for information and data and would then pass it on to the partners. In that capacity, the organization could keep the partners informed on the current status of their main objectives as the partners worked to attain their part in the project goals.

As a 'systems integration' approach, residents began to work side-by-side with professionals, including university-based scientists and their students, and paraprofessionals linked through collaborative activities in the various environmental justice projects. Within this bridging network (Briggs 2003), all parties worked together towards common programmatic goals within the existing socio-environmental system and local political structure, with the overarching goal of bringing about change from within the system. Bridges were thereby created between scientists and community residents through the sharing of lay and professional knowledge and experience, which may lead to mutual trust built upon a common concern for the community's well-being (Viswanathan et al. 2004). Such collaborative planning of research design and methodology discloses unexplored strategies and solutions to existing problems and allows the residents to develop sensitivities towards the early detection of problems. The community-based research process that emerged from this style of foresight and planning involved the collaboration of lay community members and experts to produce new knowledge for social change (Murphy, Scammell and Sclove 1997). This practice carries on the work of community development researchers so influential in creating the philosophical underpinnings for America's urban agenda since the late 1960s (Warren 1971, Bennis, Benne and Chin 1985). As 'action researchers', they valued the involvement of community residents in all aspects of need and data analysis so that when action strategies are developed, the people most affected by their consequences will have a substantial investment in the action (Stringer 2007). Their approach to urban transformation also promises some assurance that community residents will continue to be participants over the long term.

Moreover, the style of community-based participatory action research used in the CARE project—one that employs accurate risk assessment techniques to detect and monitor biological and chemical exposures, and also seeks to understand the social environment in which these exposures occur—clearly fits within the 'New Ecological Paradigm', as developed by environmental sociologists to acknowledge the 'ecosystem dependence of human societies' (Dunlap and Marshall 2007). Within ecological anthropology, there is a related trend, namely toward the integration of human and environmental (biophysical) factors, and an acknowledgement of the role of human agency and the difference it makes in the way members of social groups share concerns and make decisions about cumulative impacts (Moran 2007). In the CARE project, following an action research approach first introduced by social psychologist Kurt Lewin (1946), professionals and community residents collaborated from the beginning to inform the specific objectives set forth in the proposal, to reach consensus on data collection methods, and to work together on planning the ongoing project and its sustainability. Well before the current integrative turn in ecological anthropology and environmental sociology, Lewin's emphasis on dynamic systems in the study of human behavior moved the social sciences closer to the view that 'a wider and wider realm of determinants must be treated as part of a single, interdependent field,' in Dorwin Cartwright's words (1951: xii). Further, Lewin saw the need to move beyond disciplinary boundaries in order to study social phenomena through a coherent system of constructs. Kurt Lewin's legacy, including the need for a broad interdisciplinary framework toward understanding social phenomena, for ongoing dialogue within small groups, and for experiential learning and action research, continues to influence researchers and practitioners today. This would include those of us who, like Lewin, view social phenomena as complex, the environment as a key to understanding behavior, and who share his concern for the integration of theory and practice in our work and in our lives.

Acknowledgements

This study was funded by a grant from the U.S. Environmental Protection Agency, Cooperative Agreement Program – Agreement No: RE-9891670-0 – Community Partnership: Understanding Toxic Risks. I would like to thank Karen Henry, Matthew Lakin, Marva King, Hank Topper, Michael Bandrowski, and Richard Grow, U.S. Environmental Protection Agency; Marlene Grossman, Elvia Hernandez, Nury Martinez, Blanca Nuñez, Patricia Ochoa, Fernando Rejón, and Liseth Romero-Martinez, Pacoima Beautiful; and the following CARE Level 1 grant partners: Joseph Lyou, California Environmental Rights Alliance; Joni Novosel, Valley Care Community Consortium; Tim Dagodag, Linda Fidell, and John Schillinger, California State University, Northridge; Deborah Davenport and Olga Vigdorchik, Los Angeles County Department of Public Health; Theresa Nitescu and Deborah Rosen, Northeast Valley Health Corporation; Josh Stehlik, Neighborhood Legal Services of Los Angeles County; Brian Condon, Arnold and Porter; Linda Kite, Healthy Homes Collaborative; Gretchen Hardison and Christopher Patton, Los Angeles Environmental Affairs Department; Sarayeh Amir and Gabriel Farkas, California Department of Toxic Substances Control; Dale Shimp, California Air Resources Board; Jonathon Bishop, Stephen Caine, Fran Diamond, California Regional Water Quality Control Board. I would also like to acknowledge the ongoing support and critical judgment of Sam Beck, who continues to inspire my work in public anthropology.

References

Bennis, W. G., Benne, K. and Chin, R. (1985) *The Planning of Change*, 4th edn, New York: Holt, Rinehart and Winston.

Briggs, X. de S. (2003) *Bridging Networks, Social Capital, and Racial Segregation in America.* Kennedy School of Government Faculty Research Working Paper Series RWP02–011, Cambridge, MA: John F. Kennedy School of Government, Harvard University.

Bullard R. D., Mohai, P., Saha, R. and Wright. B. (2007) *Toxic Wastes and Race at Twenty: 1987–2007 – Grassroots Struggles to Dismantle Environmental Racism in the United States,* Washington, DC: National Council of Churches of Christ.

Cartwright, D. (1951) 'Foreword', *Field Theory in Social Science.* New York: Harper & Row.

Dunlap, R.E. and Marshall, B.K. (2007) 'Environmental Sociology', 329–40; in C.D. Bryant and D.L. Peck (eds.) (2007) *21st Century Sociology: A Reference Handbook, Vol 2.*, Thousand Oaks, CA: Sage.

Evans, T.M.S. and Handelman, D. (2006) *The Manchester School: Practice and Ethnographic Praxis in Anthropology*, New York: Berghahn Books.

Faber, D. (ed.) (1998) *The Struggle for Ecological Democracy: Environmental Justice Movements in the United States*, New York: Guilford Press.

Field Museum (2006) *Collaborative Research: A Practical Introduction to Participatory Action Research (PAR) for Communities and Scholars*, Chicago: Center for Cultural Understanding and Change, The Field Museum.

Gottlieb, R. (2001) *Environmentalism Unbound: Exploring New Pathways for Change*, Cambridge, MA: MIT Press.

Hansell, Jr., W.H., Hollander, E. and DeWitt, J. (2009) *Putting Community First: A Promising Approach to Federal Collaboration for Environmental Improvement, An Evaluation of the Community Action for a Renewed Environment (CARE) Demonstration Program*, Washington, DC: National Academy of Public Administration.

Lewin, K. (1946) 'Action Research and Minority Problems', *Journal of Social Issues* 2: 34–46.

Moran, E.F. (2007) 'The Human-Environment Nexus: Progress in the Past Decade in the Integrated Analysis of Human and Biophysical Factors', 231–42; in A. Hornberg and C. Crumley, (eds.) (2007) *The World System and the Earth System; Global Socioenvironmental Change and Sustainability Since the Neolithic*, Walnut Creek, CA: Left Coast Press.

Murphy, E., Scammell, M. and Sclove, R. (1997) *Doing Community-based Research: A Reader*, Amherst, MA: Loka Institute.

Pitt, L. and Pitt, D. (1997) *Los Angeles A to Z: An Encyclopaedia of City and County*, Berkeley: University of California Press.

Sclove, R. E. (1995) 'Putting Science to Work in Communities', *The Chronicle of Higher Education* 41, no. 29 (31 March): B1–B3.

——(1996) 'Town Meetings on Technology', *Technology Review* 99: 24–31.

Stringer, E. T. (2007) *Action Research*, 3rd edn, Thousand Oaks, CA: Sage.

United States Environmental Protection Agency (2007) *Proceedings of the U.S. EPA Workshop on Research Needs for Community-Based Risk Assessment*, Research Triangle Park, NC: National Center for Environmental Research.

Viswanathan M., Ammerman A., Eng E., Gartlehner G., Lohr K.N., Griffith D., Rhodes S., Samuel-Hodge C., Maty S., Lux, L., Webb L., Sutton S.F., Swinson T., Jackman A. and Whitener L. (2004) *Community-Based Participatory Research: Assessing the Evidence*, Evidence Report/Technology Assessment No. 99 (Prepared by RTI–University of North Carolina Evidence-based Practice Center under Contract No. 290–02–0016), AHRQ Publication 04-E022–2, Rockville, MD: Agency for Healthcare Research and Quality.

Warren, R. L. (1971) 'The Sociology of Knowledge and the Problems of the Inner Cities', *Social Science Quarterly* 52: 468–85.

Zartarian, V.G. and Schultz, B.D. (2009) 'The EPA's Human Exposure Research Program for Assessing Cumulative Risk in Communities', *Journal of Exposure Science and Environmental Epidemiology* (15 April 2009) http://www.nature.com/jes/journal/vaop/ncurrent/full/jes200920a.html
Zuckerman, B. (1999) 'The Sierra Club Immigration Debate: National Implications', *Population and Environment* 20: 401–12.

Part III
Anthropologists and the Real World

8

ANTHROPOLOGY, CLIMATE CHANGE AND COASTAL PLANNING

Bob Pokrant and Laura Stocker

This chapter examines the contribution of anthropology to climate change research and policy with a focus on coastal adaptation. We begin with a discussion of the recent history of climate change response, its construction as a largely scientific enterprise, and the challenge climate change (hereafter CC) presents for anthropology. We suggest that anthropology and science have been moving towards embracing a wider range of knowledge types in order to solve what are referred to as 'wicked problems' such as CC. We go on to argue that little 'official' anthropological work has focused on contemporary anthropogenic CC debates and concerns at a global level. However, this is now being redressed, especially through interdisciplinary and transdisciplinary studies involving anthropologists. We show that present-day Environmental Anthropology and cognate areas are actively engaged in both academic and policy-oriented research relevant to climate change and climate variability. Finally we focus on the contribution of anthropology to coastal adaptation responses in coastal Western Australia and Bangladesh, presenting several case examples. We conclude that anthropology has an important role in 'post-normal science' and transdisciplinary approaches aimed at assisting coastal populations to adapt to the impacts of CC.

The Construction and Challenge of Climate Change

Until recently, academic and policy discussion of CC was dominated by natural scientists who sought to explain the growth of greenhouse gas emissions (GHGs) in the atmosphere and provide ways of mitigating such emissions through their removal at source or through carbon sequestration. Mitigation research focused on technical and engineering solutions to reducing GHGs with limited input from anthropologists, other humanities researchers and most of the human population. Mitigation policy continues to be made by an elite group of global decision makers and their scientific advisors (the climatocracy) in venues remote from the life worlds of most people (Jasanoff 2010). In contrast, adaptation research and policy, that aspect of CC dealing with the accommodation to the unavoidable consequences of CC, has played a less important role in global negotiations and delegated to the sphere of the quotidian, the local, and the place-based, watched over by national governments. At present national governments and local communities are implementing adaptation programs without sufficiently available, accessible and quality information to provide precise predictions about the character, magnitude and intensity of the spatial and temporal impacts of climate change (Biesbroek et al. 2009; Mearns et al. 2009). This presents anthropologists with a challenge and an opportunity. The challenge is that CC is ' ... the quintessential multiscalar environmental problem' (Lemos and Agrawal 2006), which is no respecter of geographic, ecological, national, ethnic, and psychological boundaries. It has taken on the shape of an unseen and impersonal process, which can strike at random, and potentially destabilize people's experiences and understandings of the world. Its impacts are said to be felt everywhere, but in what precise ways and with what specific impacts and consequences are not fully understood or known. The scientific modeling of climate change reflects and perpetuates this detachment of climate from daily life. This has prompted Jasanoff to ask: 'How, at the levels of community, polity, space and time, will scientists' impersonal knowledge of the climate be synchronized with the mundane rhythms of lived lives and the specificities of human experience?' (Jasanoff 2010: 238). We argue that CC provides anthropologists with an opportunity to play an important role singly and in collaboration with others in integrating this impersonal knowledge of climate into the life-worlds of ordinary people and equip communities with skills, practices, guides and other enabling mechanisms to deal with the impacts of CC-induced hazards.

Anthropology and Post-Normal Science

CC is a field of inquiry in which anthropologists can enhance their existing con-tribution to CC research and policy by moving towards a more collaborative, parti-cipatory and trans-disciplinary dialogue at the interface between science, policy and civil society. Mike Hulme, founding director of the UK-based Tyndall Centre for Climate Change Research, has argued for a much greater role for Humanities and Social Science disciplines in climate change research and policy. He states:

> If climate change is the biggest issue facing the future of human civilization, to use the rhetoric, then surely a body [IPCC] charged to assess what humans know about climate change should actually be assessing all forms of knowledge.
>
> *(Blackman 2009)*

Hulme echoes early critics of traditional approaches to the relationship between science, public policy and civil society such as Beck (1992) who proposed a model of reflexive modernization in which experts and citizens are linked together in demo-cratic networks as co-producers of knowledge and action in the world. The idea of co-production of knowledge is central to post-normal science, which seeks to extend and modify the methodology of established scientific practice to deal with situations of high risk and uncertainty where action needs to be taken quickly (Funtowicz and Ravetz 1993, 1994; Ravetz 2004; Modvar and Gallopin 2005). According to proponents of post-normal science, where there is high uncertainty regarding explanations offered for particular problems, science is to extend its traditional methods of investigation to include (i) 'extended peer community', that is, to include a wider range of 'stakeholders' in the deliberative process, and (ii) 'extended facts', extending what constitutes relevant scientific facts to include community views, narrative accounts, personal observations and the like. Science becomes one set of representations of the real rather than the mirror to reality (Jasanoff 2010). Post-normal science aims towards 'socially robust knowledge' (Maasen and Lieven 2006), which emphasizes civic science and expertise and deliberative governance as against ' ... the scientisation of environmental governance ... ' (Bäckstrand 2004: 711).

Contemporary 'Official' Anthropological Studies of Climate Change

Anthropology has long emphasized knowledge diversity and participatory approaches in the study of human–non-human relations. However, it is only recently that it has given greater attention to contemporary CC issues. Finan (2007) has asked: Is 'Official' Anthropology ready for climate change? He attributes what he considers a lack of anthropological engagement with CC to an 'Official Anthropology' dominated by an anti-scientific and anti-applied research approach to the study of human society. He calls for anthropologists to re-commit to what they do best:

> ... solid fieldwork, a holistic perspective and the ability to contribute to a problem-solving challenge grounded in a complex reality of human-environmental interaction.
>
> *(Finan 2007: 11)*

In contrast, Lahsen (2007b) argues that anthropology has focused too much on the local and needs to up-scale its theoretical and methodological interest to issues of global governance and to take a more interdisciplinary approach. Nelson (2007), an anthropologist with the UK Tyndall Centre for Climate Change Research, remarks that anthropology has much to contribute to the study of CC, especially through local level research, a greater awareness of the relationship between global environmental change and local consequences, and a more active public role on anthropology's contribution to public debate on CC and its impacts. Milton (2008) wants more research on local responses to CC, on CC discourses, and for anthropologists to speak up publicly about what they can contribute to understanding and resolving environmental challenges society faces. Townsend calls for a public anthropology on the social and cultural construction of the science of climatology and climate policy (Townsend 2004). Batterbury, a human geographer, is surprised that anthropologists have not played a major role in research and policy debates on CC given the discipline's historic engagement with human-nature interactions (Batterbury 2008). Like Lahsen, he sees value in embracing other disciplines, but echoes Finan in his criticism of anthropology's preoccupation with discourse analysis. He calls for a greater engagement with international policy and research, more research on local understandings and practices regarding weather and climate and their relationship to scientific knowledge, and a more critically realist approach to doing research that recognizes the material reality of a world external to the senses and which possesses its own causal efficacy accessible to humans via particular knowledge systems.

There is some evidence to support claims that anthropology is a late starter in the study of CC. Two recent volumes on Environmental Anthropology (Haenn and Wilk 2006; Dove and Carpenter 2008) contain no dedicated discussion of climate change, apart from brief references in a few chapters. Our examination of the titles of all articles published between 1988 and 2007 in three flagship anthropological journals – *American Anthropologist, American Ethnologist* and *Current Anthropology* – revealed not a single article focusing on contemporary climate change, although several were on environmental issues with a climate reference.

However, since 2008 *Current Anthropology* and the *American Anthropologist* have included more climate change-focused articles (Crate 2008; Nelson, West and Finan 2009) and Kelman and West (2009) reviewed the impact of CC on small island states in Ecological and Environmental Anthropology. Recently published and forthcoming publications include Crate and Nuttall's (2009) *Anthropology and Climate Change*, Mearns et al. (2009) on the social dimensions of climate change, Rudiak-Gould's 2009 study of climate change in the Marshall Islands and McDowell and Morrell (2010) on displacement and climate change. Social and cultural anthropology's sister disciplines, archaeology and physical anthropology, have contributed greatly to understanding how pre-historical and historical societies used and transformed their natural environments and how they affected and were affected by local and regional climate variability (Rosen 2007; Fagan 2008).

Since 2000 there has been a growth in literature on how winds, waves, seasons and storms shape human activities and how humans understand such phenomena (Strauss and Orlove 2003; Cruikshank 2005; Hsu and Low 2008; Orlove, Wiegandt and Luckman 2008). There has been a shift from seeing culture and nature in ontologically dichotomous terms to one in which culture and nature are viewed as mutually constitutive and co-dependent processes and networks of actors and actants, that is, non-purposive agents (Latour 2005) resulting in complex inter-dependent land and waterscapes (Castree 2005). An emerging related field is 'multi-species ethnography', which examines how a variety of organisms are affected by social and other forces (Eben Kirksey and Helmreich 2010). An example of this 'recombinant nature' (Murphy 2004: 252) is when people build embankments to protect themselves and their crops from water inundation but the waters adapt to this new humanized environment often with unintended and unanticipated consequences.

Static equilibrium notions of society and ecology in which change was considered a disturbance to otherwise stable systems have been replaced by inherently dynamic, often non-linear and unpredictable systems and their interactions (Scoones 1999; Holling 2004; Shoreman-Ouimet and Kopnina, this volume). Anthropologists working with non-anthropologists (Nelson, Badger and Brown 2007), have shown how private, public and community actions and adaptive processes (both incremental and transformational) can interact with systems to enhance or inhibit resilience, a key concept in the CC vocabulary (Holling 1978; Köhn and Gowdy 1999; Nordberg and Cumming 2008). Such work points to a methodological link between anthropological studies and Complex Adaptive Systems research, which focuses on how complex, non-linear behavior emerges from the localized interactions of a diversity of agents such as cells, species, individuals, firms and nations, a particular context and the relations that exist between the various components of the system (Harris 2007).

Anthropologists have contributed to cross-disciplinary fields of inquiry relevant to CC such as disasters and hazards research (Oliver-Smith and Hoffman 1999; Oliver-Smith 2004), studies in energy and society (Henning 2005) and the anthropology of science (Franklin 1995; Hathaway 2006; Fischer 2007; Lahsen 2007a, b). For example, Lahsen's work (2005, 2007a, 2008, 2009) on the social context of knowledge production about climate change and the culturally embedded practices of epistemic communities extends earlier philosophical and sociological studies by Kuhn (1970), Latour and Woolgar (1986), and Longino (2002). Anthropologists work with geographers, biologists and ecologists on the interface of society and nature and are increasingly participating in interdisciplinary research projects such as Past Global Changes (PAGES) and the Integrated History and Future of People on Earth (IHOPE) project.

While the flagship anthropological journals were slow to publish articles on CC, many anthropologists have published in non-anthropological journals such as *Conservation and Society*, *Society and Natural Resources*, *Environmental Science and Policy*, *Climate Research*, *Global Environmental Change*, *Disasters*, *Climatic Change and Environmental Science and Policy*. In addition, anthropology has contributed to the development of several, often overlapping cross-disciplinary approaches to the human–non-human world relationship such as Political Ecology, Historical Ecology, Environmental Anthropology, Ecological Anthropology and the Anthropology of Development. Thus, anthropological approaches and ideas are reaching a wider audience of non-anthropologists than otherwise might be the case.

Coastal Collaborations and Adaption to Climate Change: Case Studies

A growing area of anthropological academic and policy-related research is that of coastal vulnerability to CC (Engels 2009; Lazarus 2009; McDonald et al. 2010). This research builds on anthropological and other studies of social and environmental vulnerability but seeks to incorporate climate change projections into the analysis. The remainder of this chapter looks at the authors' engagement in collaborative research projects on coastal vulnerabilities and climate change in Western Australia and the southwest coast of Bangladesh in which we discuss the contribution anthropology is making to linking CC to the every-day lives of local communities.

The Western Australian and SW Bangladesh coasts share several features in common. Their land and seascapes have been modified by humans and non-humans *in situ* or forged by wider processes, including climate change. They are increasingly subject to climate- and non-climate induced pressures such as growing urban and rural populations, multiple land use demands, industrial expansion, off-shore oil and gas extraction, infrastructure development, over fishing, terrestrial and aquatic pollution, sea level change, cyclones, coastal erosion and habitat loss, storm surges and flooding. Both coasts are projected to experience increased climate variability and climate change through increased intensity of cyclones, storm surges, sea level rise, rising temperatures and ocean acidification which will impact on livelihoods, ecosystems and economies. Their capacity to respond to these pressures varies as a result of differing levels of economic development, models of policy and planning, quality of governance structures, differences in population size and densities, biophysical regions and cultural histories and background.

Both countries are shifting towards integrated coastal management strategies (ICM) such as ecosystem-based management and models of adaptive governance (Brown et al. 2002; UNEP 2002; Visser 2004; Christie 2005; Harvey 2006), which involve the bringing together, through official and informal networking, of a variety of academic specializations, policy makers, NGOs, business and local communities aimed at creating sustainable coasts, which includes planned adaptation to CC. A model of sustainable coasts differs from other cultural models (see below) in the sense that contained within its discourse is the ability and responsibility to reflect critically on itself and other models (Meppem & Bourke 1999). According to sustainability theory, community, ecological, and economic dimensions of the coast need to be consciously integrated in coastal policy in order to achieve sustainability (Kane 1999), which must now include coastal adaptation to climate change. There is a growing state and scientific recognition that ecological models must include people and their unique cultures and economies that are connected to coasts. Central to such a task, one to which anthropology is well-suited, is to translate the universalizing and decontextualized language of CC science into the everyday languages and practices of ordinary people.

Both countries also recognize adaptation to CC planning as a central pillar of climate change policy in general and coastal management in particular (Government of Bangladesh 2008; Garnaut 2008; Department of Climate Change 2010). Such planning involves a marshalling of a variety of knowledges and cultural practices that go beyond traditional top-down, expert-dominated models to ones with the potential to integrate diverse human communities into active and critical transdisciplinary communities of practice (Brown 2010). Anthropology is playing an important role here, as our own research indicates.

First, anthropology allows us to gain an understanding of the various cultural constructions or models of the coast held by different subcultures and the practices they engage in to deal with weather-related events and processes (Thompson 2007;

Stocker and Kennedy 2009). These constructions of the coast have different consequences for how coastal communities respond to climate change and climate related pressures. For example in Western Australia, the implications of seeing the coast as a site of productivity, that is, as a stock of resources that can be put to use for the betterment of society has meant that climate scientists have focused their attention on the economic impacts of the weakening Leeuwin Current along the WA coast, which has led to zero recorded recruitment of rock lobster larvae central to the state's fishing industry. By contrast, where the coast is seen as valuable real estate that can be bought and sold and as a cherished place of residence, there is resistance to acknowledging the impacts of coastal erosion due to rising sea levels. For indigenous Australians, the cultural coastscape is wholly inclusive of land, sea, humans and non-humans. For other Australians, the coast is a viewshed or place visible to the observer, valued for its aesthetic appearance.

In Bangladesh, on-going documentary and fieldwork-based research by Pokrant and his Bangladeshi colleagues reveal that the coast has several meanings for Bangladeshis, some shared with Australians. For middle class urban dwellers visiting the Sundarban mangrove forest, the world's largest continuous single mangrove forest tract, in the country's southwest, is the edge of civilized life, a place of hazard from cyclones, storm surges and flooding, the domain of the poor and the marginal, to be exploited for its resources and for the occasional holiday. For ship breakers near Chittagong, the country's main port, it is a place where used ocean-going commercial vessels are dismantled and scavenged for parts for on-sale (Buerk 2006; Hossain et al. 2008). For fishers, it is home, the place of their ancestors, a source of life and livelihood. For Hindu fishers, the relationship between land and sea has a moral and practical unity in which the sea is a 'feminine entity' (Deb 2008) 'fertilized' by the rivers to produce fish. Fishers also view the coast as a place of physical danger from rough seas and unpredictable weather, as economically hazardous through indebtedness to merchants and from pressure from shrimp farmers for land. For the state, the coast is a productive resource to be developed for a variety of uses, some compatible with existing uses, others, such as rice farming and shrimp farming, coming into conflict with each other (Ali 2006).

The Bangladesh coast is dominated by resource extraction activities central to key government policies such as the Integrated Coastal Zone Management Plan (ICZM), the National Adaptation Programme of Action (NAPA) and the Bangladesh Climate Change Strategy and Action Plan (BCCSAP). Few Bangladeshis consider the coast as a place of recreation but there have been official moves to turn parts of it into tourist centers for domestic and international travelers. For example, there are now expensive boat trips for well-off eco-tourists into the Sundarban mangrove forest to view the forest's megafauna. For local people, the forest's northern tip attracts large numbers of day-trippers who arrive by boat and move phalanx-like along wooden platforms viewing 'nature' and observing some of the forest's tamer wildlife confined to pens. Similar to Australia, the Bangladesh state recognizes the threat of CC to these resources. The attempt to turn the coast into sites of consumption is placing added pressure on coastal peoples dependent on the ecological services the coast provides.

Anthropology can also help inform the coastal adaptation debate through its methodological and substantive emphasis on meaning and interpretation. In Australia, the prevalent approach to coastal adaptation, where it exists at all, is technical, which sits comfortably with the technocratic approach to decision-making. The risk assessment approach to coastal adaptation is recommended by the federal government and is being adopted by most local governments already familiar with this methodology. Most coastal risk assessment approaches are linear, reductionist, and focused on physical threats to buildings and infrastructure, less commonly on threats to ecosystems, and rarely on threats to human experience of the coast and the meaning that gives to people's lives. In Bangladesh official thinking is shifting to more integrated approaches that seek to incorporate social, cultural and political processes into planning activity. However, progress is slow and governance arrangements remain sectoral, fragmented, and short-term. There have been few long-term, in-depth anthropological research projects on how coastal peoples understand and utilize the coast compared with short-term rapid appraisal research, which lack 'thick description' of local peoples' understandings of weather and climate.

A third way in which anthropology can contribute to the study of coastal adaptation to climate change is by 'being there' (Roncoli, Crane and Orlove 2009). Long term involvement with local communities allows the anthropologist to build up a picture of their life-worlds, institutions, and cultural understandings and practices and their experienced-based interaction with their social and natural worlds. It also provides an opportunity to promote the trans-disciplinary way of working mentioned earlier and to examine those seeking to intervene in the lives of local peoples. Thus, at one and the same time, the anthropologist can act as field worker, cultural broker, critical observer and cultural advocate. This mélange of skills fits well with new approaches to the science–policy interface that move beyond the linear thinking of earlier planning to what are referred to as 'wicked problems' (Brown, Harris, Russell 2010; Rittel and Webber 1973). These are problems difficult to solve because they emerge from a highly complex and interdependent set of factors (ecological, cultural and socio-economic) operating at different scales. In the case of coastal adaptation to climate change, we are dealing with shifting parameters, many intersecting and sometimes non-linear variables and dimensions (conceptual complexity); many methodologies and technologies (techno-methodological complexity), and a diverse range of 'stakeholders' interested in finding solutions to their problems (social complexity). Anthropologists have long recognized the importance of taking a more holistic approach to understanding social and cultural life and have worked in multi-disciplinary teams and with local communities in diverse social and ecological environments. They are well-placed to contribute to working with others on open-ended problems that defy easy solutions.

Adaptation and Coastal Development in Bangladesh and Western Australia

The concept of adaptation, a central concept in anthropology since its beginnings as an academic discipline (Orlove 2009), has taken on new significance as a central pillar of climate research and policy. It refers to collective or individual adjustments to unavoidable climate change impacts that reduce their disruptive effects and turn negative impacts into opportunities to improve a community's, nation's, or wider system's capacity to sustain itself. Adaptation is of particular importance to the least developed countries where development gains and aspirations will be jeopardized by climate change (UNDP 2007; World Bank 2010).

Anthropological interest in adaptation to climate change in Australia is recent. However, one Australian government funded project that seeks to bring together social scientists, natural and environmental scientists, business, policy makers and local communities is called 'Enabling Science Uptake in Australia's Coastal Zone'. It recognizes the importance of building cultures of resilience along Australia's coastline, which require the skills of both social and natural scientists in collaboration with local stakeholders. In Western Australia, the research team, which includes one anthropologist, has recently developed the use of overlay mapping and Google Earth. In this approach, diverse community members and stakeholders (local government, academics, community representatives, NGOs, business) are brought together in a one-day deliberative workshop. Using both physical maps and Google Earth, they map the cultural, social, economic and ecological aspects of coastal locations they identify as significant to them within a prescribed area. Key significances identified include the history of fishing, Aboriginal cultural use of land and sea, heritage, place and the built environment, festivals, public space and its uses, and tourism and recreational activity. These aspects are mapped onto separate layers onto clear acetate sheets over the physical base map and provide spatial explicit information about the values, uses and attributes of the chosen locations. Ideas can be drawn or written on the plastic sheets. The information can be qualitative and can be about the meaning and significance of these places to the various participants. The information can also be quantitative and technical. In this way no type of information is overly privileged. When the four layers are complete and laid on top of each other, participants can see how the layers potentially interact and synergize. This process enables different cultural models of the coast to be included and respected. The information is simultaneously transferred to Google Earth in digital format, which enables all perspectives to be annotated or 'Placemarked' in a spatially explicit manner in Google Earth, using the same four layers. The layers can then be turned on and off to assess the interaction among layers. When all four layers are switched on there are areas where there are high levels of activity in all four layers. This means that there are places with strong social, cultural, ecological and economic values, which we term 'Hotspots' as they are rich in meaning for participants.

In the next workshop activity, the participants hear from a range of speakers about the possible climate change impacts on the locations under consideration. Participants then return to their mapping process and Placemark in Google Earth any specific concerns they have for the coastal Hotspots identified. These might include the loss of a surf break, homes, public infrastructure or a fishing site. Finally, the participants develop and Placemark in Google Earth some adaptive pathways or solutions for their concerns about their coastal hotspots. Here they might consider for example whether planned retreat from the coast or hard defenses represent a better option for coastal adaptation. This methodology (Stocker and Burke 2006, 2009) enables the interaction among anthropological, sociological, ecological and economic perspectives in a more democratic and inclusive way. The resultant Google Earth file can be shared with participants as a record of the workshop, and it can be converted to a shape file and used as part of a local government GIS planning process (see Moran, this volume). This methodology has been used for the local government area of Fremantle and for Rottnest Island, both in Western Australia.

A second example comes from Bangladesh where governments, NGOs and others are working to make development planning more climate-change resilient. One component of this is community based adaptation to climate change (CBA) where NGOs, practitioners, anthropologists, and other researchers work with coastal and other communities on community-based adaptation to climate change projects (Ayers and Forsyth 2009; Ayers and Huq 2009).

CBA extends pre-CC community-based development approaches through incorporating climate change issues into wider development planning. Where it differs from these approaches is in its promotion of adaptive practices that anticipate longer-term and uncertain climate trends. This approach recognizes that climate change policy needs to be multi-purpose, targeted at a wider range of social and environmental changes and form part of development planning. For example, if adaptation strategies are too narrowly conceived to deal with a locally defined 'climate' problem, the result may be maladaptive. Thus, building an embankment may keep the water from inundating one community but affect another community downstream. A development program such as expanding irrigation schemes can lead to water shortages if future rainfall and temperature trends are excluded from program planning.

Central to this more development-based view of adaptation (Ayers and Dodman 2010) is detailed and reliable knowledge of how local communities have adapted to natural and human-induced hazards, how these communities are likely to be affected by CC, and the relevance of 'traditional' adaptive strategies to CC. The collection and systematization of such knowledge is an essential part of participatory learning and action research (PLA) in which cross-disciplinary teams work with local communities to facilitate improved adaptive strategies (Reid, et al. 2009a). In Bangladesh there is a growing body of literature and experience based on the PLA model, which, *inter alia*, complements new and more refined macro-level climate modeling systems which allow planners to provide different climate change scenarios. For the full potential of such models to be realized, they must be translated into terms understandable to the targeted communities and be relevant to the development concerns of those communities (Baas and Ramasamy 2008). Through collaboration with local communities, scientific information about CC can be integrated into people's everyday lived experiences rather than remaining as abstract notions remote from their experience.

Pokrant is collaborating with Bangladeshi academic and NGO colleagues on a program of research to link local understandings of climate change to regional, national and international scales through more deliberative forms of participation, information sharing, collective mobilization, cooperation with national planning bodies, and representation at international fora. As a first step, the program focuses on establishing a data base on coastal people's understandings of the relationship between local weather, climate change and the value of 'traditional' forms of adaptation to changing environmental and climate-related conditions. One current project is in two villages abutting the Bangladesh state-owned Sundarban mangrove forest, a UNESCO World Heritage site and biodiversity hotspot in the southwest of the country and shared with India. The selected villages are part of the up to one million people who depend directly or indirectly on forest and non-forest ecological goods and services. The main occupational groups who draw directly or indirectly on these goods and services are shrimp farmers, sea going fishers, local fishers (jele), crab collectors, nypa palm and wood collectors (bowali), honey collectors (mowali), shrimp fry collectors, fish traders, shrimp farm laborers and boatmen. They are highly vulnerable to existing natural and human-induced hazards such as cyclones, storm surges, flooding, salinity, attacks by tigers, river bank erosion, land grabbing, harassment by local gangs (dacoits) and corrupt practices of government foresters. CC is thought to be adding to some of these hazards in ways not yet fully understood (Alam and Ahmed 2010) but exacerbating the already fragile state of the mangrove forest and the people who depend upon it to maintain existing sources of sustenance (Gopal and Chauhan 2006; Pender 2008; Inman 2009; Loucks et al. 2010).

Preliminary interviews with selected villagers reveal their perceptions of climate and its impact on their lives are shaped by their levels of physical vulnerability and social vulnerability defined in terms of their exposure, sensitivity and response to 'natural' and human-induced hazards. Vulnerability is, in turn, a product of a complex web of interrelationships between, *inter alia*, geographic location, gender, age, occupation, political status, and wealth. For the poor and landless, who we estimate constitute some 50 percent of the village populations, their major concern is finding work and earning enough to feed their families. They live in poorly constructed homes often highly exposed to physical hazards such as cyclones and storm surges. Such physical exposure is a product of their social vulnerability as they cannot afford to protect their homes from physical hazards. In seeking to earn a living, they are highly dependent on family and ethnic ties, patronage relations with local power holders, representatives of the state and people with trading and other forms of capital. Any relevance that 'climate' has in their lives is mediated by these relations, which structure their livelihood opportunities and access to the basic means of life.

In recent years, villagers have noticed unusual changes in environmental and weather-related conditions. These changes are expressed in locally specific terms and filtered through occupational and other culturally defined lenses rather than through the language of 'climate change'. For example, ocean-going fishers pointed to an increase in rough weather conditions during the main fishing season and a growth of 'sudden and instant storm' events in the sea /coast which lasted for short periods of time. These events occurred so rapidly and for such short duration that official warning systems failed to capture them and so increased fishers' vulnerability at sea.

Most villagers had observed a decline in rainfall, less regular falls in the pre-monsoon and monsoon seasons and shorter cool, dry seasons. For fishers, fishing had become more dangerous and their fishing grounds were changing, for crab and honey collectors, poorer rains meant fewer crabs and poor quality honey, for rice farmers, planting schedules were disrupted.

People continued to explain these events within known parameters or within their historical and recent experience and their adaptive responses are consonant with that experience. For example, growing water and soil salinity was blamed on human interference with upstream water flows, siltation of river bends or shrimp farming. The growing threat of tiger intrusions into human settlements was explained by a lack of animal prey in the forest caused by cyclone Aila in 2009.

Their adaptive responses to such hazards remain largely autonomous and reactive and included harvesting of rainwater, floating gardens, raising homes on concrete plinths, diversifying income generating opportunities, modification of housing construction and spatial location of wind breaks, and the use of new strains of rice. They considered such adaptive measures as means to cope with immediate and seasonal water shortages, salinity, flooding, cyclones and the like rather than as potential packages of measures to deal with longer-term changes in climate.

These preliminary observations will be supplemented by the collection of more detailed qualitative and quantitative data across the two villages to provide a basis for comparison of their differential social and physical vulnerabilities to a range of climate-related and non-climate stressors. The researchers will work with villagers to develop more climate-sensitive anticipatory adaptive strategies, facilitate co-learning strategies about CC between local peoples, NGOs, business and government, and integrate these local initiatives into national and regional adaptive networks.

Conclusion

Anthropologists have been slow to engage with climate change but this is now changing as they are increasingly involved singly and in cross-disciplinary teams on academic and policy research across a range of climate change-related topics. They are building on anthropology's rich contribution to the study of human-rest of nature relations, climate variability and local understandings of weather. One key area of such research is adaptation to climate change. This chapter discussed coastal adaptation in Australia and Bangladesh to illustrate how anthropologists are working with different disciplinary specialists and local communities to devise ways of planning more sustainable coastal futures. We emphasized the importance of working with local people to understand how they perceive and deal with changing climate-related socio-ecological conditions. This provides a basis upon which to develop a multi-scalar approach to adaptation that recognizes the importance of integrating CC concerns into development planning and that sees CC and its impacts as the result of complex causal chains that are at one and the same time embedded within particular places and communities but that also transcend them.

References

Adger, W. Neil, Lorenzoni, I. and O'Brien, K. (eds) (2009) *Adapting to Climate Change: Thresholds, Values, Governance.* Cambridge: Cambridge University Press.
Alam, M. J. B. and Ahmed, F. (2010) Modeling Climate Change: Perspective and Applications in the Context of Bangladesh in Y. Charabi (ed) *Indian Ocean Tropical Cyclones and Climate Change*, The Netherlands: Springer.
Ali, A. M. S. (2006) 'Rice to shrimp: Land use/land cover changes and soil degradation in southwestern Bangladesh,' *Land use Policy, 23*(4): 421–35.
Ayers, J. and Dodman, D. (2010) 'Climate change adaptation and development I: the state of the debate,' *Progress in Development Studies* 10(2): 161–68.
Ayers, J. and Forsyth, T. (2009) 'Community-Based Adaptation to Climate Change. Strengthening Resilience through Development,' *Environment* 51(4): 24–31.
Ayers, J. and Huq, S. (2009) 'Community Based Adaptation to Climate Change: an update – A Briefing Note', London: International Institute for Environment and Development.
Baas, S. and Ramasamy, S. (2008) *Community based adaptation in action: a case study from Bangladesh: project summary report (phase 1), Improved adaptive capacity to climate change for sustainable livelihoods in the agriculture sector*, Rome: Food and Agriculture Organization of the United Nations.
Batterbury, S.P.J. (2008) 'Anthropology and global warming: the need for environmental engagement'. *The Australian Journal of Anthropology*, 19 (1): 62–68.
Beck, U. (1992) *Risk Society: Towards a New Modernity*, London: Sage.
Biesbroek, G.R., Swart, R.J., van der Knaap, W.G.M., (2009) 'The mitigation-adaptation dichotomy and the role of spatial planning,' *Habitat International* 33 (3), 230–37.
Blackman, S. (2009) 'Top British boffin: Time to ditch the climate consensus.' *The Register*, 6th May 2009. Online. Available http://www.theregister.co.uk/2009/05/06/mike_hulme_interview/ (Accessed 15 February 2010)
Brown, K. Tompkins, E.L. Adger, W. N. (2002) *Making Waves: Integrating Coastal Conservation and Development*, London: Earthscan.
Brown, V.A. (2010) 'Collective Inquiry and Its Wicked Problems', in V. Brown, J. A. Harris, J. Y. Russell (eds) *Tackling Wicked Problems. Through the Transdisciplinary Imagination*, London: Earthscan, 61–83.
Brown, V., Harris, J. A. Russell, J. Y. (eds) (2010) *Tackling Wicked Problems. Through the Transdisciplinary Imagination*, London: Earthscan.
Buerk, R. (2006) *Breaking Ships: How Supertankers and Cargo Ships Are Dismantled on the Beaches of Bangladesh*, New York, NY: Chamberlain Bros.
Bäckstrand, K. (2004) 'Scientisation vs. Civic Expertise in Environmental Governance. Ecofeminist, Ecomodernist and Postmodernist Responses', *Environmental Politics*, 13, 4: 695–714.
Castree, N. (2005) *Nature: the adventures of a concept*, London: Routledge.
Christie, P. (2005) 'Is Integrated Coastal Management Sustainable?' *Ocean & Coastal Management*, 48(3–6): 208–32.
Crate, S. A. (2008) 'Gone the Bull of Winter? Grappling with the Cultural Implications of and Anthropology's Role(s) in Global Climate Change,' *Current Anthropology*, 49 (4): 569.
Crate, S. and Nuttall, M. (eds) (2009) *Anthropology and climate change: from encounters to actions*, Walnut Creek, CA: Left Coast Press.
Cruikshank, J. (2005) *Do Glaciers Listen? Local Knowledge, Colonial Encounters, and Social Imagination*, UBC Press: Vancouver, Canada.
Deb, A. K. (2008) 'The Slaves of Water': Socio-cultural Construction of the Community-based Coastal Resource Management in the South-eastern Bangladesh'. Paper presented at the 2008 International Association for the Study of the Commons, Gloucester, UK.
Department of Climate Change (2010) *Adapting to Climate Change in Australia. An Australian Government Position Paper*, Commonwealth of Australia: Canberra.

Dove, M. and Carpenter, C. (eds) (2008) *Environmental Anthropology. A Historical Reader*, Oxford: Blackwell Publishing.

Eben Kirksey, S. and Helmreich, S. (2010) 'The Emergence of Multispecies Ethnography,' *Cultural Anthropology*, 25 (4): 545–76.

Engels, A. (2009) 'Local Environmental Crises and Global Sea-Level Rise. The Case of Coastal Zones' in Senegal, in M.J. Casimir (ed.) *Culture And The Changing Environment. Uncertainty, Cognition, and Risk Management in Cross-Cultural Perspective*, London: Berghahn.

Fagan, B. (2008) *The Great Warming. Climate change and the rise and fall of civilizations*, New York: Bloomsbury Press.

Finan, T. (2007) 'Is "official" anthropology ready for climate change?' *Anthropology News*, 48: 10–11.

Fischer, M. J. (2007) 'Four Genealogies for a recombinant anthropology of science and technology', *Cultural Anthropology*, 22(4): 539–615.

Franklin, S. (1995) 'Science of cultures, cultures of science,' *Annual Review of Anthropology*, 24:162–85.

Funtowicz, S.O. and Ravetz, J. R. (1993) 'Science for the Post-Normal Age', *Futures*, 25 (7): 739–55.

——(1994) 'Emergent Complex Systems', *Futures*, 26: 568–82.

Garnaut, R. (2008) *The Garnaut Climate Change Review*, Cambridge: Cambridge University Press.

Gopal, B. and Chauhan, M. (2006) 'Biodiversity and its conservation in the Sundarban Mangrove Ecosystem,' *Aquatic Sciences*, 68: 338–54.

Government of Bangladesh (2008) *Bangladesh Climate Change Strategy and Action Plan, 2008*, Dhaka: Government of Bangladesh.

Haenn, N. and Wilk, R. (2006) *The Environment in Anthropology: A Reader in Ecology, Culture, and Sustainable Living*, New York: New York University Press.

Harris, G. (2007) *Seeking Sustainability in an Age of Complexity*, New York: Cambridge University Press.

Hathaway, M. (2006) 'Environmental Anthropology and Science Studies,' Anthropology News, 46(3): 43–44.

Harvey, N. (ed) (2006) *Global Change and Integrated Coastal Management: The Asia-Pacific Region*, Springer.

Henning, A. (2005) 'Climate change and energy use: The role for anthropological research'. *Anthropology Today*, 21, 3: 8–12, June.

Holling, C. S. (1978) *Adaptive Environmental Assessment and Management*, Chichester: Wiley.

——(2004) 'From Complex Regions to Complex Worlds', *Ecology and Society*, 9(1). Article 11. No page numbers given.

Hossain, M. S., Chowdhury, S.R., Abdul Jabbar, S.M., Saifullah, S.M., and Rahman, M. A. (2008) 'Occupational Health Hazards of Ship Scrapping Workers at Chittagong Coastal Zone, Bangladesh,' *Chiang Mai Journal of Science*, 35(2): 370 – 381.

Hsu, E. and C. Low (2008) *Wind, life, health: Anthropological and Historical perspectives*, New York: Wiley-Blackwell.

Inman, M. (2009) 'Where warming hits hard,' *Nature reports climate change*, 3: 18–21.

Jasanoff, S. (2010) 'A New Climate for Society,' *Theory Culture Society* 27; 233–53.

Kane, M. (1999) 'Sustainability Concepts: From Theory to Practice', in J. Köhn, J. M. Gowdy, F. Hinterberger, and J. van der Straaten (eds.) *Sustainability in Question The Search for a Conceptual Framework*, London: Edward Elgar Press.

Kelman I and West J. (2009) 'Climate change and Small Island Developing States: a critical review', *Ecological and Environmental Anthropology* 5 (1): 1–16.

Kuhn, T.S. (1970) *The Structure of Scientific Revolutions*, 2nd ed., Chicago: University of Chicago Press.

Köhn, J. & Gowdy, J. M. (1999) 'Coping with complex and dynamic systems. An approach to a transdisciplinary understanding of coastal zone developments.' *Journal of Coastal Conservation*. 5(2): 163–70.

Lahsen, M. (2005) 'Technocracy, democracy and U.S. climate science politics: The need for demarcations,' *Science, Technology and Human Values*, 30(1): 137–169.

Lahsen, M. (2007a) 'Trust through participation? Problems of knowledge in climate decision-making', in M.E. Pettenger (ed) *The social construction of climate change: power, knowledge, norms, discourses*. Aldershot, UK: Ashgate Publishing Limited. pp. 173–196.

Lahsen, M, (2007b): 'Anthropology and the trouble of risk society,' *Anthropology News*, 48, 9–10.

Lahsen, M. (2008) 'Experiences of modernity in the greenhouse: a cultural analysis of a physicist 'trio' supporting the backlash against global warming', *Global Environmental Change*, 18: 204–219.

Lahsen M. (2009) 'A science-policy interface in the global South: The politics of carbon sinks and science in Brazil', *Climatic Change*, 97(3): 339–372.

Latour, B. (2005) *Reassembling the Social–An Introduction to Actor-Network-Theory*, Oxford: Oxford University Press.

Latour, B. and Woolgar, T. (1986) *Laboratory Life: the Social Construction of Scientific Facts*, Los Angeles, London: Sage.

Lazarus, H. (2009) 'The governance of vulnerability: Climate change and agency in Tuvalu, South Pacific,' in S. Crate and M. Nuttall (eds) *Anthropology and climate change: from encounters to actions*. Walnut Creek, CA: Left Coast Press. pp. 240–249.

Lemos. M. C., and Agrawal, A. (2006) 'Environmental Governance,' *Annual Review of Environment and Resources*, 31: 297–325.

Longino, H. E. (2002) *The Fate of Knowledge*. Princeton: Princeton University Press.

Loucks, C., Barber-Meyer, S., Hossain, Md. A., Barlow, A, Chowdhury, R. M (2010) 'Sea level rise and tigers: predicted impacts to Bangladesh's Sundarbans mangroves: A letter,' *Climatic Change*, 98: 291–98.

Maasen, S. and Lieven, O. (2006) 'Socially robust knowledge Transdisciplinarity: a new mode of governing science?' *Science and Public Policy*, 33(6): 399–410.

McDonald, J., Baum, S., Crick, F., Czarnecki, J., Field, G., Low Choy, D., Mustelin, J., Sanò, M. & Serrao-Neumann, S. (2010) *Climate change adaptation in South East Queensland human settlements: Issues and context*, unpublished report for the South East Queensland Climate Adaptation Research Initiative, Griffith University.

McDowell, C. and Morrell, G. (2010) *Displacement Beyond Conflict: Challenges for the 21st Century*, London: Berghahn Books.

Mearns, R., Norton, A., and Cameron, E. (eds) (2009) *Social Dimensions Of Climate Change: Equity And Vulnerability In A Warming World*, Washington, D.C.: World Bank.

Meppem, T. and Bourke, S. (1999) 'Different ways of knowing: a communicative turn towards sustainability,' *Ecological Economics* 30: 389–404.

Milton, K. (2008) 'Fear for the future' *The Australian Journal of Anthropology*, 19 (1): 73–76.

Modvar, C. and Gallopin, G. C. (2005) *Sustainable Development: Epistemological Challenges to Science and Technology*, Report of the workshop 'Sustainable development: epistemological 'challenges to science and technology,' Santiago, Chile, 13 to 15 October 2004, Cepal, United Nations.

Murphy, R. (2004) 'Disaster or Sustainability: The Dance of Human Agents with Nature's Actants', *Canadian Review of Sociology/Revue canadienne de sociologie*, 41(3): 249–266.

Nelson, D. (2007) Expanding the Climate Change Research Agenda, *Anthropology News*, 48: 12–13.

Nelson, D. Adger. W. N. and Brown, K. (2007) 'Adaptation to Environmental Change: Contributions of a Resilience Framework', *Annual Review of Environmental Resources*, 32: 395–419.

Nelson, D., West, C. T., Finan, T. (2009) 'Introduction to 'In Focus: Global Change and Adaptation in Local Places' *American Anthropologist*, 111(3): 271–274.

Norberg, J., and Cumming, G.S. (2008) 'Introduction,' in J. Norberg and G. S. Cumming (eds) *Complexity Theory for a Sustainable Future*, New York: Columbia University Press. pp. 1–6.

Oliver-Smith. A. (2004) 'Theorizing vulnerability in a globalized world: A political ecological perspective,' in G. Bankoff, G. Frerks and D. Hilhorst (eds) *Mapping vulnerability: Disasters, development and people*, London: Earthscan Publications.

Oliver–Smith, A. and Hoffman, S. (1999) *The Angry Earth: Disaster in Anthropological Perspective*, London : Routledge.

Orlove, B. (2009) 'The past, present and some possible futures of adaptation,' in Adger, W. Neil, Lorenzoni, I. and O'Brien, K. (eds) *Adapting to Climate Change: Thresholds, Values, Governance*. Cambridge: Cambridge University Press.

Orlove, B., Wiegandt, E., Luckman, B. (eds) (2008) *Darkening peaks: glacial retreat, science and society*, Berkeley: University of California Press.

Pender, J.S. (2008) *What Is Climate Change? And how it will affect Bangladesh Briefing Paper*, Dhaka, Bangladesh: Church of Bangladesh Social Development Programme.

Ravetz, J. (2004) 'The post-normal science of precaution', *Futures*, 36: 347–57.

Reid, H., Alam, M., Berger, R., Cannon, T., Huq, S. Milligan, A. (eds) (2009a) 'Community-based adaptation to climate change: an overview', in H. Reid, M. Alam, R. Berger, T. Cannon, S. Huq, and A. Milligan (eds) *Participatory Learning and Action 60*, London: IIED.

——(2009b) *Participatory Learning and Action 60*. London: IIED.

Rittel, H. and Webber, M. (1973) 'Dilemmas in a General Theory of Planning', *Policy Sciences*, 4: 155–169.

Roncoli, C. and Orlove, B. (2009) 'Fielding Climate Change in Cultural Anthropology,' in S. Crate and M. Nuttall (eds) *Anthropology and climate change: from encounters to actions*. Walnut Creek, CA: Left Coast Press. pp. 87–135.

Rosen, A. (2007) *Civilizing Climate: Social Responses to Climate Change in the Ancient Near East*, Lanham, MD: AltaMira Press.

Rudiak-Gould, P. (2009) *The Fallen Palm: Climate Change and Culture Change in the Marshall Islands*, VDM Verlag.

Scoones, I. (1999) 'New ecology and the social sciences: what prospects for a fruitful engagement?' *Annual Review of Anthropology*, 28: 479–507.

Stocker, L. and Burke, G. (2006) 'Overlay Mapping–A Methodology for Place-Based Sustainability Education', In S. Wooltorton and D. Marinova, D (eds) *Sharing Wisdom for Our Future: Environmental Education in Action*, Sydney: Australian Association for Environmental Education.

Stocker, S. and Burke, G. (2009) 'Teaching sustainability with overlay mapping and *Google Earth*,' TL Forum (2009), *Teaching and learning for global graduates*. Proceedings of the 18th Annual Teaching Learning Forum, 29–30 January 2009. Perth: Curtin University of Technology. Online. Available http://otl.curtin.edu.au/tlf/tlf2009/refereed/contents-refereed.html (Accessed 6 October 2010)

Stocker, L., & Kennedy, D. (2009) 'Cultural Models of the Coast in Australia: Towards Sustainability,' *Coastal Management* 37(5): 387–404.

Strauss, S. and Orlove, B. (eds) (2003) *Weather, climate, culture*, London: Berg.

Thompson, R. (2007) 'Cultural models and shoreline social conflict,' *Coastal Management*, 35(2): 211–237.

Townsend, P. K. (2004) 'Still Fiddling while the Globe Warms?' *Reviews in Anthropology*, 33(4): 335–349.

UNDP (2007) 'Fighting climate change: Human solidarity in a divided world,' *Human Development Report, 2007/2008*, New York: United Nations.

UNEP (2002) *Global Environment Outlook 3: Past, present and future perspectives*, United Nations Environment Programme, London: Earthscan Publications.

Visser, L. (ed) (2004) *Challenging coasts: Transdisciplinary excursions into integrated coastal zone development*, Amsterdam: University of Amsterdam Press.

World Bank (2010) *World Development Report 2010: Development and Climate Change*. Washington, DC: The International Bank for Reconstruction and Development/The World Bank.

9

FROM ECOSYSTEM SERVICES TO UNFULFILLED EXPECTATIONS

Factors Influencing Attitudes Toward the Madidi Protected Area

Teressa Trusty

Introduction[1]

Dramatic cases of exclusion and even the forced relocation of rural and oftentimes indigenous residents from protected areas have been well documented. Cases from North America trace the history and establishment of the first national parks including Yellowstone (Spence 1999; Jacoby 2001), which was the model for many protected areas established worldwide prior to the 1990s. Studies of conservation areas that exclude people demonstrate how this design contributes to local tension (Neumann 1998; Buergin 2001; Brockington 2002). These types of protected area demarcations regularly have a direct, adverse effect on people's livelihoods and way of life, which engenders conflict and contributes to negative, sometimes hostile, attitudes toward these areas (Hough 1988; Heinen 1993; Allendorf et al. 2006; Allendorf 2007).

Recognition of this problem led academics and conservationists to realize that in order to meet conservation goals, people living in and around protected areas need to support these goals and be involved in the conservation process (West and Brechin 1991; Wells et al. 1992). Institutionally, this led to a change in the mid-1990s in the design of some protected areas. UNESCO redefined biosphere reserves, one of the principal forms of protected areas since the 1970s, from focusing exclusively on biodiversity conservation and research to include helping local people live sustainably (Axelsson and Angelstam 2005). Concurrently, the International Union for the Conservation of Nature (IUCN) formalized a protected area category for managed resources with dual goals: to conserve natural resources and meet local community needs through sustainable resource use (IUCN 1994). Yet disputes persist at these more permissive conservation areas in large part because regulations continue to prohibit activities locals perceive as necessary to both economic and cultural survival (Fiallo and Jacobson 1995; Silori 2007; Bosak 2008). Where satisfactory access and extraction are permitted, local attitudes may be more positive (Allendorf 2007).

The 18,957.5 km^2 Madidi National Park (NP) and Integrated Natural Management Area (ANMI) in northwestern Bolivia has successfully averted most resource use conflicts along its northeastern border due in part to its location, design, and policies. The protected area was established in a region with low population density, reducing the potential for disputes. This contrasts to the norm for protected areas in the tropics and sub-tropics where high biodiversity and dense human populations frequently co-occur (Cincotta and Engelman 2000). Additionally, instead of drawing the borders solely based upon conservation concerns, the final design implemented by the Bolivian government minimized the number of people enclosed by the more restrictive national park. The government also recognized the rights of local indigenous people, who depend upon natural resources located inside the protected area, by decreeing protection of biological and cultural diversity as dual objectives. Despite initial conflict over the activities of resident populations living inside the ANMI, subsequent policies have supported subsistence use rights including hunting, gathering, and clearing land for agriculture.[2]

This chapter describes the attitudes of the resident population toward the Madidi protected area, the factors influencing them, and how they compare to findings from other sites. The methods used in this research facilitated the uncovering of a range of views amongst the study population, who lived inside or along the highway just outside the northeastern boundary of the protected area where they could clearly see the steep ridge that marks its frontier in this zone. This ethnographic study, conducted during two six-month periods in 2006 and 2007,[3] allowed informants to freely discuss their ideas, using an open-ended interview format as the principal method. As opposed to closed-ended questionnaires, which are commonly employed in non-ethnographic attitudinal studies, this approach captured the most salient concerns and opinions of study subjects instead of constraining or shaping their responses through the content of the questions or the structure of the survey (Allendorf 2007). The interview protocol included five topical areas: culture, nature and the forest, conservation, the Madidi protected area, and development. I introduced these topics and invited subjects to converse about them. I recorded 69 interviews where the informant agreed, which three assistants transcribed. I coded these transcripts in Atlas. ti along with additional ethnographic information that I assembled (Scientific Software Development GmbH 1993–2008). The latter included field notes from narrative walks,[4] participant observation, and interviews where the informant declined to be recorded.

Anthropologists have been involved with protected areas through their research about indigenous knowledge and environmental management, as practitioners in conservation programs, and as advocates for indigenous rights (Orlove and Brush 1996). Through their ethnographic assessment, they also have an opportunity to contribute to conservation policy and programs that reflect the concerns and interests of resident populations. As Kopnina and Shoreman argue in the introduction to this book, focusing on the positive aspects of the human–environment relationship may help perpetuate environmentally sound behavior. Thus interventions, such as educational programs and alternative income-generation projects, may work to strengthen or enhance existing feelings of goodwill identified by this research. However, the findings also highlight legitimate concerns that impede support for the protected area, such as failing to deliver promised jobs and development projects, which contribute to negative attitudes. If not addressed, they pose a risk to the sanctity of the Madidi protected area. At other sites, negative attitudes have contributed to retaliatory acts against park staff and the illegal use of conserved resources (Hough 1988). In addition, once entrenched, negative attitudes may be hard to overcome (Brandon 1998).

Attitudes Towards Protected Areas

Conflicts about access and extractive resource use occurred elsewhere around the Madidi protected area. However, as rural residents in the northeast indicated, they did not see these issues as primary concerns, a feature that distinguishes this case study. Nor were they contributing factors to the predominant perceptions of the protected area. The majority of informants not residing within its boundaries had never entered the Madidi protected area prior to or since its decree. They did not see themselves as directly harmed by its presence. Even though many informants indicated they learned about the protected area only after its decree, this was a minor irritant, not a source of negativity. Instead, concerns related to the lack of development benefits received since its creation, and amongst a small portion of the study population, to the size of the protected area. This was countered by generally positive attitudes related to the goals of the protected area and the various ecosystem services provided from improving wildlife populations to providing clean air and water.

Other studies have found similar results from sites in Africa and Asia where positive opinions about a protected area have been shown to reflect perceived benefits from these services (Heinen 1993; Abbot et al. 2001; Allendorf et al. 2006; Sodhi et al. 2010). However, the idea that a conserved area has the potential to supply future resources and services when there is no explicit compact to do so may contribute to negative attitudes, particularly if they do not become available (Infield 1988). In addition, wildlife issues often contribute to negative feelings about protected areas. In Asia and Africa, local people frequently view wildlife from protected areas as pests (Infield 1988; Newmark et al. 1993, de Boer and Baquete 1998; Infield and Namara 2001; Allendorf et al. 2006), something to be feared (Infield 1988; Allendorf 2007), or as something that the government values more than they value the local people (Brockington 2002; Igoe 2004). For instance, residents near Chobe National Park in Botswana noted increased problems from elephants and other animals after the park's establishment (Parry and Campbell 1992). They also stated that the conservation benefits from this wildlife accrued to professional hunters and the park and wildlife service, not local people. In a unique case from Latin America, people living within and outside Machalilla National Park in Ecuador believed that there were fewer animals after the park was founded than before (Fiallo and Jacobson 1995). These findings about wildlife contrast with those from the Madidi, which provide an opportunity to build up positive attitudes not possible at other sites.

The widespread positive attitude toward the Madidi protected area's existence, goals, and its conservation benefits appears to reflect the success of conservation activities. Since the mid-1990s, SERNAP, the municipal government, and conservation NGOs have sporadically disseminated education and public relations materials to rural residents, such as pamphlets describing why the park is beneficial and how without it, the forest and the animals will disappear. The majority of study subjects indicated they learned about the wealth of resources and services stemming from the Madidi protected area along with their conservation value from these materials, informational meetings, video viewings, references in local print and radio media, and participation in conservation projects related to tourism, agroforestry, and other income-generating activities.

Knowledge about protected area management goals for conservation has been associated with increased support (Fiallo and Jacobson 1995; Infield and Namara 2001), and participation in education and conservation projects has had a constructive effect at multiple sites (Mehta and Heinen 2001; Padmanaba and Sheil 2007; Sodhi et al. 2010). In the case of Amboró National Park in southern Bolivia, proficient facilitation by a conservation organization contributed to voluntary conservation measures in some resident communities including forest rehabilitation and protection of water sources (Moreno et al. 1998). However, protected area neighbors who have little interaction with staff have expressed more negative attitudes toward the conserved area and its managers (Newmark et al. 1993; Holmes 2003; Anthony 2007), while park managers perceived as hostile, disparaging towards local people, and as untrustworthy contribute to negative attitudes (Fiallo and Jacobson 1995; Infield and Namara 2001; Anthony 2007; Stern 2008).

Wide-spread generalized support for conservation, like that seen in this study, may persist even when people have negative attitudes toward specific issues or there are ongoing conflicts (Infield 1988). In the Madidi, attitudes toward the protected area's extent varied, while assessment of its role as a political economic actor produced a clear, negative consensus. These views reflected the interplay of multiple factors including a community's location inside or outside the protected area's boundaries, the amount of land and resources available to an individual or group, and their perception of the protected area's effect on their household and community development. Perceived and actual land shortages often contribute to negative attitudes toward conserved areas and calls for their reduction in size or their removal (Infield 1988; Newmark et al. 1993; Infield and Namara 2001). Frustration about the lack of available land has contributed to resentment at Amboró National Park, particularly amongst those without secure land titles (Moreno et al. 1998). In contrast, a study at Nepal's Royal Chitwan National Park found large landholdings were associated with a positive attitude toward the protected area (Nepal and Weber 1995).

Meanwhile, the perception of future economic benefits including infrastructure development and income has been linked to local people backing a protected area (Alexander 2000). However, studies have shown more negative attitudes when these expectations are unfulfilled (Fiallo and Jacobson 1995; Ite 1996) and where promised jobs and economic benefits do not materialize (Alexander 2000; Allendorf 2007).

Conversely, recognizing personal benefits in terms of employment, income, or payment in goods and services that stem from the protected area has been associated with positive attitudes (Infield 1988, Newmark et al. 1993; Fiallo and Jacobson 1995; Abbot et al. 2001).

Interestingly, in Costa Rica and Honduras, researchers have found people living within or adjacent to national parks share similar feelings as rural residents in the Madidi, that these benefits should be forthcoming due to the protected area's presence, both directly through government actions and indirectly through the attraction of additional resources (Schelhas and Pfeffer 2008). In a seven-year study of attitudes toward a national park in Uganda, researchers found that along with participation and knowledge of conservation activities came more requests for "support and resources" (Infield and Namara 2001: 48). Thus, education and outreach that otherwise facilitates positive attitudes may also intensify interest in development assistance.

Finally, providing expected development does not guarantee a positive attitude, nor will increased development necessarily reduce actual threats to a protected area (Brandon 1998). First, perceived benefits of any type must outweigh disadvantages associated with the protected area's presence (Fiallo and Jacobson 1995; Alexander 2000). Second, when positive attitudes form, they will not necessarily persist. Development assistance has been shown to have a short-term effect on conservation attitudes (Infield and Namara 2001). Thus, the interplay of development and conservation measures and benefits must be assessed to understand their contribution to resident people's attitudes toward a protected area.

Study Area and Background

The study site is located at the intersection of the foothills of the Andes and the Amazon basin in an area of moist humid forests with savannas interspersed in the north and east. Part of the site is within the northeastern border of the Madidi protected area, which extends westward, upslope to the top of the eastern cordillera of the Andes where the peaks are over 6000 msl. The altitudinal gradient within the protected area contributes to its high biodiversity. Conservation International[5] (CI) cited the diversity of the flora and fauna, its relatively intact state, and the presence of exceptional ecosystems, such as dry mountain forest and natural savannas, when lobbying for the protected area's designation in the early 1990s (Conservation International 1991). Following confirmation of CI's claims, the Bolivian government recommended boundaries for the protected area in 1992, officially creating the Madidi protected area in September 1995.

The majority of the study population referenced in this chapter hailed from one of seven rural communities, which belonged to one of the three principal political-ethnic assemblages found in the region. The first are lowland indigenous peoples. This includes the Tacana from Bella Altura, Buena Vista, and Tumupasa and the residents of San José de Uchupiamonas (San José). The latter distinguished themselves from the Tacana, though the history of these two groups is closely intertwined. The *colonos* or settlers, the second faction, were predominantly Quechua and Aymara who have migrated from the altiplano or the upper valleys of the eastern cordillera since the late 1980s in response to government programs promoting the lowlands, population pressure, periodic droughts, and perceived economic opportunity. They resided in Hurí Huapo and La Esmeralda. The other two study communities, San Isidro and Nueva Palestina, had a mix of residents including *colonos* from the earliest migration wave, lowland indigenous peoples, Quechua from the lower intermontane valleys located in the nearby Apolo region, and individuals who did not identify as indigenous. They were part of an assortment of communities in the region that were not politically associated with either the *colonos* or a lowland indigenous organization, nor did they have their own pan-community alliance.

Despite the different histories and ethnic composition of these communities, all had broadly similar livelihood practices and living conditions. Rural residents practiced swidden (*chaco*) agriculture centered around the staple crops of rice and corn. Bananas, yuca, and minor crops played a smaller role in their subsistence. They also raised chickens, pigs, and ducks, with some households owning from one to ten head of cattle. Hunting, gathering, and fishing contributed to household nutrition depending upon preference and the local availability of these resources. Rural residents earned income from agricultural sales, wage labor, and participation in local markets for forest products ranging from wild cacao and honey to refined handicrafts (*artesenía*), which were sold primarily to tourists. The people of San José also owned an ecolodge established with institutional support from CI and funding from the Inter-American Development Bank (IDB). Chalalán provided income to the community and the men and women who worked there.[6] The only other study community to benefit substantially from tourism was Bella Altura, where a small majority of the residents earned the greater part of their income from *artesenía*. The communities that contributed to this study had a comparable array of basic services including piped water, cistern flush pit toilets, an elementary school or access to one in an adjacent community, and a two-way radio. In addition, the larger communities of Tumupasa and San José had a high school, health post, public telephone, and a community tractor used predominantly for public works and transportation. Tumupasa also had around-the-clock electricity from a generator.

Land rights and tenure patterns however distinguished the groups that participated in this study. Lowland indigenous peoples have a history of use and occupation in the region that predates the Conquest. This entitled them to petition for large expanses of lands called *Tierra Comunitaria de Origen* (TCO), which San José and the Tacana communities in this study, all of which are affiliated with the *Consejo Indígena de los Pueblos Tacana* (CIPTA), have received. Meanwhile *colonos* only had the right to obtain 50 ha per household, which was slightly higher than the average lot size in Hurí Huapo and La Esmeralda. Like the *colonos*, most residents of unaffiliated communities had the right to 50 ha parcels, though some indigenous lowland households could have joined petitions for TCO lands. In Nueva Palestina, the average lot size was approximately 50 ha. However, in San Isidro, many households had smaller parcels on the order of 20 ha or did not hold title to any land, renting from a neighbor or using untitled state lands for agricultural activities.

Along its northeastern border, the demarcation of the Madidi protected area's boundaries disturbed the livelihood patterns of only a small portion of the resident population, primarily members of the few communities located inside the ANMI. This includes San José whose TCO lies predominantly in the ANMI, but which also crosses into the more restricted national park. Except for San José, the study communities lay outside of the protected area, where few residents entered prior to its creation because of the precipitous hills and the historic abundance of more readily accessible resources outside its current boundaries.

Results

Despite minimal direct effect on their subsistence activities from the protected area's decree, all study communities saw increased conservation and development activity by NGOs and the government starting in the late 1990s. This clearly has influenced their ideas about conservation and attitudes toward the protected area. Even amongst the study subjects who expressed concerns about its political and economic effects, this study found a generalized understanding and acceptance of its presence and purpose. For some, this developed over time. As an elderly Tacana man from Buena Vista said, "At the beginning, it was not understood what the reason was to conserve a park, but then we realized it was necessary." Informants explained that the park, the term they used most frequently to refer to the entire protected area, was created to maintain the natural resources located there. They described how it was primarily designed to look but not touch (*no tocar*), and that the goal was to prevent the forest from disappearing (*desaparacer*) and its resources from running out (*no acabar*), which they indicated has happened outside its borders. For example, a Tacana man from Bella Altura described what he knew about the Madidi protected area:

> What I have learned of the park is how to improve what was, because inside the park, there are areas where no one can enter, where no one can do any activity, but there are areas where yes, one can do some tourism activities, walk, spend time. This I have learned. What else I have learned is how to keep conserving these things, these resources that are about to end. This I have learned: how to care, how to improve, and how to continue with these resources.

Amongst the study population, there was a strong consensus that conserving nature inside the protected area was good. First and foremost, they said that the park protected wildlife, which many described as in danger or not readily available in their own communities. "They created Madidi National Park for the animals, where they can be … The animals always will live there," said one man from La Esmeralda. Many directly benefited from their protection, by hunting these animals both inside and outside its boundaries. A man from San José who lived outside the park at the time of this study, but who continued to take advantage of hunting privileges inside the ANMI due to his affiliation with the community, said:

> [The park] is good because sometimes when we go to hunt, there are animals. It is very necessary that it survives. If the whole world is going to enter, the animals will leave and it is going to be sad.

Informants generally described the conservation of other natural resources, including trees, water, and the ecosystem services they provide, subsequent to wildlife benefits. They expressed their support in terms of provisioning and regulating services. Many informants discussed shade and protection from the wind provided by the trees, while others mentioned conservation of soil and water. And, as one woman from San José said, the park also "protects the water so that it is not contaminated." Another common reference study subjects made was to the forest as the lungs of the world, phrasing that appears frequently in conservation literature which people living near other parks in Latin America similarly cite (Pfeffer et al. 2001; Schelhas and Pfeffer 2008). In addition, study subjects discussed oxygen, like an Aymara man from Nueva Palestina who had lived in the region for over 20 years. He explained:

> I think the park is good because the oxygen is nearly finished. If all the world moves, we clear all the trees, and we will have pure industry … The trees are important in the fabrication of oxygen and pure air. They make the air better. It is an important part, to maintain, well, everything. But Bolivia carries much of the weight, more than others where they have decimated the land.

With respect to consumption of conserved resources, such as timber-yielding trees and the seeds they produce, some saw themselves as having a right to use them in the future, though it was unclear how these would be available and whether for subsistence only or commercial extraction. Other informants with use privileges inside the ANMI recognized these benefits in the present. Additionally, a universal objective fulfilled by the park was saving these resources for their children and future generations. A man from San Isidro understood these aims but not how they would be achieved.

> This park is for the animals, also for the forest, the wood, the timber-yielding trees, because with time for new generations, there is going to be none. For this reason, I believe that the park is maintaining, but I do not always have an understanding of the end. What is the park going to do, what help they are going to give, how is it going to be?

Inside the ANMI, the residents of San José had the right to use these resources at the time of this study. However, informants from the community initially envisioned economic hardship when after the park's decree administrators announced prohibitions against necessary subsistence practices including hunting, firewood collection, and clearing land for agriculture. Restrictions on the sale of natural resource products were less of an issue, due to the community's remote location and inability to access regional markets. Because of the lack of respect shown to them, *joseanos* also were concerned about SERNAP's ongoing presence in the community. Informants mentioned how park staff would enter unannounced, measuring *chacos*, inserting themselves into multiple areas of their daily subsistence, and without notice, impose new rules. Negative interactions as well as unrealistic regulations prohibiting necessary subsistence activities provoked San José's residents to object directly to SERNAP. The park administration relaxed the rules affecting subsistence and agreed to ask permission to enter the community's lands to meet with residents about their environmental activities. The woman below describes how, with respect to hunting, negotiations resolved the situation.

> In the beginning, they put their conditions like, 'You are in the park so you cannot hunt even a bird.' But we have put the condition, 'You as the park have come to help us to protect. This is good that you have come, but you cannot prohibit this because here there is nowhere to make purchases, and we cannot buy where we are not earning money.' So, we said to the park, 'Look for work for us or for sure employment and put in a place to buy meat, and we will not consume meat from the forest.' Clearly, that's why we have our reservation area to not go hunting, for example, from Chalalán up above one or two hours by boat it is prohibited to hunt, and because the animals have to be tame for the tourists, and we have till there where we can go to look for hunting. So, at first the park was very negative and did not want that, but we have said to them to get us employment where we earn monthly and with the same resources, we will be able to consume that which they put here to sell to us. And they have understood that they could not do this here. It is too difficult, so they have accepted it.

While a few *joseanos* remained frustrated at the time of this study by the remaining limitations imposed on them, which allowed hunting and gathering for subsistence only and suggested small *chacos*, the majority did not consider the restrictions to their subsistence practices an issue. Meanwhile, outside the park, only a handful of Tacana and non-affiliated rural residents raised this concern with respect to their subsistence practices. They were from Tumupasa, which sits next to the dirt track that enters the protected area from the highway and continues on to San José, and from a few nearby communities that used this same path to access the foothills. As one Tacana man said, since the park was created, they "can no longer enter quietly" without requesting permission. Another man from a nearby, unaffiliated community who had lived in the region for more than 20 years complained, "We are neighbors with the park, and we know that [the right] has been lost to enter to hunt animals. We have lost this up above." Though this vocal minority felt their loss keenly, often complaining about how park guards, commercial loggers, and other people (*terceros*) continued to enter the protected area to hunt and log illegally along this road, theirs was not a prevalent complaint amongst the study population.[7]

Instead, two other factors contributed to the predominant negative attitudes toward the Madidi protected area, one specific to *colonos* and unaffiliated communities and the other ubiquitous amongst the study population. First, the extent of the park was a pervasive concern outside of the lowland indigenous populace. Many study subjects without extensive TCO lands considered conserving a large space like the Madidi protected area to be detrimental to their survival and the development of their communities. They despaired about the future, saying when combined with lands titled privately and collectively as well as concessions for logging in the region that were held by large, national companies, the Madidi protected area left little land available for the large-scale agriculture they wanted to practice and for impending needs as the population grows. Even in cases where they accepted the park's goals and appreciated the ecosystem services it supplied, the majority of these study subjects questioned or outright contested its magnitude. In the Madidi, an Aymara woman from Hurí Huapo who had a 50 ha parcel of land with her husband explained her concerns:

> I agree with conserving nature in the Madidi protected area, but only in part. I believe that there are many people that cannot survive in the future in this way. We want to plant in big areas, to put in sugar cane … Now, what is saving us is only rice, and it does not supply us, and it does not provide because there is no market. And this is the disadvantage, but the advantage is that in the park, it conserves also all the things.

Many of the *colonos* and residents of unaffiliated communities were very vocal about the extent of the protected area. A man from La Esmeralda stridently asserted that the Madidi protected area will be destroyed, that the lure of the trees and the land will be too much to resist if rural peoples are not supported better in their efforts to obtain additional land. This has occurred in the southwest where *colonos* and unaffiliated residents without TCOs have illegally entered the Madidi protected area to log, sometimes leading to tense confrontations (La Razón 2007a; La Razón 2007b; La Razón 2009).

While only informants in *colono* and unaffiliated communities demonstrated negative attitudes toward the Madidi protected area's expanse, nearly all informants vociferously complained about the lack of financial benefits and development assistance received since its declaration. Many found the idea that the protected area was designed partially with the intent to provide economic benefits to the rural residents of the Madidi ludicrous. Tourists were seen as benefiting directly from the protected area through their visits, and the state was frequently cited as a principal financial beneficiary. A few informants called Madidi a private park, saying all the profits go to the exterior of the region or the country, and in more than one instance, they specifically referenced North America.

Aside from their belief in the actual destination of these funds, informants clearly indicated money associated with the protected area did not reach their communities, even in San José, which had the successful tourist business. Additionally, San José has received the most conservation-associated development aid along the northeastern border in terms of time, money, and resources, yet still no one I spoke with there believed the benefits were adequate. As one man from San José told me the park staff and administration is only concerned with their own survival, not the support of his community. However, a small number of informants recognized they would have received even less without the Madidi protected area as an attraction. For example, a young man from Bella Altura said:

> The cacao that I have has been financed by the park, which has resources to manage this type of project, because if we were not outside the park, nobody would bring any type of project. There would be nothing.

Many informants inside and outside the park believed that because they acted like caretakers (*cuidantes*) or because they lived adjacent to the protected area, SERNAP should provide direct payments. Residents of San José frequently used their location inside the park and past instances when they notified park guards about people illegally entering to mine or log as a rationale. However, being located near the park was seen as sufficient as well. For instance, an Aymara woman from La Esmeralda discussed how the park provides no compensation, yet they ask the people to restrict their extractive activities and the amount of land they clear.

> Well, the park does not want us to work, but the park does not give anything to us in exchange, rather we give to the park, you see? It gives nothing to us. If we work, we eat. If we do not work, no, but meanwhile they want to maintain all the environment, that is to say conservation, while in return, they give us nothing.

Informants clearly understood that there was a lot of money associated with the Madidi protected area, often donated by the United States and other countries.[8] They said some goes to those who work for the park, the guards and the administrators. While a handful of study subjects had relatives who worked in conservation, many more did not, and they complained about the lack of employment and other economic benefits. There have been some SERNAP-sponsored development projects, most recently to expand cacao production, and many more by NGOs ranging from installing potable water systems to microenterprise development. Each study community had participated in more than one of these projects as of 2007. However, informants unanimously expressed dismay at the lack of financial resources and support provided. They thought they should receive development assistance to improve basic services and find economically viable alternatives to their low-rent agricultural activities, both from SERNAP and the NGOs working in the area. Additionally, informants commonly stated that their community did not receive anything, but that other communities in the region did. Actual inequity in aid was clearly visible,[9] and it frustrated those who had received fewer projects and less financial assistance, particularly the residents of La Esmeralda, including the man quoted below, and members of unaffiliated communities.

> We know that the park has a lot of financing, a lot of money, that is one aspect. I do not know; I am not well informed, but we know that there are

non-governmental organizations that give money to them, but we here in the community of the park, we do not receive any benefit, none, not a single one.

However, lowland indigenous informants said that the park does not trouble itself with them either. As a Tacana man from Tumupasa declared:

The park should facilitate having a living, to generate for our livelihoods, to improve our conditions. Although they have given us little projects that do not provide enough to survive, they have not given us a project for a better future.

At the time of this study, despite these negative attitudes, generalized support remained for the Madidi protected area's existence. While few envisioned the inequitable land tenure situation being resolved satisfactorily, study subjects continued to be hopeful that development assistance was forthcoming. Sometimes they expressed it subtly as with a Tacana woman from Bella Altura who said optimistically, "Perhaps the park will begin to help the community, but until now, nothing has been seen on behalf of the park. Perhaps now with everything they will think to collaborate." Other informants like the man from San Isidro cited below used their own enthusiasm with the potential benefits to convey they had not despaired yet, recognizing the ongoing conservation and development activities in the region and indicating they are open to receiving them.

If the park would be able to support us with a project, that would be magnificent. We would be in agreement, but the National Park, like I said, is SERNAP. SERNAP has different projects, but till this moment, there has not been one thing from a project from Madidi National Park here ... If the park brings us a benefit from a project, good. 'This is a benefit for you so that you can move ahead.' This would be magnificent. But, meanwhile, we are making our small agriculture that really is little benefit to us.

Discussion

This hope for improvement, which persisted amongst many of the study subjects, provides an opportunity to address the negative attitudes that have developed toward the Madidi protected area. In addition, widespread knowledge about the protected area's management goals and identification of the benefits conservation provides, an often unrecognized view held by resident populations (Allendorf et al. 2006), offers an opening to enhance their support for the park. However, resident people need a detailed understanding of how wildlife populations will improve and what are the specific ecosystem services the protected area provides along with how these are relevant to their own lives. Some informants in the Madidi vaguely stated that the protected area is "good for the environment." For example, one woman from La Esmeralda noted without the forest in the protected area, everything becomes *barbecho* and the soil becomes nothing, and this affects "many people," but she did not connect this to her own livelihood activities. This superficial recognition may not ensure continued appreciation for the protected area or conservation in general.

Alternatively, those with the strongest beliefs about the value of conserving the Madidi expressed an appreciation for conservation's advantages that was detailed and directly related to their way of life. They often shared a story to describe them. For example, in Bella Altura and San Isidro, multiple informants illustrated instances where troops of peccaries (*Tayassu pecari*) crossed the road from the Madidi protected area, entering their communities where they then hunted them. They said these peccaries no longer lived along the highway outside of the protected area, attributing their availability to their protection inside. In San Isidro, where a stream dried up following the removal of trees around it to create a pasture, multiple study subjects recognized the value of maintaining forest cover near waterways, including those that fed their community from above near the protected area's border. These informants saw their access to water and their own survival as vested in the preservation of the park.

Regular, targeted outreach is necessary to build upon the past success of conservation activities in generating positive attitudes. Study subjects complained that these activities had tapered off in recent years. They need to continue with consistent programs designed for each community or subpopulation. They should focus upon how conservation's successes can improve resident people's lives. In communities where they have not directly recognized this benefit, SERNAP and conservation NGOs working in the region need to make the connection clear. How is the park improving or protecting the soil, water, trees, and animals, and how does this help them? As one man from La Esmeralda said, "I tell you, we want evidence that it succeeds. The park has much good income, also a little goes to the communities, but concerning something like deforestation or other things, are they necessary? That would be the question." Additionally, a man from San Isidro cited above clearly conveyed his lack of understanding about how conserved resources would benefit his community in the future. The park administration needs to establish clear policies that ensure the continuation and availability of these ecosystem services and natural resources to resident peoples both inside and outside of the protected area, and they need to convey this information to the residents.

Negative attitudes related to the extent of the park and concerns about the lack of development require a different approach to ameliorate. Addressing the first problem directly would require structural changes to land rights and tenure policies that the Bolivian government, conservation NGOs, and indigenous associations like CIPTA would not support.[10] In addition, the lack of land not otherwise titled or committed to another use makes this physically impossible. The most practical solution remains to ensure that migrants and non-affiliated community members have title to the smaller parcels that they have the right to acquire, and to find an economic livelihood strategy for this land that provides both for their subsistence and meets their need for income and advancement.

This first requires more attention to these particular communities, the *colonos* and unaffiliated, who had received less assistance than lowland indigenous communities as of 2007. Next, this requires recognition that many of the proposed income-generating projects to date were not feasible for all community members to join. For example, in the community of La Esmeralda, a cacao agroforestry project that started with less than a quarter of the households in the community ended in 2007 with only three having participated fully. For nearly a quarter of the community, the project was not an option due to the water retained on their parcels that prevented them from establishing the permanent tree crops that were the centerpiece of the project. In addition, those who did not participate or complete the project cited the inherent risk of growing and marketing cacao, the onerous labor requirements including weeding four times per year, and the delayed economic returns in comparison to their current livelihood activities. Addressing these concerns may require a novel approach grounded in the realization that poor, rural residents do not have the wherewithal to participate in these types of income-generation projects without direct cash payments to offset lost productive activities and labor inputs required, along with guarantees of assistance should these projects fail. In addition, the one-size-fits-all approach may not work in a heterogeneous landscape like the study site. Local ecological, economic, and cultural conditions need to be addressed, even within communities.

Solutions to the more extensive concern about insufficient economic and development benefits are no less difficult to address. Whether through jobs or other means, economic benefits with an unmistakable link to the protected area's existence need to be increased in order to leverage this means of support. This requires improving the development assistance given to resident communities and spreading it more equitably amongst them. For example, the organizations and government agencies active around the Madidi protected area need a coordinated effort to bring projects and improved basic services to all communities in the area regardless of political-ethnic affiliation. This may improve both the perception and the actual inequalities that exist.

However, there are risks to this strategy. Trying to meet the persistent, boundless desire for development expressed by study subjects poses risks to the long-term sustainability of the protected area. Paige West describes how in her work with the Gimi of Papua New Guinea, the requests for development aid that they gave to her upon each visit increased (West 2006). They asked for more advanced items which built upon the earlier achievements made in education, sanitation, and market-participation. Study subjects in the Madidi have similar expectations (Trusty 2010). As Kopnina and Shoreman note, anthropologists have not studied the role of poor and indigenous populations in environmental degradation (this volume), nor have they explored how their increasing level of development affects the environment, an oversight to remedy in cases like the Madidi.

Positive feelings toward the protected area engendered by economic and development benefits also may dissipate as they have in San José. Residents received assistance from SERNAP and conservation and development NGOs for both basic services and to initiate alternative income generation activities. In addition, the revenues from Chalalán, their ecolodge, have provided funds to build and staff the health clinic and high school they now have. Yet, as discussed, frustrated study subjects in San José had the same perception as other informants of receiving too little assistance. One solution is to continue to address resident people's interest in development by maintaining long-term relationships with communities, which few NGOs in the Madidi have done to date, while tailoring the assistance provided to meet conservation goals. This requires overcoming institutional barriers like the preference for short-term projects and continuously shifting priorities within conservation organizations, along with attending to the problems encountered by development projects as described above and as detailed extensively elsewhere (see Chambers 1983; Brandon and Wells 1992; Crewe and Harrison 1999).

Not addressing development interests is not an option. Development is a powerful, goal-oriented cognitive model amongst study subjects in this area (Trusty 2010). They focus much of their energy on both household and community development, and they clearly make decisions in their daily lives designed to achieve these goals. In addition, informants' concerns about unfurnished development associated with the Madidi protected area were some of the strongest shared during research, both in terms of the emotion expressed and the detailed explanations provided. While the perception of insufficient economic benefits has yet to lead to actions against the park, this may change in the future if the situation continues.

Lowland indigenous residents along the northeastern border previously have protested in support of the Madidi protected area and conservation, marching to La Paz in 2006 to demonstrate their disgust with proposed changes to the administration with which they disagreed. Other residents generally have remained neutral. However, to garner desired development and economic benefits, they may reverse their positions. Recently, residents of the region have spoken of the Madidi protected area as a "white elephant," indicating this massive venture has not led to expected outcomes (Lopez 2010). Basically, all the options the resident population gave up when the government decreed the Madidi protected area may become attractive again. While outside interests may drive extraction of known petroleum resources located along the northeastern border of the Madidi protected area (Stronza 2006), local people may turn in support of this option as well as other projects that are contrary to the park's conservation objectives. In addition, illegal logging may increase as it has on the southwestern side of the park. Alternatively without attention to their development objectives, rural residents may turn to other activities like gold mining or they may enter the park in search of agricultural land, which to date they have not done extensively within the study area. The Bolivian government has limited capability to prevent these types of incursions, and their potential implications for conservation objectives are profound.

Conclusion

When considering the case of the Madidi protected area's northeastern border, negative attitudes about its presence, purpose, and benefits do not fall neatly into the archetype of displacement and disenfranchisement that leads to conflicts over livelihoods and subsistence. In fact, in the study communities, widespread understanding of the park's purpose and support for its goals to protect and ensure the continuation of environmental resources mirrors the concerns of conservationists, who have actively worked to engender these attitudes. Instead, negative opinions reflect local concerns related to land availability, which they see as inhibited by conservation activity in the region and the presence of the Madidi protected area, and development, which they expect but feel they have not sufficiently received. The former affects a subset of the rural population, those without tenure and access to large expanses of land. The latter is a concern of all the study subjects. Both are risk factors for the success of the Madidi protected area, while the generalized concern for conservation and understanding of the park's purpose provide opportunities to improve the people–protected area relationship.

The similarities and differences between the findings from this study and those from other sites highlight the need to understand the local context when studying attitudes toward protected areas. Factors ranging from design to regulation to the broader political economy, ecological conditions, as well as social and cultural aspects may influence attitudes.[11] These must be understood from the point of view of local residents, who may have different perceptions of the state of affairs depending upon their positionality and their own experiences.

However, comparing studies, including findings from this research, reveals broad patterns amongst sites. First, unresolved access and resource use issues invariably lead to dislike and often conflict around protected areas. However, resolving them, as in the Madidi where the park administration relented and permitted necessary subsistence activities inside the ANMI, can improve perceptions about the protected area and may even overcome hostile attitudes. Second, showing respect for resident populations and improving communication is important as management's negative interactions with them is a contributing factor to poor opinions about protected areas. Third, the perception or reality of land scarcity outside a park contributes to negative attitudes toward the amount of land conserved, while having sufficient land attenuates this trepidation. Where there is not sufficient land to increase holdings, other solutions must be found to address concerns about resource availability. Fourth, the perception that economic and development benefits are not forthcoming when they are expected or promised leads to disgruntlement with the protected area. However, improvements may not ensure lasting support as seen in San José, and their environmental impact is uncertain, requiring further study. Fifth, knowledge about a protected area's purpose and recognition of its ecosystem services, achieved through context-appropriate outreach and bolstered by experience, facilitates positive attitudes. Finally, only when the perceived benefits, be they environmental, economic, social, or cultural, outweigh perceived negative consequences from the protected area's presence will conservation goals be secure.

Notes

1 This material is based upon work supported by the National Science Foundation under Grant No. 0717916. Any opinions, findings, and conclusions or recommendations expressed in this material are those of the author and do not necessarily reflect the views of the National Science Foundation.

2 While the park administration allowed subsistence activities on these TCO lands, in order to harvest products for sale from within the ANMI, these groups had to follow applicable environmental laws including preparing required management plans. However, the new Bolivian constitution, passed by popular referendum in 2009, provides additional rights to indigenous peoples to manage their lands and affairs. As of the submission of this chapter for publication, these had not been legislated. Thus, it is unclear what effect the new constitution may have on the management and utilization of TCO lands that overlap with protected areas.

3 The findings presented in this chapter are the result of a broader dissertation project that explored patterns and variations in rural residents' ideas and beliefs about the environment, conservation, and development.

4 I utilized narrative walks as a technique to elicit study subjects' thoughts about the research topics in an effort to reduce the distortion often introduced by the content and order of direct questioning (D'Andrade 2005). While the informant and I walked through their parcel of land or the community, the environs served as a prompt for the direction of the conversation. I would ask the informant to talk about what we saw and what was significant to them, posing clarification questions or prompting them to continue by asking about a natural or human-made feature in the landscape if there was an extended lull in the conversation.

5 I worked at CI in their Washington, DC office from 1994–96 in the Conservation Enterprises Department.

6 The community owns 50 per cent of Chalalán, while individual households in San José own the rest. A director and paid staff, all residents of San José, manage the lodge with input from the community. Dividends are paid occasionally to the member households, and investments have been made in community development projects with profits from Chalalán. Profits also have paid for necessary upgrades to infrastructure at the lodge.

7 The general consensus amongst the local population was that illegal incursions to the park in the study area were limited in scope, with only a few individuals entering. This opinion was seconded by conservationists and protected area staff who were concerned with the much larger scale of illegal logging and forest clearing for agriculture taking place in other areas around the Madidi protected area, particularly the southwestern side near Apolo.

8 Most funding comes from international donors with the mix of funding agencies shifting over time. The main contributors historically have been various bilateral aid agencies including US AID and the German, Canadian, Danish, and Japanese equivalents, the Inter-American Development Bank, and the Global Environmental Facility (GEF). The main international conservation NGOs active in the region are CI, since the early 1990s, and Wildlife Conservation Society (WCS), since 1999. They often manage projects financed by the donors. Numerous smaller conservation and development NGOs, national and international, also operate in the region and receive funds from the larger organizations and the bilateral and multilateral agencies with limited financing received through their own fundraising.

9 With regards to the disparity in development assistance, SERNAP attempted to address the issue with a cacao project funded by GEF in 2006 and 2007 that specifically targeted more remote communities and those that had not previously received assistance. Lack of institutional support and limited funding impeded its success. A few conservation NGOs had made an effort to reach more remote communities as well, especially WCS. However, none had yet tackled the disparity between communities associated with different political-ethnic groups effectively.

10 The government has had difficulty securing land for new 50 ha parcels for migrants who do not yet have a titled parcel. The conflict between lowland indigenous people and the migrants turned violent in 2009 as they fought over a logging concession returned to the state which both demanded. Thus, titling even small parcels to migrants is fraught with tension.

11 In some cases, demographic factors including age, education, and wealth have been shown influence attitudes (Fiallo and Jacobson, 1995, Infield, 1988, Newmark et al., 1993, Mehta and Heinen, 2001). However, the majority of studies I have reviewed which tested these relationships found no significant effect. In general, demographic factors are the least likely to have clear patterns across sites as opposed to contextual factors.

References

Abbot, J. I. O., Thomas, D. H. L., Gardner, A. A., Neba, S. E. and Khen, M. W. (2001) 'Understanding the Links Between Conservation and Development in the Bamenda Highlands, Cameroon', *World Development*, 29: 1115–36.

Alexander, S. E. (2000) 'Resident attitudes towards conservation and black howler monkeys in Belize: the Community Baboon Sanctuary', *Environmental Conservation*, 27: 341–50.

Allendorf, K. (2007) 'Residents' Attitudes Toward Three Protected Areas in Southwestern Nepal', *Biodiversity and Conservation*, 16: 2087–2102.

Allendorf, T., Swe, K. K., Oo, T., Htut, Y., Aung, M., Allendorf, K., Hayek, L.-A., Leimgruber, P. and Wemmer, C. (2006) 'Community Attitudes toward Three Protected Areas in Upper Myanmar (Burma)', *Environmental Conservation*, 33: 344–52.

Anthony, B. (2007) 'The dual nature of parks: attitudes of neighbouring communities towards Kruger National Park, South Africa', *Environmental Conservation*, 34: 236–45.

Axelsson, R. and Angelstam, P. (2005) 'Biosphere Reserve and Model Forest: A Study of Two Concepts for Integrated Natural Resource Management,' in B. Frostell (ed.) *1st VHU Conference*, Västeros, Sweden.

Bosak, K. (2008) 'Nature, Conflict and Biodiversity Conservation in the Nanda Devi Biosphere Reserve', *Conservation and Society*, 6: 211–24.

Brandon, K. (1998) 'Perils to Parks: The Social Context of Threats,' in K. Brandon, K.H Redfordand S.E. Sanderson (eds) *Parks in Peril: People, Politics, and Protected Areas*, Washington, D.C.: Island Press.

Brandon, K. E. and Wells, M. (1992) 'Planning for people and parks: Design dilemmas,' *World Development*, 20: 557–70.

Brockington, D. (2002) *Fortress Conservation: The Preservation of the Mkomazi Game Reserve, Tanzania*, Bloomington, IN: Indiana University Press.

Buergin, R. (2001) 'Contested Heritages: Disputes on People, Forests, and a World Heritage Site in Globalizing Thailand,' in T. Krings, G. Oesten and S. Seitz (eds) *SEFUT Working Papers*. Freiburg, Germany: Working Group Socio-Economics of Forest Use in the Tropics and Subtropics at the University of Freiburg.

Chambers, R. (1983) *Rural Development: Putting the Last First*, New York: Longman.

Cincotta, R. P. & Engelman, R. (2000) *Nature's Place: Human Population and the Future of Biological Diversity*, Washington, DC: Population Action International.

Conservation International (1991) 'A Biological Assessment of the Alto Madidi Region and Adjacent Areas of Northwest Bolivia: May 18–June 15, 1990,' In T. Parker and B. Bailey (eds) *RAP Working Papers*, Washington, DC: Conservation International.

Crewe, E. & Harrison, E. (1999) *Whose Development? An Ethnography of Aid*, London: Zed.

D'Andrade, R. (2005) 'Some Methods for Studying Cultural Cognitive Structures', in N. Quinn (ed.) *Finding Culture in Talk: A Collection of Methods*. New York: Palgrave Macmillan.

De Boer, W. F. and Baquete, D. S. (1998) 'Natural resource use, crop damage and attitudes of rural people in the vicinity of the Maputo Elephant Reserve, Mozambique,' *Environmental Conservation*, 25: 208–18.

Fiallo, E. A. and Jacobson, S. K. (1995) 'Local Communities and Protected Areas: Attitudes of Rural Residents Towards Conservation and Machalilla National Park, Ecuador,' *Environmental Conservation*, 22: 241–49.

Heinen, J. T. (1993) 'Park-People Relations in Kosi Tappu Wildlife Reserve, Nepal: A Socioeconomic Analysis,' *Environmental Conservation*, 20: 25–34.

Holmes, C. M. (2003) 'The Influence of Protected Area Outreach on Conservation Attitudes and Resource Use Patterns: A Case Study from Western Tanzania,' *Oryx*, 37: 305–15.

Hough, J. L. (1988) 'Obstacles to effective management of conflicts between national parks and surrounding human communities in developing countries,' *Environmental Conservation*, 152: 129–36.

Igoe, J. (2004) *Conservation and Globalization: A Study of National Parks and Indigenous Communities from East Africa to South Dakota*, Belmont, CA: Wadsworth.

Infield, M. (1988) 'Attitudes of a rural community towards conservation and a local conservation area in Natal, South Africa,' *Biological Conservation*, 45: 21–46.

Infield, M. and Namara, A. (2001) 'Community attitudes and behaviour towards conservation: an assessment of a community conservation programme around Lake Mburo National Park, Uganda,' *Oryx*, 35: 48–60.

Ite, U. E. (1996) 'Community perceptions of the Cross River National Park, Nigeria'. *Environmental Conservation*, 23, 351–57.

IUCN (1994) 'Guidelines for Protected Area Management Categories', Gland, Switzerland: IUCN.

Jacoby, K. (2001) *Crimes against Nature: Squatters, Poachers, Thieves, and the Hidden History of American Conservation*, Berkeley: University of California Press.

La Razón (2007a) 'La tensión por la disputa de tierras regresa a Apolo', *La Razón*, 24 de agosto.

——(2007b) 'Los campesinos declaran la guerra contra las TCO', *La Razón*, 19 de julio.

——(2009) 'Apolo inicia paro y bloqueo indefinido en contra de TCO', *La Razón*, 24 de septiembre.

Lopez, E. (2010) 'Discussion about dissertation research in the Madidi,' Chat conversation (31 May 2010).

Mehta, J. N. and Heinen, J. T. (2001) 'Does Community-Based Conservation Shape Favorable Attitudes Among Locals? An Empirical Study from Nepal', *Environmental Management*, 28: 165–77.

Moreno, A., Margoluis, R. and Brandon, K. (1998) 'Bolivia: Amboró National Park,' In K. Brandon, K.H Redford, K. H. and S.E Sanderson (eds.) *Parks in Peril: People, Politics, and Protected Areas*, Washington, D.C.: Island Press.

Nepal, S. K. and Weber, K. E. (1995) 'The Quandary of Local People-Park Relations in Nepal's Royal Chitwan National Park,' *Environmental Management.*, 19: 853–66.

Neumann, R. P. (1998) *Imposing Wilderness: Struggles over Livelihood and Nature Preservation in Africa*, Berkeley: University of California Press.

Newmark, W. D., Leonard, N. L., Sariko, H. I. & Gamassa, D.-G. M. (1993) 'Conservation attitudes of local people living adjacent to five protected areas in Tanzania,' *Biological Conservation*, 63: 177–83.

Padmanaba, M. and Sheil, D. (2007) 'Finding and Promoting a Local Conservation Consensus in a Globally Important Tropical Forest Landscape,' *Biodiversity and Conservation*: 137–51.

Parry, D. and Campbell, B. (1992) 'Attitudes of Rural Communities to Animal Wildlife and Its Utilization in Chobe Enclave and Mababe Depression, Botswana,' *Environmental Conservation*, 19: 245–52.

Pfeffer, M. J., Schelhas, J. W. and Day, L. A. (2001) 'Forest Conservation, Value Conflict, and Interest Formation in a Honduran National Park,' *Rural Sociology*, 55: 382–403.

Schelhas, J. and Pfeffer, M. J. (2008) *Saving Forests, Protecting People? Environmental Conservation in Central America*, Lanham, MD: AltaMira Press.

Scientific Software Development Gmbh (1993–2008) 'ATLAS.ti: The Knowledge Workbench'. WIN 5.2.21 ed. Berlin, Germany: Scientific Software Development Gmbh.

Silori, C. S. (2007) 'Perception of Local People towards Conservation of Forest Resources in Nanda Devi Biosphere Reserve, north-western Himalaya, India,' *Biodiversity and Conservation*, 16: 211–22.

Sodhi, N. S., Lee, T. M., Sekercioglu, C. H., Webb, E. L., Prawiradilaga, D. M., Lohman, D. J., Pierce, N. E., Diesmos, A. C., Rao, M. and Ehrlich, P. R. (2010) 'Local People Value Environmental Services Provided by Forested Parks,' *Biodiversity and Conservation*, 19: 1175–88.

Spence, M. D. (1999) *Dispossessing the Wilderness: Indian Removal and the Making of the National Parks*, New York: Oxford University Press.

Stern, M. J. (2008) 'The Power of Trust: Toward a Theory of Local Opposition to Neighboring Protected Areas,' *Society and Natural Resources*, 21: 859–875.

Stronza, A. (2006) *Madidi a través de Nuestros Ojos: La Historia del Ecoalbergue Chalalán de Bolivia*. La Paz, Bolivia.

Trusty, T. (2010) *The Politics of Representing Nature, Culture, and Conservation in Northwestern Bolivia*. Ph.D. dissertation, University of Washington.

Wells, M., Brandon, K. and Hannah, L. J. (1992) *People and Parks: Linking Protected Area Management with Local Communities*, Washington, D.C.: World Bank, World Wildlife Fund, and U.S. Agency for International Development.

West, P. C. and Brechin, S. R. (eds.) (1991) *Resident Peoples and National Parks: Social dilemmas and Strategies in International Conservation*, Tucson, AZ: The University of Arizona Press.

10

WHO'S GOT THE MONEY NOW? CONSERVATION-DEVELOPMENT MEETS THE *NUEVA RURALIDAD* IN SOUTHERN MEXICO

Nora Haenn

Introduction

Since the year 2000, migration to the United States from the Mexican municipality of Calakmul has grown exponentially.[1] Observing this, I commented to one of Calakmul's 'local policy-makers' (see below) that I might examine the topic. Calakmul is home to Mexico's largest protected area for tropical ecosystems, the Calakmul Biosphere Reserve. The region ranks third in the nation for state-sponsored conservation-development funding.[2] On the topic of international migration, this policy-maker, a man with 20 years of experience in local conservation-development, reacted swiftly and with careful calculation: 'They're the ones with money now.'

Conservation practitioners have persistently sought ways for protected areas to financially benefit local people. In the 1990s, conservationists created 'integrated conservation development projects' (ICDPs) to raise local incomes and preserve natural resources (Campebell and Vainio-Matilla 2003). In Mexico, the idea sits at the heart of a program administered at Calakmul and other biosphere reserves, PRO-CODES or the Conservation Program for Sustainable Development. PROCODES supports projects such as habitat restoration, energy efficient stoves, and water catchment systems.[3] Conservation ideals also underpin a program administered mainly by Mexico's department of agriculture, *Activos Productivos*, or Productive Assets. Both programs include a mechanism for popular participation. In these forums local residents debate what sustainable development might look like in the region and enact this vision by voting on aid projects requested by the broader Calakmul community.

The structure of ICDP and sustainable development funding in Calakmul reflects global trends, which encourage the democratization and decentralization of environmental decision-making (Alcorn et al. 2005; McCarthy 2005). Within these efforts, people regularly compare conservation with an array of economic opportunities. Because of this, understanding the economic context associated with conservation entails more than a grasp of the social hierarchies that can make ICDPs inaccessible to marginalized groups (Gibson and Agrawal 2001; Igoe and Fortwangler 2007). It requires understanding the variety of economic opportunities available in given places, why different groups prefer some opportunities over others, and how certain economic activities become constructed, discursively, as appropriate objects of conservation.

Taking as a case study the municipal economy of Calakmul, this chapter asks: 'Who's got the money now?' And, what relationship, if any, is there between conservation programs and Calakmul's more lucrative financial opportunities? While the boundaries of a municipal economy can be arbitrary—Calakmul is well integrated into national and international structures—the idea is locally relevant. Similar to U.S. counties in size and governing authority, Mexican municipalities are a basic building block of the state, framing the flow of state funding. Authorities report welfare, agricultural, and other expenditures according to municipality. The municipality also shapes localized policy-making. Since 2005, this policy-making has included the participatory forums associated with PROCODES and Productive Assets. Both bodies include publically elected municipal officials, federal agents, and representatives of cattlemen's, forestry and other associations. Between 2005 and 2009, the same 30 or so individuals participated in both forums. Throughout the chapter, I refer to this group, collectively, as 'local policy-makers'.

In outlining Calakmul's municipal economy, I begin by depicting the region's main economic activities as described by local policy-makers. During a twelve-month period spanning 2009–10, I documented 12, day-long meetings of the public, participatory bodies (4 meetings of the Reserve's Advisory Council and 8 meetings of the department of agriculture's Municipal Council on Rural Sustainable Development). I also gathered archival information, including lists of programs approved by the participatory bodies. I supplemented these observations with both formal and informal interviews with local policy-makers. In 2004, their vision of the regional economy was published in a planning document known as a *diagnóstico*, a 'diagnostic.' The document analyzes the municipality's economic and social qualities, suggests state interventions to foster economic growth, and forecasts future social life. Calakmul's diagnostic surprised local policy-makers by asserting the region had changed from a forest-based economy to a cattle ranching economy.

In the paragraphs below, this surprise provides an entry to comparing those ideas of the Calakmul economy circulating among local policy-makers with data on the value of primary production, state welfare aid to households, and remittances from migration (The larger research goal for 2009–10 aimed at teasing out relationships between international migration and conservation.) A comparison across this information reveals aspects of Calakmul's economy overlooked by local policy-makers: international migration, women's increasing authority over household expenditures, and a growing populace dependent on salaried employment. As I explain, silence on these matters is partly due to the use of participatory forums by members for personal and political goals, but also to important identity differences between members of the forums and the larger Calakmul population.

This broader economic picture has implications for the use of ICDPs as conservation tools. The diagnostic implicitly questioned the value of ICDPs, as Calakmul seemed to be following the well trod path of cattle expansion and rain forest depletion (Fearnside 2005). The data reported here offer a different lesson. Since ICDP expenditures began in Calakmul in the mid-1990s, the region's economic and political structures have changed. The chapter's discussion section explains how Calakmul now reflects what Latin American researchers call the *nueva ruralidad* or new rurality. In these circumstances, the financial import of ICDPs may be diluted, and the model of conservation that pays people to protect biodiversity needs reconsideration.

This regional approach to ICDPs has little precedent in the academic literature. Thus, before delving into the case material, I review how economics and geographic scale have been treated in social science writing on ICDPs and point to the need to connect diverse bodies of writing on socio-ecologies to address the situation at Calakmul.

Economics and Scale in Conservation Research

The role of Calakmul's local policy-makers in conservation connects two issues in research on natural resource management. First, what counts as an ICDP, and how should researchers measure the ability of ICDPs to achieve their goals? Second, what role do regional decision-making bodies have in ICDPs and other kinds of environmental management? For the most part, ICDP examinations are carried out by researchers interested in conservation as a unique social phenomenon (Brechin et al. 2003). These researchers take as a point of reference the ICDP itself and pay less attention to regional bodies. Contrastingly, research in political ecology and natural resource management institutions suggests regional forums can be important places where people debate the content of ICDPs and influence their success. Collectively, these three strands of research call for detailed descriptions that convey the inner workings of regional institutions in order to connect their activities with environmental outcomes.

At the most specific level, ICDPs seek to conserve a particular species, aid ecosystem functioning, and improve human livelihoods (Robinson and Redford 2004). At the broadest level, ICDPs aim to improve relations between a protected area and surrounding communities (Hughes and Flintan 2001). ICDPs are usually associated with a protected area, instigated by NGOs or government-based conservationists, and target people living in that park or reserve's vicinity. ICDPs operate on the assumption that development aid will ease antagonisms toward conservation and, perhaps, produce desired ecological outcomes. As such, they differ from a formal economics approach, which measures whether 'it is worthwhile to protect nature' based on people's willingness to pay for conservation (see Folke 2006: 686).[4]

Given their localized quality, ICDP research has tended toward case studies, and a cottage industry has developed in the form of periodic reviews of the cases. This structure has a particular geographic quality, as reviewers move between the local and global levels (see, for example, Brosius and Russell 2003). Two reviews of the conservation literature illustrate these divided attentions. Both West et al. (2006) and Naughton-Treves et al. (2005) begin their accounts by describing the expansion of protected areas in the late 20th century. Both reviews then outline global agreements on biodiversity protection and the transnational institutions that put these agreements into effect. An economy of conservation must certainly exist at the international level (Igoe and Brockington 2007), but these reviews tend to conceptualize conservation as fostering localized economic consequences.

In this regard, both reviews find ICDPs fail to live up to their promises. West et al. are the more pessimistic, cataloguing relocations from protected areas that can force a loss of livelihoods. In place of subsistence practices, protected areas offer ICDPs that convert the local environment into a marketable good. West et al. fear the ecological consequences of such projects, citing how 'certain species have gone from being little known or valued by local people to being highly valued commodities' (2006: 283).

Naughton-Treves et al. agree that 'reviews of ICDPs consistently have found ... it is hard to identify substantial achievements either in improving social welfare or in protecting biodiversity' (2005: 240). At the same time, the authors describe as 'truth' that 'desperate poverty' is a threat to biodiversity (ibid: 239). Consequently, their review describes a growing commitment in the global conservation community to poverty alleviation. Notably, the authors disagree with this change, arguing the responsibility is simply too much for conservation programs. An emphasis on poverty alleviation, they say, also distracts consideration from those 'large-scale actors and policies' that influence social ecologies (ibid: 243). Instead, Naughton-Treves and colleagues assert, conservation research and practitioners should employ alternative geographies that address conservation's social complexities. They call for 'landscape-level initiatives' and offer zoning as an example of an alternative geography.

How do researchers define 'landscape' or its companion concept, the 'regional' economy? What kinds of institutions would operate at this level? Naughton-Treves and colleagues are vague on the answers to these questions, a response that leads some anthropologists to fear a kind of geographic creep. These skeptics focus on the political dynamics of landscape-level institutions. The bigger the 'landscape' the greater the environmental restrictions demanded by protected areas. These same researchers also observe that 'landscape' management risks creating geographies of scale too big for local-level decision-making (Peterson et al. 2010). In such settings, the default decision-makers become people with the finances and technological resources to undertake such management.

The ideal landscape might, thus, be a geographic level at which sufficient natural resources exist to merit conservation and where local level knowledge remains valid and applicable. Mexican municipalities fit this description, and the participatory bodies at Calakmul's Reserve and department of agriculture arose as part of a zoning process operating on these principles (see below). These kinds of groups have the advantage of filling in gaps between the 'local' and the 'global' and demonstrating how these two are connected. Conservation researchers increasingly agree these kinds of institutions are key elements of conservation programming (Oldekop et al. 2010; Waylen et al. 2010). The fields of political ecology and institutional research on resource governance offer tools to examine regional decision-making bodies. Researchers in both fields cite the need for careful descriptions that locate questions of power and social connectedness at the center of conservation decision-making.

By taking into account the power relations that shape regional decision-making bodies (Adger et al. 2006; Berkes 2008), institutional researchers are beginning to look more and more like political ecologists (Robbins 2004). As institutional researchers move from the local-level studies that previously dominated the field to regional scales, they note the complications these larger associations pose:

> Just as distant managers are apt to be ignorant of and insensitive to local considerations, local managers tend to know little about linkages to larger systems and the interests of those who are not physically present at the local level but exert economic pressures involving land use and the production of commodities. In addition, local managers are often not provided with financial means to achieve proposed goals of decentralized authority.
>
> *(Brondizio et al. 2009: 269)*

Hesitant to theorize these relationships just yet (ibid), institutional researchers again parallel those political ecologists who critique the field for arriving at conclusions while weakly delineating the politics, economics, and ecologies under consideration (Paulson et al. 2003). For both intellectual traditions, regional institutions are, at this stage, a black box that requires closer examination.

The following paragraphs take a step toward illuminating that black box by describing how members of Calakmul's regional institutions conceptualize the municipality's economy. In this example, the economic question is also a geographical question. The economic flows reflect people's spatial commitments. In some cases, these economic and spatial ties are represented by specific members of the participatory bodies. Some economic and spatial connections, however, have no physical representative, and these are precisely the trends that challenge ICDPs as conservation tools.

Calakmul: Municipality and Biosphere Reserve

The municipality of Calakmul is located in Campeche State on the Yucatán peninsula, where Mexico borders Guatemala and Belize. At roughly 723,000 hectares, the Calakmul Biosphere Reserve covers half of the municipal territory. The remaining territory is a patchwork of more than 80 communities. The 25,000 people who live in Calakmul are spread out among a few large towns (four locales house 1,000–3,300 people) and numerous, smaller villages (INEGI 2007). By Mexican standards, the region is not prosperous, although its circumstances have been improving. Mexico's National Population Council maintains an 'Index of Marginalization' that compares municipalities on issues such as urbanization, literacy, and household income. The Council, then, locates each municipality within five categories ranging from 'very high' to 'very low' marginalization. In 2000, the Council ranked Calakmul a zone of 'very high' marginalization, but by 2005, the municipality had moved up a rank to 'high' marginalization (Anzaldo and Prado 2006).

This improvement has its roots in ICDPs, which heralded the expansion of state welfare in Calakmul. Calakmul was an agricultural frontier with little government infrastructure until the early 1990s. The area's poor farming soils and periodic droughts meant economic hardship, and, while the frontier saw a regular influx of new migrants, it also experienced regular outflows of people who found they could not survive the region's harsh conditions. Then, Reserve authorities founded an ambitious ICDP agenda (Haenn 2005).

Between 1992 and 1996, the Reserve's agenda operated at three scales. At the household level, authorities encouraged the diversification of household economies in areas such as organic agriculture, intensive cattle-ranching, and agroforestry. At the community level, conservation programming reckoned with the common property quality of the villages—or *ejidos*—where most county residents live. Within ejidos, landed farmers (90 per cent of whom are men, see Radel 2005) exercise collective responsibility for community resources. Reserve staff worked with ejido members to demonstrate the economic value of an array of forest goods. Collaborating with the Reserve, ejido members established protected areas within ejido boundaries and created systems of sustainable hunting and timber extraction. At a third level, Reserve authorities created a peasant organization whose thousands of members sent representatives to a regional forum to debate the area's future and press for more financial aid. In 1995, collective expenditures for ICDPs neared 1 million U.S. dollars a year, an amount little changed fifteen years later (see below).

This movement ended for a variety of reasons, including the creation of new, rival peasant organizations, the end of funding cycles that underwrote the programs, and the creation of the municipality. Some ejidos still maintain their protected areas, and a number of people active in the movement now count among local policy-makers. Their understanding of ICDPs reflects this earlier time period with its emphasis on men's work in the primary sector. The municipality, however, replaced the Reserve as the main geographic lens through which both state authorities and local residents viewed the region. Today, the municipality is the largest government entity in Calakmul, commanding a budget 14 times that of the Biosphere Reserve. The municipality is the largest formal employer in the region, and its elections are fiercely contested.

The municipality's financial weight is made possible by federal monies. Calakmul's tax base is almost null. Instead, the municipality relies on federal funds channeled directly from Mexico City or administered by Campeche State.[5] (Supplemental funds are available to regions of 'high' marginalization.) This financial dependence is widely recognized among local-policy makers, and, sometimes, increases the prestige of locally posted federal agents—at the Reserve and department of agriculture – whose own budgets are considerably smaller than the municipality's.

Alongside these agencies, one additional federal office is involved in natural resource management in Calakmul, the National Forestry Commission (CONAFOR). At present, the forestry commission is the biggest environmental spender in

Calakmul, offering payments to landholders for ecosystem services. The Commission has no local staff, and local policy-makers complain the agency does not participate in regional participatory bodies.

Defining a 'Conservation Economy'

This section uses the municipal diagnostic and an analysis of projects supported by PROCODES and Productive Assets to establish how local policy-makers define a 'conservation economy'. In all, three federal agencies make financial contributions to conservation in Calakmul. Figure 10.1 lists the total amount offered by these agencies in household subsidies in 2009. (I discuss the 'Opportunities' category below.)

PROCODES, which disbursed 2.2 million pesos in 2008 and 2009, and Productive Assets, which disbursed 550,000 pesos in the same period, are only part of their respective agencies' larger offerings.[6] Nonetheless, the public forums linked to these programs allow researchers to witness how local policy-makers conceptualize and put into practice sustainability.

Originally published in 2004 (Arreola, A. et al. 2004), the diagnostic was part of a project funded by the German development agency, the Deutsche Gesellschaft für Technische Zusammenarbeit (or GTZ), to zone the municipality for sustainable resource use. In gathering information for this task, the diagnostic identified the municipality's principle economic activities: subsistence farming, forestry, cattle ranching, bee keeping, cash crop production, tourism, and various subsidy programs. The document then examined data published by the state (where available) to assign a financial value to each of these and evaluate their relative weight in the local economy. The GTZ simultaneously worked to bolster the Reserve and department of agriculture's public participatory bodies. The economic categories outlined in the diagnostic closely reflect the framework within which these groups operate.

To the surprise of local policy-makers, the diagnostic concluded cattle ranching was the most valuable economic activity in the municipality. The document makes

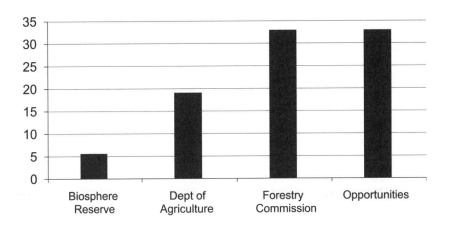

this estimate by evaluating the municipality's 'gross domestic production' (GDP), the market value of goods and services produced inside municipal borders. The authors estimated that ranching is responsible for 40 per cent of the municipality's annual GDP. Forestry generated 15 per cent, services 10.7 per cent, cash crops 6 per cent, commerce 5.4 per cent, and honey just 2.5 per cent. Subsistence corn farming was ranked among the least remunerative of activities, even though corn is an important part of the social safety net in this 'marginalized' region.

For all the products mentioned, the authors estimated their value based on actual sales, but for cattle, they estimated the sector's value based on the number of animals in the municipal herd. (The calculation method is unstated.) In other words, they based the value of cattle on *potential* sales (Ibid.: 7). The authors added to this inaccuracy by relaying data from the state uncritically, even though interviews with officials in 2010 indicated that problems in the quality of this data were longstanding (see below). These mistakes, nonetheless, changed how local policy-makers thought about economic activity in Calakmul. Previously, policy-makers viewed residents as mainly combining forestry with slash-and-burn farming, activities that can be consonant with conservation. Subsequent to the diagnostic, Calakmul seemed to be following the well trod path of cattle expansion and forest depletion. The process seemed inevitable, as even Reserve officers argued ICDPs needed to support ranching: 'With these projects we're going to try to semi-stabilize cattle ranching. Because, as I mentioned, you cannot argue with the ranchers. They have a production system. And, you cannot tell them to limit themselves.' [Author interview, Aug. 19, 2009.]

With these categories in place, the Reserve and the department of agriculture's participatory bodies set about prioritizing the distribution of sustainable development funds. Table 10.1 outlines the distribution of funds by sector as decided by each of these participatory bodies for 2008 and 2009. Despite their overlapping membership, the two bodies show institutional differences when it came to supporting different sectors. The department of agriculture has demonstrated no interest in financing forestry, while Reserve offices have a long-term commitment to forestry activities. Policy mandates for the Reserve's ICDPs allow for greater latitude in the kinds of projects PROCODES can support. PROCODES can pay for technical studies and training workshops. Programs of these sorts sit within the 'Other' category. Concerns about ranching's negative effect on forest cover led to a collaboration between the Reserve and the department of agriculture in the conceptualization of a large-scale project that introduces methods to reduce the hectareage required to raise a

TABLE 10.1 Distribution of development funds by participatory bodies.

	Ranching	Agriculture	Honey	Forestry	Ecotourism	Other
Dept of Ag 2008	26%	24%	39%	0%	0%	11%
Dept of Ag 2009	44%	22%	20%	0%	7%	7%
Reserve 2008	12%	5%	19%	18%	14%	32%
Reserve 2009	10%	2%	0%	21%	21%	47%

single head of cattle. This project's approval led to the department of agriculture increasing its commitment to ranching between 2008 and 2009.

Activities listed in Table 10.1 convey what might be thought of as Calakmul's 'conservation economy'. These are the activities that receive attention in Calakmul's participatory bodies, where conversation moves between two poles: local production and state subsidies that support this local production. Households involved in Calakmul's primary sector rarely cover their costs by farming, forestry, or cattle ranching alone. Instead, they rely on the kinds of subsidies outlined in Figure 10.1. It is worth noting that the funds available to the Reserve and department of agriculture's participatory bodies are only 5 per cent of all federal subsidies associated with natural resource management entering Calakmul. This fact is well recognized by local policy-makers who complain that federal agencies decline to allow public input into their spending. The disparity confirms critiques which note that decentralized bodies allow local citizens some say in state development efforts, but fall short of allowing citizens to change the overall direction of those efforts (Paley 2004). In Calakmul, this minimal commitment to decentralization also translates into an ongoing disconnect between land managers and bureaucrats who subsidize certain kinds of land use.

A Conservation Economy in Context, Part 1

This conservation economy merits contextualization in two ways. The first examines these economic categories in light of additional state information on these sectors. The second contextualization examines these activities in light of economic activities not contemplated in the conservation economy (see below). In the case of ICDPs, contextualization helps delineate the impact of sustainable development interventions beyond the household and community levels. At the same time, the state plays a crucial role in both conservation and the Calakmul economy. Thus, contextualization indicates the manner in which conservation and specific economic activities are legible to various state authorities (Dove 1994).

Published in 2004, the diagnostic argued the principal economic activities in Calakmul, in descending order of importance, were: cattle, timber, pork, services, cash crops, commerce, and honey. For example, the diagnostic assigned a valued of 32 million pesos to the municipal cattle herd. Timber stood as a distant second at 12.2 million pesos. Where do these data come from? How reliable are these findings?

For the most part, local policy-makers and diagnostic authors worked with data generated by the department of agriculture and state environmental offices (SEMARNAT). In cases where these offices did not have information available, diagnostic authors turned either to local production associations or made their own calculations. The estimation of ranching's value is an example of the authors' own calculations. The authors never explain exactly how they arrived at this figure. The state data available to them at the time estimated not the value of the herd but the value of meat production. And, the state's estimations provide a markedly different picture. The state valued beef production around the time of the diagnostic's writing at 4.6 million pesos. In other words, state figures for beef production are only

15 per cent of the diagnostic's valuation. The department of agriculture lists total meat production (beef, pork, mutton, and chicken included) at one-fourth the value listed in the diagnostic (INEGI 2007).

Exploring this discrepancy with state department of agriculture officials, I learned their data collection methods cast doubt on the reliability of all their agricultural production figures. Authorities calculate beef production by periodically surveying municipal butchers, even though Calakmul's largest beef producing regions are located near urban areas. Cattle raised in Calakmul and butchered in these urban areas fall outside the accounting. Estimates of cash crop production are based on farmers' self-reports. At no time do state authorities undertake an independent confirmation of crop production of any sort. In the case of corn, this led to an intriguing methodology for estimating the value of corn harvests.

Department of agriculture officials assessed local corn production based on the amount the agency pays in crop subsidies. One particular subsidy, known as PRO-CAMPO, came into effect in the mid-1990s and originally aimed at compensating subsistence producers for the drop in corn prices expected with Mexico's entry into the North American Free Trade Agreement (NAFTA). Over the years, the crops that qualify for the subsidy have expanded in number. Someone receiving PROCAMPO may or may not be planting corn. This point aside, policy-makers in Calakmul commonly acknowledge that people receive PROCAMPO without planting their registered amount (payments are by hectare) and, sometimes, without planting at all. Thus, even though corn is a central part of the social safety network in 'marginal' regions, actual corn production in Calakmul is largely illegible to state authorities.

For corn, state authorities are apt to focus on their own bureaucratic efforts associated with the crop, a tendency repeated in the case of timber production. Recall the diagnostic argued that timber was the second most valued economic activity in Calakmul. State environmental authorities calculate timber sales based on harvesting permits issued. Suspecting that illegal timber harvests are common, local policy-makers view this amount as an undercount. Figure 10.2 summarizes recent figures for those parts of the conservation economy where data is available.[7] The multiple years of data attempt to capture the flux of agricultural production (2007 production was affected by a hurricane) but also aim to delineate the range of earnings possibilities for these activities.

This brief assessment of official data on primary production shows the extent to which Calakmul's local policy-makers necessarily operate in the dark about some of the municipality's main economic activities. State authorities are pressed to fulfill their own bureaucratic accounting, but those pressures do not necessarily extend to producing reliable data. Without accurate knowledge of the economy in which ICDPs intervene, it is impossible to assess their relative success. Instead, local policy-makers are left to work with their own qualitative assessments of the relative value of different sectors and the relative importance of ICDPs. Numerical assessments, even if calculated in error, can sometimes shape the thinking of local policy-makers, in part, because they offer the illusion of concreteness in decision-making processes that otherwise function under rules of thumb.

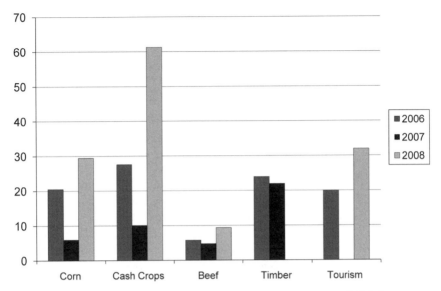

FIGURE 10.2 Estimated values in Calakmul's conservation economy, 2006–8.

These decision-making processes are also closely tied to competition over development monies. The projects reported in Table 10.1 are partly the result of prioritizing activities according to conservation criteria and partly the result of local policy-makers' jockeying for influence. Local policy-makers have a financial interest in the approval of certain projects. They may apply personally for these funds or charge a fee for championing a project in the voting process. The outcome, as a local department of agriculture official notes, is that members of these bodies 'have directed the majority of the funds toward themselves' [author interview, January 20, 2010]. In 2009, just two individuals, long-term members of the body, received nearly 20 per cent of the funds administered by the department of agriculture's participatory body. Decision-making related to the Reserve's ICDP expenditures could be even less transparent. Contrary to past years, the Reserve's participatory body never convened in 2010, and Reserve staff determined the successful applications.[8] I revisit the more covert aspects of sustainable development funding after considering economic trends that go unconsidered by the Reserve and department of agriculture's participatory bodies.

A Conservation Economy In Context, Part 2

If the data on Calakmul's primary sector is unreliable, reports on other aspects of Calakmul's economy tend to be more trustworthy. These include data on salaried employment and household subsidies. Data on remittances is only partially available, and, below, I explain my calculation methods for remittances. Where debates at the Reserve and department of agriculture's participatory bodies give the impression that the male-dominated primary sector is the most salient portion of Calakmul's economy (it certainly employs the greatest number of people), this additional information offers a different economic scenario. It suggests the feminization of household financial management and a growing proportion of rural families connected to cash economies via salaried labor, state welfare, and remittances. These qualities are part of larger changes in Latin America that researchers characterize as a *nueva ruralidad* or new rurality (Kay 2008). Ideas of a new rurality ask researchers to consider the relationship between ICDPs and those rural people who are *not* active in the primary sector.

The largest employer offering salaried positions in Calakmul is the state, which hires soldiers, teachers, healthcare professionals, and municipal employees. For example, the National Defense Secretary supports a military base housing 300 soldiers, whose salaries amount to at least 25 million pesos a year or 75 per cent of the diagnostic's figure for cattle production.[9] Statistics on the number of school teachers and healthcare staff, along with their salaries, were unavailable. Although likely significant, their contribution to the Calakmul economy is affected by perceptions that they are outsiders who only stay in the municipality during the work week. The municipality tends to import its professional class. Local policy-makers, thus, view teachers and healthcare staff as people who spend their money elsewhere, in their home communities where their families live full-time. (Also unavailable are data on Calakmul's tertiary sector, the shops that are a presumptive beneficiary of household spending.)

The military, educational and health sectors are rarely discussed at Calakmul's participatory bodies, even though the law framing the department of agriculture's body stipulates the forum as a site to coordinate the primary sector with health and education (SAGARPA 2001). In contrast, local policy-makers pay very close attention to employment possibilities in the municipality.

The municipality offers 300–350 jobs and an annual payroll of some 50 million pesos. About one-third of these jobs are reserved for unionized staff. The other two-thirds are doled out to supporters of the winning candidate for municipal presidency. Municipal presidents are elected every three years, and, upon their installation, non-unionized municipal staffing undergoes an almost complete turnover. The winners of these (temporarily) secure salaries include people who volunteered in the campaign, made hefty campaign contributions, or otherwise positioned themselves as someone who can deliver the vote.

The reserve and department of agriculture's participatory bodies are deeply implicated in these electoral machinations. (Some federal agents used perceptions of the forums as subject to electoral shenanigans as an excuse not to participate.) The 30 people who dominated the forums between 2005 and 2009 included one future municipal president and three losing candidates. Many more members are believed to harbor aspirations to the office. The forums might be a springboard for mounting a candidacy or a means to increase a person's position within his or her political party. In interviews, local policy-makers charged their colleagues with awarding projects to cultivate a network of political activists and voters. While nobody admitted to personally carrying out this practice, members of opposing parties accused one another of the same deed, suggesting a generalized electoral strategy.

These electoral considerations help explain a certain myopia within the participatory bodies regarding remittances and women's growing importance in household financial management. Politics in Calakmul is very much a man's game. Only 7 per cent of the county's elected officials are women. Prior to the region's incorporation into international migration, no women held public office, and migration appears associated with subtle shifts in women's public authority (cf. Taylor et al. 2005). Despite their growing numbers, elected women still encounter obstacles to wielding authority similar to that of men. In Calakmul, a woman who travels alone or speaks with men outside their families inspires intense community gossip which typically accuses her of licentiousness and marital infidelity. As a result, female elected authorities tend to be silent in regional meetings.

In this way, women's public power belies their private power. Financially, women's authority rests on government subsidies and remittances. A government subsidy associated principally with women is 'Opportunities' (see Figure 10.1). Opportunities is a poverty alleviation program that supports some 75 per cent of Calakmul households. This compares with half the Calakmul households who receive PROCAMPO, the most popular subsidy for subsistence farm production. Women receive Opportunities payments in exchange for regular check-ups and for showing up at healthcare talks. Children qualify for Opportunities with continued school attendance (payments are made to the children's mother). Average bi-monthly payments in the municipality are roughly equal to 15 days of wage labor. On an annual basis, this amounts to 25–100 per cent more money than PROCAMPO.[10] PROCAMPO's relative weight in household finances is further diminished by the fact that the farm subsidy arrives once or twice a year, and its timing can be unpredictable. Opportunities provides families with a regular and reliable income.

Opportunities has become internationally fashionable; its model of cash transfers exported to other countries (Valencia Lomelí 2008). Researchers argue one of the program's qualities has been its ability to stay out of electoral disputes (although its ability to politically empower recipients is debated, see Hevia de la Jara 2007). In Calakmul, this assertion might also be applied to remittances linked to international migration. In fact, former migrants describe frustration with the way municipal old boy networks shut them out of the job market: 'Here in Mexico, the government supports you only to win your vote. The government gives benefits to the same government workers. They live off the backs of the poor.' [Author interview, April 3, 2010.]

State census figures report that 1 per cent of the Calakmul population worked in the United States in 2005 (INEGI 2007). A 2003 survey of 203 Calakmul households found the number to be much higher; 7.4% of the population older than 17 years was in the United States (Schmook and Radel 2008: 899). Migrants are typically young men in their 20s who leave behind a wife and young children. These migrants earn as much as four times their counterparts who choose not to migrate, and, in general, the income of migrating households is twice that of non-migrating households (ibid.).

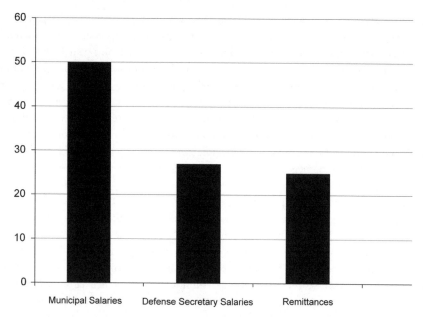

FIGURE 10.3 Salaried employment and wage labor earnings in Calakmul, 2009.

Official data on remittances entering Calakmul are unavailable. The estimate listed in Figure 10.3 of 25 million pesos/year is based on interviews with local financial houses where many residents receive their money. The amount excludes remittances sent to banks in urban areas. The upper limit of remittance receipts in Calakmul is, thus, unknown. Certainly, though, remittances appear roughly similar to what the municipality receives in Opportunity payments or the value of any single category in the region's primary sector (see Figure 10.2). Remittances may even rival what the municipality pays in salaries.

Because men constitute 90 per cent of Calakmul's international migrants (ibid.), women in migrating households tend to be responsible for household administration. Rather than assume agricultural labor themselves, migrants' wives take on the role of employer, hiring relatives and neighbors to undertake farm work. Women do not always find these new duties empowering (McEvoy 2008). Even so, women's new duties upset household structures in a region where women were previously categorized as 'helpmates' to male farmers (Radel 2005b). In this patriarchal, patrilocal society, women who channel money to their kin (as opposed to their in-laws) increase their standing in their natal family. Importantly, migration has created the possibility for women to become landowners.

Discussion

Demand for ICDP and sustainable development funding in Calakmul far outstrips what the Reserve and department of agriculture offer. In 2010, residents submitted

600 proposals to Productive Assets. Roughly 50 would be funded. PROCODES requests totaled 12.6 million pesos for a program budgeted at 2.5 million pesos. The conservation economy is clearly a socially vibrant entity in Calakmul, even if local policy-makers overlook the region's broader economic setting.

In recent years, this setting took on the qualities of a *nueva ruralidad*, or new rurality. The idea of a new rurality arose in the mid-1990s as researchers examined the effects of neo-liberal policies on rural communities. The notion has received little attention in English-speaking academic circles (although see Kay 2008 for an overview). In Latin America, however, the framework has become a common one for understanding the social and economic structures that shape rural life. Where before, researchers focused on rural areas as isolated sites, dependent on a farm economy, and governed by a few strongmen, the new rurality Kay (ibid.) notes emphasizes: farming as one, and not necessarily the most important, economic activity; the feminization of rural workforces; growing rural-urban interactions; and the increasing importance of migrants' remittances.

Local policy-makers in Calakmul acknowledge these trends in a very general way, but they have not incorporated women or migration into their understanding of Calakmul's economy. Not once during interviews or meetings did local policy-makers volunteer an observation about international migration, even though a handful of policy-makers had sojourned themselves to the United States. During 2009–10, only three or four of the 30-plus people attending the participatory bodies were women. Men might call on these women to speak up in the interest of gender equity, but they hesitated to connect these women's presence with underlying economic shifts.

'Who's got the money now?' And, what are the implications of that distribution for ICDPs? In Calakmul, the answer to these questions depends on one's standpoint. From a household perspective, people with secure sources of income include the minority with a full-time wage, such as a soldier or a municipal employee. Another typical money manager might be a woman administering Opportunities and migration remittances. From a political perspective, the people with the money are those who control the municipal budget. For the former groups, ICDP and sustainable development funding are, largely, inconsequential. These funds support the environmental work of a handful of men. Ideas of sustainable development in Calakmul, still rooted in the mid-1990s, have yet to consider whether and how to connect the Reserve to people located in a consumer economy.

Although exceptions exist, local control of ICDP and sustainable development monies in Calakmul have become part of a certain political tumult that accompanies decentralization and new ruralities. Researchers observe that under decentralization empowered local policy-makers take advantage of their newfound authority to press for diverse notions of democracy and the state. Writing on Chiapas, Leyva Solano (2001) notes that increased participation does not always translate into increasing citizenship or pluralism. In Calakmul, this participation has been revelatory in delineating local policy-makers' relationship to a welfare state.

Once distributed, ICDP and sustainable development funds in Calakmul often find a destination other than that proposed. There are few consequences for the misapplication of funds (cf. Blaikie 2006). For three years leading up to 2010, the Reserve officer charged with auditing ICDP projects was among the 25 per cent of Reserve staff *not* assigned a vehicle for travel. In 2009, only one-third of department of agriculture projects were audited and half of these failed to fulfill their proposed activities. An administrator of these projects asserted, with no hint of irony, participants had excelled in filling out the associated paperwork, 'it's the physical aspect of the projects that is lacking' [Author notes, June 30, 2010].

These findings might be different if my research had taken the more localized approach usually associated with ICDP research. For individual households and communities, ICDP and sustainable development funds can make quite a difference. In Calakmul, these monies have helped assure some people access to a year-round supply of water, created temporary jobs, and identified endemic strains of corn. However, given the goal of ICDPs to change the way people actually interact with the environment, the regional perspective raises the question of whether these benefits are enough.

As phrased here, the importance of a regional perspective to ICDPs is particular to Calakmul. Since the new century, Mexico is experimenting with a democratic openness that has increased electoral competition in a way that impacts all levels of government. Mexico's history as a welfare state and the importance of the municipal government as a rural employer may also be unique. Nonetheless, the case raises deeper questions about ICDPs anywhere a diverse economic setting creates a sizable group of people working outside the primary sector. (In the misallocation of funds, even local policy-makers tend to situate themselves in a consumer economy.) How might ICDPs focus on people other than impoverished natural resource users?

This question places Calakmul residents on the same economic terrain as people who similarly participate in a global economy as consumers and salaried employees, including members of the developed world and conservationists, themselves. The question, thus, demands a flattening of the global-local dichotomies that currently shape social science thinking on conservation.[11] It also makes even more urgent a fundamental re-thinking of how environmentalists counter destructive economic tendencies. Reviews of ICDPs have found successful projects, but not so many as to suggest the model reliably delivers conservation success. In the developed world, some researchers argue, ecology movements have similarly failed to create broad-based environmental solutions that combat consumerism and models of never-ending economic growth (Blühdorn 2000). Where might conservation go from here?

The next step in Calakmul appears to be a change in tactic that shifts attention away from the primary sector, where monies are easily monopolized by local policy-makers for personal and political gain. Through its environmental education programs, the Reserve is looking to experiment with establishing connections to adolescents and people other than local policy-makers. A focus on education connects conservation to a new generation and, given women's role in educating children, creates the possibility of making conservation more gender inclusive. If enacted, the environmental education programs would change conservation in the region, from one that focuses on buying out opposition to one that emphasizes experiential, even joyful, connections to local ecologies. The tactic is partly opportunistic. Reserve authorities have been invited by UNESCO officials to submit an environmental education proposal. The change also responds to economic realities. As argued above, ICDP and sustainable development monies have an indirect impact on the region via their use in electoral politicking, and a Reserve that seeks greater social leverage via these expenditures has few chances for success. A creatively constructed environmental education program, however, may be poised to insinuate conservation into other parts of Calakmul's social life (cf. Waylen et al. 2010).

Notes

1 My thanks to Birgit Schmook, Luis Melodelgado, Helen Kopnina, and Elle Shoreman-Ouimet for their helpful comments on earlier drafts of this article. Luis Melodelgado also aided in data collection for this project. This research was carried out under the auspices of a Fulbright-García Robles Fellowship.
2 The Calakmul Biosphere Reserve ranks third in the country in PROCODES funding, a program explained below.
3 PROCODES also supports research. For a complete list, see http://www.dof.gob.mx/nota_detalle_popup.php?codigo=5126638 available August 18, 2010.
4 Additional economic approaches are used to assess conservation settings (see, for example, Lynch et al. 2007). The two approaches listed here are those most commonly associated with research on ICDPs.
5 Federal authorities collect 94% of the country's revenue and account for 63% of government spending. States and municipalities account, respectively, for 29% and 8% of spending (Lazos Garza 2010).
6 Amounts listed for the Reserve include PROCODES and PET (the Temporary Employment Program), and *Maíz Criollo* (a program that seeks to conserve endemic corn strains). Amounts reported for the department of agriculture include 'Productive Assets, PROCAMPO (see below), a ranching and honey subsidy (PROGAN), and emergency aid distributed after natural disasters.' Amounts for the Forestry Commission include the program *ProÁrbol* or Pro-Tree. Pro-Tree supports activities associated with reforestation, tree nurseries, and biodiversity protection.
7 Tourism estimates are based on calculations of tourist expenditures made by Anaïs Jaud.
8 State policy encourages, but does not require, Reserve staff to take into account opinions emitted by its participatory body. See http://www.conanp.gob.mx/pdf_procodes/Lineamientos%20PROCODES%202009%20FINAL.pdf, available August 18, 2010.
9 This figure uses information gathered in interviews, i.e. the number of soldiers posted at the base multiplied by the minimum monthly salary a soldier might receive.
10 Average PROCAMPO payments in Calakmul for 2009 were 4,726 pesos for the spring-summer cycle. One-third of recipients earned, on average, an additional 2,200 pesos for the fall-winter cycle. Average Opportunities pay-outs per recipient for 2009 were 8,500 pesos. Wage labor rates at this time ranged between 100 and 150 pesos per day.
11 See Lomnitz Adler (1999) and Escobar (2008) for in depth discussions of the relationship between geography and social distinctions.

References

Adger, W. N., K. Brown, and E. L. Tompkins.(2005) 'The political economy of cross-scale networks in resource co-management', *Ecology and Society*, 10(2): 9 [online] URL: http://www.ecologyandsociety.org/vol10/iss2/art9/

Alcorn, J., A. Luque, and S. Valenzuela (2005) 'Global Governance and Institutional Trends Affecting Protected Areas Management'. Online. Available. http://www.earthlore.ca/clients/WPC/English/grfx/sessions/PDFs/session_1/Alcorn.pdf (Accessed September 6, 2010.)

Anzaldo, C. and M. Prado (2006) *Índices de Marginación, 2005*, México, D.F.: Consejo Nacional de Población.

Arreola, A., R. Delgadillo, A. López, and G. García Gil (2004) *Diagnóstico de la Situación de Desarrollo en el Municipio Calakmul, Campeche*, internal document. Proyecto Prosureste, GTZ/CONANP.

Berkes, F. (2008.) 'Commons in a multi-level world'. *Int. J. Commons* 2:1–6.

Blaikie, P. (2006) 'Is Small Really Beautiful? Community-based Natural Resource Management in Malawi and Botswana', *World Development*, 34: 1942–57.

Blühdorn, I. (2000) *Post-Ecologist Politics: Social Theory and the Abdication of the Ecologist Paradigm*, New York: Routledge.

Brechin, S., P. Wilshusen, C. Fortwangler, and P. West. (2003) *Contested Nature: Promoting International Biodiversity with Social Justice in the Twenty-First Century*, Albany: State University of New York Press.

Brondizio, E., E. Ostrom, and O. Young (2009) 'Connectivity and the Governance of Multilevel Social-Ecological Systems: The Role of Social Capital', *Annual Review of Environment and Resources*, 34: 253–78.

Brosius, J.P. and D. Russell (2003) 'Conservation from Above: An Anthropological Perspective on Transboundary Protected Areas and Ecoregional Planning,' in U. Goodale, M. Stern, C. Margolius, A. Lanfer, and M. Fladeland (eds.) *Transboundary Protected Areas: The Viability of Regional Conservation Strategies*, Binghamton, NY: Food Products Press.

Campebell, L. and A. Vainio-Matilla (2003) 'Participatory Development and Community-Based Conservation: Opportunities Missed for Lessons Learned?' *Human Ecology*, 31: 417–37.

Dove, M.R. (1994) 'The Existential Status of the Pakistani Farmer: Studying Official Constructions of Social Reality', *Ethnology*, 33: 331–51.

Escobar, A. (2008) *Territories of Difference: Place, Movements, Life, Redes*, Durham, NC: Duke Univ. Press.

Fearnside, P. (2005) 'Deforestation in Brazilian Amazonia: History, Rates, and Consequences', *Conservation Biology*, 19: 680–88.

Folke, Carl (2006) 'The Economic Perspective: Conservation against Development versus Conservation for Development', *Conservation Biology*, 20: 686–88.

Gibson, C. and A. Agrawal (2001) *Communities and The Environment: Ethnicity, Gender, and the State in Community-Based Conservation*, Pisctaway, NJ: Rutgers University Press.

Haenn, N. (2005) *Fields of Power, Forests of Discontent: Culture, Conservation and the State in Mexico*, Tucson: Univ. of Arizona Press.

Hevia de la Jara, F. (2007) 'El Programa Oportunidades y la construcción de ciudadanía: Ejercicio y protección de derechos en un programa de transferencias condicionadas en México'. Ph.D. thesis, Centro de Investigaciones y Estudios Superiores en Antropología Social.

Hughes, R. and Flintan, F. (2001) *Integrating Conservation and Development Experience: A Review and Bibliography of the ICDP Literature*, London: International Institute for Environment and Development.

Igoe, J. and D. Brockington (2007) 'Neoliberal Conservation: A Brief Introduction', *Conservation & Society*, 5: 432–49.

Igoe, J. and C. Fortwangler (2007) 'Whither communities and conservation?' *International Journal of Biodiversity Science, Ecosystems Services & Management*, 3: 65–76.

INEGI (Instituto Nacional de Estadística, Geografia e Informática) (2007) *Cuaderno Estadístico Municipal: Edición 2005*, Aguascalientes: Instituto Nacional de Estadística, Geografia e Informática.

Kay, C. (2008) 'Reflections on Latin American Rural Studies in the Neoliberal Globalization Period: A New Rurality?' *Development and Change*, 39: 915–43

Lazos Garza, F. (2010) 'Municipal Finances and Participatory Budgets,' paper presented at workshop sponsored by the Consejo Regional Indígena y Popular de Xpujil, Xpujil, Mexico. April, 2010.

Leyva Solano, X. (2001) 'Regional, Communal, and Organizational Transformations in Las Cañadas,' *Latin American Perspectives*, 28: 20–44.

Lomnitz Adler, C. (1999) *Modernidad Indiana: Nueve Ensayos Sobre Nación y Mediación en México*, México, D.F.: Editorial Planeta Mexicana, S.A. de C.V.

Lynch, L., W. Gray, and J. Geoghegan (2007) 'Are Farmland Preservation Program Easement Restrictions Capitalized into Farmland Prices? What Can a Propensity Score Matching Analysis Tell Us?' *Applied Economics Perspectives and Policies*, 29(3): 502–9.

McCarthy, J. (2005) 'Devolution in the Woods: Community Forestry as Hybrid Neoliberalism', *Environment and Planning A*, 37: 995–1014.

McEvoy, J. (2008) 'Male Out-Migration and the Women Left Behind: A Case Study of a Small Farming Community in Southeastern Mexico', M.S. Thesis, Utah State University.

Naughton-Treves, Lisa, Margaret Buck Holland, and Katrina Brandon (2005) 'The Role of Protected Areas in Conserving Biodiversity and Sustaining Local Livelihoods', *Annual Review of Environment and Resources*, 30: 219–52.

Oldekop, J. A., A. J. Bebbington, D. Brockington, and R. F. Preziosi (2010) 'Understanding the Lessons and Limitations of Conservation and Development', *Conservation Biology*, 24: 461–69.

Paley, J. 2004 'Accountable Democracy: Citizens' Impact on Public Decision Making in Postdictatorship Chile' *American Ethnologist* 31(4): 497–513.

Paulson, S., L. Gezon, and M. Watts (2003) 'Locating the Political in Political Ecology: An Introduction', *Human Organization*, 62: 2–5–217.

Peterson, R. B., D. Russell, P. West, and J. P. Brosius (2010) 'Seeing (and Doing) Conservation Through Cultural Lenses', *Environmental Management*, 45: 5–18.

Radel, C. (2005) 'Women's Community-Based Organizations, Conservation Projects, and Effective Land Control in Southern Mexico', *Journal of Latin American Geography*, 4: 7–34.

SAGARPA (Secretaria de Agricultura, Ganadería, Desarrollo Rural, Pesca y Alimentación) (2001) 'Ley de Desarrollo Rural Sustentable', *Diario Oficial*, December 7, 2001.

Schmook, B. and C. Radel (2008) 'International Labor Migration from a Tropical Development Frontier: Globalizing Households and an Incipient Forest Transition in Southern Yucatán', *Human Ecology*, 36: 891–908.

Robbins, P. (2004) *Political Ecology: A Critical Introduction*, Hoboken, NJ: Wiley-Blackwell.

Robinson, J. and K. Redford (2004) 'Jack of All Trades, Master of None: Inherent Contradictions among ICDP approaches', in T. McShane and M. Wells, (eds.) *Getting Biodiversity Projects to Work: Towards More Effective Conservation and Development*, New York: Columbia University Press.

Taylor, M. et al. 2005 'Land, Ethnic, and Gender Changes: Transnational Migration and its Effects on Guatemalan Lives and Landscapes' *Geoforum*, 37(1): 41–61.

Valencia Lomelí, E. (2008) 'Conditional Cash Transfers as Social Policy in Latin America: An Assessment of their Contributions and Limitations', *Annual Review of Sociology*, 34: 475–99.

Waylen, K. A. A. Fischer, P. J.K. McGowan, S. J. Thirgood, and E.J. Milner-Gulland (2010) 'Effect of Local Cultural Context on the Success of Community-Based Conservation Interventions,' *Conservation Biology*, 24: 461–69.

West, P., J. Igoe, and D. Brockington (2006) 'Parks and Peoples: The Social Impact of Protected Areas', *Annual Review of Anthropology*, 35: 251–77.

11

MIDDLE-OUT CONSERVATION

The Role of Elites in Rural American Conservation

Eleanor Shoreman-Ouimet

Introduction

> Between Delta blacks and the realization of their goal of economic as well as political independence, lay the determination of the region's planters, who throughout the upheaval of war, emancipation, and Reconstruction fought to regain their political, racial, and economic dominance and, insofar as possible, recapture the dream of a Delta where the planter's power was absolute and his wealth unrestricted.
>
> *James C. Cobb (1992)*

This may seem a strong, and even controversial sentiment to cite in a discussion of conservation, but it bears important significance to the conservation efforts underway in the Mississippi Delta. In the Delta, wealthy local landowners and conservation organizations are mobilizing a historically well-known oft-cited cultural aversion to federal regulation over, and interference in, agricultural affairs in order to encourage local residents to participate in environmental programs. By publicizing the real possibility of federal regulation if certain environmental improvement goals are not met, these rural elites are recruiting residents to implement conservation measures, join their boards, and advocate on behalf of the organizations and their objectives (Shoreman and Haenn 2009). And while there is evidence of an evolution of environmental concern among those participating residents, this growing ethic does not appear to be the pivotal impetus.

Like their ancestors before them, these modern-day Delta planters have a mission to recapture absolute control over their property and income. This scenario exemplifies Toqueville's assessment of American's 'self-interest rightly understood' – for the rural elite are indeed protecting and repairing the environment while effectively keeping federal regulators off of their land, out of their water, and ultimately out of their checkbooks. In this way, their actions epitomize what I here refer to as 'middle-out' conservation, in which along with local conservation organizations, individuals with social influence and a stake in local affairs, mediate between federal officials and local level players. Although Delta landowners, long partial to terms such as 'stewardship' to describe their relationship to the land, have only recently adopted the term conservation to describe their activities, the fact remains that 'conservation' in the Delta is used to describe the steps that farmers and local landowners are taking to satisfy and rid themselves of federal regulators. In most cases, the wellbeing of the environment has little bearing on their actions. This scenario raises the question to anthropologists and environmentalists: How can we harness the power of internal motivation in our own efforts to understand and motivate community-based conservation across cultures, in different geographic locations?

The Delta's previous reluctance to cooperate with federal officials to protect their environment has earned it a reputation for 'anti-environmentalism' (Shoreman-Ouimet 2010). Thus of primary importance to this research is ethnographic data that explains not only *how* the rural elite of the Mississippi Delta have utilized their understanding of local history, norms, values and beliefs to motivate farmers to invest in conservation in ways that federal authorities were unable to do; but also the reasons why *only* the rural elite were capable of exerting the necessary social pressure to accomplish this task. This example complexifies the issue of motivation by contrasting the powerful role of social influence and the relatively small role that environmental ethics plays in the establishment of community-based conservation in the Delta. In this way, it calls for a detachment of conservation from Western environmental values and emphasizes the need to expand our focus to include new communities and to pay greater attention to community relations, economics, cultural history, values, norms and beliefs.

The ethnographic accounts presented in this chapter do not depict a community convinced of conservation – rather they demonstrate the difficulties involved in organizing community conservation projects, the multiple interests and personalities at play and the pains taken to reach various community members. While some Delta farmers disagree with the politics of environmentalism, others are cultivating an environmental ethic of their own. Despite the wide array of opinions, however, nearly every large Delta commodity farmer is now participating in these programs.

Thus, this chapter also aims to demonstrate how the process of reintroducing the environment into environmental anthropology must include the analysis of the ways in which some communities are, in fact, making an effort to repair environmental damage. For, embedded in these community efforts is local environmental knowledge which is both important to understanding the relationship between a community and the environment, as well as, how to perpetuate environmental wellbeing. Furthermore, these types of positive actions are in themselves, examples of how a community can be brought together and motivated to take communal action in the name of the environment. How this motivation is cultivated may provide an important model for similar efforts to motivate community conservation projects around the world and may also inform environmental anthropological studies of underrepresented demographics, as well as those attempting to understand the relationship between culture, history, and the environment.

Accentuating the positive, however, does not mean neglecting the negatives or turning a blind eye to the ways in which daily life conflicts with the project to repair the local habitat or how cultural values, beliefs and ideologies may or may not support these local efforts. The anthropology of conservation is thus, not just meant to demonstrate the ways a community helps or hurts its environment – it is constructed around the age-old anthropological conundrum that culture is complicated, and the relationship between culture and environment is often counterproductive to cultural survival or environmental well-being. It thus behooves environmental anthropologists interested in conservation, for either its theoretical significance or applied usages, to present the full picture of a community's process of reconciling its place in the local environment.

The Mississippi Delta is an agricultural region replete with mud, hunters, chewing tobacco, trucks, racial tension, and discrimination; but it is also a community where a man's word, specifically a white farmer's word, and reputation is of the utmost importance. Church, school board meetings, and farm councils – all of these activities attract a large crowd for personal as well as social reasons. Conservation is no different. While it may be beneficial for the environment and the long term welfare of private land, in the Delta it has become a way that farmers can stand up for their community, in their community and show their neighbors as well as federal regulators that not only are they doing 'the right thing' but that they can be trusted to take care of their land, themselves.

This research was conducted between 2006–7 as part of the author's doctoral fieldwork in the Mississippi Delta, specifically, Coahoma, Bolivar, and Washington counties in the state of Mississippi.[1] Although initially designed to study rice cultivation in the Mississippi Delta, this research project quickly evolved into an analysis of land and water conservation amongst the region's largest farmers and in so, some of the country's staunchest opponents of liberal politics and green ideologies. The ethnographic data presented in this chapter was collected during more than 200 formal and informal interviews with area farmers, conservationists, agricultural scientists, politicians, federal employees, and various other members of these communities. Interviews were arranged through word of mouth recommendations from other community members, sign-up sheets at meetings of the local Farm Bureau and through daily interaction with farmers and other community members.[2]

The Delta Conservation Organizations

The Mississippi Delta houses a number of conservation agencies that range in their purpose and authority. While there are federal and state agencies, including the Natural Resource Conservation Service (NRCS), Mississippi Department of Environmental Quality (MDEQ), Soil and Water Conservation Board (SWCB) etc., the most active in their recruitment and publicity are the private organizations, founded by local citizens including wealthy landowners, large farmers, and/or those with a vested interest in Delta agriculture and property.

The establishment of these organizations was largely stimulated by a 1996 lawsuit in which the Sierra Club successfully sued the Environmental Protection Agency

(EPA), Region Four[3] for not upholding the Clean Water Act. As a result, the EPA was instructed to determine which southeastern U.S. streams were impaired and to establish, as well as implement, Total Maximum Daily Load (TMDL) limits for the impaired waterways (Shoreman and Haenn 2009: 99–100). As Mississippi came up as having more impaired waterways than any other state in the region, the EPA was forced to take regulatory action. In response to these threats, local elites formed private conservation organizations and got to work encouraging farmers to participate and convincing federal officials to lift regulations if area farmers could meet the minimum requirements. Since this time, the majority of Delta farmers have joined in these efforts and, for the most part, have both surpassed the minimum requirements and successfully kept outside regulatory officials from interfering in their property and production practices.

Despite the fact that NRCS monitors the federally funded conservation programs available to farmers, they are not as successful as the private organizations at recruiting farmers to participate, nor have they been able to inspire farmers to go above and beyond the minimal conservation practices, as the local level organizations have been able to. In the Delta, these private organizations are simultaneously promoting Delta farmer conservation efforts, and moderating the attentions of state and federal environmental regulatory agencies. While the mission statements of these private offices vary slightly, their stated-overarching goal to keep regulatory authorities out of Delta agriculture remains consistent (Shoreman and Haenn 2009). These conservation groups include Delta FARM (Farmers Advocating Resource Management), the YMD (Yazoo-Mississippi Joint Water Management District), and the DCDC (Delta Conservation Demonstration Center).

These local organizations serve as the institutions that govern the course of conservation and environmental reform in the Delta. They are locally constructed, locally run and responsive to the preferences of their board members and constituents. It is this flexibility and honing to the desires of the Delta farmers that has gained them such acclaim across the area, but it is despite this flexibility that they appear strong to external, federal authorities and can appear accountable for the actions of Delta landowners. This fits with Agrawal and Gibson's (1999: 637) argument that institutions remain the primary mechanisms available to mediate, soften, attenuate, and structure particular outcomes and actions. Even more applicable to the Delta scenario, however, is Agrawal and Gibson's (1999) insight into the importance of institutions when local actors do not share one another's goals for conserving resources and/or are unequally powerful – a common situation in an area that has strong opposition to liberal environmentalists, as well as a wide economic and influential disparity among landowners, renters, and laborers. According to Agrawal and Gibson (1999: 637), in these situations, institutions represent some of the power relations that define the interactions among actors who created the institutions while also helping to structure the interactions that take place around the resources, thus providing validation to the former and assistance to the latter, less powerful community members. By bridging this difference within the community, and appealing to the needs of both sides, institutions help to align local behavior and goals (Shoreman and Haenn 2009).

Agrawal (2005: 163) observed that within the Kumaon regulatory community or governmentalized locality:

> The shift from dynamic coercion and resistance toward involvement in regulatory practices and transformations in environmental subjectivities may be an uncertain process, but it is the goal toward which regulatory communities strive.

The conservation organizations of the Mississippi Delta, are, likewise, trying to initiate a private property/common water 'regulatory' community without imposing any regulation and maintaining the perspective that all participation is voluntary and for the sake of agricultural autonomy in the Delta. To do so they have to remove all overt aspects and explicit language of regulation from their communications, and extricate the federal authorities from Delta environmental affairs. In the course of this process, they are promising to maintain local authority over agriculture and environmental improvements, and to promote a new, albeit moderate, conservation ethic among residents.

Mark Charles, director of the Delta Council – a longstanding organization responsible for initiating a number of social, agricultural, and political reforms in the Delta, as well as for acting as the central mediator between local commodity farmers and decision makers in Washington, D.C. – summarized the Delta's approach to conservation and the threat of regulations over water use, as follows:

> ... We wanted to get the best answer to water quality and adopt it here. We have state of the art TMDL program being built here by the waterways experiment station. It's engineering research done by the corps at Vicksburg, with one of the foremost and widely renowned water quality scientists. The research going on is to establish water quality standards for Delta streams, which are obviously not the same as those for Rocky Mountain streams. The reality is that this river was always going to be 'The Big Muddy.' We need to break down the stereotypes of what this really is, what the water quality should be and how we can comply with it. We are going to have a scientist on our side when we go to court with the EPA ... We simply don't work with regulations that tell farmers what they can do.

Conservation, Capitalism, The Rural Elite

The term conservation has been defined in various ways by a number of researchers. Smith and Wishnie (2000: 493) qualify as conservation, any action or practice that not only prevents or mitigates resource over-harvesting or environmental damage, but is also designed to do so. Alvard (1995), meanwhile, argues that in order for something to count as conservation, there must be a quantifiable personal cost leading not necessarily to immediate reward. Meanwhile, research by Little (1994: 350) concludes that "cases in which local communities in low income regions manage their resource bases with the prime objective of conservation – rather than improved social and economic welfare – are virtually nonexistent." Such communities, Little (1994) remarks, are more likely to pursue enhancement by outsiders and allocate subsistence to the most rewarding areas and resources currently available. Their choices may have the effect of conserving habitats and biodiversity, but they will rarely have been designed to do so and may at many times have the opposite consequence (ibid).

Despite the agricultural wealth of the Delta region, this last point has largely characterized the relationship that area farmers had with the local environment. Their priority has long been on their crop yields and they have rejected environmentalist efforts to sway them otherwise. However, as we will see, it was this very same fear of being forced to decrease their yields and income that led this community to adopt conservation.

Conservation, as discussed in the current literature is largely focused on natural parks and the people that inhabit them, primarily in places such as Africa and South America where Western, capitalist notions of conservation and environmentalism are being implemented, largely in spite of indigenous populations (Brockington 2001; Igoe 2004; Trusty in this volume). These analyses have much to say about the ways in which conservation is becoming a capitalist enterprise in which the wealthy sequester and/or siphon off natural resources for their own economic ends while the local populations and environment continue to suffer. Very few critiques, however, address the nature of Metropole conservation (Haenn forthcoming) – that is, conservation in Western, industrialized countries, where both the modern ideals of conservation and preservation were largely conceptualized, as well as where many of the organizational mechanisms to profit off such enterprises were designed.

The Delta is not a park and is certainly not off limits to users – instead, it hearkens back to the day when conservation was better known as stewardship, when the notions of 'wise use' made a certain amount of sense to the native farmers. The Delta, perhaps in a more blatant fashion, demonstrates what the locals would consider a very necessary link between conservation and capitalism. The farmers of the Mississippi Delta are aware of what anthropologists have been quick to point out, that capitalism depletes the very natural resources that underpin wealth creation (ibid). Yet, they argue that in order for the land to stay in the hands of those most knowledgeable of it, farmers must be able to survive economically while preserving and repairing their environment. Thus, the Delta scenario seems to support the notion of ecological modernization that profits and conservation should not be considered mutually exclusive (Bluhdorn 2000; Poncelot 2001).

Although for many Delta farmers, income production and yield are still their highest priorities there are some farmers who are moving towards practices that put the environment first. For, as Agrawal (2001) demonstrates in 'Environmentality', there is something to be said for the influential process of managing resources that creates environmental subjects out of those who formerly didn't care. The ethnographic data presented in this chapter supports this by demonstrating that those farmers who have taken charge of their effect on the environment and who have taken it upon themselves to influence others to do the same, have changed their long term approach to farming and land management. This gets us to the question of how does the conservation movement engage with and come to understand those whose motivation is so very different from their own? This example demonstrates how getting to the very root of motivation – the cultural and historical origins of beliefs, values, norms and behaviors – has actually inspired conservation in a very unlikely place.

In this situation, there was no one better equipped to motivate than the rural elite, for not only were they familiar with the culture and beliefs, but by the nature of their family name and the importance of such legacy in the Delta, they were inherently more persuasive than any outside force. The term 'elite' has been defined as a group of persons 'with access to and control of values' (Gould and Kolb 1964: 234), in the Delta; this definition must be expanded to include those who display and epitomize community values, as well. In this region, dedicated to maintaining tradition and conservative moral values, individuals are judged largely on their community partici-pation. Not surprisingly it is those with the longest family history in the area and typically those with the greatest resources and abilities to contribute and participate, who have also been rewarded the greatest reverence. Traditionally these elites are landowners – old-money families who have worked Delta land for generations and defended its honor against outside forces and/or, as discussed above, who have represented the region in important matters at the state and federal level. Today, it is these families who are using their social influence and historical knowledge of and experience with the community to inspire conservation efforts across the Delta. This example thus demonstrates that in addition to understanding the history, politics, values and beliefs of a particular group, it is also important that environmental efforts recognize the influential members of a community who can be trusted by the community to represent them (see also Hirsch et al. in this volume).

Elites are not well studied in anthropological literature largely because of the dif-ficulty of access (Marcus 1983). Ryan Thomas Adams (2009) writes about his experiences trying to gain access to landowning elites in Brazil, describing:

> ... the lack of trust by many large scale landowners is understandable in this region, as government regulators, environmentalists, and popular opinion all characterize large-scale landowners as socially and environmentally irresponsible ... the landowners feel that they are unfairly targeted and inac-curately stereotyped in an internal political climate that equates large-scale landownership with an oppressive upper class and an external political climate that equates ranchers and farmers in the Amazon with the destruction of the Amazon rainforest.

An analysis of the Deltan and Brazilian elites would seem to imply that there is common distrust of outsiders by elites for the very reason that they believe outsiders associate them with corruption, the siphoning of resources, and collusion with state authorities. Like in Brazil, the Delta elites, like the majority of the community, indeed harbor great distrust of outsiders who have long criticized inhabitants of the region and the south, in general, as rebellious, racist, backward, and slow (see Cash 1941; Odum 1947; Killian 1970; Goldfield 1981; Fischer 1989; Cobb 1991; Nisbett and Cohen 1996; D'Andrade 2002; Harkins 2004). These same elites are also known in the US for their subsidized, over intensified farming practices and their conservative politics. And yet while critics of 'neoliberal nature' (Igoe and Brockington 2007) that depict elites capturing state and environmental resources for their own profit, are supported by this scenario, these critiques don't account for the fact that in terms of Delta conservation, the elites are making every effort to distance themselves from the state and its regulatory authorities while simultaneously fighting for monetary support and the continued subsidization of commodity farming, as well as for their conservation efforts.

Drawing from this, we see that the Delta elites are a complicated example in the discussion of capitalism and conservation. They are implementing conservation to prevent further government regulation of their farming practices yet they fight for support. They claim that such subsidies are in place as much for the consumer as they are for the farmers – that Americans need to subsidize farming so they can secure a safe and affordable food base – and that they deserve to make a profit just as everyone else in the country does. Yet, as Polanyi (1944) points out, capitalist enterprises rely on and are largely responsible for the existence of a welfare state. This perspective is well demonstrated in the Delta, where not only are farmers now being compensated for land, time and effort that goes into conservation, but also by the fact that the hundreds of millions of dollars that come to farmers through the Farm Bill each year are tied to the monies that are distributed through food stamps and other social programs to the impoverished communities that surround Delta farmland – a fact that has led to much resentment and concern amongst Delta farmers and landowners.

Based on interviews I conducted with several members of the Delta elite, it appears as though the continued subsidization of Delta commodity agriculture has long been the veiled jurisdiction of the local elite. This may be one reason why they are so well respected in the Delta and thus trusted by others when they promote something like conservation in order to maintain autonomy over the land. John Semmer, a former President of Delta Council, summarized the subsidy debate as follows:

> When it comes right down to it there have long been two arguments: subsidies or no subsidies. What people don't know is that there are artificial subsidies for a lot of crops that never make paper. Right now [2007] Ag[ricultural] secretary, Mike Johanns, says he's going to fight, but I assure you that it's rarely the Ag secretary that has any influence over the outcome of the bill. People think the Secretary of Ag has something to do with it but the Ag committee has never written a farm bill. In '85 for instance, seven of us wrote the farm bill one night in a hotel room in D.C ... I remember another farm bill writing period, sending up a group of farmers to speak on behalf of maintaining support programs. We sent a widow up there, the widow of a black landowner to speak before Congress and to tell them that those subsidies: "that's all I have."

The Delta elites have proven their ability to work with the federal government and get the Delta farmers what they want. Thus its not surprising that their influence and their knowledge of how much farmers dread the regulation of agricultural practices and their incoming producing activities – would be able to persuade farmers in the Mississippi Delta to adopt conservation.

Thus while Adams' and Marcus' discussion of elites is certainly applicable to the Delta in many ways and while capitalist critiques are certainly partially accurate in their assessment of this elite group – neither discussion can fully account for a group so tied to the government and yet so intentionally distant that it can do what it wants with its land and water, influence federal legislation, garner tremendous natural resources and federal support, and still win the favor and allegiance of its fellow, yet less profiting, farmers.

The Role of Elites in Delta Conservation

Although many of the farmers I interviewed, as well as theorists, would like to believe that individuals are moved to voluntary, sacrificial action because of the morality of the cause, in most cases, such action requires some sort of social capital to act as a discreet form of pressure to encourage individuals to participate. The Delta is no exception. The Delta is a region supported by individualism and social pressure, and although these two forces can cause friction within a community, they also feed one another and push individuals to contribute at the community level. Agrawal (2005) describes a situation in which once introduced to the concept of forest conservation, Kumaon residents continued because it was the right thing to do. Deltans, however, seem to require a more powerful incentive – a social incentive – to push them into action. As discussed above, this incentive came from wealthy local landowners who understood how to motivate community members to take communal action against potential regulation.

One of the oldest Delta families and the leader of the ongoing conservation effort is the Percy family. Recently resurrected by John Barry's *Rising Tide: The Great Mississippi Flood of 1927 and How It Changed America*, the Percys are known for first cultivating the wild Delta landscape, for establishing a levee board immediately after the Civil War, for keeping the Ku Klux Klan out of the Delta, and for contributing resources, money, literature and fame to the city of Greenville, Mississippi. Although few of them remain, Percy is still an important name in the Delta. To the majority of Delta farmers it represents hard earned money, as well as honor, history, and pride in their homeland. It is Billy Percy, one of the few remaining members of the family, who is responsible for instigating conservation in the Delta by establishing the primary conservation organization, Delta F.A.R.M (Farmers Advocating Resource Management). As F.A.R.M's executive Director, Carl Trake, explained:

> The Percy's were crucial to the early stages of information gathering because they were trusted by the community ... With people like the Percy's, F.A.R.M. could gain a key to the 'farm gate' and find out what was going on, on the

other side. These gates were built so that the outside world didn't know what farmers were doing. It took people like the Percy's to enter it so that it's long-term security could be maintained. Slowly but surely F.A.R.M.'s reputation for representing the right thing to do, confidentiality, and prestige, grew … But it was the Billy Percy and other wealthy, landowning, influential residents that brought the concept of local conservation to the table and that it was only they who were able to rally community support …

From the beginning, Percy's idea and F.A.R.M's strategy was to hand pick about ten of the most respected people in the Delta to sell our mission. It was sold as the right thing to do, and important for the sake of developing an organization that could represent the voice of agriculture when future regulatory issues were being discussed … But it was key that these selected individuals go around to different farms and tell people about our method and then bring them in and hash over our approach with everyone.

Although, as Trake says, "people's motivation for participation is starting to change" and farmers are beginning to practice conservation for many reasons, the influence of elite local residents was crucial to the establishment and continued success of Delta conservation.[4] "The south is very proud," says large cotton farmer, Clarence Burrows, "we don't like people telling us what to do, but we do want to do the right thing."

The Role of Cultural Norms, Values, and Beliefs

While some researchers (Agrawal and Gibson 1999) have scoffed at the role of community norms in the success of community-based conservation, many (Milton 2006, Stern et al. 1999) believe that an understanding of community norms, values, and beliefs can have a significant effect on the long term success of conservation projects and are key to establishing a sense of social identification among community members. Much of the supporting literature comes from social movement theory – and is applicable as it addresses sustained local level action in support of an, oftentimes, local cause. Stern and Dietz (1999: 83) propose that the base of general movement support lies in a conjunction of values, beliefs, and personal norms – feelings of obligation that are linked to one's self expectations that impel individuals to act in ways that support movement goals. The authors further contend that movement success depends on movement activists and organizations building support by activating (or reshaping) personal norms to create feelings of obligation (ibid). To understand how this happens, Stern and Dietz (1999: 83) apply a version of Schwartz's (1973, 1977) moral norm-activation theory, proposing that norm based actions flow from three factors: acceptance of particular personal values, beliefs that things important to those values are under threat, and beliefs that actions initiated by the individual can help alleviate the threat and restore the values.

The Delta's local conservation organizations gained support, not necessarily through their own actions, although their local employee base and knowledge did help with their introduction into the community, but more importantly, by applying effective social pressure and mobilizing knowledge of what could incite Delta residents to act. With the help of local elite, they notified long time Deltans that their farms were under threat of federal regulation; that their autonomy over their own land was in danger as was their greatest source of income, and their most sacred family asset. These sons and daughters of Delta Confederates and plantation owners were familiar with the ramifications of federal regulation. Although they had accepted certain parameters in the name of subsidies, they had fought since the dawn of the Civil War to prevent further federal interference in Delta agriculture.

Ethnographic data collected during interviews with local farmers and conservationists support these anti-regulatory sentiments and further illustrate that while the farmers who are participating in conservation agree with the need to keep regulators off of their land, there is little agreement over the importance of environmental conservation. As one farmer explained, "We simply don't work well with regulations around here." Agricultural consultant, Trey Miller, reiterated this sentiment in his assessment of the rural community's perspective on outsiders, as well. " … We don't want anyone to come here," he said. "We don't want anything from the outside. We're all a well-kept secret."

Small rice and soybean farmer, Charlie Martin, exemplifies the Delta farming community in his opposition to heavy handed, regulated environmentalism and in his support of conservation initiatives to keep farmers farming and free of federal interference. Martin was named young farmer of the year just a few years back – an honor, I was told, that typically implies heavy on-farm conservation practices. Yet, in his opinion:

> There's too much focus on conservation, right now. Farmers are the best conservationists there are. Wildlife preservationists, too, cause we've been doing it for ourselves for years … All these organizations are different, just like every farmer is different, but the whole concept is the same. We used to trash the land and now everyone is going low or no till. Minimum till, working it in the fall, after harvest, seems to work best, though. We rarely do conventional tillage anymore.

Similarly, large cotton farmer, Clarence Burrows admits that he does practice conservation though not to the degree that he should or plans to. "It still takes more money than most people are willing to spend," he says. "I think that Delta F.A.R.M. is on the right track and that we do need to police ourselves so that somebody else doesn't do it for us. I think they've done a good job."

Other farmers like Brad Cowell, a large rice farmer from Tunica County, claims to want to increase efficiency but only on his own terms:

> I don't want to cut down on chemicals or fertilizers because I don't want my yields to drop. I don't want to go no till because my tractors are paid for and the cost of tillage will be incurred anyway. I don't use GPS to monitor because I can't afford to put machines in all my tractors and I don't want data before

I know how to use it to make management decisions, so I'm becoming more efficient by trimming labor. I'm down to six employees and cutting overhead that way.

Farmers like Brad, however, are becoming the exception to the rule in the Delta as farmers not only realize, thanks to the local conservation organizations, that they can maintain greater autonomy over their farms by implementing conservation, but also that there are large money saving benefits to efficient water use, soil conservation, and decreasing inputs. Large rice farmer Jerome Howard describes how his family learned early on that saving money and protecting the environment went hand-in-hand.

The Howard's started moving dirt in 1980. By 1981 their last contour levee (or crooked levee, depending on who you talk to) was replaced with straight levees:

> We spent so much less on water and planting, harvesting, etc. took about half as long as it did on crooked leveed fields. We also saved a lot of money on pesticides with grading the fields. This was much more efficient.
>
> The husband of my daddy's secretary at the time was a soil conservationist and when he saw daddy's computer system and leveling techniques, they started working together leveling other people's fields for the sake of soil conservation. It took a few years for the soil conservation scientists to catch up with the computer system that daddy was using ... We've played with water outlets and went to smaller wells when we broke the fields into smaller blocks. Precision leveling, though, is what really changed the way rice farming is done in the U.S., you just can't imagine how much water those crooked levees require. We were the first ones to start with water outlets, in fact, and now you see them everywhere. Our outlets were made with slats stacked on top of each other that can be added to or removed to hold or release water.

Other farmers, like James Maker are new to conservation, but recognize its myriad benefits:

> We pump water out of the lake and use about 75 per cent surface water. I designed my own fields and I use a concrete dam and pump all the run-off water back on to the field at night. My ditch is never dry.
>
> ... We just don't respond well to legislation down here, so we take the opposite approach. We act before regulation can come in. Anytime the government gets involved, even if it got good intentions, you never know what will happen.

Local conservationist, Walter Clark, whose job it is to instruct farmers on how to implement various soil and water conservation practices, summarized the local perspective on conservation as follows:

... Farmers aren't here because they're conservationists. There's a big difference between environmentalists and farmers. They're on opposite sides of the spectrum. Farmers have a vested interest in maintaining the land, but they're doing it for money ... We can't all be as environmental as the environmental folks want us to be, it don't make sense. I agree that we have to protect the environment, but environmentalists are extremists. Truth is, though, most folks around here are willing to work with you.

Middle-out Conservation

Although this conservation effort is not as 'bottom-up' as many examples in Central and South America (Escobar and Alvarez 1992; Haenn 2006) and elsewhere in which the farmers and/or local residents themselves instigate protests against external interference in their local environment, this Delta scenario is locally based and inspired. While Delta farmers are motivated by their cultural disposition and their historical experience with federal regulation (Shoreman 2009; Shoreman and Haenn 2009), their coordinated actions were conducted by wealthy and respected local landowners and organizations aiming to satisfy the upper echelon of federal officials as well as the lower level community members. Thus, this whole process may be considered an example of a 'middle-out' conservation effort, rather than a bottom-up or top-down process. The majority of research on community-based conservation emphasizes the importance of bottom-up movements and the critical role of ordinary community members in the effective implementation of conservation. We see their effectiveness in this middle-out situation as well. Just as certain social elites helped to instigate environmental efforts, local farmers also encouraged each other to participate by expressing their opinions on federal interference and through their own participation in environmental organizations and activities.

The essence of what I here call the middle-out flow of information and influence in the Delta, however, derives from a hegemonic system of influence established by the wealthy landowners and revered Delta natives. According to Gramsci (1992 [1947]), a social group or class can be said to assume a hegemonic role to the extent that it articulates and proliferates throughout society cultural and ideological belief systems whose teachings are accepted as universally valid by the general population. The organizers of this dispersion, or the 'organic intellectuals,' become the organizers and educators of society and become the intermediaries through which the dominant class and subordinate classes are organically linked (ibid). In the Delta scenario, the federal authorities can be equated to Gramsci's dominant class. In this situation, however, the organizers or 'intellectuals' are not necessarily working to promote the ideology of the dominant classes. In the Delta, the intellectuals, depicted by families such as the Percys, simply resolve the contradiction that Gramsci (1992 [1947]) believed to exist between the alta cultura (the culture of the ruling groups) and the cultura populare (the culture of the subaltern masses) by mediating between them and convincing both to modify their behavior and/or plans in opposition to federal and state government regulations (see Shoreman and Haenn 2009).

In the establishment of local conservation organizations, door-to-door recruitment of local farmers, and articulation of cultural beliefs in the right to agricultural autonomy, these 'intellectuals,' according to Gramsci's theory, render the existing power structure acceptable to subordinate masses. They also convince federal authorities to relinquish control over agricultural conservation in exchange for effective farmer participation and real change in mode of production (Shoreman and Haenn 2009). The intellectuals are thus shifting the power of the government to local authorities and securing their own goals of decreased regulation. As demonstrated by the Deltans' feelings towards regulation, the Delta can largely be characterized by Gramsci's (1992 [1947]) depiction of hegemonic equilibrium in which the sociopolitical order is based on a "combination of force and consent, which are balanced in varying proportions, without force prevailing too greatly over consent."

The regulation of the environment is an ideal context in which to study this creation of subject-hood, hegemony, and the imposition of various manifestations of power. According to Timothy Luke (2006: 261), "environmentalized places become sites of supervision, where environmentalists see from above and from without through the enveloping designs of administratively delimited systems." Many argue (Hardin 1968; Johnston 1996, Berkes et al. 2006) that this reality stems from and is necessitated by the fact that people acting separately will not necessarily act in their best interests and that they need others to impose rules which ensure that they do act consistently with their objective self-interests, in ways which are also in the collective best interest (Johnston 1996: 131).

From one perspective, this argument could be framed in the context of Hobbes' *Leviathan*, in which according to Johnston (ibid): "every man's power resists and hinders other men's search for power, so pervasively that many men's power is simply the excess of his above others." From a more community-oriented perspective however, this notion bears more resemblance to social contract theory in which one willingly gives up some rights in order to preserve social order. Given the fact that, in the Delta, farmer income is dependent upon common pool water resources and the cultivation and manipulation of private land, state and federal regulators with an apparent Hobbesian bent had little faith that farmers could be trusted to monitor their own water use or pollution rate. From the federal perspective, tightening regulation over water use as well as imposing regulation on certain practices such as discharge from and the erosion of private land was a way to stave off a further tragedy of the commons (Hardin 1968) and appeared to them as the only solutions for long-term improvement. Although many farmers subscribe more to contractarianism, agreeing that all must cooperate so that all may benefit, most believe that they themselves, rather than the government, are best equipped to supervise resources and determine their appropriate use.

Conclusions

When high profile, politically active, Delta landowners caught wind of the possibility of federal regulation over Delta agriculture in the name of increasing soil and water conservation, they formed the organizations discussed above. These organizations were then charged with recruiting local membership, garnering local participation, and convincing federal officials to deregulate Delta resources. Their accomplishments demonstrate that while motivation for conservation may not matter in terms of promoting sustainability, motivation does matter in regards to the fact that the knowledge and understanding of that motivation is necessary to garner support and cooperation in the local community.

In this situation, the power that in theory ought to be held by governmental and federal level officials has been transferred to the local level organizations, which because of the sway of local elite, were able to provide the community with the proper incentives and rationales for adopting conservation practices. The citizens involved in creating these organizations used their social capital as well-respected landowners, as well as their knowledge of cultural history and sentiment, to rally enough participation so as to deter federal regulation. While it may be argued that the organizations themselves have become another sort of regulatory office, their financial dependence upon the community, as well as the local composition of their boards of directors, will likely keep these local organizations focused on local interests in pursuit of their environmental goals. Although the diversity of actors and self-interests involved in this situation makes coordination seem impossible, we here see how cultural knowledge – historically specific, but relevant to modern day economics and values – is an effective tool in the recruitment of individuals to community-based conservation projects.

This study demonstrates an evolution of environmental subjects (Agrawal 2005), the importance of social influence, local level institutions, and cultural beliefs; and the relatively minor role that Western environmentalism plays in the initiation of conservation. However, it also hastens the adoption of new methods by environmentalists and researchers alike, for it illustrates the wealth of conservation potential amongst long considered 'anti-environmental' communities and demonstrates the effectiveness of a broader investigation into a community's historical, sociocultural and political behaviors. Such detail enables researchers and/or environmental workers to discern a more realistic basis for resident action, as well as the community's larger, institutional objectives.

Like any community, the Delta consists of a multiplicity of players – various personalities within local organizations and a variety of culturally and historically patterned farmer perspectives and penchants. All of these individuals not only need to be able to express their self-interests, but they also have to be able to see some sign that their self interests, as they understand them, and the interests of the community as a whole, will be met before they agree to participate in conservation. Although the strength of civic society in the United States has been questioned (Putnam 2000), Tocqueville noted long ago that Americans tend to voluntarily come together in associations to further the interests of the group and, thereby, to serve their own interests (Tocqueville [1835] 1969; see also Weber 1985). For Delta farmers, this very American tradition of voluntary collective action has huge personal benefits – not only does it further their quest towards agricultural autonomy but it lessens the role of government in their daily lives.

If collaborations over conservation can make new agents out of ultra-conservative highly subsidized farmers such as those in the Mississippi Delta – a new breed of conservationist, perhaps, stripped of the term's present, more liberal, connotations – then, environmentally speaking, the actor's original motivation for conservation does not matter. Furthermore, it is possible that the spirit of collaboration and the ethic of conservation, impelled by a realistic accounting of economic benefits, may lead these farmers to continue their efforts to restore their environment. This situation thus encourages us to recognize the variability of terms and identity markers such as 'conservationist,' 'green,' and 'environmental;' as well as 'anti environmentalist,' 'conservative,' and 'southern.' Barth (1993: 104) warns that we should not assume that formal groups, statuses, etc., because they endure, comprise the most salient components of persons in the sense of being the most important identities they conceive of and embrace, and in terms of which they act. We must not project our own definitions and symbolic meanings of these aforementioned terms on to their use in this environment; nor use them to preemptively characterize groups because of externally observable traits such as wealth, region, religion, or politics (Smith-Cavros 2006).

Terms such as 'conservation' have been adopted by the Delta community to describe their activities, perhaps for lack of better descriptors, or perhaps for the sake of collaborations with external authorities. Either way, of greatest importance is the fact that, in collaborations between Deltans, they are not used, acknowledged, or granted the same significance with which an urbanized, educated, wealthy, white population, associated with universities, and/or the politically liberal, tend to imbue them (Kempton et al. 1996). If we, as anthropologists, fail to recognize new and various approaches to sustainability as viable local options, then not only do we eliminate possible environmental solutions but we deny cultural heritage and history.

I have here argued that it is crucial to any environmental project to first investigate the history, values, and beliefs of a community in addition to understanding their environmental ethics in order to determine how, why, and when they can be motivated to take communal action in the name of the environment. The Delta's previous reluctance to cooperate with federal officials to protect their environment has long been misconstrued as 'anti-environmentalism' (Shoreman-Ouimet, 2010). However, as has been frequently documented (Williams 2005; Howell 2005; Hufford 2005; Berkes 1999; Rikoon and Goedeke 2000, Haenn 2006, Johnson 1999), this type of behavior is more of a reflection of distrust for the federal government and environmentalists, rather than actual ambivalence or disregard for the land. The fact that it took local elites to unlock the farm gate and motivate conservation demonstrates the, perhaps necessary, detachment of conservation from Western notions that environmental efforts be aimed only at meeting non-utilitarian goals and preserving the environment for the environment's sake. If we are to truly acknowledge that environmental discourse and conservation efforts are and should be culturally specific, then we must also recognize the diversity of forms that such discourses may take and the dissimilarities they may bear with the Western version of environmental care, concern, and action (Howell 2002).

Notes

1 The Mississippi Delta is a lens shaped stretch of land that runs 200 miles in length from Memphis, Tennessee to Vicksburg, Mississippi and is approximately 70 miles wide.
2 The names of all individuals interviewed during this research have been changed to protect their identities.
3 Provides environmental information, and enforces laws and regulations to protect human health and the environment in Alabama, Florida, Georgia, Kentucky, Mississippi, North Carolina, South Carolina, Tennessee and six Tribes.
4 See Shoreman and Haenn 2009 to read more from this interview.

References

Adams, R.T. (2009) 'Conflict or collaboration: Two kinds of rural elites in the Amazon,' paper presented at the meeting of the American Anthropological Association, Nov. 2009.

Agrawal, A. (2005) *Environmentality: Technologies of Government and the Making of Environmental Subjects*, Durham: Duke University Press.

Agrawal, A; Gibson, C. (1999) 'Enchantment and Disenchantment: The Role of Community in Natural Resource Conservation', *World Development*, 27(4) 629–49.

Barry, J. (1997) *Rising Tide: The Great Mississippi Flood of 1927 and How It Changed America*, New York: Touchstone.

Barth, F. (1993) *Balinese Worlds*, Chicago: The University of Chicago Press.

Berkes, F. (1999) *Sacred Ecology: Traditional Ecological Knowledge and Resource Management*, Philadelphia: Taylor and Francis.

Berkes, F.; Feeny, D; McCay, B.J.; Acheson, J.M. (2006) 'The Benefits of the Common,' in N. Haenn and R. Wilk, (eds) *The Environment in Anthropology: A Reader in Ecology, Culture, and Sustainable Living*, New York: New York University Press. pp. 355–60.

Bluhdorn, I. (2000) *Post-Ecologist Politics: Social Theory and the Abdication of the Ecologist Paradigm*, New York: Routledge.

Brockington, D. (2001). *Fortress Conservation: The Preservation of the Mkomazi Game Reserve, Tanzania*, Oxford: James Currey.

Cash, W.J. (1941) *The Mind of the South*, New York: Vintage Books.

Cobb, J.C. (1992) *The Most Southern Place on Earth: The Mississippi Delta and the Roots of Regional Identity*, New York: Oxford University Press.

D'Andrade, R. (2002) 'Violence without Honor in the American South,' In Tor Aase, ed. *Tournaments of Power: Honor and Revenge in the Contemporary World*, Burlington, VT: Ashgate.

Escobar, A. and Alvarez, S. (1992) *The Making of Social Movements in Latin America: Identity, Strategy, and Democracy*, Boulder, CO: Westview Press.

Fischer, D. (1989) *Albion's Seed: Four British Folkways in America*, New York: Oxford University Press.

Goldfield, D. (1981) 'The Urban South: A Regional Framework,' *The American Historical Review*, 86(5): 1009–34.

Gould, J. and Kolb, W. (1964) *Dictionary of Social Sciences*, New York, NY: Free Press of Glencoe.

Gramsci, A. (1992 [1947]) *Prison Notebooks*, Vol 1, edited and translated with introduction by J.A. Buttigieg, New York: Columbia University Press.

Haenn, N. (2006) 'The Power of Environmental Knowledge: Ethnoecology and Environmental Conflicts in Mexican Conservation,' In N. Haenn and R. Wilk (eds) *The Environment in Anthropology: A Reader in Ecology, Culture, and Sustainable Living*, New York: New York University Press. pp. 226–37.

——(forthcoming) 'Capitalism and Conservation: Mexico's Contribution to a Global Debate.'

Hardin, G. (1968) 'Tragedy of the Commons,' *Science*, 162(3859): 1243–48.

Harkins, A. (2004) *Hillbilly: a cultural history of an American icon*, New York: Oxford University Press.

Howell, B. (2002) 'Appalachian Culture and Environmental Planning: Expanding the Role of the Cultural Sciences,' in B. Howell (ed.) *Culture, Environment and Conservation in the Appalachian South*, University of Illinois Press: Chicago. pp. 1–17.

Hufford, M. (2002) 'Reclaiming the Commons: Narratives of Progress, Preservation, and Ginseng,' In B. Howell (ed.) *Culture, Environment and Conservation in the Appalachian South*, University of Illinois Press: Chicago. pp.100–121.

Igoe, J. (2004) *Conservation and Globalization: A study of national parks and Indigenous communities from East Africa to South Dakota*. Belmont, CA: Wadsworth/Thomson Press.

Igoe, J, and Brockington, D. (2007) 'Neoliberal Conservation: A Brief Introduction,' *ConservatSoc* [serial online] [cited 2010 Oct 18], 5:432–49. Available from: http://www.conservationandsociety.org/text.asp?2007/5/4/432/49249.

Johnson, B.H. (1999) 'Conservation, subsistence, and class at the birth of superior national forest,' *Environmental History*, 4(1): 80–99.

Johnston, R.J. (1996) *Nature, State, and Economy: A Political Economy of the Environment*, 2nd Edition, New York: John Wiley and Sons.

Kempton, W.J.; Bolster, J.; Hartley, J. (1996) *Environmental Values in American Culture*, Massachusetts Institute of Technology: Woburn, MA.

Killian, L. (1970) *White Southerners*, New York: Random House.

Luke, T. (2006) 'On Environmentality: Geo-Power and Eco-Knowledge in the Discourses of Contemporary Environmentalism,' in N. Haenn and R. Wilk (eds) *The Environment in Anthropology: A Reader in Ecology, Culture, and Sustainable Living*, New York University Press: New York. pp. 257–70.

Marcus, G. (1983) 'Elite as a Concept, Theory and Research Tradition,' in G. E. Marcus (ed.) *Elites: Ethnographic Issues*, Albuquerque: University of New Mexico Press. pp. 2–27.

Nisbett, R. and Cohen, D. (1996) *Culture of Honor: The Psychology of Violence in the South*, Boulder, CO: Westview.

Odum, H. (1947) *The Way of the South*, New York: Macmillan Co.

Polanyi, K. (1944) *The Great Transformation: The political and economic origins of our time*, Boston, MA: Beacon Press.

Poncelot, E.C. (2001) 'The Discourse of Environmental Partnerships,' In C. Crumley (ed.) *New Directions in Anthropology and Environment: Intersections*, Maryland: Rowman and Littlefield. pp.273–304.

Putnam, R. (2000) *Bowling Alone: The Collapse and Revival of American Community*, New York: Simon and Schuster.

Rikoon, J.S. and Goedeke, T. (2000) *Anti-environmentalism and Citizen Opposition to the Ozark Man and the Biosphere Reserve*, Symposium Series, v. 61, Lewiston, New York: Edwin Mellen Press.

Schwartz, S. (1973) 'Normative explanations of helping behavior: A Critique, proposal, and empirical test,' *Journal of Experimental Social Psychology*, 9: 349–64.

——(1977) 'Normative Influences on Altruism,' In L. Berkowitz (ed.), *Advances in Experimental Social Psychology*, 10: 221–79, New York: Academic Press.

Shoreman, E. (2009) *Regulation, Conservation, and Collaboration: Ecological Anthropology in the Mississippi Delta*, Doctoral Dissertation, Boston University. Boston, MA.

Shoreman-Ouimet, E. (2010) 'Concessions and Conservation: A Study of 'Anti-Environmentalism among Commodity Farmers,' *Journal of Ecological Anthropology*. 14(1): 52–66.

Shoreman, E. and Haenn, N. (2009) 'Regulation, Conservation, and Collaboration: Ecological Anthropology in the Mississippi Delta,' *Human Ecology*, 37: 95–107.

Smith-Cavros, E. (2006) 'Black Churchgoers and Environmental Activism' *Ecological Anthropology*, 10: 33–44.

Stern, P.; Deitz, T.; Abel, T.; Guagano, G. and Kalof, L. (1999) 'A Value-Belief-Norm Theory of Support for Social Movements: The Care of Environmentalism,' *Human Ecology Review*, 6(2): 81–97.

Tocqueville, A. (1969 [1835]) *Democracy in America*, New York: Anchor Books.

Weber, M. (1985) 'Churches and Sects in North America,' *Sociological Theory*, 85.

Williams, M.A. (2002) 'When I can read my title clear: Anti-Environmentalism and sense of place in the Great Smoky Mountains,' in B. Howell (ed.) *Culture, Environment and Conservation in the Appalachian South*, Chicago: University of Illinois Press. pp. 87–100.

12

LEARNING BY HEART

An Anthropological Perspective on Environmental Learning in Lijiang

Rob Efird

'Humans and Nature are Brothers'

This is the caption on the giant mural that fills one wall of the airport in Lijiang, a small city in China's Yunnan province. The mural is inspired by a traditional expression of Lijiang's indigenous Naxi people, whose religious texts describe humans and the nature deity (*shu*) as children of the same father but different mothers.[1] Each brother was given a separate domain: Humans took charge of crop growing and livestock grazing in the valleys, while *shu* ruled the natural world beyond human habitation and cultivation, including the mountains, rivers, springs, and streams and all wild animals. Over time, however, humans grew greedy and began to violate *shu*'s realm by overcutting the trees, killing game, and fouling water sources. People were then punished with disasters and diseases until three agreements were negotiated. These agreements allowed humans to clear land and cut wood, but not excessively. Humans could also hunt an appropriate amount of wild game if their domestic animals did not provide them with enough food. But people were strenuously forbidden from excavating mountainsides or polluting water sources. Research on Naxi communities (Yang Fuquan 1999, 2009) suggests that the patient teaching of beliefs such as these helped motivate both individual stewardship and sustainable forms of collective resource management. Studies also document the emotional intensity that surrounded these beliefs: people did not just know the rules. They felt them.

Over the past half century, however, Naxi children have come to know their environments in much different ways. In China's schools, homes and media, environmental issues are now overwhelmingly phrased in the secular terms of science rather than the emotionally resonant idioms of kinship and divine retribution. Yet once again, it seems, humanity's insults to nature are mounting. In order to better cope with its array of environmental crises and motivate sustainable behavior, China's government in 2003 joined many other nations around the world in mandating environmental education for its public schoolchildren. Will these efforts in the world's largest school system suffice to motivate sustainability? Much is at stake in this attempt at behavioral change. China is already the largest single source of greenhouse gases, but if each Chinese were to live the profligate American lifestyles to which so many aspire, their carbon emissions would be four times as great. Thus the entire planet's environmental future may pivot on the choices and values of China's 1.3 billion citizens and consumers.

Unfortunately, recent studies show that the Chinese government's environmental education mandate is going largely unfulfilled due to a host of structural obstacles. As the governments of China and other nations adopt policies to foster the teaching of environmental education, this chapter considers historical examples of environmental learning among the Naxi people of Lijiang in China's Yunnan Province in order to document the role of emotion in this process. Against the tendency to see environmental education as a strictly rational process of text-focused learning that leads to sustainable behavior, these examples show how direct, emotional experience may be a more powerful motivator for environmental stewardship.

As the Introduction to this volume notes, we all confront the imperative of finding solutions to our pressing environmental challenges. Understanding how children learn environmental stewardship is obviously not just China's problem, it is everyone's problem. As we search for solutions, anthropological fieldwork can significantly refine our understanding of the processes in which environmental stewardship and sustainable behavior are learned. In particular, anthropologists Gene Anderson (1996, 2010a, b) and Kay Milton (2002) have demonstrated the crucial role of emotion in environmental learning, and their insights serve as a lens through which the problems and possible solutions in China's environmental education snap into focus. As humans increasingly acknowledge our ecological dependence (Catton and Dunlap 1980), it is worth bearing in mind that scientific explanations of this dependence have not been enough to motivate sustainable behavior. In order to be motivated, it seems we must also be moved. By examining traditional and contemporary approaches to environmental learning in Lijiang, this chapter seeks to enhance environmental education practice by exploring how human relationships with the non-human world are learned by heart.

Anthropology and Environmental Learning

How do children come to know and cherish their environments? A wide range of unsustainable behaviors and ecological phenomena (including anthropogenic climate change, biodiversity loss, and resource exhaustion) urgently require us to change our behaviors and reorient our relationship with the non-human world. In order to address this need for a change in environmental values, environmental education and education for sustainable development are being promoted internationally by numerous non-governmental organizations and the United Nations, for which 2005–14 is the Decade of Education for Sustainable Development. Beginning in the 1970s, national governments began to address the need for changes in values by mandating environmental education in public schooling. In Mainland China, some two decades of increasing environmental education initiatives were capped in 2003 by the official elevation of environmental education as a mandatory subject in public education.

Like people everywhere, Chinese people's choices are shaped by their cultural context. Given the lengthy and nearly universal experience of formal education in China, the content of their education is an obvious source of such cultural beliefs. While some Chinese children have arguably benefited from an increasing governmental emphasis on environmental education, a growing body of evidence suggests that in practice the effectiveness of environmental education in China is seriously compromised by a number of major structural obstacles (Efird 2010 and forthcoming; Lee and Williams 2009; Lin and Ross 2004a, b; Ma 2007, 2010; Wang et al. 2010; Zeng, Yang and Lee 2009). One result is that children often have few if any opportunities to establish an emotionally compelling relationship with their non-human neighbors, including local flora, fauna and unbuilt landscapes. Before and after school, Chinese children have less and less contact with the out of doors due to homework demands and a growing preference for indoor leisure like computer games. Although research on the impacts of these trends is lacking, the consequent atrophy in local knowledge and emotional attachment may be inferred from anecdotal evidence and the extensive literature on children's environmental experience in North America.

Under such challenging circumstances, how can Chinese children learn to live environmentally sustainable lives? Surely there are many ways to effectively learn and teach sustainable behavior. But anthropological research and environmental education practice suggest that sentiment plays an important role in motivating stewardship. Indeed, the role of sentiment is explicitly acknowledged by China's Ministry of Education. Following the 2003 mandate making environmental education obligatory in all of China's public primary and secondary schools (Ministry of Education 2003), the general goals of environmental education were officially described as 'leading students to appreciate and care for Nature, to attend to the environmental problems of their homes, communities, nation and planet, to correctly understand the interrelationship between the individual, society and nature, to help students acquire the knowledge, means and ability needed to harmoniously coexist with their environments, to cultivate students' environment-friendly feelings, attitudes and values, and to guide students to choose environmentally beneficial lifestyles.'[2] Nevertheless, while the importance of sentiment is clearly expressed, it is unclear how these sentiments are to be successfully cultivated in the classroom.

The growing anthropological literature on environmental learning[3] shows that ethnographic fieldwork can help us answer such questions. As several researchers have noted, the anthropological methodology of extended, intimate participant–observation is a very effective way to document and assess the transmission and acquisition of environmental behavior and belief (Ross 2007; Zarger and Stepp 2004). This chapter draws upon the work of anthropologists Anderson (1996, 2010a,b) and Milton (2002) and their discussions of the role of emotion in motivating environmental conservation. Anderson's *Ecologies of the Heart* (1996) offers extensive cross-cultural evidence for both the importance and the context of emotion in learning sustainable resource management. In a separate review of research on environmental learning among indigenous peoples, Anderson (2010b) identifies several recurring characteristics of this process. He notes that in many cases, learning occurs in the form of an informal or extended apprenticeship in which the child learns by helping. It also often takes place with little discussion or lecturing—in sharp contrast to the pedagogy practiced in formal educational settings. When verbal teaching occurs it is often in the form of stories that are 'graphic, dramatic, exciting, and personally compelling.' Finally—and perhaps crucially—learning is frequently enhanced by emotionally powerful rituals and ceremonies. Similarly, Milton's work *Loving Nature* (2002) analyzes the relation-ship between emotion and learning and the development of sentimental commit-ments to conservation. She identifies in these commitments and motivations a 'personal understanding' of nature rooted in direct experiences of the non-human world. In light of Anderson's and Milton's demonstrations of the importance of emotional experience in motivating sustainable practice, the following sections are an attempt to assess the importance of emotion to environmental learning in Lijiang.

Lijiang's Local Culture and Ecology

Back in Lijiang's airport, the giant mural is a silent, seemingly unmarked backdrop to the ebb and surge of travelers, mostly Chinese and international tourists who come to Lijiang for the attractions of its Old Town. Though many of the Old Town's quaint wooden homes and cobbled lanes endure, the past half century has brought a series of wrenching changes for the Naxi people of Lijiang. People of the Naxi nationality now compose just a sixth of the city's population, and many of the Naxi children in the Old Town no longer speak Naxi, while the Naxi's traditional Dongba religious teachings have largely yielded to secular explanations for humanity's relationship with nature. Now humanity's insults to nature and their devastating consequences are discussed in impersonal, scientific terms in Lijiang's media, homes, and classrooms, and schoolchildren in Lijiang relate to the land much differently than those who sustainably stewarded it before them. Now, in the absence of these old relationships, local schools and NGOs (non-governmental organizations) grapple with the question of how to motivate children to care for their environment.

The Lijiang area lies in the northwest of Yunnan Province, a largely poor, rural region of southwest China bordering on Burma and Viet Nam. It is also a region of spectacular biodiversity (Yang et al. 2004) and cultural complexity. Many of the indigenous cultural groups—which include 26 of China's 56 official 'nationalities'—have traditional practices that appear to foster and maintain the region's rich biolo-gical variety (Xu et al. 2005). Even within this diverse province, the Lijiang area is notable for both its biological and cultural wealth.[4] The abundance of medicinal plants has fostered a venerable local tradition of herbal healing, and Lijiang's Old Town has a cosmopolitan history of more than eight centuries as a long-distance trading nexus that brought the deep influences of not only Chinese Han culture, but Tibetan Buddhism as well. Recently the pace and intensity of these influences have accelerated, however: in addition to the sweeping political and cultural shifts of

China's past sixty years, Lijiang has also become a major destination for tourists and labor migrants. One consequence of these changes has been the evaporation of traditional ecological practices and the belief systems that sustained them.

Naxi scholar Yang Fuquan grew up in Ljiang's Old Town in the late 1950s and 1960s, his childhood suffused with the sounds of water running through the web of canals, the fragrance of flowers brought into the Old Town for rituals, and the iridescence of the Old Town's 'five color stones', a local term for the rain-washed sparkle of the glistening, foot-polished cobbles.[5] As children, Yang Fuquan and his friends would go in the evenings to the Old Town's central market square, Sifangjie, to listen to the older men tell stories from Naxi legends (53). Elders still played an important role in teaching proper behavior, and this included how a child was to behave toward the natural environment: 'Since the time that they were small,' writes Yang,

> young children were patiently schooled in the prohibitions by their elders, who told them that they were not allowed to do anything that would pollute or destroy the natural environment. In the 50s and 60s, residents of the Old Town would get water directly from the rivers for drinking. One of the housework duties I did when I was little was to wake every day at dawn in order to go to the river to get the day's drinking water, and you didn't need to worry about people throwing in dirty things. The blue-green river grass undulating at the river's bottom, the water limpid like jade, people dipping gourd ladles right into the river to drink their fill—these sights will forever remain in my memory.
>
> *(Yang Fuquan 1999: 72)*

Clean water is an essential component of Naxi religious rituals, and the Dongba religion lays sacred stress on maintaining the purity of water sources: the nature deity, *shu*, is also the god of water and resides in water (Yang Jiehong 2005: 73). In the Old Town and Naxi rural communities throughout the region, water purity and resource abundance were protected by a triple foundation of communal rules, sacred belief, and institutions for common property management (Yang Fuquan 2009b). Stone tablets inscribed with people's covenants on village regulations (*cungui minyue*) were prominently displayed in Naxi villages. These rules typically included the requirement to protect water sources and forests, to strictly avoid polluting or obstructing waterways, and to leave stone and soil next to water sources untouched. Severe penalties were also spelled out, and both in principle and recorded practice, no one in the community was excepted. These civil regulations were backed up by threats of divine punishment for transgressors, and the images and scriptures of the Naxi Dongba religion include many vivid illustrations of punishments for unsustainable activities like wanton deforestation and overharvesting of wild game. Based on his decades of fieldwork in Naxi communities and his reading of Naxi religious scriptures, Yang Fuquan believes that Naxi religious teachings reflect a 'sentiment of awe'[6] towards the non-human world, which was treated with a caution and dignity befitting its importance in sustaining human life. In this worldview, writes Yang, 'nature [is] a being with life and feelings' (Yang Fuquan 2004).[7] This emotionally resonant, almost interpersonal relationship can be closely linked to Naxi conservation:

> It was precisely due to this personification of nature, this notion of the 'unity of life' (*shengming yitihua*) in which humans and nature are treated equally, that the region in which the Naxi lived was able to long maintain a healthy ecological environment and human harmony with nature.
>
> *(Yang Fuquan 2009b: 496)*

Seeing the characteristics of a person (such as the capacity for feelings and an intentional life) in the non-human world closely resembles the 'personal understanding of nature' that Milton (2002) finds in many people committed to environmental conservation. Both also suggest comparisons to indigenous peoples of North America and elsewhere who see personhood in the non-human world (cf. Callicott 1994, Callicott and Nelson 2004). In Milton's (2002) sophisticated formulation of the relationship between emotion and conservation, our identification of personhood in non-human entities correlates with how we value them, and this 'valuing' is fundamentally an emotional process. In surveys of environmentalists by Milton and others (e.g. Palmer 1998, Chawla 1998), emotionally-charged, direct experiences of the non-human world, often in the company of a friend or relative, are frequently cited as the basis for later conservation behavior.

By contrast, in Lijiang—as in North America (Louv 2005)—children are increasingly detached from their non-human neighbors and the sources of their subsistence. Urbanization, a precipitous drop in the farming population, labor migration, the mounting demands of schoolwork and the increased availability of indoor recreation are some of the factors that are contributing to this separation. Both in the provincial capital of Kunming and the rural areas around Lijiang I heard parents speak of their children's increasing alienation from the outdoors and fixation with indoor, often electronic, forms of entertainment. As in many other countries (Pilgrim et al. 2008), China's rapid urbanization and economic growth appear to be accompanied by a precipitous decline in ecological knowledge, which coexists with increasingly unsustainable use, and often, environmental abuse, of local resources. In order to counter the negative effects of this physical detachment, North American environmental education has come to emphasize hands-on learning and community engagement (Sobel 1999, 2004). But this type of education is difficult in China, where parental anxiety about student safety coupled with the time constraints of exam preparation conspire to confine student learning to the classroom. Field trips and opportunities for hands-on learning beyond the school are rare.

The socio-cultural values of environmental learning have also changed for Lijiang's children. After the ideological campaigns of the 1950s and 1960s that stigmatized traditional belief as 'superstition,' it seems that few if any children have inherited their ancestors' personal understanding of the non-human world. As in other parts of

China, Naxi children and their parents appear to prioritize educational success, material acquisition and affluence, and the desirability of First World lifestyles (Fong 2004), and these priorities are evident in local responses to the teaching of Naxi traditional culture. In the summer of 2009 I spoke about efforts to teach traditional culture with the creator of the mural in the Lijiang airport, He Pinzheng, who is a Naxi artist and senior scholar at Lijiang's Naxi Dongba Culture Research Institute. Mr. He's calligraphy and painting incorporate traditional cultural motifs and the pictographic script of the Naxi Dongba religion, which he has studied for decades. As a child in Lijiang's Old Town he would go with his young friends to gather mushrooms on the hill above Black Dragon Pool, a sacred, spring-fed water source that still supplies the Old Town's network of canals. In the early 1970s, during the waning years of the Cultural Revolution, he was sent down from the city to work as an 'intellectual youth' (*zhiqing*) in the nearby village of Baisha, where he was able to witness firsthand the sustainability of Naxi traditional resource management. From the late 1950s to the early 1970s, a period that included political movements like the Great Leap Forward and the Cultural Revolution, an intense top-down pressure to harvest the region's timber led to the clear-cut of local State forests by armies of loggers from outside the region. By contrast, said Mr. He, traditionally managed Naxi village forests preserved much of their timber due to deeply held local customs and moral convictions.[8]

These customs and morals appear to have little relevance to Naxi children today. In 2005, Mr. He was part of a sophisticated project to create Naxi 'local learning materials' for use in Baisha's public elementary school. Led by Yang Fuquan and funded by the Ford Foundation, this impressive project mobilized Naxi children in Baisha to directly investigate and document the traditional culture of their hometown.[9] However, even after the new materials were developed the local primary school (while supportive) continued to emphasize the standard test-focused curriculum. When the project team attempted to offer Naxi culture classes during the school's summer break, they suffered from poor attendance: Mr. He said parents preferred to pay for their children to take English classes rather than send them to learn about Naxi culture for free.

This stark expression of values reminds us that attempts to instill stewardship and sustainable practice in China must accommodate the cosmopolitan aspirations of China's students and parents. Chinese efforts at environmental learning must also acknowledge the practical constraints on teachers who have enormous class sizes, few if any opportunities for outdoor learning and intense pressure to ensure student success on China's standardized exams. Under these circumstances, attempts to reanimate the natural world with, for example, the theme of brotherhood appear to have little traction. What, then, will persuade local children to care for their land?

Transnational Environmentaliam in Lashihai: Yunnan Eco-network and the Lijiang Green Youth School

From a big outdoor market at the edge of the Old Town, take a local minivan taxi west through the sprawl of concrete buildings in the Lijiang basin. After several kilometers you reach the basin's edge and suddenly climb and twist amidst the exhaust of dump trucks, tractors and long distance buses before crossing not only from one basin into another, but also from Lijiang's built environment to a verdant farming valley that is centered on the sparkling Lashihai Lake. As you descend on a road that eventually bends away northward towards Tibet, orchards and fields of row crops on your right grade gently towards the lakeshore, while to your left and beyond the lake the land rises three to four thousand meters above sea level in slopes of reddish soil with mixed conifer and broad leaf forest. Above the bowl of hills juts the glaciered wedge of Jade Dragon Mountain, a traditionally sacred peak for the entire region's Naxi and the incarnation of the Naxi protector god, Sanduo. Although Lijiang city and the Old Town have experienced a recent heavy immigration of Han Chinese, around Lashihai Lake people of the Naxi nationality still compose some 90 per cent of the watershed's approximately 18,000 residents. Naxi farming villages are concentrated in the low-lying arable areas ringing the lake, while most of the watershed's non-Naxi population—largely represented by another minority group, the Yi nationality—moved to the area in the 1920s and 1930s and is concentrated on the mountain slopes ringing the lake. While the lifestyles of the two cultural groups may differ considerably, each developed sophisticated means to teach environmental ethics to their children and sustainably manage their natural resources.[10] The local ecological treasure is the key wetland area of Lashihai Lake. Over the course of the year Lashihai hosts nearly sixty varieties of waterfowl, many of which are rare, and offers a key resting and feeding site for more than 1,000 migratory birds every winter. It was named Yunnan's first provincial highland wetland reserve in 1998, and in 2005 was listed as an internationally important wetland. When the large international NGO The Nature Conservancy (TNC) set up their biodiversity protection operations in China in 1998 at the invitation of Yunnan's provincial government, they established their headquarters not in Beijing but in Yunnan's provincial capital of Kunming. The Lashihai wetlands outside of Lijiang became their first major project, one that included a nine-week course of environmental education for public schools that blended teaching approaches developed outside of China with local content (He 2010).

The many threats to Yunnan's rich biodiversity are among the reasons why the province has become a 'cradle of NGOs' and has a heavy representation of both international and domestic environmental NGO offices and projects.[11] Many of these NGOs are engaged in environmental education activities on environmental themes ranging from biodiversity conservation to pollution to renewable energy. In a relatively poor and rural province such as Yunnan, this type of NGO-led environmental education may well be a child's only formal experience of environmental learning.

In one recent NGO-led activity in the Lashihai Lake area, local schoolchildren fanned out under the highland summer sun to uproot and record invasive plants and gather trash on the fringe of the village's outdoor basketball court. Over the course of their two day summer camp, nearly sixty local fourth, fifth and sixth-graders participated in a series of small group activities that included the hands-on collection of trash and invasive plant removal as well as presentations and demonstrations on topics like biodiversity, computer literacy and renewable energy (biogas). Most of the children were of the Naxi nationality and still speak Naxi, but in their parent's generation the transmission of tradition—and traditional ecological knowledge (Berkes 2008)—suffered a severe blow. Prior to the 1950s, most Naxi children learned the relationship between humans and the non-human environment from parents, elders and ritual specialists in their families and communities. In the political campaigns of the 1950s and 1960s these individuals and their traditional forms of knowledge, practice and belief were subject to intense criticism. For this and other reasons, awareness and respect concerning traditional knowledge and practice have waned in subsequent generations. During the same period, environmental abuses have increased, and the Lashihai area's ecological degradation has attracted the interest of both international and domestic environmental NGOs.

Yunnan Eco-Network (YEN) is one of these NGOs, and the host of the summer camp mentioned above. Its fifty-year-old director Chen Yongsong has been conducting environmental education and remediation activities in the Lashihai area for almost a decade, beginning with tree-planting and now focusing on the promotion of biogas. Chen is not Naxi, and he grew up far from Lashihai in Yunnan's southern region of Xishuangbanna. Though Xishuangbanna is home to indigenous sustainable resource management traditions such as those of the Dai minority, Chen is a member of the majority Han Chinese. Like many in China, Chen is also a fairly recent convert to environmentalism. He told me that his first encounter with environmental protection occurred as a volunteer with the 1998 World Horticultural Exposition in Kunming, the capital of Yunnan Province. The theme of the exhibition concerned 'the harmonious coexistence of humans and nature.' 'Before, we never thought about the question of how people and nature could co-exist harmoniously,' he said. 'There was never this kind of slogan.'(Chen 2009). For Chen, it was the exhibitions on 'the harmonious coexistence of humans and nature', coupled with recent failures to achieve this harmony (such as the devastating 1998 Yangtze River floods) that catalyzed his personal change in consciousness.

Chen began his involvement in the Lashihai region by organizing afforestation activities in the lake basin, where trees were being overharvested for fuel and building materials. In 2003, Chen began promoting the local use of biogas in the Lashihai area as a sustainable alternative to wood, and in 2007 he rented one of the traditional Naxi farmhouse-courtyard complexes in Lashihai's Anshang Village as a base for his educational outreach and other activities. The tiled wooden buildings that comprise his Lijiang Green Youth School include simple accommodations for the many young people who come to volunteer, an exhibition space that introduces visitors to biogas, local biodiversity and other local and global environmental concepts, and a kitchen and restroom areas which serve as working examples of the biogas principles and practices that Chen teaches to local schoolchildren.

There are three key characteristics of Chen's approach to environmental education. First, Chen focuses on school-age youth as the catalysts for community-wide change through the principle of *'xiao shou la da shou'* – 'little hands leading big hands.' Second, in contrast to Yang Fuquan's emphasis on Naxi culture, Chen adopts a 'universal' approach that gives little importance to the Naxi traditions of Lashihai.[12] For him, it isn't any package of traditional culture that is worth preserving, but rather the cultural elements that allow one to live sustainably. 'You live in Lashihai: whatever it is that allows you to preserve the water's cleanliness and maintain your ability to use it … that's what I see as worth preserving,' he says (Chen 2009). Finally, like many underfunded NGOs, Chen relies heavily on young volunteers.

In fact, the summer camp was largely planned and executed by over one dozen college-age volunteers roughly split between Chinese and U.S. universities. Working in pairs with small teams of students, the volunteers engaged local children in a dramatically new learning style that encouraged their personal expression and active involvement. Chen sees the involvement of both Chinese and foreigners as critical to his teaching process. As he explained, when foreigners and Chinese from other regions join local children in picking up trash, planting trees and pulling up invasive plants, the children see that these things are universal.

Although Chen's teaching model is explicitly non-traditional, the use of older peers in environmental education resembles the way in which many children around the world have traditionally learned their environment. In many indigenous societies, other children—and particularly older children—play key roles in the transmission of environmental knowledge, a fact that 'has important implications for studies of environmental knowledge change' since 'it is likely that transmission of environmental knowledge may depend on sibling or peer teaching, particularly during early childhood' (Zarger 2010: 358–59; see also Nabhan 1997).

Moreover, despite the vast cultural gap between today's Lashihai children and the traditions of their great-grandparents, the evaluations filled out by students in the summer camp testified to the enduring importance of direct and often emotionally resonant experience in fostering environmental stewardship. In both the evaluation immediately following the camp and a second survey one year later, virtually all of the students described how they enjoyed the camp and wished they could do it again. Amidst these generally positive expressions, strong opinions clustered around two of the activities. One of these activities was the trash collection and invasive eradication exercise, which several students criticized in the first evaluation by complaining about the heat and their discomfort. In the one-year follow-up, however, nearly half of the students mentioned this exercise as that which left the deepest impression. 'Because picking up trash was hard work (*xinku*), and my hands and clothes got all dirty,' one student explained. 'But in order to protect the environment of my hometown, it felt good to do my part.' 'I feel really happy,' wrote another student, 'because we went out and through our own actions did something meaningful for our home.'

By contrast, an equal number of students wrote that the computer class made the deepest impression. While a few students in the initial evaluation were strongly critical of computers and their potential as a distraction and even an addiction, over half of the follow-up respondents expressed a desire to learn more about them. Poised thus between the outdoors and the world of electronic media, elementary school children in Lashihai seem drawn to both. In the future, which will lay greater claim to their time and affections?

Conclusion: Loving Nature

'We cannot win this battle to save species and environments without forging an emotional bond between ourselves and nature as well,' wrote Stephen J. Gould, 'for we will not fight to save what we do not love (but only appreciate in some abstract sense)' (1993: 40). As nations around the world mandate some form of environmental learning in their public school curricula, how can environmental learning go beyond textual abstractions to directly engage students in the kind of emotionally compelling relationships that motivate sustainable behavior?

Nearly a decade after China's environmental education mandate was adopted, environmental learning in Chinese public schools remains severely constrained by resource limitations, lack of time, and a shortage of trained and willing teachers. But perhaps the greatest constraints are the classroom context and abstract content of much environmental education: unfortunately, it remains largely true that 'despite the curriculum rhetoric and the actions of a few schools, [Chinese environmental education] is predominantly *about* the environment rather than *in* or *for* the environment in any meaningful way' (Stimpson 2000: 72). Perhaps, this type of teaching will suffice to motivate students to learn and practice environmental sustainability. But contemporary environmental education practice in Europe and North America instead emphasizes direct experience of the non-human world in order to establish the emotional and ethical relationships that in turn motivate stewardship. Despite the obstacles to hands-on learning, environmental educators in China may still find ways to create such opportunities in the form of (for example) school gardens (Zarger 2008). They can also explore the potential synergy between environmental education and the subjects of study that students, teachers and parents seem to value most, such as English. Outside of the schools, Chen's summer camp represents another innovation that deserves to be replicated where such extracurricular support is available. Indeed, the environmental education efforts of NGOs like Chen's serve as a crucial supplement to school-based instruction.[13] In North America, summer camps and short multiday camps during the school year have proven to be powerful, emotionally compelling learning experiences, and such programs can serve as useful references for Chinese initiatives.

As teachers in China and around the world experiment with environmental learning inside and outside the classroom, the breadth and intimacy of anthropological fieldwork promise to enhance our understanding of what makes this practice effective. In studies that range in focus from traditional resource management to contemporary conservation, anthropologists have repeatedly demonstrated the importance of an emotional relationship with the non-human world that is grounded in direct experience. The challenge now lies in adapting this insight to the institutions and priorities of contemporary life and devising new opportunities to learn nature by heart.

Notes

1 The description of this traditional teaching is based on Yang Fuquan (1999, 2009b) and Yang Jiehong (2005).
2 Accessed at http://www.sepa.gov.cn/xcjy/wxzl/200511/t20051118_71829.htm (8/2/2010).
3 Notable examples of this literature include Anderson 1996, 2010; Hunn 2002; Milton 2002; Stross 1973; Wyndham 2002; Zarger 2002, 2010; Zarger and Stepp 2004.
4 Chinese ethnobotanist Pei Shengji cites studies that document the use of between 350 to almost 600 varieties of medicinal plants among Naxi communities within the north-western Yunnan Region, which he classifies as one of China's Important Plant Regions (Pei, Huai and Yang 2006).
5 Unless otherwise noted, details of Yang's childhood are drawn from Yang Fuquan 1999.
6 The Chinese original is *jingwei zhi qing* (2009b: 495) in which 'awe' (*jingwei*) literally means 'respect and fear' and is translated as such in Yang Fuquan 2004, which is essentially an English translation of Yang Fuquan 2009b.
7 The fact that such teachings still held emotional force into recent times can be appreciated in the story of a middle-aged Naxi high school teacher who I interviewed in Lijiang. He had grown up in the countryside with strict warnings against polluting water sources, and when he first came to the city and encountered a Western style toilet filled with water he had a visceral aversion to using it.
8 Yang Fuquan (2009: 504) reports that the forest coverage of Lijiang County dropped from 63% to 37.8% between 1947 and 1985, and places the blame on overcutting due to irresponsible government policy and the 'decline' (*chenlun*) of traditional morality and the longstanding systems of community forest management.
9 See Yang Fuquan (2006) and Efird (forthcoming).
10 Natural resource management patterns and conflicts in this area are discussed in Yu (2001).
11 See Lu (unpublished dissertation). Yunnan is the headquarters for The Nature Conservancy's large-scale involvement in China.
12 This difference is clear from a look at Chen's 2008 textbook for schoolchildren, which he titles in English 'The Knowledge on Rural Biogas and Environment Protection' [sic] (*Nongcun zhaoqi huanbao changshi*). In contrast to the detailed exploration of local particulars typical of 'local educational materials' (Efird 2010), Chen's text and the accompanying images and photos are almost entirely devoid of references to a specific Chinese locale (though they are of course focused on *rural* China). Instead of uncritically celebrating traditional local culture, Chen stresses the importance of teaching children scientific answers to the questions of how to conserve and live sustainably.
13 For a fuller discussion of environmental education conducted by NGOs, see Efird, ed. (2010) and Efird (forthcoming).

References

Anderson, E. N. (1996) *Ecologies of the Heart*, Oxford: Oxford University Press.
——(1999) 'Child-raising among Hong Kong Fisherfolk: Variations on Chinese Themes', *Bulletin of the Institute of Ethnology, Academia Sinica*, 86: 121–55.
——(2003) *Those Who Bring the Flowers*. Chetumal, Quintana Roo, Mexico: ECOSUR.
——(2010a) *The Pursuit of Ecotopia: Lessons from indigenous and traditional societies for the human ecology of our modern world*, Santa Barbara, CA: Praeger.
——(2010b) 'Tales Best Told Out of School', Online unpublished essay. HTTP: http://www.krazykioti.com/articles/tales-best-told-out-of-school-2/ (accessed 20 August 2010).
Berkes, F. (2008) *Sacred Ecology*, New York: Taylor and Francis.
Callicott, J. B. (1994) *Earth's Insights*, Berkeley: University of California Press.

Callicott, J. B. and Nelson, M. P. (2004) *American Indian Environmental Ethics*, Upper Saddle River, NJ: Pearson.

Catton, W. R. and Dunlap, R. E. (1980) 'A New Ecological Paradigm for Post-Exuberant Sociology', *American Behavioral Scientist*, 24 (1): 15–47.

Chawla, L. (1999) 'Life Paths into Effective Environmental Action', *The Journal of Environmental Education*, 31(1): 15–26.

Chen, Y. (2009) 'Interview', Kunming China. 7/24/2009.

——(2008) *Nongcun zhaoqi huanbao changshi* ('The Knowledge on Rural Biogas and Environment Protection'), Kunming: Yunnan Renmin Chubanshe.

——(2010) 'The Yunnan EcoNetwork's Path of Environmental Education', *Chinese Education and Society*, 43(2): 16–26.

Efird, R. (2010) 'Guest Editor's Introduction: NGOs and institutions of higher education in China's environmental learning', *Chinese Education and Society*, 43(2): 3–5.

——(forthcoming) 'Learning the Land beneath Our Feet: local learning materials and environmental education in Yunnan Province', *Journal of Contemporary China*.

Efird, R. (ed) (2010) 'NGOs and Institutions of Higher Education in China's Environmental Learning', *Chinese Education and Society*, 43(2).

Fong, V. (2005) *Only Hope*, Stanford: Stanford University Press.

Gould, S. J. (1993) *Eight Little Piggies: Reflections in natural history*, New York: W.W. Norton.

Gruenewald, D. and Smith, G. (eds) (2007) *Place-based education in the global age*, New York: Taylor and Francis.

Hart, P., Roch, M-C., Wilkenning, K.E. (2007) 'Global to Local: International conferences and environmental education in the People's Republic of China,' *International Research in Geographical and Environmental Education*, 16(1): 44–57.

Hunn, E. (2002) 'Evidence for the Precocious Acquisition of Plant Knowledge by Zapotec Children', in J. R. Stepp, F.S. Wyndham, P.K. Zarger (eds) *Ethnobiology and Biocultural Diversity*, Athens, GA: University of Georgia Press.

Lee, J. C-K. (2010) 'Education for Sustainable Development in China: experiences of the Environmental Educators' Initiative (EEI)', *Chinese Education and Society*, 43(2): 65–83.

Lee, J. C-K., and Williams, M. (eds) (2009) *Schooling for Sustainable Development in Chinese Communities*, New York: Springer.

Lin, J. and Ross, H. (eds) (2004a) 'Environmental Crises, Governmental Policies, and 'Green Schools' in China', *Chinese Education and Society*, 37(3).

——(2004b) 'Theories and Practices in Environmental Education', *Chinese Education and Society*, 37(4).

——(2005) 'Addressing Urgent Needs: The Emergence of Environmental Education in China,' *China Environment Series 7, Wilson Quarterly*, Woodrow Wilson Center.

Louv, R. (2005) *Last Child in the Woods*, Chapel Hill, NC: Algonquin Books.

Lu Y. (2009) 'The Political Environment for NGO Development in Yunnan, China', Unpublished doctoral dissertation (in Chinese), University of Technology-Sydney, Australia.

Ma, G. (2007) *Huanjing jiaoyuxue (di erban)*, Beijing: Science Publishing.

——(2010) 'The Practice and Idea of Environmental Education at Normal Colleges and Universities', *Chinese Education and Society*, 43(2): 55–64.

Milton, K. (2002) *Loving Nature: Towards an Ecology of Emotion*, London: Routledge.

Ministry of Education (2003) 'Guide for Implementing Primary and Secondary Environmental Education (Trial)' (*Zhongxiaoxue huanjing jiaoyu shishi zhinan [shixing]*), Online. HTTP:http://wwfchina.org/wwfpress/publication/ecb/eduFinal.pdf (accessed 17 July, 2009).

Nabhan, G. P. (1997) 'Children in Touch, Creatures in Story', in G.P. Nabhan (ed.). *Cultures of Habitat*, Washington, D.C.: Counterpoint Press.

Palmer, J.A. (1998) 'Spiritual ideas, environmental concerns and educational practice', in D.E. Cooper and J.A. Palmer(eds) *Spirit of the Environment*, London and New York: Routledge.

Pei S, Huai H. and Yang L. (2006) 'Important Plant Areas for Medicinal Plants in Chinese Himalaya: National Report of China,' Unpublished paper for Regional workshop on identification and conservation of important plant areas for medicinal plants in the Himalayas, 19–22, September, 2006, Kathmandu, Nepal.

Pilgrim, S. E., Cullen, L. C., Smith, D. J., and Pretty, J. (2008) 'Ecological knowledge is lost in wealthier communities and countries', *Environmental Science & Technology*, 42(4): 1004–9.

Ross, N. (2007) 'Understanding Children's Environmental Knowledge', *Anthropology News*, 48 (5): 47–48.

Sobel, D. (1999) *Beyond Ecophobia*. Great Barrington, MA: Orion Society.

——(2004) *Place-based Education*. Great Barrington, MA: Orion Society.

——(2008) *Childhood and Nature*. New York: Stenhouse.

Stimpson, P. (2000) 'Environmental Attitudes and Education in southern China', in D. Yencken, J. Fien, and H. Sykes (eds) *Environment, Education and Society in the Asia-Pacific*, London and New York: Routledge.

Stross, B. (1973) 'Acquisition of Botanical Terminology by Tzeltal Children', in M.S. Mouton (ed) *Meaning in Mayan Languages*, The Hague: Mouton.

Wyndham, F. S. (2002) 'The Transmission of Traditional Plant Knowledge in Community Contexts,' in J.R. Stepp, F.S. Wyndham, R.K. and Zarger (eds) *Ethnobiology and Biocultural Diversity*, Athens: University of Georgia Press.

Xu, J., Ma, E., Tashi, D., Fu, Y., Lu, Z. and Melick, D. (2005) 'Integrating sacred knowledge for conservation: cultures and landscapes in southwest China', in *Ecology and Society* 10(2): 7. Online. Available HTTP: http://www.ecologyandsociety.org/vol10/iss2/art7/ (accessed 22 November 2010).

Yang F. (1999) *Shengshanxia de Guguo: Zoujin Naxiren de xinling he jiayuan*. Kunming: Yunnan Minzu Chubanshe.

——(2004) 'The Epistemological Concept of Nature Conservation and Human Activities as seen from the Dongba Religion of Naxi People of Southwest China', Paper for *Bridging Scales and Epistemologies: Linking Local Knowledge with Global Science in Multi-Scale Assessments*, Alexandria, Egypt. March 17–20, 2004. Online. HTTP: http://ma.caudillweb.com/documents/bridging/papers/fuquan.yang.pdf (accessed 28 May 2010).

——(2009a) *Naxixue Lunji*. Kunming: Minzu Chubanshe.

——(2009b) 'Lijiang Naxizu de Shequ Ziyuan Guanli Chuantong', in F. Yang, *Naxixue Lunji*. Kunming: Minzu Chubanshe.

Yang F. (ed) (2006) *Lijiangshi Yulong Naxizu Zizhixian Baishaxiang Baisha Wanxiao Xiangtu Zhishi Jiaoyu de Shijian*, Kunming: Yunnan Keji Chubanshe.

Yang, G. and Lam C. C. (2009) 'ESD in Chinese secondary schools: Beijing teachers' views', *Geography*, 94(1).

Yang J. (2005) *Xicun Shehui; yige Naxi cunluo de jiyi, wenhua yu shenghuo*, Huhehaote: Yuanfang Chubanshe.

Yu, X. (2001) 'Conflict in Resource Management for Ecosystem Services: Water in Lashi Watershed, Lijiang', *Economic and Political Weekly*, 28 July, 2001: 2851–58.

Zarger, R. K. (2002) 'Acquisition and Transmission of Subsistence Knowledge by Q'eqchi' Maya in Belize', in J.R Stepp, F.S Wyndham, and R.K. Zarger (eds) *Ethnobiology and Biocultural Diversity*, Athens: University of Georgia Press.

——(2008) 'School Garden Pedagogies: Understanding childhood landscapes', *Anthropology News*, 49(4): 8–9.

——(2010) 'Learning the Environment', in D. Lancy, J. Bock, and S. Gaskins (eds) *The Anthropology of Learning in Childhood*, Lanham, MD: AltaMira.

Zarger, R. K. and Stepp, J.R. (2004) 'Persistence of Botanical Knowledge Among Tzeltal Maya Children', *Current Anthropology*, 45(3): 413–18.

Zeng H., Yang G. and Lee, J. C-K. (2009) 'Green Schools in China', in J. C-K Lee, M. Williams, M. (eds) *Schooling for Sustainable Development in Chinese Communities*, New York: Springer.

13

LINKING CLIMATE ACTION TO LOCAL KNOWLEDGE AND PRACTICE

A Case Study of Diverse Chicago Neighborhoods

Jennifer Hirsch, Sarah Van Deusen Phillips, Edward Labenski, Christine Dunford, and Troy Peters

> 'The point is to learn, how does one community start and scale out. Because the best impact starts with individuals on a small level and grows out.'
>
> Community Leader, North Kenwood/Oakland
> neighborhood, Chicago

Over the past decade, environmental anthropologists have increasingly argued for the importance of inserting anthropological arguments into debates on climate change (Magistro 2001, Human Organization 2003, Crate and Nuttall 2009, Baer and Singer 2008). In a recent volume, *Anthropology and Climate Change: From Encounters to Actions*, Crate and Nuttall (2009) lay out at least three areas in need of new research that focus on human-environment relationships: 1) anthropology's role in exploring the cultural implications of climate change, 2) facilitating collaborative, community-based projects focused on mitigation and adaptation, and 3) developing culturally-sensitive strategies for communicating climate change to diverse audiences. However, few studies have examined climate change or climate action efforts in diverse urban areas or even in the United States (Crate 2008).

This chapter presents ongoing applied ethnographic research being led by The Field Museum's division of Environment, Culture, and Conservation (ECCo) to understand sociocultural viewpoints on climate change in Chicago's diverse neighborhoods (The Field Museum 2009, 2010a, 2010b). This research was commissioned by the City of Chicago Department of Environment (DOE) to help them develop locally relevant communication strategies and programs for engaging diverse communities in the Chicago Climate Action Plan (CCAP). Launched by the City of Chicago in October 2008, the CCAP aims to reduce carbon emissions to 25 per cent below 1990 levels by 2020 and 80 per cent by 2050 by implementing five strategies focused on energy efficiency in buildings, clean and renewable energy, improved transportation options, waste reduction, and adaptation (City of Chicago 2008).

To date, The Field Museum has completed studies in five communities (three of which are available on the Web at: http://fieldmuseum.org/explore/department/ ecco/engaging-chicago-communities-climate-action), and we are now in the midst of doing five more after which the project will be complete. This chapter reports on the results of our first two studies, in the South Chicago and North Kenwood-Oakland/Bronzeville (hereafter 'NKO') communities, as well as the community engagement work that has resulted from all of them.

The Field Museum's goal in undertaking this research project was to help strengthen climate action in the Chicago area by facilitating the active involvement of diverse communities. More specifically, using the research as a jumping off point for additional work with community, environmental, and government organizations (discussed in the final section of the chapter), we aim to help communities actively participate in city-led CCAP programs as well as incorporate climate action in their community-led work and lead grassroots climate action campaigns. To facilitate innovation in both, our research aims to help establish processes for collaboration and sharing of ideas. These processes should allow for a multilateral flow of information, ideas, and best practices—between the City and communities, and among communities themselves—and also result in building the capacity of community leaders to lead climate action based on their visions of what it means to be a low-carbon, sustainable city. If our projects are successful, community leaders will not only carry out CCAP strategies but will participate in long-term planning around climate action goals and strategies focused both on their specific communities and on the city and region more generally. We see this as the urban equivalent of involving local populations in the planning and management of protected areas (Introduction to this volume).

In addition to serving as an ethnography of human-environment interactions, this study addresses intersections among climate change mitigation and adaptation strategies and the varied multi-stakeholder interests at the local level, which are often situated in long-standing historical, institutional, and culturally rooted values and practices (Poncelet 2004). Our research explores what climate change and climate action initiatives look like within a context of both innovative collaborations and multiple long-standing histories of distrust of efforts initiated by outside entities, including the government. It attempts to address two fundamental questions: 1) how and under what circumstances can climate change and climate action become an issue pushed forward at the local level, and 2) what will make climate change feel relevant and urgent to urban communities? Our research suggests that even in communities where climate change may not be a predominant local concern, there still exist opportunities for widespread adoption of carbon reduction strategies by promoting local quality of life benefits of climate action in areas such as environmental health, energy efficiency, food security, heritage promotion, affordable housing, youth engagement, job creation, community safety, or other locally relevant issues. Anthropology has a great deal to contribute to these debates, and to understanding how addressing key local concerns—which may or may not be directly related to climate change—and working effectively with local partners can be central to the effectiveness of climate policy, and to generating engagement strategies that work best for policy makers and community residents alike.

The chapter has five sections. Section 1 presents The Field Museum's research methodology and approach to applied anthropology. Section 2 provides a brief introduction to the communities of South Chicago and North Kenwood/Oakland, based on our research findings. Section 3 examines findings on climate change awareness and local environmental practices and values. Section 4 explores community concerns that have the potential to link to the CCAP climate action strategies (referred to in climate change circles as 'co-benefits'). Finally, Section 5 reviews The Field Museum's on-going efforts to turn research findings into action. Throughout, we highlight the commonalities and differences in our research communities and suggest ways in which local community assets and environmental values can be built upon and enhanced by climate action. We aim to provide a specific example of the role that applied environmental anthropology can play in developing broader participatory models for democratic decision making and policy development in a complex and socially differentiated urban environment.

Section 1: The Field Museum's Approach To Exploring Human-Environment Interactions

The division of Environment, Culture, and Conservation (ECCo) is the applied science arm of The Field Museum of Natural History. Since its founding in 1995 as two separate departments (the Center for Cultural Understanding and Change [CCUC], and Environmental and Conservation Programs), the division has always viewed research as a step in a larger process of community engagement. As a respected institution embedded in Chicago's cultural fabric – and with strong connections to government agencies, area universities, and planning institutes – our work often focuses on facilitating equitable relationships between small and large organizations (Wali 2006, The Field Museum 2007). As a natural history museum with four departments focused on biological and cultural diversity—zoology, botany, geology, and anthropology—our thematic focus has always been on people and their environments.

Undergirding all of our major projects is a framework developed by CCUC's founder, environmental anthropologist Alaka Wali, termed 'Common Concerns, Different Responses.' This framework explains cultural diversity as the product of: 1) environment – the material resources available to us, 2) history – an accumulation of past actions, ideas, and values, and 3) creativity – human ingenuity that allows us to develop strategies for overcoming constraints and creating new opportunities for survival and collaboration (Wali 2006, The Field Museum 2010c). It resonates with the New Ecological Paradigm (NEP) emphasized in this volume, which recognizes that humans, though capable of complex cultural achievement, are still biological organisms that exist in a complex relationship with their ecosystem and are therefore subject to processes of ecological balance (Catton & Dunlap 1980, Dunlap 1980, 1983, Dunlap & Marshall 2007). By overtly recognizing that human cultures operate within ecological systems of scarcity, we can begin to understand how groups of people come to make sense of their place in both local and global ecological systems. Furthermore, we can encourage innovative cultural adaptations to scarcity that can mitigate some of the negative human impacts on the environment, like those that we now know result in climate change.

ECCo's focus on human-environment interactions has led us to undertake anthropological projects focused on place-making: examining and strengthening residents' and communities' relationship to and stewardship of the neighborhoods and regions in which they live through the nurturing of innovative collaborations between organizations focused on environmental and sociocultural issues (The Field Museum 2003, 2008). More specifically, the Common Concerns, Different Responses framework has led us to focus our research and action programs since the early 2000s on identifying:

1   *community concerns and understandings* that link environmental and sociocultural issues,
2   *community assets* that can serve as a starting point for broadening community involvement in work around these concerns,[1] and
3   *barriers* to increased participation in environmental practices and programs.

Climate Action Research: Methods

In the climate action research that is the focus of this chapter, we have conducted rapid ethnographic research, completing each study in approximately six months, with the ethnographic component lasting approximately four months. Each study is a participatory action research project (The Field Museum 2007), which in this case is conducted by a team including Field Museum anthropologists, staff from the Chicago Department of Environment, and leaders of community-based organizations in the communities being studied. Working with community organizations that have strong social capital has been key to the success of the project: in gaining rapid access to the community, capitalizing on existing community knowledge, and using the research process itself as the first step in climate action engagement to begin to build residents' and community leaders' understanding and awareness of climate change as well as their capacity to address it. Involving the DOE has also proven crucial, in ensuring that we accurately describe the CCAP and the City's goals, connect to DOE community partners, and help craft research questions and recommendations so that they can easily translate to action.

In each of the studies discussed in this chapter (South Chicago and North Kenwood/Oakland), we engaged or observed approximately 200 leaders and residents. Our research activities included the traditional ethnographic methods of interviews, focus groups, and participant-observation at community meetings and events. We also employed visual and performative methods (see examples in Figures 13.1 and 13.3), including drawing, object-based storytelling, participatory photography and photo elicitation, community mapping, and visual prompting (e.g., using photo collages of environmentally-friendly practices to prompt discussion). We find that these

FIGURE 13.1 Drawing from a focus group in South Chicago in response to the question, 'What does climate change look like to you?' the accompanying caption reads (translated from Spanish): 'I drew something that represents the good we can do [for the environment] and the consequences of doing so, as well as of the bad we are doing and the consequences of that.'
© The Field Museum, ECCo.

methods draw out local understandings about climate change and environment in creative ways, and thus help us access information and ideas that might not come forth using traditional research methods. For example, in South Chicago we conducted a focus group with Latino residents in which we asked participants to draw what climate change looks like to them. Some of our approaches (and interdisciplinary methods) have been influenced by our role as a natural history museum with a strong focus on material life. Two examples include 1) focus groups that use objects to prompt discussion and 2) home interviews in which we take photographs of participants interacting with objects and spaces that represent their environmentally-friendly practices.[2]

Section 2: Community Overview

We chose South Chicago and NKO (for map see Figure 13.2) as the first two research sites because they seemed fertile ground to explore the potential of making climate action relevant to a diverse range of residents. Both communities are located on the city's South Side and have significant differences in demographics, geography, and history. South Chicago is racially and ethnically diverse – with a population that is 62 per cent African American, 33.4 per cent Latino, and 5.6 per cent white – and largely working-class, with a 2000 Census median income of $34,279. NKO is racially homogeneous, with a population that is nearly 97 per cent African American,

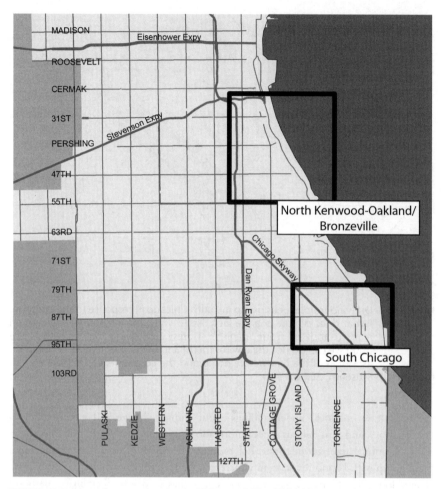

FIGURE 13.2 Map of research areas in Chicago © The Field Museum, ECCo.

but it has recently become highly class stratified with many subsidized public housing residents living next to increasingly affluent homeowners.

Like the rest of the Southeast Side in which it is located, South Chicago was born with the expansion of the American steel industry in the 19th century. Much of the community derives its identity from an interwoven history of heavy industrialization and ecological richness, as well as the subsequent histories of immigration and deindustrialization. As a result, the heritage of South Chicago is grounded in working-class origins, particularly the strong tradition of labor union activism among the largely immigrant workers who were the backbone of the mills. Many of the social and environmental practices we documented in South Chicago can be traced back to the traditions different groups brought with them and fostered through their experiences in the steel mills, from Appalachia, Eastern Europe, and Latin America (Sellers 1998 and Walley 2009).

In recent years, the Southeast Side has been defined by nearly constant and dramatic change. As a result of the steel mill closures in the 1980s, community demographics shifted and City services contracted as well. Our research suggests that during this process, residents came to believe that mainstream organizations, including the City, were not going to take care of them as their livelihoods failed. This, in turn, led to a strong culture of self-sufficiency and the birth of a plethora of community organizations that provide social services and advocate for community needs. It also resulted in a strong tradition of community-based activism that mobilizes residents to address big challenges—some of which have been related to the environmental degradation left behind in the region by heavy industry.

Discussions of heritage in South Chicago and the Southeast Side often emphasize the community's history of standing up to powerful forces and fighting for justice and a good quality of life. Stories about the steel mills emphasize not only the work itself, and how hard it was, but also steelworkers' experiences organizing for their rights through union activism—again, across lines of race and ethnicity. This particular theme is embodied in the popular play, Unfriendly Fire, by local author Kevin Murphy (2003), which details the events leading to, and the fallout from, the confrontation between police and union members at Republic Steel on Memorial Day of 1937. The important role of confrontation also emerges in discussions of the birth of the region's environmental movement in the 1980s, which stemmed from conflicts concerning proposals for increasing landfills in the area and building Chicago's third regional airport. Ongoing volunteer efforts to address pollution through restoring and rehabilitating city lots, public parks, and nature preserves are one example of how this environmental activism in South Chicago continues to this day.

In comparison, NKO has been shaped by competing needs for housing near downtown. In the late nineteenth century, Chicago's growing white middle-class built up NKO as a residential area. Shortly thereafter, the exploding African-American population—fueled by the Great Migration—was forced to crowd into the neighboring communities that would become Bronzeville. After restrictive covenants fell in the 1940s, African-American families started moving into NKO from older parts of the adjacent 'Black Belt' to find better housing, and the neighborhood was quickly absorbed into the greater Bronzeville cultural area. Over its history, NKO has been influenced time and again by government experiments in urban planning. It has been victim to discriminatory federal home appraisal practices in the 1930s and 1940s, host to thousands of public housing units in the 1950s and 1960s, neglected by city planners in the 1970s, and more recently a site of property redevelopment and gentrification as a result of changes in public housing that removed thousands of now dilapidated units and their residents (Patillo 2007: 4).

Due to constant in and out migrations, as well as the flow of those who commute for work and services, NKO area residents described strong connections with many other parts of the city, particularly African-American areas on the South and West Sides. This, in addition to the Bronzeville area's historic significance as a national center for African-American culture, results in residents identifying with a broader conception of African-American heritage than a purely location-based one. As an outgrowth of this many NKO residents support broad notions of racial uplift, but the specific shape of that identity and uplift varies by class and social aspirations. Many NKO residents are also personally committed to projects that improve the appearance and perception of their community, in response to the legacy of concentrated poverty brought on by public housing developments. Campaigns for well-managed affordable housing, resident-led efforts to keep area parks safe by involving youth in structured activities, and neighborhood councils that monitor the quality of new developments, renovations, and general property maintenance are all examples of the types of concerns that have mobilized community action in NKO.

Environmental issues have only recently begun to be talked about and addressed in NKO, partly in response to promises of green jobs and cost savings via energy efficiency spread through the wider media and Chicago's organizational networks. In addition, though, a small minority of community leaders are passionate about climate change-related issues, such as peak oil, and are actively trying to spread awareness and mobilize action, in part by framing these issues as strategies for tackling other community challenges. For example, the Bronzeville Alliance holds monthly movie nights featuring sustainability-themed movies and is creating community gardens to address a number of issues including access to affordable healthy food, job training, and beautification.

Like South Chicago, NKO also has a strong culture of self-sufficiency, but it is embedded in their close relationship with city government and with nearby research institutions like the University of Chicago and the Illinois Institute of Technology. Our research suggests community leaders warily adapt pragmatic engagement strategies: staying aware of various policy initiatives and research projects to try to harness them to their local goals. This is complicated by internal differences among community organizations, which often prevents them from forming a unified front. One of the most significant points of difference exists between those groups who work to increase property values and others who focus on developing residential capacities to improve life for the entire community without displacing its lower-income members.

Both the South Chicago and NKO communities have a mix of agencies with outside connections, local community organizations, small businesses, and activist residents who operate as primary advocates for various community concerns. But while the South Chicago community's history of rapid industrialization and deindustrialization has given rise to a vibrant set of grassroots organizations and local social networks, NKO with its changing population patterns and long history of direct government intervention is primarily led by organizational brokers: groups that act as bridges between the community and powerful institutions. Our research in the two communities suggests it is key to have both types of community assets working in concert—grassroots organizations and cultural brokers—to implement and drive successful initiatives to mobilize residents around climate issues.

Understanding the histories and social contexts of these two communities, as presented in this section, provides a basis for thinking in a more nuanced and embedded way about their environmental engagement and how to increase this engagement by linking it to other community concerns—as discussed in the next two sections.

Perspectives On the Environment and Climate Change

In both South Chicago and NKO, awareness of climate change figures into community life, but to differing degrees and in different ways. For example, in South Chicago and on the Southeast Side there is significant interest in the concepts of climate change, global warming, and 'going green' that relates to the area's long interconnected history with the natural environment. This recognition is directly tied to historical memory of the impact of mills on local air and water quality, as well as current struggles with open space, landfills impacting the region, and coal piles releasing pollutants into the area. In contrast, for residents of NKO, climate change tends to be a more abstract and distant concern that is not recognized as an immediate threat to the environment in the Chicago region.

Despite differences about the immediacy of climate change impacts, residents of South Chicago and NKO both recognize that climate change is an important concern. One area where this was particularly evident was in discussions of the weather. In South Chicago, we documented numerous examples of residents expressing concern over recent changes in weather patterns. For example, a local owner of a body shop described small talk he engaged in with clients about winters being milder and having less snow than in the past, while participants in a neighborhood focus group observed how bird migrations have changed and geese now remain in the area all year. In NKO, local awareness of changing weather patterns emerged through interviews in which participants were asked to answer the question: 'What three words come to mind when you hear 'climate change'?' Responses such as 'extremely hot,' 'extremely cold,' or some variation (see word cloud in Figure 13.3) reflected recognition that weather and climate is now or will be more variable or unpredictable; in addition, participants tied these statements to observations about recent changes in local seasons, noting warmer winters and cooler summers. Other observations in NKO highlighted changes in local growing seasons and the mix of local flora and fauna, thus demonstrating awareness that climate change is not just a global, but also a local phenomenon.

Not only do residents in both communities recognize that changes in climate are taking place, but they attribute these changes to anthropogenic causes (although speculation varies widely on the technical nature of these causes). For example, respondents in both South Chicago and NKO reported a conviction that the space shuttle going up into space pokes holes in the atmosphere that lead to changes in weather, with an NKO resident stating, 'We have emissions going out and the sun coming in.' In another example from South Chicago, an immigrant from Mexico City regretted that human pollution of the ocean is resulting in the dramatic hurricane and tsunami events she sees reported on the news.

Nevertheless, despite the fact that both communities recognize the impact of human behavior on their environment, differences emerged in views concerning individual responsibility for altering behavior to mitigate climate change. Specifically, residents in South Chicago tended to have a sense of personal responsibility vis-à-vis the environment, while those in NKO felt that personal impacts on the environment are insignificant compared to the large-scale damage caused by corporations and the

FIGURE 13.3 As part of our interviews in NKO, participants were asked, 'What are three words that come to mind when you hear "climate change?"' Their responses are depicted in this word cloud. More frequently occurring words appear larger.
© The Field Museum, ECCo/Image by Sarah Sommers.

U.S. government. For example, a young Mexican woman born in South Chicago related her distress about the polar ice cap melting and the plight of the polar bears and said, 'We need to comport ourselves well with regards to the environment.' In contrast, a resident of NKO expressed skepticism regarding the effectiveness of individual behavior when government spending and businesses are destroying the atmosphere by launching satellites and space shuttles, rhetorically asking what point there is to doing little things to address the problem when the government is sending up the space shuttle? This attitude of skepticism was also echoed by many NKO residents who believe that the scope of climate change and the solutions to address it are beyond their control.

Awareness of climate change and its human causes are further evidenced by the ways in which people in both communities report learning about these issues, specifically by relating them to personal experiences.[3] Our research shows that residents of South Chicago often have had experiences that demonstrate to them the concrete effect that humans have on the environment. For example, Mexican immigrants to South Chicago drew on first-hand experiences of water scarcity and changing temperatures in Mexico to shape their environmentally proactive behaviors in Chicago, while white families from the U.S. and Eastern Europe who survived the closing of the steel mills actively linked industrial air contamination to the high incidence of pulmonary illness, cancer, and degenerative mental illnesses experienced in their communities. In NKO, residents drew on personal experiences related to the environment more broadly—about pollution, weather, the atmosphere, and consumerism (what they can purchase to help the environment)—to construct models of how climate change works and what can be done to address it.

Beyond personal experience, the media and different social institutions play an important role in both communities as information conduits about climate change. Both communities report learning about the impacts of humans on climate change from a variety of formal and informal institutional sources, including media, schools, and community organizations. For example, in both communities, mass media is an important source, especially television. More formally, in South Chicago and NKO, a number of schools and educational programs offered by community organizations seek to explicitly raise environmental awareness and teach people about climate change. There are more of these programs, though, in South Chicago. For example, a number of South Chicago community organizations—including many that have not traditionally advocated for environmental issues, but instead have focused on housing, health care, and jobs—have expanded their programming over the last few years to include support for local gardening, campaigns for improved recycling programs, and field trips to local natural areas. Examples of such programs include a local health clinic sponsoring a community garden as a source of local, fresh produce, the South Chicago Chamber of Commerce coordinating efforts to install solar-powered trash compactors along a major street to reduce litter, and a local community center sponsoring a summer camp program that takes children on field trips to local ecological areas to learn about invasive species.

Environmentally-friendly Practices

Our research found that local practices often re-enforce CCAP goals because significant portions of both communities have already sought out creative means for conserving their scarce financial resources. For example, residents of NKO and South Chicago report taking steps in their homes to help offset some of their energy expenditures, including turning off lights and television sets when leaving rooms, turning off water when brushing their teeth or doing the dishes, and replacing incandescent bulbs with City-provided CFLs (often received from local organizations that distribute them at community events). Similarly, residents of both NKO and South Chicago reported frequent attendance of DOE-sponsored events where they learn about energy efficiency and receive weatherization kits and CFLs to help them improve energy efficiency at home.

Both communities are also actively engaged in different forms of recycling. In South Chicago, recycling has a long history and is tied to local efforts to minimize pollution and reduce the expansion of landfills into valuable wetlands. Community organizations run programs that aim to reduce the negative environmental and health impacts of landfills on the community while at the same time addressing a lack of City-sponsored recycling programs that are more readily available in other parts of Chicago. For example, a community health program worked with City offices and education organizations to increase access to recycling centers and to further increase awareness of the need to recycle in the neighborhood. In NKO, community interviews and surveys revealed a near universal awareness of the importance of recycling; however, participation is hampered by widespread skepticism of the City's ability to effectively manage recycling programs. That said, schools in the NKO area actively engage children in recycling efforts, and some parents report that the enthusiasm their children bring home from school encourages them to recycle, despite doubts of its efficacy.

Other environmentally-friendly practices that residents and community organizations engage in are cultural in origin: they are learned behaviors inculcated through heritage traditions and through the creation and maintenance of social relationships. Continuing with the topic of recycling, in both communities, specific forms of local practice have emerged around a variation on recycling: repurposing. In South Chicago, these are rooted in long standing traditions of thrift, dealing with scarcity, and entrepreneurship in the Latino community. Though community members complain about a lack of easily accessible recycling centers for large items like appliances and electronics, local organizations work hard to provide recycling outlets for smaller household items such as clothing, used furniture, metal and plastic goods, and paper. For example, a local community center collects and distributes gently used furniture and clothing to community members who need them, and then uses the cloth from worn out clothing for summer camp craft projects such as making Aztec calendars. In NKO, in keeping with the community's long standing participation in Chicago's mural movement, a community-based design center and a local artist have both created high profile recycled art projects. The design center aims to use art to raise environmental awareness and is interested in transforming its building into a green demonstration site.

In South Chicago, some environmentally-friendly practices reflect the diversity of its immigrant heritage (see tapestry made of recycled objects in Figure 13.4), while in NKO, similar practices tend to reflect strong ties to agrarian roots in the rural South. These practices also reflect the communities' working class origins and residents creatively adapting to limited financial resources. For example, one practice that is part of everyday life in South Chicago, and increasingly in other areas including the suburbs, is found in the *junqueros*—Latino scrap metal collectors—who pick up defunct appliances and other large metal items that are cast off in alleys and transport them to reclamation centers for income. Residents specifically report leaving defunct appliances on the curb for *junqueros* to collect rather than calling a removal service because they know the appliance will be recycled. This practice is complemented by appliance repair shops owned and operated by local community members that refurbish small electronics for resale—items that would otherwise find their ways into landfills. Meanwhile, Latina women reported that they prefer to use rags to clean up messes in their homes rather than paper towels because that is what their mothers and grandmothers did. Similarly, seniors in South Chicago told stories of growing up crafting quilts and other handicraft items from household odds and ends to sell in the neighborhood and for use at home—a tradition that some continue.

Gardens are also popular in both communities. In South Chicago, there are a growing number of community and backyard gardens, and even one effort to create

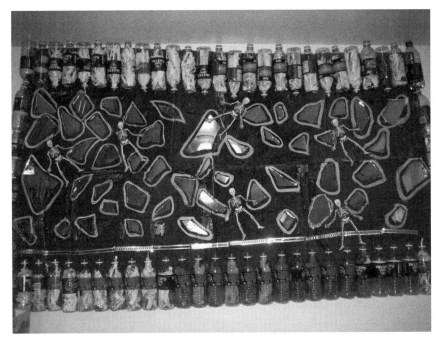

FIGURE 13.4 A partnership between a community organization and an environmental organization in South Chicago resulted in a program on creative recycling. Families involved created this tapestry, which combines recycled objects from contemporary life with skeletons, a common symbol used during 'Day of the Dead' celebrations, which are based on Mexican cultural beliefs that see death and life as an integrated whole.
© The Field Museum, ECCo/Photo by Sarah Van Deusen Phillips.

a backyard gardeners' network. Residents and organizations grow fresh vegetables that they cannot find locally, including vegetables that have cultural significance, such as chili peppers, tomatoes, and corn for Latinos and okra, greens, sweet potatoes, and watermelon for African Americans. For one senior who participated in a focus group in South Chicago, gardening is an important part of her own community heritage—and others' cultural heritage. She recalled: ' ... there was a spot ... that was put aside for the people to grow their vegetables. And the Mexican people used to call it the *jardines*. They used to grow corn, potatoes, to feed, supplement their needs, especially during the Depression that started in 1929.'

Gardeners in NKO typically garden in their backyards; there are very few community gardens and a few new school gardens. Residents attributed their horticultural interest to family or the community where they were raised (e.g. Iowa, and Tennessee), while members of both communities recall gardening as an important part of their past. A number of community members in NKO expressed a nostalgic connection to their childhood chores tending plants in the rural South, while others recounted memories of their grandparents gardening, though they do not engage in the activity themselves.

These examples of how South Chicago and NKO engage in locally meaningful practices that are also environmentally friendly represent key opportunities for generating participation in CCAP work. We recommended to the DOE that CCAP programs should recognize, reward, and build on the diverse conservation practices that already exist in communities—and which are often ignored in climate change discourse focused on the importance of behavior change. As our research in South Chicago and NKO demonstrates, a variety of sustainable practices exist in low income communities where residents have developed innovative strategies for maintaining a high quality of life based on minimal resource use, re-use, and extensive sharing. Furthermore, in both NKO and South Chicago, community heritage is central to how residents view themselves and confront challenges, thus much effort is put into preserving this important cultural history. Climate action programs can work to encourage heritage preservation efforts to also identify eco-friendly community traditions and valorize them as an important part of local heritage and a means of meeting broader-scale mitigation and adaptation goals.

Barriers to Participation in Climate Action-related Programs and Implications for Action

As the examples above demonstrate, our research uncovered a number of ways in which heritage traditions and lifestyles of low income populations facilitate environmentally-friendly practices. However, we also identified patterns in both communities in which past experiences and cultural norms serve as barriers to conservation behavior. For example, in the same focus group referenced above in South Chicago, many seniors reflected on how hard life was for them as children and expressed relief at no longer having those hardships. One resident captured this sentiment by saying she was grateful for paper napkins and other disposable items that make life easier now. Relatedly, one community leader in South Chicago told us that the African-American youth she works with are not very interested in recycling or re-using old products. She said that they equate these concepts with 'used,' and the youth tend to feel that they 'aren't good enough to get new stuff.'

Our research found cultural barriers to climate-friendly practices even more prevalent in NKO, due to its socioeconomic diversity and concern that some residents have about raising the community's image. While African-American cultural traditions of frugality, outdoor socializing, and growing food can be seen as community-rooted climate action, some cultural expectations and community rules discourage these practices. For example, when researchers showed one community leader and long-time NKO homeowner a set of photographs that included a clothesline, she told us (paraphrased):

> [A woman down the street] made the mistake of hanging clothes on a line. …
> I think everybody within two blocks was down at her house telling her to
> take those sorts of clothes off the line! 'Where do you think you are?' And I'm
> sure she's got a dryer in the house, but she thought she was going to get some

clothes dried on a line and get the fresh open air. ... disastrous (laughs). This is just not that kind of community.

The key here is that hanging out clothes carries a stigma because it suggests people cannot afford basic modern amenities and thus conflicts with a local identity of middle class respectability. These expectations are reinforced in the lease terms at mixed-income developments that prohibit the use of clotheslines on balconies and thus encouraged residents in part through the provision of dryers, to practice a more energy intensive, urban middle-class lifestyle—in this, cultural barriers are reinforced by institutional barriers. Raising chickens—a practice that is becoming increasingly popular around the Chicago area—is another practice that interviewees suggested would not be tolerated in NKO.

These ambivalent sorts of sentiments toward environmentally-friendly practices reveal some of the cultural complexity involved in pushing people to change their behaviors—especially when, as is the case with some of the practices called for in the CCAP, the behaviors being promoted counter American markers of success, signaled by a more consumptive lifestyle. But this does not mean that such sentiments have to be barriers to climate action success. Rather, the DOE can build on existing cultural practices that promote conservation to develop creative strategies for diverse engagement. Key to this is recognizing and rewarding practices that mainstream society frequently denigrates by emphasizing how such practices can come to indicate a high quality of life that is not based on excessive material possessions. A truly successful climate action engagement plan will help people recognize and take pride in the expertise they already have in conservation and sustainable living, thus changing their behavior in proactive ways that become locally meaningful. Indeed, our research illustrates that communities are interested in such changes. For example, in NKO a staff person from the local design center responded to our research findings by suggesting that the center start a community-wide clothesline art project to validate and promote the reintroduction of clotheslines, which for him brings to mind memories of his grandmother socializing with the neighbors while hanging out the clothes.

Our research in both communities also revealed that distrust of the City, large institutions, and major efforts initiated by them is another major barrier to climate action—especially when the action desired is participation in the City's climate action plan. In both South Chicago and NKO, there is significant suspicion among both community leaders and residents about 'green' initiatives that are introduced to the community from outside. South Chicago is a community that feels it was cast aside when the steel mills closed because it was no longer valuable to the city. There, residents suspect that current interest in 'helping' their community by improving environmental conditions is more about gentrification and displacement—the potential value of new lakefront residential properties to the City and developers—than about a genuine desire to help current residents or even improve the environment. This attitude of suspicion has some of its roots in a particular case concerning Waste Management (the local garbage collection company), in which the company disguised a proposal for a five-year extension for dumping at a landfill slated for closure as a plan for redeveloping the landfill as a park. When the community discovered Waste Management's duplicity, they took their complaint to the City, where they encountered what they perceived to be strong support for Waste Management's position over their own. Ultimately, the community prevailed and the landfill was closed as scheduled, but the experience left behind resentful feelings. Further evidence of distrust manifests as concern that redevelopment will push residents out of homes that some families have lived in for generations. This fear was represented most clearly in signs posted around the South Chicago neighborhood that said: 'Jobs 4 Green not Green 4 Condos,' sighted by a researcher during a bus tour sponsoring green development initiatives in the area. As with the Waste Management proposal, residents see green redevelopment as a City-sponsored process that overlooks their concerns and problems rather than addressing them, a stance that is captured particularly well in one woman's ironic response to being asked to participate in an energy savings challenge on the City of Chicago's CCAP Web site: 'Does having your gas and electric shut off count as energy conservation?'

In NKO, distrust of City and outside institutional programs stems from the community's long history of racial segregation and what some community leaders see as the City's efforts to capitalize on community assets—including its close proximity to downtown and Lake Michigan—to benefit outside businesses and government. One recent example can be seen in the abortive 2016 Olympic bid, during which a shuttered local hospital on the lakefront was acquired by the City of Chicago for the Olympic village rather than for community needs. Subsequent to the loss of the Olympic bid, the City has abandoned its promise to build proposed housing regardless of the bid's outcome. Even as many residents sense that the area is 'on the cusp of something big,' this history of outside influence has encouraged many to be suspicious of new initiatives, as demonstrated by one community leader's statement, 'The City of Chicago has always known how to keep its blight close … The City sees where money is coming from. When money was coming for public housing they built them. When there was no money in that they dismantled the buildings to salvage the copper and sell that … They are looking at this neighborhood to find gold.'

This cynicism also extends to the CCAP. Community leaders fear that the City and its outside collaborators are once again going to reap the benefits of externally driven change without gains accruing to area residents, or that resources will, as one resident and climate action advocate put it, travel 'down well worn paths' and completely bypass the area for better connected communities and constituencies. However, this distrust does not translate into a lack of interest in working with the City. On the contrary, the fear that resources will not make it to the community is prompting community organizations to seek meaningful partnerships to ensure they are not left out. For example, the director of an area development partnership, who is well aware of the City's history of implementing top-down housing policies, said that she still believes 'win-win' partnerships are possible to address climate change, because it is an issue around which they can design programs that meet both government and community stakeholders' expectations.

As the discussion above illustrates, people in NKO and South Chicago encounter very real barriers—particularly in terms of trust and historical memory—that may prevent them from readily engaging with CCAP programs. In response to this distrust, we recommended that the DOE expand its work around energy efficiency focused on existing buildings and raise its visibility. Though residents in both communities express skepticism of the motives underlying green development, they are open to environmentally friendly building projects as long as they do not result in gentrification and displacement. The DOE is already actively partnering with a number of community organizations in South Chicago through distribution of resources such as weatherization kits and CFLs—efforts that have proven popular with local residents. By extending these efforts in NKO and demonstrating their value to improving and maintaining historically important building stock, the DOE can contribute to community efforts to preserve its heritage and support residential stability.

Co-Benefits—Linking Climate Action To Community Concerns

In our research we look for local concerns that could be addressed through climate action work around the five CCAP strategies: energy efficiency in buildings, clean and renewable energy, improved transportation options, waste reduction, and adaptation. We start by exploring what efforts are already underway that are directly or indirectly related to the strategies. For example, as mentioned earlier, in South Chicago we found community organizations helping residents reduce their energy bills by installing CFLs and weatherizing their homes, and we also identified a successful collaboration between the South Chicago Chamber of Commerce and community organizations to launch a low emissions community trolley. Likewise, in NKO we found a network of community organizations advocating for a new train route and a number of efforts, both organizational and individual, to raise awareness of peak oil and energy efficiency issues. These types of efforts—climate action that is emerging from the local community—provide useful starting points for engaging the communities directly in the CCAP strategies.

We also look for co-benefit opportunities: for action and interest around issues that are indirectly related to the CCAP strategies. Economic development, cost savings, health, and transportation are co-benefits of climate action that are often cited in national discussions about climate change and are mentioned specifically in the CCAP. These issues are considered co-benefits because addressing any one of them has the potential to help improve day-to-day life for residents *and* reduce carbon emissions. We found action around all of these issues in South Chicago and NKO. For example, in both communities, there are emerging efforts to develop awareness of green jobs and to provide residents with healthier food options, through community gardens and farmers' markets.

But even concerns that look similar can vary significantly from community to community depending on ecological landscapes, community demographics, and the social, economic, and political history of the area. People in post-industrial South

Chicago, for example, are used to thinking about air quality as both a health issue and an environmental issue. This offers an opportunity for building on concerns about health and pollution to make connections to CCAP strategies that may affect air quality. On the other hand, people in NKO, a largely residential community, did not often express deep concern about pollution or air quality. They did express concern about ground-level pollution from cars and bus exhaust, however, and connections might be made between this kind of pollution, climate action, and another big concern in the area, respiratory health. In our work we aim to identify local variations of common co-benefits in order to help the City and its partners develop climate awareness and action programs that match local issues, values, and practices.

In addition to the most commonly considered co-benefit areas, our research suggests that many other community concerns can in fact provide building blocks for creative entryways into increasing climate change awareness, knowledge, and action. The following table (Table 13.1) shows the community concerns in South Chicago and NKO that have the potential to link to climate action, and where and how these concerns overlap and vary.

In South Chicago *and* NKO, these productive co-benefits relate to housing (South Chicago: affordable, NKO: residential stability, restoration and preservation), youth development, use of space (South Chicago: open space, NKO: public space), heritage (South Chicago: community and multiple cultural traditions, NKO: African-American), and crime and safety. In South Chicago, our research also highlighted healthy food as a strong potential co-benefit as well as an overall interest in 'living local'—related to the strong sense of self-sufficiency that pervades that area (as explained earlier). In NKO, our research identified a broad focus on economic development as a potential co-benefit, encompassing not just the traditional focus on green jobs but a broad array of activities from marketing the community as a destination neighborhood and establishing commercial corridors to offering financial literacy training for former public housing residents to help with resident stability.

TABLE 13.1 Community concerns in South Chicago and NKO.

South Chicago Issue	Both	NKO/Bronzeville Issue
Affordable	Housing	Residential Stability, Restoration & Preservation
	Youth Development Crime and Safety	
Open Space	Use of Space	Public Space
Community/Cultural (multiple traditions)	Heritage	African-American
Healthy Food		Economic Development (broadly defined)
'Living Local'		

Following is a discussion of how residents in South Chicago and NKO have very different perspectives on two of these concerns: housing and use of space. The comparison illustrates the importance of developing a nuanced understanding of community concerns to make CCAP community engagement recommendations that residents will welcome and that will result in significant action. For example, a nuanced understanding of these issues and how they differ by community can help explain why many residents in South Chicago are interested in 'living local' and might support affordable, energy-efficient maintenance or renovation programs that benefit long-time home-owners; and why many residents in NKO are more interested in supporting programs that either preserve or maintain historically and aesthetically significant housing stock or that build or maintain newer, mixed-income housing developments that are attractive to a changing, economically diverse influx of home owners.

Housing: Affordable v. Residential Stability, Restoration and Preservation

Residents in South Chicago and NKO have different histories with housing, different types of housing, and different concerns about housing. Our research suggests that South Chicago residents are primarily concerned with maintaining affordable local housing options, and would participate in programs that help them improve their current homes. Many residents in NKO would also participate in programs that maintain or improve existing homes. But due to NKO's history as a historic African-American community as well as its participation in major housing initiatives over the decades and the wide socioeconomic spread of its current residents, there are a number of other housing concerns in this community that can also serve as links to climate action.

Many residents in South Chicago see their homes as their primary personal asset; they want to keep their homes in good shape; and they want to stay in the community. Over the past few years, a majority of the most visible 'going green' efforts in South Chicago have revolved around development of new affordable housing and green design. This largely stems from the work of the Claretian Associates, a non-profit developer that focuses on building affordable housing that is easy to maintain.

While some South Chicago residents welcome new, energy-efficient housing, many expressed worry that green building initiatives will result in greater scrutiny of the neighborhood by outsiders, gentrification, and displacement of current residents (see examples of new developments in Figure 13.5). Because of this fear, some organizers in South Chicago have critiqued the definition of 'affordable,' arguing that most residents cannot afford to rent or buy 'green' housing, and have also observed that the jobs that this development brings are generally non-union and go primarily to non-residents.

On the other hand, residents do welcome initiatives that help them retrofit existing structures. This concern was expressed in terms of an expanded time horizon of green initiatives related to energy efficiency, durability of construction, and conserving water as meeting generational needs for durable, easy to maintain, and affordable

Recent construction and green development are signs of new opportunity for the community, according to some South Chicago residents. However, many more are concerned that the community will gentrify and eventually they will be forced to move.

FIGURE 13.5 Recent construction and green development are signs of new opportunity for the community, according to some South Chicago residents. However, many more are concerned that the community will gentrify and eventually they will be forced to move.
© The Field Museum, ECCo/Photographs by Sarah Van Deusen Phillips/Sarah Sommers/Jennifer Hirsch.

housing for future generations. Based on these findings and concerns about gentrification, we recommended that the DOE connect its energy efficient buildings strategy to residents' desire to improve their own homes and their interest in cost effective and long-term affordable housing for current and future generations. We also suggested that they de-emphasize their standard message around housing, which is that weatherization will increase home value—a proposition that can seem negative to people whose primary concern is to stay in their homes for the long-term, not sell them.

In NKO housing is a key mobilizing issue that has many facets. Beautiful greystone homes are seen as one of the community's primary assets; most of the major community organizations in the area make housing a priority; and all major community-planning projects over the past decade list housing as a concern. There have been dynamic shifts in housing stock and resident type throughout NKO's history, and the last 30 years have been no different. During this period—as thousands of subsidized housing units were demolished, and many residents were displaced—the African-American community changed from what many saw as a gang controlled model of urban blight located around a number of public housing buildings to being one of the hottest real estate markets in the city. Some of the demolished public housing was replaced with new, mixed-income housing developments; and a wave of new construction along with a great location close to downtown drew affluent home-buyers to the area. While NKO might be an attractive option for all new home buyers, the area's history as an African American neighborhood just next to the historic Bronzeville community made it particularly attractive to middle- and upper-class African Americans who were welcomed 'back' by most of the remaining home-owning residents.

While the economic downturn has slowed the pace of housing construction and sales in NKO and throughout the city, many community leaders and residents believe it can and will become a stable, mixed-income community with nearby commercial amenities. Different community leaders, however, have different visions of stability and different motivations for achieving it. Some want to expand existing affordable housing and support for low-income residents because they believe good housing is essential for people struggling to get an education, raise a family, or maintain employment. Others want to expand mixed-income housing to include a combination of market-rate, public, and subsidized housing and renting options because they fear an over emphasis on lower income affordable housing might concentrate poverty in the area and drive down property values. Many community residents engage in significant activity around maintaining and improving their homes. Several respondents singled out the physical aesthetics of their homes as the primary reason they moved to the area in the 1980s and 1990s. They explained that they purchased homes in NKO because they saw beauty and history beneath disrepair and dilapidation and were excited to rehabilitate their homes. Residential and political leaders as well as a powerful local community council place a high value on preserving historically significant landmark buildings and maintaining the visual aesthetics of the housing stock more generally.

Based on these findings we recommended that the DOE support initiatives that use energy efficiency as a strategy for addressing the shared concern of residential stability, by helping residents afford to stay in their homes. We also suggested that they increase awareness and knowledge of green options for home restoration, remodeling, and repair specifically by focusing on green technology and practices that are consistent with maintaining the historic character of the built environment.

Use of Space—Open Space v. Public Space

Local place-making practices and the use of space are important community interests in both South Chicago and NKO, but concerns differ in each community. Residents in South Chicago are primarily concerned about open spaces, including natural areas (many of which were degraded from decades of exposure to industrial pollution), parks, and community gardens. South Chicago residents often talk about past or current experiences outdoors. Some talk about how these experiences (like fishing, walking, or restoration of natural areas) have been key to building personal attachments to and understandings about nature; others talk about how interacting in the outdoors has been important in building relationships between diverse groups of residents. In contrast, residents in NKO are primarily interested in controlling outdoor public space, like undeveloped lots or vacant areas, parks, boulevards, and even private yards and other outside areas that are visible to the public.

Environmental restoration and open space have been significant concerns in South Chicago and on the Southeast Side more generally for many years, largely due to the industrial history and unique ecology of the region—the lake shore, the Calumet River, and the wild lands near the industrial corridor and mill areas—and a strong community tradition of cross-cultural interaction in outdoor spaces. As a result, there are many active restoration efforts operating within the South Chicago community. Alongside these are community initiatives related to securing or maintaining open space in neighborhoods. For example, at a local subsidized housing development, residents and the local tenants association are working with a teacher at an elementary school and other community residents to reclaim a series of vacant lots as an outdoor learning classroom, while local restoration efforts organized by C3 leaders (an environmental stewardship training program offered by the city), local high school teachers, and the City seek to rehabilitate city lots, public parks, and forest preserves for public use. South Chicago as a community is also focused on building a sustainable agricultural system, and a number of organizations are operating community gardens as a strategy for growing healthy food and building community, in part by drawing on different cultural traditions (heritage gardens). Open space initiatives, particularly gardens, have also been seen as a strategy for addressing crime, by reclaiming vacant land and providing youth with jobs and something to do. Community organizers are adamant that crime in their community has decreased in the summertime because so many youth have been working in the community gardens through a youth employment program sponsored by the state.

Because open space is a strong community asset in South Chicago, and gardens in particular are gaining so much momentum, our report to the DOE (The Field Museum 2009) recommended that they help the organizations running community gardens turn them into hubs for community engagement around climate action. We suggested that the organizations could be trained to use gardening as an entry point into education and action related to climate change and accompanying co-benefit issues that will improve quality of life. As an environmental practice linked to multiple community concerns and embedded in the cultural heritages of a number of populations, community gardening could be used to validate and encourage sustainable behaviors that reduce emissions and encourage low-resource, collective lifestyles connected to the outdoors.

In contrast, leaders and residents in NKO are concerned about *how* public spaces—including publicly visible private spaces—are used. These spaces include parks, sidewalks, boulevards, vacant lots, store fronts, and even front porches. Public space in NKO is valued for providing opportunities for people to socialize, do business, and exercise. Photographs taken during our research capture men playing chess, cyclists, people carrying their groceries, people catching public transportation, and runners. But use of public space is also highly contested due to concerns about community respectability and fears about safety. Many residents disapprove or are suspicious of unstructured activities in public spaces even as they support collective and purposeful efforts to beautify them.

Responses to certain public behaviors exemplify these concerns about the correct use of public space and how they connect to other concerns, not the least of which is building community among different people from different socioeconomic strata. Loitering is one kind of public behavior that connects to concerns of crime and safety (see Figure 13.6). Several respondents, including seniors and recent arrivals to the neighborhood, complained about men who stand in front of area grocery and convenience stores, and some reported that such behavior discouraged their patronage of those stores. Other residents expressed concern about public activities that they perceive as bad etiquette. For example, one middle-class homeowner complained that she is frequently awakened at five in the morning by honking as someone picks up a neighbor who lives in subsidized housing. She suggested that there should be a required orientation for these types of residents on proper community etiquette. Another respondent complained that one of the main boulevards has too many benches.

However, not all uses of public space in NKO are so contested. Many residents value creative uses of public space that bring together diverse residents to foster positive impressions of the community, around art. In fact, NKO has a history of public art projects that seek to bring the community together around collective representations. It is the site of at least two historically significant Black Arts Movement era murals from the 1970s—'A Time to Unite' (1976) and 'Black Women Emerging' (1977). A local artist in NKO has also gained significant recognition across

FIGURE 13.6 Signs prohibiting loitering hang in storefronts along the Cottage Grove commercial strip in NKO. A banner for 'The Grove' hangs from the lamp post by the street as part of a marketing strategy to attract new customers and business to the neighborhood.

© The Field Museum, ECCo/Photograph by Sarah Sommers.

the city for turning a vacant overgrown lot across from his house into a sculpture garden and open air art museum (Spicer and Rivera 2004). As members of a histori-cally marginalized community, many long-time residents are deeply concerned with the community image and welcome public and private efforts to 'beautify.' The artist got approval from the local alderman and planning council, involved local gang members to help protect the artwork, and was encouraged in his efforts by neighbors who gave him flowers to plant around the statues—ultimately creating a space owned by the whole community.

Because strengthening communities' connections to the outdoors is key to climate action, and public space in NKO has been the site of both contestation and vision, we recommended that the DOE support organizations' efforts to build bridges (and reduce suspicion) between residents by means of creative and collaborative uses of public space. In particular, we suggested that they encourage climate action work that brings together different sets of community members to create, maintain, beautify, and take ownership of public green spaces.

Moving From Research To Action – Impacting The City's Climate Action Programs

This final section provides an overview of the initial impact that our research has had on the development of the City of Chicago's climate action programs. It discusses our efforts to build on anthropological insights to help connect climate-focused programs to community goals, link service delivery to engagement, and assist community organizations in gaining access to and some sense of ownership of a large-scale, government-sponsored initiative.

As explained at the outset of this chapter, our community studies have had a very applied goal since the beginning: to recommend strategies to the City of Chicago and its partners in the Chicago Climate Action Plan for engaging diverse neighborhoods in the plan's implementation. In all of the reports that we write, our recommenda-tions focus partly on process: building strong relationships with community stake-holders. They also focus on program design: developing climate action programs that start with local understandings, resonate with issues that communities care about, and build on existing values and practices.

Originally we expected that our role would more or less end once we submitted our research reports to the Department of Environment. However, soon after sub-mitting the report on our pilot study in South Chicago and the city-wide focus groups we had conducted with community leaders, ECCo was asked to work with the DOE and its partners to help them build on the research findings to design community engagement programs focused on residential retrofits, under the CCAP strategy, 'Energy Efficient Buildings.' Our role in program design and implementa-tion has continued to expand and has proven to be crucial in ensuring that the research findings have significant impact.

Our biggest impact has been on the development and facilitation of the City's first major CCAP community engagement program, the Energy Action Network (EAN),

FIGURE 13.7 Members of the Energy Action Network at the second quarterly meeting of Program Year 1.
© City of Chicago.

a pilot program that launched in November 2009 (see Figure 13.7). The EAN comprises 21 community-based organizations that are receiving extra funding and training to work with residents to expand heating assistance and reduce energy use through utility subsidies, weatherization, and housing retrofits. It is administered by the Community and Economic Development Association of Cook County (CEDA), a nonprofit organization that contracts with community-based organizations throughout the county to administer social service and training programs, and has participation from the utility companies ComEd and Peoples Gas. ECCo receives funding to help run the program with CEDA staff and City consultants, as part of the EAN Planning Committee.

The concept of the EAN developed in part in response to some key recommendations that we made in our initial report on South Chicago about the importance of working through trusted community organizations to engage residents in climate action. Specific EAN guidelines followed a number of the suggestions embedded in this recommendation:

> *Help build the capacity of community organizations to take the lead on climate action,* individually and in collaboration with other organizations and agencies. To do this, DOE should help community organizations become role models and demonstration sites (not just distribution sites) by providing them with both material resources (e.g., funding, compact fluorescent light bulbs [CFLs]) and symbolic resources (e.g., t-shirts, public acknowledgment). DOE could also nurture collaborative relationships that result in innovative programs aimed at

creating sustainable communities by simultaneously addressing environmental and social issues. This could be accomplished by offering workshops and expanding networking opportunities that help organizations: 1) understand climate change as well as mitigation efforts and their co-benefits, and 2) diversify their organizational partnerships and constituencies.

(The Field Museum 2009: 37)

The influence of the research—and of ECCo's participation in the network's development—can be seen initially in the EAN goals and requirements (developed by the EAN Planning Committee), in three ways. First—and overall—they aim to build the capacity of the member organizations to become climate action *leaders* in their communities, as opposed to just having them implement outside programs. For example, we made the specific goals, such as increasing the number of weatherization applications, open-ended—in the end the DOE/CEDA provided no set required increase across-the-board—to allow for broader interpretations of 'success' that would account for a combination of increased social services, outreach, awareness, and effort. We are also working with utility companies to provide member organizations with energy assessments and facilitate free building retrofits to help them become community-based demonstration sites for climate action. Second, they emphasize the importance of member organizations working to increase the community's awareness of and engagement in energy conservation and climate change/climate action overall (including all five CCAP strategies). Third, they require that organizations collaborate with other organizations in their communities and emphasize the importance of the network itself as a mechanism for peer learning.

The network has now been running for one year, and in that time ECCo has assumed what one DOE staff person describes as a 'visionary' role, which basically involves working with the Planning Committee to ensure that we provide member organizations with materials, trainings, and networking opportunities that will help them move beyond service delivery and energy subsidies—signing more residents up for utility assistance and weatherization—to community engagement and organizational capacity-building. Additionally, we also focus on helping member organizations connect their energy service work with their communities' assets and values related to environment and place. This is important because many of the members came into the EAN with very little understanding of environmental issues, let alone climate change, and understood the network as an energy-focused program but did not relate to the big picture of the program as part of the CCAP. Even with the narrow focus on energy and social services, we try to help them broaden the work that they do by talking to residents ('clients' as they refer to them) not only about available subsidies and services, but also about home-grown, inexpensive or no-cost conservation measures such as unplugging appliances when not in use or using a clothesline instead of a dryer.

As we now enter the beginning of program year two, our challenge continues to be striking a balance between the need to demonstrate immediate quantitative successes—evaluated primarily by the increase in utility assistance and weatherization applications processed by each member—with ECCo's main interest in building the capacity of member organizations to incorporate energy efficiency and other climate action work into their core agendas for long-term change. In 2011, we will continue addressing this issue, both with the EAN and a new pilot program being launched by the DOE in South Chicago focused on developing models for 'co-delivering' residential services for green and healthy homes and, ultimately, increasing the number of residential retrofits. In the South Chicago project as in the EAN, we will be responsible for helping the lead community organizations bring together a broad range of stakeholders to link home energy issues to other organizational and community concerns, such as those discussed in our report. This project will be our first opportunity to build directly on report recommendations that are community-specific.

Conclusion: Broadening The Discussion On Climate Change

Ecological paradigms in cultural anthropology necessarily take into account both the physical and social environments in which people live. This has been the case in our research on engaging diverse Chicago communities in the Chicago Climate Action Plan. While climate change frequently has a popular dimension informed by mass media, political interests, and global opportunities and markets, our research looks at climate action as a culturally relevant and historically situated local concern. Rather than a one size fits all program for carbon reduction, or a single approach to research methods, our approach has been to accentuate local diversity, the resilience of local communities to adapt to changing environmental circumstances and scarce resources, and new opportunities for collaboration between policy makers and local stakeholders.

Our research also takes the diverse urban environment as a distinct challenge for policy development and suggests ways to build upon an existing history of human-environment interactions that are already present in communities and are meaningful to residents (although people may not always understand them as such). We've documented in our research how two distinct communities in Chicago have very different histories, social demographics, and relationships with the natural environment. South Chicago was dominated by the steel industry and the rapid social and environmental adjustments required by its collapse. The history of NKO, on the other hand, has been dominated by shifting City government interventions to meet competing housing needs: segregating African Americans and then poverty on one hand, and satisfying the demand for middle-class residences near downtown on the other. While these particular experiences have shaped everyday attitudes about the environment and the purposefulness of government action, they also encompass common concerns (e.g., about food security, changing weather patterns, crime, housing, and jobs), and it has been the point of our research to draw out some of these important commonalities and differences.

The City faces a number of important challenges in making climate action relevant to local residents. So far, policy makers have been enthusiastic about new ideas and approaches suggested by our research. Where other approaches have focused on the most cost effective means of carbon reduction, or global political frameworks and challenges, our research suggests a myriad of other avenues for engaging communities in climate action. These include:

- building on culturally relevant local practices;
- addressing local barriers—many of which are embedded in complicated histories related to social exclusion; and,
- connecting climate action to multiple co-benefits, including but beyond cost savings.

These approaches should help the City attain community buy-in on larger policy related goals as well as identify and develop more creative strategies for facilitating widespread engagement across diverse communities. This can be done in part by figuring out how to implement climate action initiatives that begin in the community and 'scale out'—as suggested by the community organizer in the opening quote to our chapter.

In sum, our research suggests that climate action can help advance community agendas addressing everyday concerns. It also brings to light some of the ways in which the diverse social and institutional focus of anthropology can assist in illuminating the human-environment interactions in urban environments and provides opportunities for developing broader participatory models for democratic processes and policy development in climate action.

Notes

1 ECCo's asset-based approach builds on the asset-based community development model pioneered by Kretzmann and McKnight (1993) by adding a focus on cultural values and beliefs and on human-environmental interactions.
2 Some of our studies also include social network analysis, which adds a quantitative component. We have been collaborating with Northwestern University's Science of Networks in Communities (SONIC) Research Lab to draw on ethnographic research findings to design and administer computer-based social network surveys. The surveys, which are given to community leaders and residents—many of whom participate first in the ethnographic research—aim to better understand and map communication and knowledge networks related to environmental issues. Findings result in recommendations regarding how the City and its partners can disseminate information through existing networks and work through trusted organizations to mobilize the community around climate action—even when those organizations have not traditionally focused on environmental issues. The first full-scale SONIC research project was conducted in North Kenwood/Oakland and the data are currently being analyzed; thus the results are not discussed in this chapter.
3 This finding is in line with other research on public perceptions of climate change. See Kempton (1997).

References

Baer, H. and Singer, M. (2008) *Global Warming and the Political Ecology of Health: Emerging Crises and Systematic Solutions*, Walnut Creek, California: Left Coast Press.
Catton, W. and Dunlap, R. (1980) 'A New Ecological Paradigm for Post-Exuberant Sociology,' *American Behavioral Scientist*, 24: 15–47.

City of Chicago (2008) 'Climate Change Action Plan (CCAP)', [Online] Available at: http://www.chicagoclimateaction.org/pages/introduction/10.php.

Crate, S. (2008) 'Gone the Bull of Winter? Grappling with the Cultural Implications of and Anthropology's Role(s) in Global Climate Change,' *Current Anthropology*, 49(4): 569–95.

Crate, S. and Nuttall, M. (Eds.) (2009) *Anthropology and Climate Change: From Encounters to Actions*, Walnut Creek, California: Left Coast Press.

Dunlap, R.E. (1980) 'Paradigmatic Change in Social Science: From Human Exceptionalism to an Ecological Paradigm,' *American Behavioral Scientist*, 24:5–14.

——(1983) 'Ecologist Versus Exemptionalist: the Ehrlich-Simon Debate,' *Social Science Quarterly*, 64: 200–203.

Dunlap, R.E. & Marshall, B.K. (2007) 'Environmental Sociology,' In *21st Century Sociology: A Reference Handbook*, Vol. 2. Thousands Oaks, California: Sage, pp. 329–40.

The Field Museum (2003) 'Journey Through Calumet: Communities in Motion in Southeast Chicago and Northwest Indiana.' [Online] Available at: http://www.fieldmuseum.org/calumet/

——(2007) 'Collaborative Research: A Practical Introduction to Participatory Action Research (PAR) for Communities and Scholars.' [Online] Available at: http://www.fieldmuseum.org/par/

——(2008) 'New Allies for Nature and Culture.' [Online] Available at: http://www.fieldmuseum.org/ccuc/allies.htm.

——(2009) 'Engaging Chicago's Diverse Communities in the Chicago Climate Action Plan – Community #1: South Chicago.' [Online] Available at: http://www.fieldmuseum.org/ccuc/ccuc_sites/Climate_Action/pdf/FINAL_Community1.pdf.

——(2010a) 'Engaging Chicago's Diverse Communities in the Chicago Climate Action Plan – Community #2: North Kenwood-Oakland/Bronzeville.' [Online] Available at: http://www.fieldmuseum.org/ccuc/ccuc_sites/Climate_Action/pdf/FINAL_Community2.pdf.

——(2010b) 'Engaging Chicago's Diverse Communities in the Chicago Climate Action Plan – Community #3: The Polish Community.' [Online] Available at: http://www.fieldmuseum.org/ccuc/ccuc_sites/Climate_Action/pdf/FINAL_Community3.pdf.

——(2010c) 'The Cultural Connections Guide to Teaching Diversity.' [Online] Available at: http://www.fieldmuseum.org/research_collections/ccuc/ccuc_sites/culturalconnections/pdf/TeachersGuide_19.pdf.

Human Organization (2003) 'Special Issue: Toward an Anthropological Understanding of Sustainability,' *Human Organization*, 62(2): 91–201.

Kempton, W. (1997) 'How the Public Views Climate Change: Research Points to Better Ways to Address Widespread Misconceptions about the Problem and How to Solve It,' *Environment*, 39(9): 12–21.

Kretzmann, J. and McKnight, J. (1993) *Building Communities from the Inside Out: A Path Toward Finding and Mobilizing a Community's Assets*. Chicago: ACTA Publications.

Magistro, J., Roncoli, C., Hulme, M. (2001) 'Special Issue: Anthropological Perspectives and Policy Implications of Climate Change Research,' *Climate Research*, 19(2).

Murphy, K. (2003) 'Unfriendly Fire: Dramatized account of the 1937 Republic Steel Memorial Day Massacre.' [Online] Available at: http://www.booklocker.com/books/2989.html.

Poncelet, E.C. (2004) *Partnering for the Environment: Multistakeholder Collaboration in a Changing World*. Lanham, Maryland: Rowman & Littlefield Publishers, Inc.

Patillo, M. (2007) *Black on the Block: the Politics of Race and Class in the City*. Chicago: University of Chicago Press.

Quad Communities Development Corporation (2005) 'Quad Communities: Connecting Past, Present and Future.' Chicago: Local Initiative Support Corporation, pp. 6. [Online] Available at: http://www.newcommunities.org/communities/douglas/

Sellers, R. and Pacyga, D.A. (1998) *Chicago's Southeast Side (Images of America)*. Chicago: Arcadia Publishing.

Spicer, C. and Rivera, G. (2004) 'Building on the Past: A New Foundation for Community in North Kenwood-Oakland,' Urban Research: Perspectives on Civic Activism and City Life, III:50–61. [Online] Available at: http://www.fieldmuseum.org/ccuc/Perspectives_III/7_Spicer_Rivera.pdf.

Wali, Alaka (2006) 'Beyond the Colonnades: Changing Museum Practice and Public Anthropology in Chicago,' Sociological Imagination, 42(2): 99–114.

Walley, C.J. (2009) 'Deindustrializing Chicago: A Daughter's Story.' In The Insecure American, (Eds, Gusterson, H. & Basteman, C.). Berkeley: University of California Press.

INDEX

technology 3, 7, 107, 109; green 288; policy as 76, 82

temporal vulnerability 149–57 *see also* vulnerability

Townsend, P. K. 2, 76, 181

toxic substances 161, 167

tradition and society 19–20, 57, 62, 63, 64, 69–71, 88, 240, 248, 257, 261–62, 273, 278, 280, 288; and modernization 16

transnational environmentalism 259–63

United Nations 39, 124, 255

understanding of nature 256, 258 *see also* Personal understanding of nature

values: economic 134, 188, 217, 220, 221, 224–25; environmental or green 4, 41–42, 121–22, 124, 134, 188, 198, 207, 235, 254, 258–59, 292; *see also* cultural values

Vayda, A. 2, 8, 12, 79, 107

Vulnerability 142–45, 183; social 146–57, 189; temporal 149–57

water 99, 128–29, 182, 190, 236–38, 245–46, 257

West, P. 82, 86, 208,

Western: civilization 19, 69–70; environmental values 235, 239, 248–49; tradition and philosophy 15, 16, 17, 43, 66–67, 70–71, 142, 143

White, L. Jr. 38

wilderness 17–18, 46, 61